# Embracing Vocation

Also by Dianne C. Luce
*Reading the World: Cormac McCarthy's Tennessee Period*

# Embracing Vocation

## Cormac McCarthy's Writing Life, 1959–1974

Dianne C. Luce

THE UNIVERSITY OF
SOUTH CAROLINA PRESS

© 2023 University of South Carolina

Published by the University of South Carolina Press
Columbia, South Carolina 29208

www.uscpress.com

Manufactured in the United States of America

32 31 30 29 28 27 26 25 24 23
10 9 8 7 6 5 4 3 2

Library of Congress Cataloging-in-Publication Data
can be found at http://catalog.loc.gov/.

ISBN: 978-1-64336-354-7 (hardcover)
ISBN: 978-1-64336-355-4 (paperback)
ISBN: 978-1-64336-356-1 (ebook)

Unpublished letters and documents from the Albert Erskine Random House Editorial Files are quoted with the permission of his daughter Silvia Erskine, and unpublished letters of Lawrence Bensky are quoted with his permission. Permission to quote from Peter Josyph's as-yet unpublished interview, "Damn Proud We Did This: A Conversation with Larry Bensky," was granted by both Lawrence Bensky and Peter Josyph. I am grateful to Anne De Lisle and to David Styles for their permission to include the photographs in this book. Joe McCamish, of McCamish Media, also has my thanks for his work on preparing the photographs for publication.

# Contents

## Part Three. *Child of God*, 1966–1973

# Preface

Early in his career, Cormac McCarthy came to realize that maintaining privacy is a necessary condition for his work, both to minimize distractions and to prevent the self-consciousness that could cripple his creativity. His most profound statement of this instinct appears in a letter he wrote to the Lyndhurst Foundation's Deaderick Montague in early October 1986, when he turned down Montague's request that he speak at a literary conference in Chattanooga, Tennessee. McCarthy declared that he could not speak publicly about his writing. He did not know how to explain this fully even to himself, but since Montague and Lyndhurst had so generously supported his career, he tried to convey what he almost superstitiously believed: "in order to write you have somehow to preserve the freedom—both delicious and bewildering—of that first day when you sat down . . . like God with the creation of the world before you and . . . no one expected anything of you" (Letter to Deaderick Montague, received Oct. 6, 1986, 2). In other words, he felt he needed to protect himself from awareness of others' expectations and especially from "adulation," which he felt was one of the two greatest threats to writers, the other being alcohol. McCarthy is neither shy nor anti-social, but he has rigorously protected his talent from the pernicious effects of fame, choosing not to make public appearances and granting few interviews, especially in nationally distributed periodicals.

Consequently, scholars have long had only a sketchy understanding of the circumstances of his life and how they relate to his work. As late as 1998, when Edwin Arnold and I edited *Perspectives on Cormac McCarthy*, our introductory account of his life and the reception of his works comprised only sixteen printed pages, even though we each had independently researched and written biographical/critical articles on McCarthy for literary reference works. Scholars also knew little about McCarthy's drafting and revising processes other than that he tended to work on at least two creative projects at a time. This dearth of information has changed dramatically since 2008, when McCarthy's correspondence with his Random House editors Lawrence Bensky and Albert Erskine became available with the University of Virginia's acquisition of Erskine's Random House Editorial Files, and 2009, when McCarthy's own vast collection of his papers opened at Texas State University in San Marcos. Gradually other archival holdings of McCarthy's correspondence have come to light. Among the most significant of these are the two collections of Robert Coles's papers at the University of North Carolina (UNC)–Chapel Hill and at Michigan State University in East Lansing, and the papers of the Lynd-hurst Foundation, also at UNC–Chapel Hill. Other valuable collections include the papers of Howard Woolmer at Texas State University, San Marcos, the correspondence of Guy Davenport at the University of Texas in Austin, the McCarthy Collection of John Fergus Ryan at the University of Tennessee in Knoxville, and the Ecco Press Records at New York Public Library. The Coles, Lyndhurst, Woolmer, Ryan, and Ecco Press archives are of special relevance to the middle and later portions of McCarthy's career.

To a large degree, this book is made out of archival papers. My purpose has been to create a fully documented, scholarly narrative of McCarthy's writing life in the first half of his career with Random House, one that supplements my interpretations of his first three novels in the early chapters of *Reading the World: Cormac McCarthy's Tennessee Period* (2009). Although much of the present study is biographical, it is not a conventional biography. I have accepted as a given that there is much about McCarthy's personal life that we still cannot know. My emphasis here is largely on his writing processes—the genesis, composition, editing, and revision of his first three novels. I have been interested in looking closely at McCarthy's activities as a professional writer and tracing his strategies, practices, and the ongoing drama of his thought processes (as much as they can be inferred) as he created each individual work and across the first decade and a half of his career. Further, this is a close study of McCarthy's texts across the evolution of each novel through several drafts, pursued in hopes that this kind of comparative and interpretive attention to the Ur-texts will provide enriching contexts for our readings of the published novels, allowing us to perceive them as they exist in multiple time dimensions—as they do for McCarthy himself. Another way of looking at it is that the accumulated drafts for each novel comprise a multidimensional metatext to challenge and enlarge our readings of the published versions.

The scope of this volume includes examination of McCarthy's participation in the professional and business activities of being a fiction writer in the 1960s and 1970s and treatment of those processes that have contributed to the emerging public recognition of his creative work: the efforts of his editors, agents, and allies to garner the attention and appreciation of reviewers, periodical editors, the reading public, and award committees. Naturally, within the scope of these large themes, I have traced McCarthy's working relationships with editors Lawrence Bensky and Albert Erskine and to a lesser degree his relationships with friends and family as they have affected the circumstances of his writing.

My goal has been to synthesize what can be learned from the archives for the period covered by this study with insights from the published interviews and to supplement these materials with published and some unpublished accounts of individuals or foundations that influenced McCarthy's early career, in an effort to create a coherent interpretive history of his first fifteen years as a professional writer. As firmly grounded in documented evidence as this study has aimed to be, I also freely acknowledge when I rely on inference and even speculation. My liberal use of qualifiers such as "perhaps," "likely," and "probably" flags inferences that are open to reinterpretation as new evidence emerges, as I hope it will.

My interpretations of McCarthy's drafts have been guided by insights about McCarthy's working methods that have evolved as I worked with them. Primary among these principles is that one cannot draw conclusions about the evolution of a novel simply from McCarthy's labeling of his drafts or the order of the pages within them. Throughout my study of the creation of McCarthy's first three novels, I have been guided by dates and the internal evidence of the typescripts—more than by page numbers and draft labels—to determine the sequence and direction in which any given scene or draft has evolved.

For the novels under consideration here, the completed typescript versions McCarthy submitted to Random are labeled either "Final Draft" or "Late Draft," and these are succeeded by the versions he revised with editorial feedback. Often the submitted draft exists in more than one copy, and for clarity I have designated the document showing such feedback as the editorial draft. Because McCarthy tended to work intuitively in his first drafts, gradually working his way to his final structures, he did not necessarily compose his scenes in the order in which they would appear in the finished novel. Nor did he always complete a scene before moving on to another. His practice in the first draft of *Outer Dark* reveals that at least in that novel, he paginated his leaves in the order in which he wrote them. As he worked, he freely moved pages within each draft, renumbering as the structure evolved. He also moved pages with which he was satisfied from one draft into the next, so that each successive draft until the final typing is a composite of leaves from different drafting stages. Sometimes McCarthy's dating of a leaf helps to identify the stage at which a scene was composed. Sometimes he works out a new scene for a draft and numbers the scene as a discrete entity, 1 through x, before repaginating for placement or simply redrafting. Clearly, such page numbers are not placement numbers, nor do they reflect the stage in a draft at which McCarthy composed them. Because McCarthy often repositioned leaves as his drafts evolved, most have two or more numbers. My in-text documentation cites all the paginations for any given leaf since these help to distinguish leaves bearing the same page number.

We are fortunate that McCarthy tends to preserve superseded or leftover material from his drafts. Thus, for *Outer Dark* his papers include two files each of the "Rough/First Draft" and "Early Draft." These identically labeled folders do not hold identical typescripts nor the two halves of one draft. In each case, the first folder is the more finished of the two, and I have designated these the A versions. The second file for each draft contains more superseded or discarded material, and I designate these the B versions. In *Outer Dark*'s "Early Draft [B]" are filed several scenes that McCarthy had first drafted for that novel but then revised for *Child of God*. For *Child of God*, there is no first-draft folder, but the Ur-material in the *Outer Dark* draft gives us much information about the genesis and early conception of Ballard's novel, and McCarthy also saved first-draft material from *Child of God* at the end of its "Middle Draft." Also preserved in the drafts, as one would expect, are scenes McCarthy deleted or substantially revised during the editorial stage.

The surviving drafts of the three novels examined here offer somewhat different but complementary insights into his working processes. No first draft survives for *The Orchard Keeper*, but correspondence and draft documents provide a nuanced picture of McCarthy's substantial revision in response to his editors' reactions, as well as much information about his views of his own work. The very complete *Outer Dark* archive includes a rare example of McCarthy's earliest drafting stages and allows for a step-by-step appreciation of the evolution of the novel's structure and its method of strategic opacity: McCarthy's moving away from direct revelations of Culla's thoughts, to dream expressions, and finally to objectifying his inner life in the triune. The draft material of *Outer Dark* also reveals how *Child of God* emerged as McCarthy worked on his second draft of Culla's novel, when he deleted or downplayed material related to the auction/eviction theme, the sheriff, and local color tales, and adapted them for Ballard's novel. And early material saved in *Child of God*'s "Middle Draft" allows us to see more fully his initial conception of the novel, before he added the serial murders and necrophilia. Together the drafts of McCarthy's first three novels provide a fairly comprehensive view of McCarthy's creative processes and the evolution of his aims and strategies in the earliest years of his writing career. Indeed, the drafts are a window into the emergence of a creative genius.

# Acknowledgments

Several people who have known McCarthy have generously shared information, anecdotes, and memories with me. My foremost debt is to Anne De Lisle, who was McCarthy's wife while he created *Outer Dark, Child of God,* and *Suttree.* Our visits and many telephone conversations have given me new information, insights, answers to long-pondered questions, and many delightful hours, and she graciously vetted my use of her information in this book. Anne introduced me to Carolyn Hare, who was Lee Holleman McCarthy's roommate at the University of Tennessee and a longtime friend of Lee, Cormac, and Anne; and to David Styles, who photographed McCarthy for the jacket of *Child of God.* Our conversations in Maryville, Tennessee over two days in the fall of 2019 were too brief but highly valued. In 2000 my friend and colleague Edwin Arnold and I spent a glorious afternoon at the home of McCarthy's friend, Bill Kidwell, one of the grand storytellers of East Tennessee. Bill filled us in on details of his and McCarthy's constructing large stone mosaics on the sidewalks of Maryville's Main Street and told us many Bill-and-Cormac anecdotes. In March 2020, Deaderick (Rick) Montague, formerly director of the Lyndhurst Foundation, spoke to me cordially and candidly over dinner and graciously submitted to a long, filmed interview with me about Chattanooga's Lyndhurst Foundation, its financial award to McCarthy, its role in the paperback issue of *Suttree,* and its board member Robert Coles. Finally, in August 2021, McCarthy's sister Barbara (Bobbie) McCooe, curator of her family's history, spent a day with Bryan Giemza and me as we interviewed her on film about her family, her memories of Knoxville, and her brother.

This study has been greatly enriched with information shared by Dustin Anderson, Edwin Arnold, Lydia Cooper, Bryan Giemza, James Grimshaw, Peter Josyph, Christian Kiefer, Wesley Morgan, Stacey Peebles, Katie Salzmann, Zachary Turpin, and Markus Wierschem. The willingness of researchers to share their work outside of the channels of formal publishing always impresses me and earns my admiration. May our community of McCarthy scholars always be so. In addition to these generous individuals, my thanks go to several colleagues who have long encouraged my work in various ways: Edwin Arnold, who introduced me to the work of Cormac McCarthy; James Meriwether, who introduced me to archival research methods; Gail Morrison, who shared my earliest ventures in archival work when we were graduate students and who has read portions of this work; and also Steven Frye, Rick Wallach, Scott Yarbrough, and the anonymous referees of my submissions to various journals: they know who they are.

My work in the archives at Texas State University in San Marcos was supported by a William J. Hill Visiting Researcher Travel Grant in 2019. I am especially grateful to Mr. Hill for his interest in the culture of the southwest and for his generosity to researchers. My thanks go as well to archivist Katie Salzmann and her staff for their unfailing helpfulness. They make every visit to the archives welcoming, comfortable, and productive. Special thanks also go to Bryan Giemza, who was the director of the Southern Historical Collections at the University of North Carolina–Chapel Hill, when I first traveled there to work on the Robert Coles papers. His own work had made me aware of the correspondence between Coles and McCarthy, and during our conversations on-site, he called my attention to the Lyndhurst Foundation Records, which, we discovered, preserve McCarthy's correspondence with Deaderick Montague. Sincere thanks go to Dr. Robert Coles for granting me access to his papers at UNC. Finally, thanks are due to the staff of the Southern Historical Collections at UNC for their assistance with the Coles and the Lyndhurst papers and to Grace Hale and the staff of the Special Collections Library at the University of Virginia for their assistance with the Albert Erskine Random House Editorial Files.

Parts of this study were read in early versions as keynote addresses for the American Literature Association's Fiction Symposium in Savannah in 2010 and for the Cormac McCarthy Conference sponsored by the John F. Kennedy Institute of Berlin's Free University in 2016. I am grateful to conference directors Olivia Carr Edenfield, James Dorson, and Julius Greve for their interest in and support of my work. Other extracts of this book were presented at Cormac McCarthy Society conferences held in Austin in 2011, 2017, and 2019; in Memphis in 2015; at the American Literature Association (ALA) conference in Boston in 2015; and at ALA Fiction symposia in Savannah in 2009 and 2011. The questions and reactions of audience members at these readings have been invaluable in shaping my work.

Portions of this study that deal with McCarthy's relationship with his Random House editors appeared in "Cormac McCarthy and Albert Erskine: The Evolution of a Working Relationship," *Resources for American Literary Study* 35 (2012); and portions that treat his early awards from foundations and the individuals who endorsed them appeared in "Robert Coles and Cormac McCarthy: A Case Study in Literary Patronage," *Resources for American Literary Study* 41 (Fall 2019). For their adept editing of these pieces, my thanks go to Jackson

Bryer, Paul Thifault, and Donna Brantlinger Black. A section of Part Two was published in earlier form in the *Cormac McCarthy Journal* as "Projecting Interiority: Psychogenesis and the Composition of *Outer Dark*," 16, no. 1 (Spring 2018); and a portion of Part Three appeared there as "Ballard Rising in *Outer Dark*: The Genesis and Early Composition of *Child of God*," 17, no. 2 (Fall 2019). I am grateful, as always, to editor Stacey Peebles for her interest in my work and for her thoughtful and informed editing and for the friendly copyediting and shepherding of Helen Myers. In addition, many of my major findings about the typescripts of McCarthy's southern works were summarized in my two contributions to Steven Frye's collection, *Cormac McCarthy in Context* (Cambridge University Press, 2020). I thank Steve, too, for his confidence in my work, for recruiting me for the volume, and for his able editing.

# Abbreviations

AEF    Albert Erskine Random House Editorial Files, 1933–1993
CMP   Cormac McCarthy Papers
*CoG*    *Child of God*
*OD*    *Outer Dark*
*OK*    *The Orchard Keeper*
*S*     *Suttree*

# Part One
## *The Orchard Keeper,* 1959–1965

# Apprentice Work and Biographical Context

When the typescript of Cormac McCarthy's first novel, *The Orchard Keeper*, arrived at Random House in early May 1962, McCarthy was unknown in publishing circles. He had published nothing in nationally distributed periodicals, and nothing he wrote as an adolescent or in his apprentice years was available to readers beyond Knoxville. To the editors, the novel must have seemed one of those miraculous manuscripts that sometimes materialize unheralded. Random's publicity release about the novel indicates that it came to them as an unsolicited manuscript, one of a very few submissions of merit "out of thousands" received. And Random's readers quickly recognized that it was an extraordinary accomplishment, outshining the first novels of many highly respected writers. How had it come to be?

McCarthy told Knoxville interviewer Mark Owen that he had chosen to write not long after learning the alphabet and began a book at age eight but only managed fifteen or twenty pages. "It took me another 20 years to get around to writing again," he quipped (Owen, "McCarthy Is One"). He also told Oprah Winfrey that he had written when he was a boy, but that he had produced nothing during his teen years. This is not entirely the case, as a few pieces of juvenilia survive in the files of the *Gold and Blue,* the student-produced newspaper of Catholic High School. As far as we know, there followed a gap of several years until McCarthy began writing his first novel and two related stories at age twenty-six in 1959, when he was enrolled for the second time at the University of Tennessee. However, his commitment to his writing was already firm. He told interviewer Richard Woodward in 1992, "I never had any doubts about my abilities. I knew I could write. I just had to figure out how to eat while doing this" (Woodward, "Venomous Fiction" 31). This dilemma persisted throughout the first two decades of his writing career, but it seems to be one that he understood and embraced from early on.

Indeed, that McCarthy's commitment to his craft, his confidence that he could write, was in place by 1959 suggests that his four years in the Air Force (about which we still know very little) may have been a time not only of the intensive reading he mentioned to Woodward (Woodward, "Venomous Fiction" 31), but also of drafting, of exploring and developing his skills, a self-directed apprenticeship undertaken in his hours off duty, while reliably fed and housed by the federal government. His sister Barbara (Bobbie) McCooe reports that although his first assignment in the Air Force was as a navigator, he preferred his second role as a radio disc jockey for the base in Alaska, not only because it gave him more autonomy, but also because it allowed him to work at night and fish in the daytime (Interview with Bryan Giemza and Dianne Luce). Along with fishing, he clearly was doing a great deal of reading and perhaps trying his hand at writing as well. His enlistment not only allowed for distancing from his birth family, crucial to a young person's maturing, but also from his circle of lively friends in Knoxville, whose camaraderie would provide material for *Suttree,* but whose desire for rowdy socializing might have proved a distraction from developing his talent. One suspects that when his term of enlistment was up, McCarthy returned to the University of Tennessee in 1957 with the intention of further honing his literary talent in preparation for his chosen career. Moreover, one imagines that his return to Knoxville with eligibility for support under the GI bill was calculated to put him back in touch with environs that were the setting for his novels of the Tennessee period.

McCarthy received encouragement for his fiction writing at the university, where in 1959 and 1960 the student literary magazine, *The Phoenix,* published his two short stories, "Wake for Susan" and "A Drowning Incident," both of which explored ideas and strategies he revisited in *The Orchard Keeper* and later works. Because these short pieces display competence but little of the explosive mastery with which McCarthy blossomed as a writer in his first novel, his talent seeming to arise without precedent in his apprentice writing, scholars have usually assumed that they preceded his work on *The Orchard Keeper.* However, it is also possible, since McCarthy was already at work on *The Orchard Keeper* in 1959, that the stories were offshoots of that novel. Either way, they form some of our best evidence of the genesis of the longer work, of the concerns and strategies that were central to it at its beginning.

Both stories employ the third-person indirect discourse that typifies McCarthy's novels, and the protagonists of both are preadolescent boys living in proximity to the natural world and coming to terms with their innate compassion for other people and animals. As its title suggests, "Wake for Susan" depicts a boy, Wes, whose empathy for an unknown young woman awakens through his solitary contemplation of her tombstone. His imagination builds on the terse engraved details of Susan's life—her age at death, her gender—to create for her a story that moves him to tears. The tale Wes imagines is constructed out of his own experience, and his empathy is at least partly self-centered and sentimental, but the story is a parable of the creative process. In its narrative frame, Wes walks through the woods looking for historical artifacts such as musket balls or Indian arrowheads, then stops in an old mountain cemetery to enter imaginatively into Susan's brief life through the touchstone of her tombstone. As I discuss in "'They aint the thing': Artifact and Hallucinated Recollection in McCarthy's Early Frame-Works," the structuring device of a frame in a narrative present bookending a reconstructed past is one McCarthy also deploys in *The Orchard Keeper*, where the similarly named John Wesley returns to Red Branch and stands in meditation at his mother's tombstone in the opening and closing scenes. The bracketed narration can and, I believe, should be read as John Wesley's imaginative recovery/reinterpretation/"writing" of his and his mentors' experiences during one year of his early adolescence. A character's framing and reconstruction of the past also figures importantly in *Suttree*, *The Gardener's Son*, and *The Stonemason*; and in a different sense the whole of *Blood Meridian* can be read as an act of historical/imaginative recovery as the unsituated, unidentified narrator invites us to join in his project to "see the child" and that bloody period of America's past.

In "A Drowning Incident," a boy discovers that his father has tied the puppies of the family dog Suzy in a sack and cast them into the nearby creek to drown. The boy retrieves the bloated body of one puppy and places it beside his baby sister in her crib in affirmation of the equivalent value of their young lives, then awaits the inevitable confrontation with his callous and perhaps punitive father. The boy's courageous rebellion against the utilitarian ethics of his father and the wider society they inhabit parallels John Wesley Rattner's rejection of the hawk bounty offered by the county government in *The Orchard Keeper*. Further, it adumbrates the novel's exploration of the broader conflict between the values of the mountain people and the new social order in East Tennessee: urbanization, the machine age, and the advent of the Tennessee Valley Authority, for which McCarthy's own father served as chief counsel in charge of property acquisition by eminent domain. When McCarthy developed this unifying theme in the novel, he distributed the alienation from the newly dominant socioeconomic order among his three main characters. John Wesley Rattner comes to reject the order emblematized by his corrupt father and the community's law officers, an order based on utilitarianism and the devaluing of the mountain people. Marion Sylder actively rebels against the governmental mandate that the mountaineers forfeit their traditional whiskey-making and articulates his disgust for those who sell their *own neighbors out for money*" (215, italics in original). And old Arthur Ownby wants to live in peace but feels compelled to protest against the government installation that regards the land on which it was erected with "contempt" (93). Greatly increasing its complexity over his taut tale, "A Drowning Incident," McCarthy organized his novel around three interwoven narrative arcs that trace their parallel rebellions and challenged himself to work out linked resolutions for the key characters, including the remains of John Wesley's corrupt father. At the same time, his creation of the living characters Sylder and Ownby, who follow their own consciences, places the fatherless John Wesley within a structure of emotional support that encourages his inner moral sense and his courage to live by it—something the lonely boy of "A Drowning Incident" does not enjoy. *The Orchard Keeper* is far more ambitious than "A Drowning Incident," but the germ of the novel's central issues is explored in the short story McCarthy wrote at about the same time.

As Rick Wallach discusses in "Prefiguring Cormac McCarthy," the motif of the drowned puppies is reused in *Blood Meridian,* where Judge Holden, that powerful agent of the will to disvalue and discard life, buys two puppies solely so that he can toss them into a river, where one of his disciples shoots them as they are carried, struggling, downstream (192–93). The scene is one of many that suggest the nature of the judge, against whose values that declare war is God the Glanton gang members too rarely and too weakly protest. Of broader significance than the specific trope of drowned puppies, the youth who finds himself at odds with his father's and/or his culture's blindness to the value of others became a dominant theme in McCarthy's work from the 1950s through the 1990s, recurring in Robert McEvoy's alienation from the mill system in *The Gardener's Son,* in Suttree's repudiation of his father's and his city's middle class values, in Ben Telfair's rejection of his father's business endeavors in favor of his grandfather's older values of "the craft" in *The Stonemason,* and in the kid's halting and ineffectual opposition to the judge in *Blood Meridian.*

The theme reappears in the Border Trilogy, where John Grady must confront the social consequences in Mexico for a young woman like Alejandra whose naïve claim of sexual freedom marks her as ruined even in the eyes of her father, and where John Grady will subsequently fall in love with the innocent Magdalena made into a "whore" by her society. In both *All the Pretty Horses* and *Cities of the Plain,* the story with which the trilogy originated, John Grady acts on his own sense of the worth of these young women, withstanding the practical discouragement of his friends and older mentors. But even more than *The Orchard Keeper,* the Border Trilogy dwells on the terrible cost to self and loved ones of adhering to one's own moral sense when the world opposes it. In its middle volume, *The Crossing,* the theme is explored in an ecocentric context, when Billy Parham repudiates his cattle culture's (and his father's) view of the wolf as a pest to be exterminated. Billy's attempt to honor the wolf's life and her mystery ends in her death and his despair. Moreover, he is left with guilt that his doomed choice to save her has cost the lives of his parents; similarly, John Grady's attempt to save Magdalena by taking her across the border to America results in her murder.

"A Drowning Incident" lies behind all these fictional and dramatic treatments of the young man at odds with conventional value structures, and in that sense the story adumbrates not only *The Orchard Keeper* but also much of McCarthy's mature work. McCarthy seems to have found himself out of sync with the familial and social expectations he was born into, as well as with some of Knoxville's and America's social norms. In 1968 he remarked to Lexington interviewer Blithe Runsdorf, "Any artist is outside the mainstream of society . . . they just don't fit in well with American society" (Runsdorf, "Recognition Acceptable" 5). Howard Gardner's study *Creating Minds* shows that the experience of such asynchrony is common to highly creative people, even fruitful if it is not excessive (40–41). To be sure, McCarthy's devoting himself to the uncertainty and independence of a creative life rather than a career in law like his father Charles Joseph Sr. and brother Dennis, or in academia like his classicist paternal aunt Barbara and folklorist brother William, or the priesthood (William's initial career choice) was one manifestation of what he meant when he reported that he was not what his parents "had in mind" (Woodward, "Venomous Fiction" 31). McCarthy's ex-wife Anne De Lisle has remarked that McCarthy's analytical, pragmatic father "didn't know what to make of him" (Conversations). And his sister Barbara McCooe recalls that it was the impracticality of his chosen career in the arts to which his parents objected (Interview with Bryan Giemza and Dianne Luce).

McCarthy certainly had the option of pursuing a profession. His lifelong breadth and depth of reading and his tremendous range of interests—"I had every hobby there was," he told Woodward of his childhood (Woodward, "Venomous Fiction" 31)—speak to his remarkable intelligence and curiosity, which must have been evident to his parents and teachers even when he underperformed in school. His high school peers recognized his flexibility of mind, naming him "Most Talented" of those in his senior class (Luce, "Cormac McCarthy in High School" 3). When he left the university to pursue his writing career in early fall 1960, he turned his back on fellowships for graduate work in three different fields—and thus on academia (McCarthy to Larry Bensky, [late Oct. or Nov. 1962]). But as he told Woodward, fiction can "encompass all the various disciplines and interests of humanity" (Woodward, "Venomous Fiction" 30).

Sheer intelligence was not the determining factor. Temperamentally, McCarthy was unsuited to a career within a hierarchical structure, restive under obligations imposed by others. This was one factor behind his steadfast refusal to take a job teaching writing at a university or to promote his books through public readings or lectures. As a child, like John Wesley, he would climb out his family's second-storey window at night to explore the surrounding country-side, a habit that may be linked with his adult wanderlust and his tolerance for living for months at a time without the comfort and security of a home. As much as he was liked and respected by his peers, he disliked school. "What could the nuns have taught me?" he once asked his sister Bobbie (McCooe, Interview with Bryan Giemza and Dianne Luce). And by his own report in the sketch "Two Hour Scholar Loses His Dollar," he played hooky at least once to visit the fairgrounds. It seems telling, too, that his wife Anne thought of him during their years together as "a rebel" (Williams, "Annie DeLisle" E2). His discomfort within the structures of family, church,[1] work, and community made engagement in a self-directed creative life attractive to him, even necessary. Moreover, his alert skepticism about the values revealed in a society's actions lies behind his repeated exploration in his writing of a young person's adhering to his own value structure in conflict with the conventions consciously or thoughtlessly adhered to by others.

Thanks to the sleuthing of Wesley Morgan, we may now infer that some of McCarthy's works in this vein may have arisen from the productive conjunction of his innate temperament with his exposure by age eleven to Marjorie Kinnan Rawlings's Pulitzer Prize-winning novel *The Yearling* (1938). His imaginative inhabiting of the character of Jody Baxter in January 1945, when he auditioned for that role in the film adaptation, so impressed the talent scouts that he was selected as a finalist from the Knoxville area (Wesley Morgan, "McCarthy and *The Yearling*" 71). It is almost certain that McCarthy read the novel or at least some of it to prepare for his auditions, and its influence surfaces in several of his own works, especially those that treat a young boy's feeling for the natural world. Morgan reports that the audition announcement specified that candidates for the role should have an affinity for animals, a trait that was central to Jody's character ("McCarthy and *The Yearling*" 71). In *The Yearling*, Jody longs to adopt a wild animal as a pet as his strange friend Fodder-wing frequently does, but his mother foresees only the expense and trouble involved. Eventually Jody is allowed to foster a fawn, but when it grows bigger and destroys some of the impoverished family's crops, he is forced to kill it. This aspect of *The Yearling* resonates with "A Drowning Incident," with John Wesley's having to return Lady's puppy to Sylder in *The Orchard Keeper*, and especially with the long tragic story of Billy and the she-wolf that opens *The Crossing*.

Like *The Orchard Keeper*, *The Yearling* is a coming-of-age story about a rural boy who learns about death, loss, love, and sacrifice, and the two novels develop similar themes and incidents. Jody shares his father Penny's love for the Florida wilderness that surrounds their small farm, but the boy is often at odds with his worried mother, whose primary concern is for the family's survival. She resists his hunting with his father and their neighbors, but his father believes that hunting is crucial to Jody's learning to be a man. Like John Wesley, Jody relishes the mentoring he receives in the masculine world of hunting. In addition, he confronts the naturalistic realities of the dangers to human livelihood posed by predators—wolves, panthers, and bears—as when the big bear Slewfoot takes livestock, for instance (Rawlings, *Yearling* 22–23, 293). Like Ownby, Jody learns that a panther cub can be tamed (79), but he also learns to fear the panther as an avatar of Death (141–42). A female panther with two cubs figures in *The Yearling* (231), and an avenging she-bear reclaims her cub (331–32). The hunters warn Jody that a raccoon can drown a dog (49), and McCarthy develops this idea in his episode of Lady and the big raccoon (*OK* 121–24).

A measure of how related *The Yearling* was to McCarthy's interests and how strong an influence it has been on his boy stories and wilderness writing is his returning to it for incidents and details of his later novels. Like Lester Ballard, as well as John Wesley Rattner, Jody encounters a world "devastated with . . . flood" (222). His father kills a seven-foot rattlesnake and hangs its skin on the wall (205), an image McCarthy deploys in *Outer Dark*. And like Culla Holme, Jody becomes lost in the swamp (ch. 33), which McCarthy transforms into a strange psychic terrain in *Outer Dark*. Fodder-wing's visions of the old Spaniards in Florida (59) anticipate John Grady's visions of the Comanches in *All the Pretty Horses* and *Cities of the Plain*. Finally, like Billy Parham in *The Crossing*, Jody witnesses the mysterious spectacle of a wolf playing in the moonlight (353). His father patiently explains to him that wolves know nothing of human boundary lines (39), and Penny is distressed to learn that his neighbors the Forresters are killing wolves by setting poison bait from horseback (268; 272). So many plot affinities lie between *The Yearling* and McCarthy's treatments of boys, men, and animals in the natural world that one is tempted to see his childhood exposure to Rawlings's novel as a formative influence on his own choice in his adult years to become a writer. Yet there must have been many other influential stories that inspired him as well. We know that Shakespeare, Melville, Dostoyevsky, Joyce, Hemingway, Faulkner, and O'Connor have all been important influences, and McCarthy may well have been reading them during his adolescence.

Among Faulkner's works, the child Sarty Snopes of "Barn Burning" and the intellectually disabled Ike Snopes of *The Hamlet* seem significant influences on McCarthy's conception of John Wesley's moral choices. Both of Faulkner's innocent characters emerge from a state of relative confusion to take stances that repudiate the values of the Snopes adults around them. As painful as it is to him, Sarty, the son of a bitter sharecropping father, foils his father's vengeful burning of the landowner's barn and then strikes out from his family at an early age, carrying guilt for having betrayed his father and for possibly causing his death, yet affirming his own values of justice and courage. While John Wesley does not betray the memory of his father in so profound a way, he chooses loyalty to his foster father Sylder over the vengeance his mother has urged him to internalize. On a more bathetic level, in the "Afternoon of a Cow" section of *The Hamlet,* Ike Snopes rejects the cash valuation of his beloved cow when he lets the coin fall from a bridge. To stop his inappropriate attentions to her, his family has slaughtered her and given him the coin in compensation. Their act in service of respectability does not recognize his love, but his gesture of repudiation affirms it. McCarthy reinscribes the principled refusal of coin and of conformity to the accepted social order in John Wesley's return of the hawk bounty. Faulkner depicts both his characters' struggling toward the insights that impel their acts of liberation, and McCarthy's drafts do so even more explicitly than does the published novel.

# Drafting *The Orchard Keeper*
## Remnants of the First Draft

W hile still in college, in 1959 McCarthy received a $125 award in support of his writing from the Ingram Merrill Foundation ("Charles McCarthy"). McCarthy's prize, the first of many he would receive from private foundations, was among the earliest awarded by Ingram Merrill, which had been established that year by poet James Merrill with his inheritance from his father Charles, of Merrill-Lynch renown. In McCarthy's letter offering *The Orchard Keeper* to Random House, received by the fiction editor on May 3, 1962, he records that the prize was "renewed," but the drafting of his novel took longer than the support could have lasted. McCarthy's letter makes it clear, then, that although the two stories he published in *The Phoenix* may have been some of the materials he submitted with his application, the Merrill award was to support his work on the novel; his need for paid employment accounted for the novel's three-year composition process more than "any struggle with the writing of it."

Indeed, the first draft seems to have come together rather steadily in 1959 and 1960 although we have little surviving evidence of that version. Remaining from the initial draft are a few dated pages from 1960 and possibly some of the undated leaves carried forward into the "Late Draft," which is the earliest type-script of *The Orchard Keeper* among McCarthy's papers. For the most part, the "Late Draft" comprises second- or third-draft leaves. The leaves from 1960 are numbered in the upper left corner and later repaginated in the right margin, sometimes more than once, to indicate their changing positions in subsequent drafts. As few as the surviving first-draft pages are, they show that by summer 1960, when he was still enrolled at the university, McCarthy had formulated the complicated design and narrative frame of his novel and had roughed out the interwoven plotlines of at least three of his four main characters. Two con-secutive leaves carried forward from McCarthy's first draft are dated June 17, 1960, and the first of these carries the notation, "last ¼ in school" ("Late Draft" 134/230). This is an early draft of the scene in which John Wesley leaves the courthouse after returning the hawk bounty, the choice that resolves his ethi-cal dilemma and confirms his value system. Its date is evidence that John Wes-ley's repudiation of societal norms was central to McCarthy's earliest thinking about the novel.

Two pages dated "Sat June 18" were also composed in 1960, since the 18th fell on a Saturday that year. McCarthy wrote these pages the day after he drafted John Wesley's return of the hawk bounty, but here he turned to Own-by's teasing the men at the store about the panther's scream ("Late Draft" 139/149/156–140/150/157; cf. *OK* 149–50), evidence that Ownby's story and his sense of the panther as a symbol of wilderness had also been part of the novel's first draft. In the "Late Draft" and the published novel, when Ownby tells this anecdote to the boys on a snowy afternoon, it segues into his un-voiced memory of the panther kit he and his wife Ellen adopted with disas-trous results. With its treatment of the contradictory desires to protect and to domesticate a wild creature, the panther kit episode is among those most indebted to *The Yearling*. Although the evidence for that memory's presence in the lost first draft is inconclusive, Ownby's panther tale at the store and John Wesley's return of the hawk bounty suggest that from the novel's inception McCarthy also had in mind the theme of human regret for impinging on the wilderness.

Since in this period McCarthy usually recorded dates of composition only in his first drafts (although there are some rare exceptions to this), it seems likely that a page in the "Late Draft" dated July 7 was also composed in 1960. On this page of the graveside epilogue, McCarthy jotted a note—possibly in 1960, possibly as late as early spring 1962, when he was finishing the novel—in which he considered having an intoxicated John Wesley staggering "among the . . . stones to find father" and thinking that "A skull and a gallon of bones shouldnt need much space" (156/258). If the leaf and the note were both com-posed in summer 1960, it would mean that by mid-year not only had McCarthy devised the narrative frame in which John Wesley has his "hallucinated recollection" in the cemetery, but also that he had worked out incidents surrounding the recovery of Rattner's remains. No page from 1960 features Sylder, but if the note about Kenneth Rattner's bones in the first draft's epilogue was recorded in 1960, it would suggest that McCarthy had already conceived something of his killer. He may well have composed Sylder's story in his first draft but revised it so heavily that no dated first-draft leaves survive.

The holograph dating of a half-page on August 5 and another page on September 11 suggests that they too are first-draft leaves advanced into the "Late Draft." If so, judging from their pagination, McCarthy had written some two hundred pages of first-draft material by mid-September 1960. The first of these is a description of Ownby's wielding his spiderstick as he walks the orchard road ("Late Draft" 194; cf. OK 55). The other reflects an early conception of Ownby's arrest, in which he is detained at the store by Constable Gifford rather than the published version's unnamed agent in his starched clothes, a stranger to Ownby ("Late Draft" 218/238; cf. *OK* 201 ff.). As McCarthy revised in the late-draft stage, he reconceived the details of Ownby's arrest, but this leaf suggests that in his earliest conception, the persecution of the citizens of Red Branch was to be carried out predominantly by their own neighbors, especially Gifford.

Finally, the dated, first-draft material in the "Late Draft" shows (as the extensive first draft of *Outer Dark* does even more conclusively) that McCarthy did not compose the sections of his novel in the order in which they would appear. Rather, he seems to have held the broad shape of his novel in his mind and worked on scenes as the mood struck him, perhaps as he felt some urgency to get down on paper a particular way of expressing a scene.

Although McCarthy had attended the university for four years (1951–1952, 1957–1960) before and after his tour of duty in the Air Force (1953–1957), he left after the summer term of 1960 without finishing the language requirement for his degree (Fields, "Knoxville Author"; Owen, "McCarthy Is One" 4B). In a letter to his first Random House editor, Larry Bensky, written in late October or November 1962, McCarthy provided a fanciful autobiographical sketch, which his second editor, Albert Erskine, abbreviated two years later for the biographical note on the dust jacket of *The Orchard Keeper*. In the sketch, McCarthy explained that he had not earned a degree because instead of ticking off the requisites, he had taken courses that appealed to his interests until his funding under the GI bill ran out. By this time, the small Merrill awards had run out as well. As the jacket description partially based on this sketch states, "the necessities of life delayed [the novel's] completion." The evidence of his substantial progress on the first draft through summer 1960 suggests that the delays started after he left school.

In addition to the need to eat, two primary "necessities of life" likely resulted from his marriage to Lee Holleman on January 3, 1961, as McCarthy reported in *Who's Who* (34th ed.), and her pregnancy in 1962. Lee had attended high school in Wynne, Arkansas, and she moved to Knoxville when she enrolled at the University of Tennessee. She was five or six years younger than Cormac, so their meeting occurred no earlier than 1957, during his second period of enrollment. Wesley Morgan has shared with me that Lee graduated from the university on December 15, 1960 (email, Apr. 25, 2018), and Barbara McCooe recalls that the couple moved to Chicago after their marriage in January (interview with Bryan Giemza and Dianne Luce).

Cormac and Lee seem to have lived in Chicago's counter-cultural Old Town neighborhood, an historic area made affordable by middle-class flight to the suburbs. According to recollections he jotted in 1966, McCarthy spent Thanksgiving 1961 on North Park, which lies partly in Old Town (*OD*: "Early Draft [A]" 126), and Lee McCarthy refers to walking between Division and North, the streets bounding Old Town on the south and north, in her poem "It's in the Cards" (l. 5). In his letter to Bensky, McCarthy described this time in Chicago as a period of "living in cellars, on unemployment and welfare," but the couple's financial situation was probably not quite as dire as he suggests (letter, [late Oct.-Nov. 1962]: 2). He acknowledged that he had a part-time job; in addition, Wesley Morgan has discovered that Lee held a job as a clerk-typist in the Walter F. Bennett advertising and public relations agency in 1961–1962 ("Lee Holleman McCarthy" 3459; Morgan, Email to the author, Apr. 25, 2018). Thus, they had regular earnings, but in these jobs they were both underemployed, and their income was not lavish even if they supplemented it with food stamps or some other form of welfare. By the time McCarthy wrote his life sketch for Bensky in late October or November 1962, in which he explained the delays in the composition of his first novel, the baby's birth was imminent. Probably the couple's financial pressures made it seem to McCarthy that it had taken him a long time to bring his first book to completion, but its composition period from 1959 to 1962 was much shorter than many of his subsequent books would require.

Little is known about McCarthy's life in Chicago, but in January 1980 he wrote to Robert Coles revealing the genesis there of a novel that would occupy him for the rest of his writing career. He wrote that in a Chicago bar he had often heard a friend recite an unpublished poem by Louis Diehl, who had been a member of the International Workers of the World movement in the 1930s. The poem was about innovative New Orleans jazz clarinetist Leon Roppolo and the legend that he threw his clarinet into Lake Pontchartrain in a fit of despondency and self-destructiveness. McCarthy confided to Coles that the poem had given him the idea for a novel set in New Orleans, although the narrative would not be about Roppolo himself. There is no solid evidence that McCarthy began drafting such a novel in the 1960s, but by August 1980 he wrote to Deaderick Montague that he thought the New Orleans novel would be his next after the publication of *Blood Meridian*. What is clear, then, is that McCarthy partially conceived his long-awaited work *The Passenger* before May 1962 and that he was mulling the project intermittently while finishing *The Orchard Keeper* and drafting *Outer Dark, Child of God,* and *Suttree,* the novels he worked on during the period of this study.[2]

From fall 1960 through spring 1962, McCarthy twice revised the novel that would only later be titled *The Orchard Keeper* (McCarthy, Letter to Bensky, July 12, 1962). In his letter of submission, received May 3, he wrote from Chicago that he had just finished the final draft (McCarthy, Letter to Fiction Editor). In his fall 1962 sketch for Bensky, McCarthy wrote that in Chicago he had worked for a year in an auto-parts warehouse, "the longest I have ever held a job" (letter, [late Oct.-Nov. 1962]: 2). This implies that he was employed in Chicago from around January or February 1961 through January or February 1962. If so, he may have given up his job in February in a push to complete the novel. McCarthy's holograph note in the novel's "Late Draft" indicates that he hoped to complete revising and retyping the draft up to page 136 (the start of section III) by February 26 [1962] and that he anticipated completing pages 136 to 161 between March 6 and 9, although he still had "stuff to add" (136). McCarthy composed the remaining pages of the novel and incorporated them into the "Final Draft" that spring. He had not been halfway through revising his "Late Draft" in February, but the recognition that Lee was pregnant, which they may well have suspected by March, would have made the completion and publication of the novel seem more urgent.

# The "Late Draft"

The pagination of "Late Draft" is quite regular through page 143, with only one page number recorded per leaf, evidence that the typescript began as a clean retyping to incorporate the revisions from the previous stage. Pagination of its later leaves is more irregular, with new material inserted and some repositioning of passages. It is among these later pages that we find first-draft leaves carried forward, with some holograph notes for their revision.

The "Late Draft" reveals that McCarthy had designed his plot resolution to make it much tidier than it would become at the behest of his editors. To deter him from taking revenge on Gifford, Sylder tells John Wesley on the second of three unnumbered leaves that the boy is not obligated to him, "and I hope to God youll never find out why. The reason is right out there on that mountain. But youll never find it . . . [.]" He adds that he doubts John Wesley will live his whole life there and partially confesses, "I wouldnt of if . . . [.]" The reader might guess that Sylder's reason for staying relates to his wife or the persistence of state and local prohibition laws, which make his job possible, but as he continues it becomes clear that his remaining in Red Branch has much to do with his having assumed responsibility for the son of the man he has killed. He tells John Wesley that no one chooses to live on a mountain top unless there is a compelling reason, but he declines to share it with the boy, saying only, "If a man is a man, well. . . [.]" On the next unnumbered leaf, John Wesley insists they are still not square, that he owes Sylder, who replies "Square be damned. . . . I ast you jest to stay away from Gifford." But John Wesley will not swear to it, so Sylder says, "Alright . . . We'll do it the hard way," repeating that there is a reason the boy does not owe him anything, and that he would "rather you never knew what it was." He asks John Wesley to take his word for it, and the boy agrees but will not agree to leave Gifford alone, so Sylder repeats that they will "do it the hard way." A line break follows, and in this narrative gap, the reader infers, Sylder reveals that it was he who killed the boy's father in self-defense. The revelation absolves John Wesley from his felt need to take revenge against Gifford for Sylder's injuries, but unknown to Sylder, it also releases the boy from his impulse to avenge the death of his father.

In the "Late Draft" are notes and three draft versions of the next scene. In the first version, when John Wesley leaves the jail, he observes that now everything is "bright with the air of a reckless freedom." He feels newly "purposeful" (228), and as he walks toward the courthouse with the dollar of bounty in his hand, "his throat ached with holding back" his tears "of so fierce a joy" (229). The next version makes it clearer that the boy's newfound sense of freedom and confidence derives from his knowledge that Sylder killed his father in self-defense, a circumstance that requires no retribution. As John Wesley leaves the jail, he reviews his friend's revelation: "In a fight, . . . and he got accidentally killed and he put him in the peach pit and . . . The fire" (228A).

A paragraph break before "The fire" suggests a darker leap in John Wesley's train of thought—a sudden recognition that he and Warn, playing with matches, were themselves responsible for the burning of his father's bones. But McCarthy realized as he worked on the scene that John Wesley's painful recognition could emerge only after Ownby tells him that a fire consumed the body. McCarthy typed a note about what should follow the boy's terrible insight: "[which] was why he went back—sequence? How get him to visit old man?" He penciled further revisions, bracketed his references to Rattner's remains and jotted: "No. he gets this part of it from old man" (228A).

It was probably after writing this version, in which John Wesley comes to understand not only that Sylder has killed his father but also that he is himself responsible for burning the remains, that McCarthy decided to add an explicit note of anguish to the joy and freedom that John Wesley feels. He drafted this in notes he inscribed between the lines on his first version of the scene ("Late Draft" 229) and at the top of the first page of the courthouse scene he had originally dated June 17, 1960 ("Late Draft" 134/230). These notes are incorporated only in his third typed version of the scene, which now ends with John Wesley's decision to return the hawk bounty. Clutching the dollar, he approaches the courthouse, "his throat hot and constricted with a joy more fierce than any anguish" ("Late Draft" 228B). The scene shows the boy coming to terms with his new knowledge and his new awareness of his own ignorance, and groping toward a new insight: "that the darkness and ambiguity in which he . . . felt his way . . . was a universal shroud and pall upon all . . . lives." Then comes John Wesley's explicit realization of his freedom from avenging his father: "I dont have to. . . . Perhaps he thought: I hurt now, and so now I am free" ("Late Draft" 228B).

John Wesley's final conversation with Ownby in the "Late Draft" also differs from the published book. Three undated leaves of this scene were initially numbered 22–24 and were likely composed in spring 1962 when McCarthy wrote the cat's story in the rain sequence paginated 1–18. When John Wesley tells Ownby that Sylder has been arrested for running whiskey, Ownby asks if he has been charged with anything else. Sylder has told the boy the half-truth that he killed Kenneth Rattner accidentally, so John Wesley asks the old man what else Sylder might have been accused of. Without realizing what he is revealing, Ownby replies, "Seems to me . . . he's the same feller I seen back seven eight year ago on the mountain one night. Somebody leastwise had put somebody in the peach pit. . . . Could of been this feller" (22/242). He also innocently discloses that the body was burned when boys set fire to some dead cedars the winter before (23/243). Ownby knows neither Sylder nor Rattner, but he intuits that the corpse was placed there for cause: "You find a feller in a peach pit you can genly figger he got hissef there and even not, it wouldnt hep him none to holler about it" (24/244/227). Ownby's account of the body confirms what Sylder has confessed and expresses attitudes toward killer and victim that reinforce John Wesley's sense of freedom from any obligation to avenge his father, as well as from conventional attitudes about law and justice. In thinking about his resolution, McCarthy briefly considered that if John Wesley were to kill Sylder after all and place his body in the pit, where Ownby could find it and cover it with cedars, it would create a cyclical structure for the plot ("Late Draft" 135/231). (This leaf bears the date June 17, 1960, the date on which McCarthy first drafted John Wesley's return of the hawk bounty, but the notation may have been added later.) Instead, the two complementary conversations in the "Late Draft" give John Wesley knowledge of his father's killer and the location of his remains yet paradoxically release him from seeking revenge. When the boy leaves Ownby, he murmurs, more to himself than to his elderly friend, "It's all alright. It has to be alright" ("Late Draft" 24/227/244 verso).

These resolution scenes in the "Late Draft" show that McCarthy had deployed his strategy of converging main characters not only in the novel's opening but also in its ending, where he structured the meetings of John Wesley sequentially with his two mentors for their final conversations. And he deployed the strategy of convergence as well in John Wesley's synthesis of their separate pieces of knowledge to solve the mystery of his father's disappearance. In effect, this made the boy a detective figure, an archaeologist of the past, and it emphasized the problem of what to do with uncovered knowledge of violence, death, corruption, and injustice.

A related page begins "Which is why the boy went back then" and reveals that John Wesley goes to the pit in the orchard to recover the bones of his father—"some artifact to speak for the silent and unrecorded events that there transpired." He works half a day, and "even the archaeologist from the University . . . found no more" ("Late Draft" 264/260). John Wesley's recovery of his father's remains in the "Late Draft" would have prepared for his search for his father's gravestone in its epilogue, a passing idea McCarthy jotted on a first-draft leaf along with the year of Rattner's death, 1934 ("Late Draft" 156/258). Had McCarthy followed through on his idea that John Wesley would visit his father's grave in addition to his mother's, it would have reinforced that the young man was fully aware of the fate of his father and of his bones. It would also have conveyed more explicitly that John Wesley closes the book on his vexed relationship with his father as well as his mother when he visits their graves. Even without the search for his father's gravestone, the passages about the recovery of Rattner's bones implied quite clearly that the young man's hallucinated recollection of the whole story in the graveyard completes his recovery of the past, his imaginative moving beyond bones and stones to a full comprehension of the lives of the people involved. As in "Wake for Susan," then, John Wesley is not only a detective and archaeologist, but a "writer" who imagines the story presented in the novel, making mere ashes and bones the medium for the recovery of history and the construction of meaning. In opposition to John Wesley's imaginative recovery of the past, the sterile search through ashes is assigned in all McCarthy's drafts to the inept and greedy "humane" officer Legwater, in whom it is a profane sifting for bounty.

One discrete scene and two other sequences in the "Late Draft" appear to be added there for the first time, although none of them seems material that

McCarthy had just conceived. Rather, they are the "stuff" he knew in February 1962 he still needed to compose. The most straightforward addition in the "Late Draft" was the scene of Legwater's shooting Scout. McCarthy reminded himself twice that he needed to create a resolution for the dog: "What about the dog?" ("Late Draft" 228); "what haps to dog?" ("Late Draft" 251). On the leaves that immediately follow his second reminder, he drafted the new scene (252–53), making only minor changes before publication.

Each of the longer sequences added in the "Late Draft" remained somewhat problematic for McCarthy's editors and/or readers. One is the cluster of scenes dealing with the boys' and Ownby's day in the snow. These scenes comprise necessary background to Ownby's unintentional revelation in the "Late Draft" that John Wesley has burned the corpse of his father, but McCarthy was somewhat uncertain about the order in which the evidence about the fire should be revealed to Ownby and the reader. McCarthy had queried himself, "Squirrel Hunt here?" on the first page of the earlier scene which ends with the line, "That was how winter came that year" ("Late Draft" 76–77; cf. *OK* 73). So he had in mind the boys' winter hunting, but there is no evidence that he followed through on writing a squirrel-hunting scene or placing the other winter hunting scenes at this location. In both the "Late Draft" and the published novel, the advent of winter is followed by Sylder's road chase and then John Wesley's memory of collecting the hawk bounty so that he can buy muskrat traps (see *OK* 74–87). McCarthy thought of the boys again when he composed the description of the December snowfall. He introduced them with the line, "They all went to school at Vestal" (he later crossed out "Vestal," the name of the little community where he himself had lived as a child), and he specified that John Wesley knew only one of them. This detail established that John Wesley did not attend school, which is far less explicit in the published version. The leaf continues with the story of how John Wesley had met Warn Pulliam flying his pet buzzard, but McCarthy also wondered in the margin whether he had introduced Warn yet ("Late Draft" 138).

Soon after, McCarthy listed a tentative sequence for the December scenes: "Need old man here. / Where GF Inn used to be/ owl/ Store/ Then:" ("Late Draft" 145/150). We can infer that he drafted and discarded his first attempt at this sequence on leaves numbered 1–4 that do not survive. He kept a draft of the culminating scene of Ownby's discovering the burned corpse, leaves 5/6 and 7. Then he backtracked and started over with three short scenes of the boys' and Ownby's day in the snow, leaves numbered 5–9. These pages are the earliest surviving draft of the antecedent winter scenes, beginning with Ownby's walking past the Green Fly Inn site, as McCarthy had planned. He subsequently revised and reorganized the scenes on new pages 5–9, which he later renumbered 144a–144E. Now the sequence began with the incident of the four boys' starting the fire in the cave (5/144a–7/144c; cf. *OK* 139–42), which had not been anticipated in his sketch outline for the scenes. Next came the scene of Johnny Romines and Boog at Eller's store (8/144d; cf. *OK* 142–43). Placed last in this version was the scene of Ownby's emerging from the woods near the site of the burned Green Fly Inn and seeing the dead owl dangling from the lightwires (9/144E; cf. *OK* 143).

As planned, the scene of Johnny and Boog at the store explains their separation from John Wesley and Warn, who wander on to the pesticide pit. In the cave, Boog is the one most fascinated by fire, but the store scene precludes the possibility that he might have burned the corpse, and the boys' separation intensifies the reader's and John Wesley's recognition of his own involvement when Ownby later tells him that the body in the pit was burned by "some boys." Ownby has only the anonymous pair of boy-sized tracks in the snow from which to infer how the corpse has burned, but the reader brings to bear additional information about which boys were there, information known to John Wesley.

To judge from his jotted outline of the scenes, McCarthy's initial aim was to bracket the events of the snowy day between Ownby's visits to the sites of two fires, the Green Fly Inn and the pesticide pit; but as he rearranged, McCarthy apparently decided that Ownby's scene at the burned inn functioned better after the boys' scenes in the cave and at the store. In this revised order, the reference to the fire at the inn resonates with the boys' careless playing with fire, already introduced; and the image of the desiccated owl hanging from a lightwire rhymes with the decomposed corpse that they burn, presumably by throwing lit matches into the dried cedar covering it. The two other leaves McCarthy first drafted for the sequence, the scenes of Ownby's late afternoon trek to the pit, numbered 5/6 and 7, were later renumbered for their new position some twenty pages after Ownby's walk past the burned Green Fly Inn. Intervening are the scenes in which the old man hosts Warn and John Wesley at his cabin, telling them stories and serving them wine. On his walk, Ownby sees the "drunken lanes" in the snow, detects the scent of burning cedar, and follows the tracks to the pesticide pit, where the cedar smolders ("Late Draft" 7/168/167; cf. *OK* 158). During the initial drafting of this scene, McCarthy had queried whether the tracks in the snow should be those of three, two, or four boys, the question that was resolved when he wrote the store scene separating Boog and Johnny from John Wesley and Warn.

McCarthy's holograph notes for the burned corpse scene record his openness to alternative fates for Rattner's remains: "gone to white ashes as Ethan Brand? OR: Boy plays w/ skeleton of his father? or skull/ . . . he ate possum that ate man in pit" ("Late Draft" 5/6/160/166). So although the idea that the corpse would burn was foremost in McCarthy's mind, he was considering other possibilities derived from literary models in Shakespeare and Haw-thorne. With the idea that the youngsters might discover the bones or the skull and play with them without knowing their identity, McCarthy was working toward the unsettling frisson that John Wesley might experience when, like Hamlet holding Yorick's skull in the graveyard, he encounters death without anticipating that it will touch him so closely (*Hamlet* 5.1). John Wesley retro-spectively realizes he has casually burned the bones of his father, as Hamlet progressively realizes that the skull he has been casually handling belonged to the jester Yorick, loved in his childhood, and further that he has been talking with Horatio about death and corruption of the flesh without yet knowing that his beloved Ophelia has died and will be buried in the same graveyard on that day.

McCarthy's notion that John Wesley might once have eaten a possum that had fed on the corpse of his father also derives from *Hamlet*, where Hamlet taunts Claudius that a dead king, eaten by a worm, in turn eaten by a fish, might go "a progress through the guts of a beggar" (4.3.32–33). This idea might have been problematic to implement, however, since John Wesley could not plausibly link his possum dinner with his father's corpse except through mor-bid imaginings more characteristic of Hamlet or Suttree.

McCarthy's marginal reference to Nathaniel Hawthorne's short story "Ethan Brand" relates, of course, to the burning of Rattner's corpse, his foremost idea. In the tale, Brand, who has once tended a kiln where marble is burned to lime, goes searching the world for the Unforgiveable Sin. He belatedly rec-ognizes that his search for evil in the hearts of his fellows comprises his own deepest transgression, and he returns to the kiln and throws himself into the oculus of the furnace. In the morning, the current lime-burner and his impres-sionable son find Brand's bones reduced to powdered lime but not his heart, which remains cold marble. The image of human bones refined to ash is a haunting one; moreover, the reference to "Ethan Brand" documents that Mc-Carthy conceived a parallel between the outsider Kenneth Rattner and Haw-thorne's Brand, whose eyes burn like fires in a cavern (1186) and who functions within the village as a principle of darkness oppressing many who encounter him. Moreover, in contrast to his sensitive son and his fellow villagers, the dull and pragmatic lime-burner who finds Brand's ashen remains is delighted at the prospect of profiting from his predecessor's death, like McCarthy's Leg-water, who sifts Rattner's ashes in search of the platinum plate reputed to be in his skull (Hawthorne, "Ethan Brand" 1196; *OK* 237–41).

McCarthy's notes illuminate his sense of the importance of John Wesley's exposure to mortality and the boy's recognition of his implication in his fa-ther's burning. McCarthy invented and shaped all the scenes of the snowy day to lead logically to the one in which Ownby sees that the body has burned and only partially puts together how that has come to be, while the reader and later John Wesley infer his involvement. However, the implication became more obscure when, at his editors' request, McCarthy revised Ownby's revelations to John Wesley.

The second set of scenes that McCarthy still needed to compose in spring 1962 developed the story of the feral housecat. In the first draft, McCarthy had introduced the feline motif, as evidenced by Ownby's tales about panthers to the men in Eller's store. Undated leaves 262–63 from deep in the "Late Draft," where the consecutive pagination has broken down, may have been carried forward from the first draft as well, as suggested by their pagination in the upper left corner, typical of the novel's first-draft leaves. In this asylum scene, when Ownby tells John Wesley about the corpse in the pit, the old man explains his idea that the soul of an unburied person might transmigrate into the body of a cat and remain there for up to seven years (cf. *OK* 227). Another passage, which does not appear in the published novel, links the cat specifically to Rattner: "That feller in the pit, his cat come round near ever night for seven year. . . . Then one night . . . I heard it go over—up in the air. It was him leavin out, cat and all." Ownby heard the cat yowl twice and he hopes he will never hear it again, because "It tried to hant me, in a way" ("Late Draft" 262).

McCarthy knew that to prepare for Ownby's account of Rattner's cat, he would need to backtrack to trace its movements. At the top right of the scene in which Rattner drinks at Jim's Hot Spot, McCarthy jotted "CAT?" ("Late Draft" 21), as if he were thinking of including a cat reference in Rattner's memory of the porch collapse, or as if he still needed to draft and position the incidents dealing with the cat. When McCarthy completed his draft in 1962, he composed a new sequence of at least eighteen pages, numbering them consecutively from page 1 on, among which are the cat's scenes. Heading the first of these leaves, McCarthy penciled "RAIN," and the sequence is unified around the spring storms that cause the tree to split and concuss Ownby, that drench the cat, and that dilute the gasoline in Eller's pump, causing Sylder's car to stall on the bridge—the opening incidents of section IV. The first two leaves are the scene in which Ownby is hit by the falling limb and hears "Valkyrie descend with cat's cries to carry him away" ("Late Draft" 2/176; cf. *OK* 172), and the last page in the sequence is of his awakening in the dark presumably on that same day ("Late Draft" 18/193/230 "3rd draft"; cf. *OK* 184).

Problematically, the second scene in the sequence describes Ownby sleeping at the cabin on a rainy day while the cat emerges from the outhouse on feet "wincing" in the wet and gazes at Scout in his dry cellar. At the top of this leaf, McCarthy jotted "Where'd cat com[e] from?" perhaps feeling that the transition from the mythic Valkyrie to the pitiful cat was rather abrupt ("Late Draft" 3/177), perhaps thinking he needed a preparatory scene linking the cat to Rattner or establishing her presence in Red Branch. But there is no evidence in the "Late Draft" that he then backtracked to introduce the housecat any earlier, and her late appearance in the novel remained abrupt and somewhat mysterious. Furthermore, Ownby's presence at his cabin in this first cat scene was a jarring shift since he has just been knocked unconscious by the falling tree limb. McCarthy noted the apparent inconsistency as he revised his carbon "Final Draft" for Erskine, jotting in the margin, "old man is in the woods" (195). He bracketed the reference to Ownby at his cabin for deletion, but this change did not eliminate readers' confusion over how long the old man lies unconscious in the rain.

The Valkyries' screams foreshadow those of the feral cat as the owl carries her off, and the cat scenes that intervene between Ownby's concussion and his reawakening trace her experience seeking food and shelter from the rain. These incidents, originally paginated 4–7, include a very brief reference to her walking the highest portion of the road, "bedraggled" and with a "hunted look" ("Late Draft" 4/178). Perhaps the passage was McCarthy's attempt to provide at least a minimal sense of where the cat had come from, an answer to the question he had posed on the previous page. On this leaf, McCarthy marked where "Cat in smokehouse" should be inserted, and on the next leaf he composed the smokehouse scene, in which the cat gnaws on the dangling pork ribs before Mildred interrupts her, thus associating the cat with the Rattners' environs ("Late Draft" 5/179; *OK* 174). Next McCarthy composed the paragraphs in which the cat is harassed by raucous swooping crows that anticipate the owl that will carry her away; then the scene in which she tries to eat the gritty-furred mink in John Wesley's trap, echoing her attempt to eat the salted meat in the Rattners' smokehouse; and finally one in which she returns to the road, where she "squalled once, hugging the ground with her belly, eyes turned upward" ("Late Draft" 6/180–7/181; *OK* 174–76). All of this, and especially her yowling at the sky in drenched misery and cringing dread, prepares for the scene in which she is attacked by the owl, but McCarthy did not draft that scene as part of this rainy sequence, which moves on to John Wesley's checking his traps ("Late Draft" 8/182/180T). Rather, he composed the scene of her demise in a dry, warm-season setting on three leaves first numbered 11–13 and then renumbered 232–33 for placement in the summer section of the novel. Thus the scenes McCarthy composed for the spring torrent sequence were intended to link Ownby's fall thematically but not temporally with the demise of the cat and the release of Rattner's ghost, since the cat's death needed to occur in August, on the seventh anniversary of Rattner's. McCarthy would further consider the placement of the cat's final scene when he addressed his editors' concerns.

In addition to filling gaps in the narrative during the late-draft stage, McCarthy was still working out solutions to a few problems and subtly adjusting the implications of his narrative. For example, at this stage he knew that Ownby would spend his final years in the asylum, but he was still considering how the old man would be sent there. As mentioned above, on a surviving first-draft page, Gifford arrests him at the store in the mountains, but in the late-draft stage, on the bottom of the leaf in which the sheriff and Gifford try to apprehend Ownby at his cabin, McCarthy jotted a new idea: "Gifford catches him trying to carry his housewares to the mtns/ has an axe" ("Late Draft," a/194). There is no archived draft of such an incident, which would have constituted another scene of Gifford's self-determined harassment of his neighbors. Since it seems more likely that Ownby would be carrying an axe among his belongings than that Gifford would, we may speculate that McCarthy had in mind either that Ownby would kill Gifford or that there would be a stand-off until the store scene when Gifford would finally arrest him. Ownby's killing Gifford would have been a provocative parallel to Sylder's killing Rattner and would have reinforced the links between the two corrupt "officers," as opposed to the two mountaineers who resist them. It would also have created a more plausible reason for Ownby's incarceration. But McCarthy may have abandoned the idea because Ownby's killing the constable trying to arrest him would have been less justifiable than Sylder's killing Rattner in self-defense. On the verso of "Late Draft" page 217, a revised version of Gifford's arresting Ownby at 218/238, McCarthy drafted instead Ownby's arrest by an unnamed agent; and on 219 he mentions the "starched and rattling clothes" that mark the agent as a citified officer and outsider rather than a rural constable. McCarthy held the idea of an axe murder in the back of his mind until he drafted *Outer Dark*, where he considered deploying it as Culla's revenge against the arrogant authority of Squire Salter.

The "Late Draft" also reveals that McCarthy wrote brief references to the deaths of Ownby and Eller. Page 255 is a draft of the opening of the epilogue, when John Wesley visits the old log house where he once lived. On its verso is a typed note for what appears to be a different start for the epilogue. McCarthy first typed that John Wesley "was surprised to hear that Mr Eller had died too." That is, Eller is gone in addition to his mother, whom he already knows has died. Then McCarthy typed reminders that the house scene should come next, with its reference to fallen leaves ("Late Draft" 255 verso). In addition, on an unpaginated leaf close to the end of the draft, John Wesley sees the morning sun "reaching to the slope where the old man [Ownby] rested now." Had these specific deaths remained in the novel, they might have emphasized John Wesley's sense of loss not only of his family but also of his community; however, they might also have made the resolutions for these characters seem overdetermined. McCarthy had already drafted the elegiac line that "their names are myth, legend, dust" ("Late Draft" 259/266 [3rd]/ 278), and he realized that the reader could well infer the deaths of John Wesley's elderly friends during the seven years he has been away. As he considered the novel's resonant closing line, he jotted that it was "generic" while the book's plot was more "personal." He may have been unsatisfied that it might appear to be a stepping away from John Wesley's sense of personal grief, or he may have been affirming that very move toward the lament of a broader cultural loss. Since he carried the line forward into the published novel and since he did not develop scenes in which John Wesley learns of the deaths of Ownby and Eller, it seems the lament for the loss of a whole people and their way of life was foremost in McCarthy's thinking.

On the same page, McCarthy noted that he might emphasize images of dust in the framing scenes. Then in the "Late Draft's" unpaginated one-leaf prologue, McCarthy penciled in a potential new first line: "DUST & chips of wood lay deep over the kept lawn?" But apparently he decided that the connections between the sawdust in the prologue and the dust of mortality in the epilogue were too tenuous, and he did not carry the line into the published novel.

One of the more interesting changes between the late draft and the final, submitted draft was that McCarthy reduced the direct narration of John Wesley's thoughts and feelings, especially concerning his alienation from his mother, still a domineering presence in the boy's early adolescence. Rick Wallach notes the Oedipal anxiety and rejection of parental control in the short stories McCarthy wrote in 1959/60 ("Prefiguring"), and it seems likely that these themes were as pronounced in the first two drafts of *The Orchard Keeper* as in the shorter, related works. But as he revised from the "Late" to the "Final" draft, McCarthy seems to have decided that it would be most effective to convey John Wesley's anger at his mother obliquely.

In the "Late Draft," when the boy is eagerly awaiting fall and the beginning of trapping season, McCarthy initially wrote, "These nights he could not bear to be in the house with her" (69), which made John Wesley's restiveness specifically a manifestation of his troubled relationship with his mother. But McCarthy placed the last two words in parentheses and did not carry them into his "Final Draft" (72/74; cf. *OK* 66). Moreover, in the "Late Draft" John Wesley's resentment of his mother is not merely internal. Early in the typescript he acts on it, too. When he finds a lizard in the empty milk can, he childishly decides to leave it there to frighten her ("Late Draft" 67). This is a far cry from leaving a drowned puppy in a baby's crib, the protest of the protagonist of "A Drowning Incident," but it speaks to a similar alienation in the boy whose narrative arc moves toward principled protest against the civic order and ultimately toward a more mature forgiveness of his mother in the scene at her tombstone.

McCarthy also was exploring a variety of reasons for the tensions between John Wesley and his mother. When Sylder gives him a puppy, the "Late Draft" has John Wesley recognizing that his mother will insist on his returning it since "She wasn't fit to live with after the incident of the overall pants." But unless the pants incident refers to John Wesley's getting soaked in the river when he pulls Sylder from the wrecked car or when he rescues Lady from drowning, McCarthy never composed or had already deleted it. On the same leaf, he changed the reason for Mildred's anger at her son to his having stopped going to church. Furthermore, McCarthy noted that the boy's rebellion against his mother's obsessive religiosity had begun in the spring, which means that the two have been embattled for six months or more ("Late Draft" 141).

In the "Final Draft," John Wesley's resistance to his mother is never conveyed through his resentful thoughts but is implied through her harsh actions and Sylder's inference, after John Wesley has returned the puppy to him, that "She must be a pistol" (carbon 152; cf. *OK* 135–36). Although maternal pressure was suggested in John Wesley's oppressive sense that he owed vengeance to the memory of his unremembered father, the scene of Mildred's mad insistence that he must avenge his father's death does not appear in the "Late Draft," but seems to have been added in the "Final Draft" as a late strategy to clarify the opposition between them (carbon 73/75–74/76). If so, the impulse toward vengeance, aroused and quieted in his conversations with Sylder and Ownby, was self-generated within the boy until very late in the drafting of the novel.

The "Final Draft" also reformulates the idea from the "Late Draft" that Mildred's relentless self-righteousness drives a wedge between them. When John Wesley returns from hunting with Sylder, his mother is waiting for him in his pitch-dark room, where she sits silently on his bed until he accidentally touches her and starts back in shocked surprise. Then she speaks: "Whoremonger. . . . Dry tired voice, a rasping hopeless hiss. Godless whoremonger"—a word the boy does not know ("Final Draft" carbon 146/147). McCarthy removed her unjust accusation when he revised for Bensky, but Mildred remains an unsympathetic character presented largely through her lack of empathy for her son and her blind valorizing of her contemptible husband. Interestingly, she is the most extended negative portrayal of motherhood in McCarthy's works, the only mother except for Lester Ballard's absent one whose love for her child is inadequate. (De Lisle says that McCarthy "adored" and "revered" his own mother, Gladys [De Lisle, Interview with Bryan Giemza and Dianne Luce]). In the published novel, the boy's resistance to her remains evident in his desire to escape the domestic sphere and enter the worlds of nature and of the male mountaineers. But McCarthy's deletion of John Wesley's passive aggression against her and of any direct representation of his hostile feelings makes the boy both more innocent and more mature, an adolescent of good will struggling as adolescents must against the restrictions of his life.

# Revision for Lawrence Bensky

The final draft of *The Orchard Keeper* was completed by early May 1962. In his letter of transmittal to the Random House Fiction Editor, McCarthy noted that he was sending the typescript without proofreading it since he was planning to return to Tennessee from Chicago in two days. Possibly he needed to vacate his rented cellar at the end of April. Initially he and Lee stayed with McCarthy's parents on Martin Mill Pike in Vestal, south of Knoxville (the childhood home he describes in *The Road,* 25–27). But by that fall the young couple had moved to a house outside of Sevierville and were living, McCarthy wrote, "on what might be described as below subsistence. My nearest neighbor makes good whiskey at $2.00 the quart, food is cheap, rent free, and I roll my own cigarettes" (Letter to Bensky, [late Oct.-Nov. 1962]). McCooe recalls that the owner gave her brother the house rent-free on the condition that he make renovations (Interview with Bryan Giemza and Dianne Luce). Indeed, this is where he repurposed bricks salvaged from James Agee's house in Knoxville, which was demolished in 1962 (Paul Brown, *Rufus,* 251–52). But McCarthy did not mention his construction work to Bensky, saying that he spent his days "walking, reading, and talking to strangers" (Letter to Bensky, [late Oct.-Nov. 1962]).

McCarthy's relationship with Lee had ended by the time *The Orchard Keeper* reached publication in May 1965, three years after its submission. This personal trauma, his relocation to Asheville, and his desire to turn back to composing *Suttree,* which he had begun drafting in 1961 or 1962,[3] intermittently delayed McCarthy's revising the first novel for his editors, and in December 1962 he had begun drafting *Outer Dark* as well. But most of the delay in his first novel's publication resulted from the two-layered editorial process itself, which was complicated by McCarthy's unfamiliarity with the procedures and the editors' unfamiliarity with him.

Woodward implies that the manuscript languished at Random House until it came to the attention of Albert Erskine, who would edit McCarthy's novels until he fully retired in 1987 (Woodward, "Venomous Fiction" 31; Lambert, "Albert R. Erskine, 81"). However, Erskine's correspondence files and Peter Josyph's extensive and invaluable 2015 interview with editor Larry Bensky paint a more complex picture. The novel immediately garnered attention. Bensky recalled:

There was a protocol in the place where you read from the slush pile. The manuscripts came in by the cartloads. Really: every day a hand-truck full of manuscripts arrived. Jimmy, the drunken mailboy, would bring them upstairs and dump them in this office . . . at the reception area. . . .

The office had shelves up to the ceiling. You read them in order of arrival. Usually the readers, Maxine [Groffsky] and Natalie [Robins], would read three or four pages, decide if they wanted to read more, or say: "This is ridiculous." (Josyph, "Damn Proud" 16–17)

Groffsky alerted Bensky that McCarthy's novel had potential, jotting "Larry/ This might be good" in a note she affixed to McCarthy's cover letter (Groffsky, Note to Larry Bensky, [May 1962]). Bensky read the typescript less than three weeks after its receipt, and like Groffsky he was impressed, drawn to the novel equally because of its powerful language and its sympathetic treatment of underrepresented Appalachian people. "This was a creative writing spirit who had a subject and a voice that was professional and was publishable and was really really interesting and good," he told Josyph ("Damn Proud" 23).

Bensky was then a twenty-six-year-old associate editor who had been with Random for four years. He was young, but he had excellent credentials. He had been actively engaged in journalism since high school, and at Yale he served as managing editor of the *Yale Daily News.* There he studied American literature under Erskine's friend, Cleanth Brooks. After graduation, Bensky interviewed with several publishers in New York until senior editor Albert Erskine interviewed him over lunch, when they talked about Faulkner, Brooks, and Robert Penn Warren. Erskine hired him as one of Random's proofreaders and copyeditors, the typical entry-level position with the publisher (Josyph, "Damn Proud" 20, 17). Initially Bensky worked together with the others in the editorial cubicles on the firm's first floor and reported to Bertha Krantz, the crackerjack copyeditor who worked on all of McCarthy's books for Random. Within a year Bensky was promoted. Thereafter, Erskine supervised him, taking special interest in the young man who had studied with his friend. Bensky recalled, "One of the things that Albert did, one of the reasons that he was such a wonderful man, is that he threw me right into the water. Erskine was smart, funny, enormously competent as a literary editor. I've always been grateful for what was, in fact, his mentoring." One early project Bensky had worked on with Erskine was the galley proofs of Faulkner's *The Mansion* (1959), which Erskine asked him to read with an eye to spotting "indecipherable" sentences. Bensky recalls that since Faulkner's writing was so good, he found few passages that needed revision (Josyph, "Damn Proud" 12).

It was rather rare for a submission to make it this far, but impressed by McCarthy's talent, Bensky alerted Erskine on May 21, 1962, writing that

McCarthy's book was "A strange and, I think, beautiful novel in the Southern tradition, which has confused me quite a bit on a quick first reading, but which I think is worth publishing. . . . It is neo-Faulknerian in its abstract, unidentified switching from character to character, but the prose is not at all imitative. One gets an intense feeling of the land and its people, while the plot is barely glimpsed. . . . I was completely enthralled by most of the book, though it lacks a final structure and a certain coherence." He felt it needed "judicious editing" because "the time scheme is probably wrong and the various sequences must be made more coherent." Three weeks later, on June 12, Bensky wrote McCarthy "a note of admiration for your extremely fine first novel." He reported that the typescript had been read by several people and that Random was "extremely interested in publishing it"; but he was about to undertake another reading to study its chronology and the sequencing of the characters' scenes to decide "just exactly what I think has to be changed . . . in the interests of clarity and coherence."

It is not surprising that Bensky should have experienced confusion about the plot on his first reading. With Rattner unnamed in the first several pages and with relatively few type breaks to signal the shifts in focus from one character to the next or from one time level to another, the submitted draft was in fact more difficult to follow than the version that was eventually published. Bensky's letter initiated a process of lengthy interchanges that McCarthy would later cheekily characterize as "arguing with my editor and the publishers" (Owen, "McCarthy Is One" 4B). In fact, however, the "arguments" with Bensky and later Erskine were for the most part cordial and cooperative negotiations motivated on both sides by good faith and a shared desire to make McCarthy's debut novel the best it possibly could be. One gets a sense of the way Bensky defined his editorial role in the comments he made to Josyph: "One of the things I've always prided myself on . . . is knowing how much to get involved with somebody else's words. When they're good, to make them better. When they're fine, to leave them alone. How to develop a relationship where they have the confidence to do it themselves—because it's them, not me" ("Damn Proud" 9).

However, despite the encouraging tone of Bensky's letter of tentative acceptance, it was also, in places, inadvertently short on diplomacy, and McCarthy may initially have felt somewhat defensive. He let Bensky's letter sit for a month before replying on July 12 that he had already revised the book twice, largely for clarity. McCarthy's holograph notations in the "Late Draft" reveal the care with which he had worked out the chronology for the novel. For example, in the epilogue he had changed the date of Mildred Rattner's birth and instructed himself to "check all dates" (156/258). On multiple pages in the "Late Draft," McCarthy had revised to reflect Ownby's seven-year theories, even reminding himself, on a draft of the first page of the epilogue, that nothing yet made it clear that John Wesley had been away for seven years (255). Considerable self-generated revising and checking behind him, McCarthy wrote Bensky that he was not certain further reworking would result in more "lucidity," but he was willing to consider the editor's response to help him identify any "weaknesses" in the novel (letter, July 12, 1962). Indeed, McCarthy's revisions for Bensky show him developing a surer sense of audience awareness, even as he resisted writing down to his readers.

Not until October 9 did Bensky send McCarthy specific suggestions for revisions. In the meantime, he had read the novel two more times and consulted with "another editor": Erskine. Bensky's letter of May 21 recommending the novel for Erskine's consideration had ended, "I'd like to hear what you think," and a six-page set of reading notes for the novel in Erskine's hand and headed "Cormac McCarthy" clearly dates from the senior editor's reading of the submitted typescript. Although later Erskine tentatively dated this document "1964?" it refers to plot details McCarthy would revise for Bensky in 1962/63 and thus actually dates from May or June 1962. For example, Erskine's notes for the first twenty-seven pages refer to Rattner as the "Man," as the unrevised "Final Draft" did, and they record the "Abstract incantation to old man" that McCarthy would remove in response to Bensky's critique (Erskine, "Cormac McCarthy" 1–2, 5). Further, many of Erskine's notes track his attempts to identify the time and focal character of each scene, a major focus of Bensky's and his own recommendations to McCarthy. Other editorial comments in Erskine's reading notes inform Bensky's long letter to McCarthy of October 9, 1962, which was, he wrote, "the result of long thought and [their] . . . conversation" about the typescript (1).

In this letter and Bensky's accompanying revision notes, Bensky praised McCarthy's style and suggested that excerpts might be sold as short stories, which must have been encouraging. But he also objected to the "obscurity of the plot," especially the discontinuity of the novel's opening forty pages, in which Sylder, Kenneth Rattner, and Ownby are introduced in disparate scenes and brought into convergence only gradually or in Ownby's case not at all. Bensky suggested that the opening might become less disorienting if McCarthy named Sylder each time he appears, did not intersperse his story with Rattner's and Ownby's, and began the novel with page 35, except that that might sacrifice the "fine incident" of the Green Fly Inn's burning down at the end of section I. He felt that the opening pages "seem irrelevant and confusing to what you finally direct the story towards: Marion, John Wesley, and Arthur Ownby" (1). Bensky conceded that the dates McCarthy had provided in the text "make sense after I've charted them," but he still found "the fragmentary nature of the opening section . . . confusing" (list 1). Most problematic for both editors was the interweaving of Rattner's storyline with Sylder's, especially since Rattner's name was not revealed until page 27. The returns of both men to Red Branch in the opening pages further encouraged the reader's conflation of the two, even though Rattner's return in August or September 1934 does not coincide with Sylder's in March, asynchrony that would continue to trouble Erskine when he took on the editing of the novel after McCarthy had revised it for Bensky. In Bensky's attached three-page, single-spaced list of notes for specific passages that he and Erskine thought needed clarification, he addressed motivations, the identity of the focal character in various scenes, and the time relationships between adjacent sections.

In offering this kind of feedback, Bensky and Erskine defined their editorial roles similarly to that of the esteemed Maxwell Perkins of Scribner in the preceding generation: knowing "what to publish, how to get it, and what to do to help it achieve the largest readership" (Berg, *Max Perkins* 4). Neither Bensky nor Erskine would perform such intrusive editing as Perkins had, for instance, on Thomas Wolfe's *Look Homeward, Angel,* but they felt responsible for helping an author to shape his work in the most effective ways. Perkins had been distressed when reviewers started giving him credit for Wolfe's writing, which created a rift between him and the gifted young writer he had begun to consider a son. Late in his career, in 1946, Perkins warned a group of students at New York University, "An editor does not add to a book. At best he serves as a handmaiden to an author. Don't ever get to feeling important about yourself, because an editor at most releases energy. He creates nothing" (quoted by Berg, *Max Perkins* 6). Although Bensky and Erskine both would suggest substantive improvements or point out problems in McCarthy's drafts, they seem to have been guided by Perkins's dictum.

By early December 1962, McCarthy had reread his typescript, but instead of revising as Bensky expected, he wrote an eleven-page letter to address the editor's queries, essentially an explanation and defense of the book as submitted. He did not yet have a contract, and although Bensky had expressed strong interest in publishing the novel, it seems McCarthy was hesitant to revise before he and his editor agreed on exactly what was to be done. Such reluctance would later resurface in his work with Arena Stage on the aborted production of his play *The Stonemason* (Arnold, "Cormac McCarthy's *The Stonemason*" 147–49), and given the labor or expense of retyping in the pre-word-processing era, it seems altogether reasonable.

McCarthy's reply to Bensky comprises a rare attempt to explicate his own writing, matched only by his handwritten dialogue with Erskine on the editing copy of *The Orchard Keeper.* For later books, such explanation would occur earlier in the composition process and largely by phone or in person although Erskine would sometimes express mild frustration that McCarthy would not explain his work more fully. In his letter to Bensky, McCarthy's tone was professional, nondefensive, and workmanlike. He outlined the markers of time and identity that he had built into his draft and gently pointed out where Bensky had missed cues such as seasonal descriptions to indicate the passage of time. He explained that his idea was to move between Sylder and Rattner to create "tension . . . resolved by their meeting and the subsequent murder of Rattner" (1). Ownby is also introduced in early scenes partly to "convey a sense of ubiquitousness," especially with respect to Sylder. The two are "often . . . threatened with a face to face meeting" (3), and they have an "affinity . . . for each others [*sic*] presence without being aware of it" (6). When Ownby finds the corpse, he is not concerned about the identity of the killer. He assumes "responsibility for . . . [it] because he loves peace better than justice, the mountain is his domain, the body that of a stranger . . . and because he is at heart an anarchist" (4). McCarthy claimed not to know the tank's specific purpose but indicated that it had been installed by the government. For Ownby it represents "the encroaching of authority upon . . . his domain and . . . a threat to the secret he guards." Its imperviousness to the lightning strike appears to Ownby to reveal its "satanic quality." So he turns to "traditional devil medicine" to cross out its power with a pattern of shotgun holes (7–8).

In his early reading notes for the submitted draft, Erskine had recorded several scenes in which he felt a character needed to be named: "must identify John Wesley. Seems like still the old man"; "old man (IS THIS ATHER?)" ("Cormac McCarthy" 4). For a scene in which McCarthy identified Ownby by name, he queried "Why can't he <McC> do this more often?" ("Cormac McCarthy" 5). Accordingly, Bensky asked McCarthy to identify his characters more consistently. McCarthy responded in early December that "Names . . . serve no purpose other than immediate identification, and often they do that poorly or not at all." When a character reappears after several scenes, the reader recognizes the character only when reminded of his function in the story. Since Kenneth Rattner's character was "almost wholly symbolic," McCarthy preferred that his identity emerge as his role in the story unfolds (2). In the "Late" and "Final" drafts, Sylder is in fact identified by name in the opening scenes, while Rattner is not, and when the latter is simply referred to as "the man," it emphasizes his mysteriousness and establishes an ominous aura around this symbolic character.[4] Ownby is identified by name from his first appearance in the "Late Draft" (19), but he is also frequently referred to as the "old man." It seems, though, that the rotation among these characters together with the inconsistent naming of Ownby and Rattner had given both editors difficulty distinguishing among them.

The neat plot denouement of the submitted draft also troubled both editors. Objecting to the scene in the asylum where Ownby reveals to John Wesley that

Sylder may have hidden a body in the pesticide pit, Erskine noted, "bad revelation. Why bring it out here? ruins mystery" ("Cormac McCarthy" 6); and in his list of editorial suggestions of October 9, Bensky commented about Sylder's telling the boy that he killed his father, "You've got to be very careful with this revelation, in order not to make it seem like a typical end-of-book plot contrivance. I'm not really convinced that it's necessary for Sylder to tell John Wesley the truth at all. But this is your book and I don't strongly object to the revelation, I merely caution you to think it over" (list 3). McCarthy eventually eliminated both Sylder's and Ownby's revelations to John Wesley, revisions that made their relationships to Rattner and/or his corpse seem a product of John Wesley's imagination rather than his memory. Thus it also, paradoxically, made it more difficult for the reader to recognize that the tale is his. This would be a substantial alteration to McCarthy's conception of the novel, but initially he wrote Bensky only that excising the revelations would "entail a lot of cutting" and might make the ending too abrupt. He felt that "if the body goes unidentified (to the boy) . . . [it would] leave the reader hanging"—a statement that seems to derive from his idea that the murder of the boy's father must reach resolution for John Wesley, because it is he who reconstructs the story (letter, [early Dec. 1962]: 10).

Responding to Bensky's queries about motivation, McCarthy explained that John Wesley's return of the hawk bounty marks his repudiation of government regulations, his recognition that having anything to do with government officials "robs one of personal dignity." He feels that because the hawk is "a free spirit" as Ownby and Sylder are, he was wrong to accept the bounty (letter, [early Dec. 1962] 10). In the epilogue, John Wesley, a young man now, comes back after his Army service, but McCarthy acknowledged that this was not explicit in his novel. He has left Red Branch after his mentors are incarcerated "because . . . his world has dissolved," and he returns out of a feeling of "nostalgia" (letter, [early Dec. 1962]: 10–11).

In the December 1962 reply to Bensky, McCarthy suggested additional type breaks between discontinuous scenes and acknowledged that the time disruption of Rattner's flashback to the Green Fly Inn might confuse readers. He suggested a few revisions or repositionings of scenes, offered to delete a misleading sentence or two, and asked Bensky for his opinion about his analysis of the typescript's problematic features and possible solutions. He was eager to resume work on his second novel (*Suttree*), and he confessed that he disliked revising and found it a slow process. But he ended his long letter with a promise to start on revisions as soon as he heard from the editor.

Bensky briefly acknowledged McCarthy's letter on December 13, addressing him this time at Route 7, Walden Creek Road, Sevierville, where Cormac and Lee had relocated that fall. Then on January 25, 1963, the young editor responded to McCarthy's explanation of *The Orchard Keeper* as submitted and reinforced his earlier request for revision. He found McCarthy's arguments "interesting, well-thought out, and doubtless sincere," but he insisted that McCarthy's eloquent explanations did not alter "the pedestrian facts of time and identity, two things which must be made explicit or implicit in the narrative—and aren't right now. <u>Every</u> point which you make to me in your letter is an explanation which should be unnecessary, and will be unavailable to the reader." He asked that McCarthy rewrite on his own schedule. Since Bensky was still interested in the book, he wrote he would be happy to receive "even a slightly revised copy." On February 19, when he had not heard from McCarthy, Bensky inquired whether he planned to revise, "work on other books or go to work in a hydrogen bomb factory." He explained that his lack of further discussion of the manuscript's problems did not imply that Random no longer wanted to publish the book but that he "thought we had reached a dead end in revision through correspondence." What Bensky did not know is that by then not only had McCarthy's son Cullen Chase been born, on November 30, 1962 ("McCarthy, Cormac," *Who's Who*), but his union with Lee was dissolving.

Nevertheless, McCarthy had started revising *The Orchard Keeper* soon after receiving Bensky's letter of January 25. His undated reply to Bensky's February 19 follow-up assured the editor that he wasn't "sulking" and that he had begun the work, but it was going slowly. He anticipated that in a month he might submit a revision. This estimate was overly optimistic, yet despite the baby's needs and McCarthy's strained relations with Lee, he was working productively on three projects. An update he sent his editor on May 16, 1963, reported that he had been revising *The Orchard Keeper* and that during the same three months, he had written a hundred pages each of a second novel—*Suttree*—and of new material that was still formless—*Outer Dark*. He assured Bensky that he was addressing most of his suggestions about *The Orchard Keeper* through revision or deletion—"exorcism perhaps an apter word"—and that he was then working on its final section and newly rewriting portions of it. Although he found that his progress was incredibly slow going, especially because he was four years away from the book's inception, he now expected to send a revised version in another two or three weeks. Again his projection was overly sanguine, but the dates on the first draft of *Outer Dark* reveal that between May 16 and June 23, two days before Bensky acknowledged receiving the revised typescript of *The Orchard Keeper*, McCarthy's work on the new novel slowed drastically. This suggests that for that five-week interval he was devoting his energies primarily to reworking *The Orchard Keeper*. McCarthy revised conscientiously, naming characters, clarifying motivation, and rewriting the novel's ending.

On May 21, in response to McCarthy's query of May 16, Bensky expressed his preference for reading a clean, revised typescript rather than a marked one. For many of his changes, McCarthy worked first on his carbon copy of the final draft, making holograph revisions on its onion skin leaves or inserting replacement leaves on typing paper. He marked passages on the carbon copy with a check mark if he planned to revise them, as he noted to himself on its first page, and sometimes marked them "Done." Although he did not carry forward every revision that he tried out on the carbon final draft, it seems he recorded those that satisfied him on the original final-draft typescript Bensky had returned to him. This typescript no longer exists as a separate intact document. The surviving editorial copy is a photocopy of the cleanest pages from the corrected original final draft and McCarthy's newly drafted and typed pages. But it exhibits typed, consecutive repagination, all of which suggests that McCarthy himself created this clean copy that would mostly obscure his working process and allow his editors to read the revised novel with new eyes.

The editorial copy incorporates the changes McCarthy made in response to Bensky's suggestions, and it also displays the subsequent layers of editing the novel underwent. On it, Erskine wrote two sets of queries in red and then green, and McCarthy responded first in pencil and then in blue ink, fascinating interchanges to which I will return, but which must be disregarded when studying the revisions McCarthy made for Bensky.

McCarthy's revision addressed almost all the specific issues Bensky raised, but not always in the ways the editor suggested or might have expected. McCarthy also read through his entire draft for clarity of thought and imagery, carefully considering what could be made more transparent without condescending to his reader. Yet he maintained the original structure of his novel's opening, with its alternating scenes focused on Rattner and Sylder and with Ownby briefly introduced. Even though the two younger men's timelines differed, each had been followed chronologically along his own narrative arc; and beginning with the second subsection of Part I, their timelines had in fact synchronized in anticipation of their fatal convergence (see *OK* 28ff). Now McCarthy italicized many subsections of the book that violated strict chronology or represented memories, beginning with the prologue and Rattner's flashback to the porch collapse at the Green Fly Inn. In his list of October 9, 1962, Bensky had suggested such a change for the prologue, since he could not find another episode in the book to which it referred: "If it [the prologue] doesn't have anything to do with the book, it will have to be set off typographically so as not to unduly confuse the reader" (list 1). When McCarthy replied in December, he had suggested italics for Rattner's memory of the Green Fly Inn as well, and type breaks to flag the discontinuities between Rattner's scenes and Sylder's. McCarthy had already employed some page breaks to indicate shifts in time and focus, and he marked others as he revised. These simple techniques of signaling discontinuities went far toward making the novel less ambiguous and easier to follow.

Other changes were more substantive. McCarthy made Rattner's destination in Knoxville explicit, and he acceded to Bensky's wishes by emphatically naming Rattner at the end of his first hitchhiking scene, adding the lines, "Had he been asked his name he might have given any but Kenneth Rattner. That was his name" ("Final Draft" carbon 4; cf. *OK* 10). In later pages McCarthy named him as well. But he still meant to stress the character's uncanny and emblematic qualities. So because this figure no longer appeared in the novel's opening as "the man" but as the realistically named Rattner, McCarthy now inserted within the onion skin leaves of the "Final Draft" carbon a new page 24 on typewriter paper bearing the remarkable paragraph in which Rattner stands on the porch of the Green Fly Inn, aloof from the community of drinkers but communing instead with a figure "suspended mysteriously in the darkness"—"that being in the outer dark" (cf. *OK* 24). The scene had always implied that Rattner witnessed the incident at the inn, but this new paragraph made his presence on the porch explicit and suggested through juxtaposition that he somehow causes its collapse. He sits on the porch railing with the men who will fall. "There was a long creaking sound . . . and . . . the sharp detonation of strained wood giving way" ("Final Draft" carbon 24–25; cf. *OK* 24). This implication reinforced the subtler one that when Rattner later insinuates himself into Sylder's car, he somehow causes the tire to blow out so he can assault Sylder (*OK* 37)—a strategy McCarthy returned to in *Outer Dark* when the unnamed mute causes the triune's skiff to come unmoored, engineering the confluence of these dark figures with Culla (178). The new passage at the Green Fly Inn enhanced the sense that Rattner is a mysterious agent of collapse in Red Branch, a personification of the destructive elements of the new order. It also reinforced the other evidence that this scene is Rattner's memory, making it unnecessary for McCarthy to juggle its positioning.

McCarthy's correspondence and typescripts reveal the care he had taken to structure his novel around short, interspersed scenes focalized through the perspectives of his four key characters and their flashbacks—a cinematic technique that if presented in filmed imagery would create little confusion for the viewer. Furthermore, he was concerned about the pacing of his work and reluctant to devote too much space to a single character in any given subsection. For example, he later explained to Erskine that he had interposed scenes of the cat, Sylder, and John Wesley between Ownby's concussion and his waking up because the narrative had already stayed with the old man too long and because he wanted the sequence to be bookended with Ownby (Editorial Copy 209 verso).

Perhaps partly for similar reasons, McCarthy's new paragraph about Rattner at the inn replaced a humorous tale about the Fenner men that Ef Hobie tells the gathered drinkers. In the carbon copy of the "Final Draft," Hobie relates how Fenner and his brother-in-law Turnip took a long time to lay the foundation of a cabin because they thought they would dig the entire foundation first and remove the dirt from it later. When they marked the outlines of the cabin, they ran their strings on the perimeter of "the crookedy-assed hole they'd dug" and began laying the foundation stones accordingly. Undaunted by this wonky construction, they proceeded to the framing, but Fenner would catch the confused Turnip occasionally nailing planks to the nearby stack of firewood (24). McCarthy had first created this tale as he revised his "Late Draft," adding it on page 22X, where it followed the anecdote he had already written of how Mrs. Fenner borrowed and ruined the Hobie family soupbone by cooking it with peas (see *OK* 23). The longer story of the Fenners's dubious carpentry skills had contributed to Hobie's ongoing "monologue of anecdotes" ("Late Draft" 22). In addition, its insertion had created a sense of elapsed time between the first warning crack of the porch's timbers and its fall. After McCarthy's revision for Bensky, the ominous entrance of the outsider Rattner served that function, as well as maintaining his symbolic role.

Taken together, Hobie's Fenner tales are early examples of what McCarthy would do in more integrated fashion in *Child of God* with the loiterers who gossip about Ballard and in the submitted draft of *Suttree,* where McCarthy systematically represented the oral storytelling of the men of East Tennessee before he cut several of the longest tales to shorten the book.[5] Hobie's account of the Fenners's ineptitude as carpenters also contributed to a realistic and symbolic trope of construction and craftmanship in the novel—from the swaying inn, to Increase Tipton's hastily built cabins and their affinity for decay, to Ownby's shabby boxed cabin, and the solid traditional log house the Rattners squat in. But although the Fenner incident comments on shoddy craftsmanship, it was not essential, perhaps not humorous enough, and would have slowed the pace of the revised episode once Rattner's appearance on the porch was narrated, so McCarthy marked it for deletion ("Final Draft" carbon 24). Interestingly, however, this early, peripheral venture in exploring the trope humorously anticipated his extended tragic treatment two decades later. In his stage play *The Stonemason,* composed in the 1980s, McCarthy would return to the building craft as an analogue of the writing craft, making central the figure of the craftsman, with his ideals and failings.

As he revised for Bensky, McCarthy also rewrote a scene in Eller's store, where after church Mrs. Eller and Mrs. Rattner discuss the drinkers' fall from the porch with dour and self-righteous disapproval ("Final Draft" carbon 27). In the draft McCarthy initially submitted, Rattner had not explicitly appeared in this scene, which was somewhat problematic since the narration of the porch collapse and its aftermath at the store had been subtly established as his memories of the events, recalled as he drinks at Jim's Hot Spot. (As he nurses the scraped leg he has just received while robbing a motorist, he recalls the cut hand he suffered as he picked up the wallets of the fallen men in the broken glass below the inn.) This elision of Rattner at Eller's store had evolved some-what accidentally. In the "Late Draft," the scene shifts from Kenneth's per-spective when he picks himself up from the rubble tip below the inn, to a few lines of more objective narration about Mildred in the store, and then to John Wesley's point of view: "His father had escaped with cuts and abrasions" (25). McCarthy had recognized these abrupt shifts in narrative perspective, and in the carbon copy of the "Final Draft," there is no such breach in Rattner's mem-ory. However, neither is there any reference to John Wesley or his father in the store. When McCarthy revised for Bensky, he added a reference to Rattner's buying his son an orange drink at the store, giving both characters a presence there while maintaining the narrative perspective of Rattner's memory (Edito-rial Copy 27; cf. *OK* 26).

Bensky had not pointed out Rattner's absence from Eller's store, perhaps because he could not tell that the scene was a continuation of Rattner's mem-ory. McCarthy had used a line break and a colon to separate the flashback from the material at Jim's Hot Spot that introduced it. But Bensky's confusion about the scenes led McCarthy to realize that for him Rattner's flashback was dis-rupting "the continuity of the story," and he promised to ponder it further (let-ter, [early Dec. 1962]: 3). He considered moving the scenes, but instead when he revised on the carbon copy of the final draft, McCarthy tried out several strategies to emphasize that this section was Rattner's memory. After the line that the porch collapse "had been his windfall," McCarthy penciled "he remem-bered" (23); and before the sentence about Rattner's slashed hand he penciled, "He remembered that he had" (27). He also deleted Mildred's conversation with Mrs. Eller on pages 27–28, an interchange which had broadened the focus of the scene, and he retained only Mrs. Eller's humorous wonderment about how some of the drinkers had lost their "britches."

On typing paper, McCarthy composed "semi-final" and "final" versions of a new aftermath passage in which he continued to clarify that the store scene was an extension of Rattner's memory. His revisions also addressed Bensky's query about how the porch incident constituted a windfall for Rattner (list, Oct. 9, 1962: 1), to which McCarthy had replied that it provided him the chance "to pick pockets" ([early Dec. 1962]: 3). The two new versions emphasize Ratt-ner's sudden wealth, which he explains to Mildred by lying that it is train fare to a new job in Harlan, Kentucky. He gives her five dollars, after which they go to the store together. Then McCarthy added an explicit transition to the store scene, while still adhering to Rattner's perspective: "At the store they were tell-ing it [the porch collapse]." The new leaf ends with Rattner's memory as well:

"The twenty six dollars was little more than half spent before he found himself in a south Georgia Workhouse" ("Final Draft" carbon, "Semi-Final Version," np). This new reference reinforces the evidence of Rattner's criminal behavior and implies that he has just been released from the workhouse when he travels north through Georgia, where his path crosses Sylder's. McCarthy carried the sentence into his next draft of the page and then revised and repositioned it as a transition back to Rattner at Jim's Hot Spot ("Final Draft" carbon "FINAL VERSION" 27; 28), but he did not transfer it into the editorial copy (28), where the switch from italics back to roman type marks the end of Rattner's flashback more economically. Perhaps, too, McCarthy preferred to keep this symbolic character's movements opaque and to allow his reader to infer that Rattner's criminal activity periodically keeps him away from his family.

Bensky also requested clarification of the time relationship between Sylder's Louisiana and Tennessee experiences. The scene in which Sylder gives the Red Branch boys rides to town puzzled the editor because he did not recognize the references to Gay and Market streets as Knoxville landmarks and because he was not certain whether the scene with the boys occurs before Sylder's "exile" or after (list, Oct. 9, 1962, 1). In the published book, the reference to the car makes it clear that the trips to town had to happen after Sylder returned home with his rum-running earnings. But this was indeed less apparent in the submitted draft. McCarthy clarified by adding a new page 13a to the "Final Draft" carbon, a leaf in which he names Knoxville and alludes to its local blue laws to explain why "On Sundays Sylder turned to the mountain . . . beyond the dominion of law and sanctity" (cf. *OK* 16). He also added a new passage that sets Sylder's memory of the Coast Guard cutter within the context of his present activities as a whiskey runner in East Tennessee, differentiating the two periods in his life. The "Final Draft" had moved abruptly from Sylder's reassuring John Wesley about Gifford's threats (carbon 182/183; *OK* 160–61) to the line that Sylder still sometimes dreamed of "the sweep of the cutter's lights" (carbon 183/184), a juxtaposition that established Sylder's associating Gifford with the federal officers who violently interfered with his livelihood as a runner in the gulf. In this draft, the Gifford discussion had ended near the bottom of one page, and the cutter material had begun at the top of another; so although McCarthy may have intended a line break here, it would not have been detectable to his editors.

McCarthy had already embedded some of Sylder's memories within his driving experiences. Now McCarthy drafted the comparable passage that placed Sylder in his car, transporting liquor on a cold night, when he recalls his activities in the gulf. To prepare for this, he added a holograph reference to Sylder's mutilated toe in the early scene where he buys new socks ("Final Draft" carbon 29). As he drives on his whiskey run in Tennessee, the cold sensitivity of his truncated toe reminds Sylder of being shot in Louisiana, and McCarthy now explicitly introduced the Louisiana flashback with the phrase, "remembering again <u>the sweep of the cutter's lights</u>" ("Final Draft" carbon 184–1; *OK* 161). In addition, he marked the entire Louisiana memory for italic type. (In the editorial copy, Erskine later called for a double line break between the two scenes as well [McCarthy, *The Orchard Keeper:* "Editorial Copy" 182].) McCarthy's new treatment of Sylder's memory continued the strategy he had used with Rattner's: in both, physical pain reminds the men of past injuries. With this addition, McCarthy more firmly established a pain/memory trope that implied as well that the emotional pain John Wesley feels over his parents and mentors as he visits the cemetery elicits his memories of them.

Several other revisions clarified Ownby and Sylder's motivations. Bensky had mistaken Mildred's accusation, "Whoremonger," against her son for Mrs. Sylder's charge against Marion. The editor wrote of the scene in his October 9 letter, "A bit strange that with all Sylder's background his wife is never used as anything but a current harassment" (list 2). He suggested that McCarthy provide more information about her earlier in the novel. But McCarthy had already written the scene in which Mrs. Sylder reacts with appropriate wifely anger prompted by concern when Sylder is injured and in which Sylder teases her with the ease of a sexually and emotionally intimate partner ("Final Draft" carbon 123–24; *OK* 107–109). McCarthy did not explicitly correct Bensky's misreading, but he replied that the Sylders "get along all right—especially in view of his career," and he explained that he had not created a backstory for her because she was significant only "as she has affected Sylder's character" ([early Dec. 1962]: 8).

Nevertheless, to address Bensky's misunderstanding, McCarthy changed two scenes. He provided more imagery of the Sylders's tender relationship when Marion returns home after assaulting Gifford, a domestic scene he thought might have been "too cryptic and liable to misinterpretation" ([early Dec. 1962]: 8). Now he added the line, "He lay . . . [with] his hand over hers. She felt very small," as well as, "You sure have got cold feet she said, pressing her face into his shoulder" ("Final Draft" carbon 191/192). As revised, the Sylders's bedroom scene economically depicts their relationship as one of trust, comfort, and warm physicality. Far from being upset that Marion has come home late, his wife expects it because he does not hide what he does for a living, and she turns to him affectionately.[6] But as if to stress that this moment of marital accord makes Sylder aware of what he stands to lose, McCarthy also added the passage that Sylder recalls "the crazy old man shooting holes in the government tank . . . [with] a sharp foretaste of disaster" ("Final Draft" carbon 191/192; cf. revision 192a; cf. *OK* 168). This revised scene of intimacy artfully contrasts the passage that had confused Bensky, in which Mildred waits up for John

Wesley on his bed and greets him with harsh accusations; so it seems likely McCarthy added the new material about the Sylders first, intending it to counterpoint Mildred's scene. But as he revised further, he also deleted Mildred's passage from the carbon of the final draft, thereby sacrificing an indication of her harsh sanctimoniousness and making the reasons for John Wesley's alienation from her less explicit still (146/147).

Bensky had wondered about Ownby's reasons for placing a cedar in the pit every year, and McCarthy replied that he does this to conceal the body, for which he feels responsible. He chooses a full cedar because it will be seen as "a discarded Christmas tree" ([early Dec. 1962]: 4). Now McCarthy added a new page in the "Final Draft" carbon to convey this: annually "he ... cut a cedar ... for wreath and covering, the waxed and ciliate sprigs holding their green well into the summer." The new passage included the important observation that Ownby "was a watcher of the seasons and their work" (102A; *OK* 90), a line that alerts the reader, too, to pay close attention to the seasonal changes in the novel.

The final draft includes four lyrical interludes that do not appear in the published novel. In his reading notes from 1962, Erskine had flagged two of them at pages 211 and 275 ("Cormac McCarthy" 5–6), and Bensky objected to these and to a similar passage on typescript page 193 in his letter of October 9. He found their "tragic incantation tone" inconsistent with the rest of the novel (list 2–3). In his December 1962 reply, McCarthy confessed that he was not entirely happy with them either, and he explained that their shifts in tone and voice were meant to be transitional (4). He pointed out that only the interludes were in present tense, and his conception was that their "voices, while corresponding to the characters, are not attributable to them ... but are recorded out of the spiritus mundi" (5). One interlude focuses on summer, one on the close of winter, and McCarthy explained as well that sections of the book are unified by rain or snow, which determines the characters' actions (8; see also 5).

In a significant readjustment to the narrative voice in the novel, when he revised for Bensky, McCarthy pulled the lyrical interludes from the carbon copy of the final draft, where the leaves no longer appear. He saved pages 193 and 210 among four deleted typescript leaves that he filed together with his revision notes for the novel.[7] Erskine's reading notes and the Bensky/McCarthy correspondence about the final draft refer to the second of these interludes as page 211 and to page 210 as the scene in which Ownby is struck down by the falling tree, but the saved page 210 is presumably the interlude that Bensky and Erskine read in 1962 or a very similar version.

In his October 9, 1962, revision suggestions, Bensky questioned the interlude on page 193 because he found its switch to "a new style" rather "jarring" (list 2). It began, "I remember the slate skies that closed the winter's days" and focused on the last storm of the season, with hail and "steel-bright rain." The remembering "I" of this passage is situated in a house with "warped shakes splintering . . . under the fusillade of ice." This allusion to the roof of the Rattners's ancient log house identifies the voice as John Wesley's and reinforces the hint that he remembers and "narrates" the novel when he visits his deserted home and his mother's grave in its framing scenes. Indeed, it seems that McCarthy had composed the interludes as a strategy to reinforce that implication intermittently throughout the novel. At some point he underlined the passage in pencil, marking it for italic type, and inscribed the Roman numeral III at the top of the page. Additionally, the first leaf of a two-page version in the "Late Draft" has "prologue" penciled in the upper right corner (173/180/193 3rd). These notations reveal that McCarthy thought of this interlude as functioning similarly to the framing prologue and as a tonal introduction to the seasonal change to spring. Moreover, in his December 1962 letter to Bensky, McCarthy referred to the first of the interludes as an "overture" (5). Although the newly penciled changes on the page preserved among his deleted leaves might suggest that McCarthy at first considered keeping the interludes and inserting part numbers to emphasize their function as section prologues, page 193 may have been the first of the four he decided to delete. In his reply to Bensky's suggestions, McCarthy wrote that he had repeatedly revised the interlude, but it was "still not right and should probably be pulled out" (5). When he cut it from the "Final Draft" carbon, he wrote a new paragraph cast in the third person as an overture to section IV, one that conveys the break in the weather from winter to spring while it sacrifices the clear implication that John Wesley is its narrator (193/194; see *OK* 171).

Because McCarthy had shifted some pages into subsequent drafts, not all of the interludes appear in the "Late Draft." However, a crossed-out holograph false start for one appears there on the verso of an unpaginated leaf: "Is this where you come to earth old man?" McCarthy appears to have reconceived this line for the second lyrical passage he saved among his deleted leaves, a narrative address to Ownby in the asylum, which refers to Ownby's trek to the highest elevation of the mountains: "Old man, . . . sage of the rock, what vision did you have that you sought the land's spine here where the waters divide?" The final paragraph of this interlude poses a parallel question: "Old man, . . . voice of the leaf, what lucid parchment can you issue us from the quaking silence of your madhouse?" (210).[8] In the "Final Draft" carbon, this passage had preceded Ownby's retreat into the Smokies, as McCarthy wrote to Bensky in early December 1962 (5). In that location, the lines foreshadowed Ownby's incarceration in the asylum and gave the unidentified narrator a retrospective stance compatible with John Wesley's recollections in the graveyard. Again the interlude functioned as a narrative overture.

On another page filed together with the interludes in the revision notes folder, the dialogue in the asylum between young John Wesley and Ownby segues into the interrogative mode we see in the "voice of the leaf" interlude. John Wesley asks Ownby what he has done "to benefit yourself?" and the old man replies, "I gave myself seventy years of grief for eighteen months of love." In holograph notes in the margin of this page, McCarthy marked the dialogue "Abrupt?" and wondered if he might "use [it] at the last, w/ voice of the leaf?" (264), which suggests that he considered moving that interlude or some of its material to the end of the asylum scene or even to the epilogue. The page of discarded dialogue probably represents material McCarthy drafted while revising the asylum scene for Bensky. If so, the reference to trading eighteen months of love for seven decades of grief may be quite autobiographical, written in the weeks after Cormac and Lee had decided to separate. McCarthy penciled another line of Ownby's regret on a new page inserted in the "Final Draft" carbon of *The Orchard Keeper*. Ownby thinks that he ought not to have released the panther kit because his wife loved it: "For the sake of a few hogs he lost everything by not <u>daring</u> strong enough" (260/264). It seems possible that as McCarthy newly fleshed out Ownby's backstory, he was drawing on his own feelings about his failed relationship.

The lyrical interlude Bensky flagged on page 275 no longer exists in the "Final Draft" carbon, nor is it preserved with the overtures filed with McCarthy's revision notes. McCarthy described it to Bensky as "an apostrophe" to Ownby, which "affirm[s] his philosophy" and establishes "the mood for [John Wesley's] visit to his mother's grave" ([early Dec. 1962]: 5). A version of it survives in the "Late Draft" of the novel, a half-sheet with five paginations, the last of which, 275, is circled. It follows immediately after Legwater's shooting Scout, and like the other incantations it is a first-person passage, indirectly identified with John Wesley by the announcement that he intends to leave and by his reference to Ownby: "Hard weather says the old man." Then the passage becomes biblical, naturalistic, Eliotian, stoic: "Before word or flesh the earth, . . . inchoate even to a cohesiveness of . . . scoria . . . , a handful of dust loded in the firmament." He anticipates the harsh weathers of his life to come, "but I will be hard and hard and my face will turn rain like the stones" (275). Because Bensky had not grasped the relationship of the framing prologue and epilogue to the narrative as a whole, he found this passage "unidentifiable" and would probably have considered it inappropriate to the mind of young John Wesley (list, Oct. 9, 1962, 3).

Indeed, in a revised version, some lines reappear in *Suttree,* where the first-person perspective is easily identifiable as Suttree's and where the old man is the destitute rag picker who evokes his compassion: "Hard weather, says the old man. So may it be. Wrap me in the weathers of the earth, I will be hard and hard. My face will turn rain like the stones" (*S* 29). McCarthy's reuse of this material in the other novel he had been composing that year suggests a conceptual affinity between the voice of the boy in *The Orchard Keeper* and that of the adult Suttree, both of them concerned for the distressed old men they have befriended, both of them ambiguously framed as "narrators" or implied authors of their respective novels. When McCarthy jettisoned the incantations from *The Orchard Keeper,* he sacrificed the internal evidence that the story told within the narrative frame is John Wesley's imagined reconstruction. He had commented to Bensky in December 1962 that the prologue was "tonal and thematically prognostic rather than structural" (2), an assertion that underplays its narrative function as half of a structural frame yet reveals that McCarthy thought of the internal overtures and the novel's prologue in similar terms.

In his December 1962 reply to Bensky, McCarthy identified yet another "I remember" passage as one of the four he had composed to mark tonal changes and to introduce what follows (4–5). This one was on pages 54 and 55, now missing from the "Final Draft" carbon. Erskine's reading notes identify it as an "Italicized flashback to some inmate's vision" of the asylum (2). An earlier version of it survives on "Late Draft" pages 51 and 52, where it appeared between the burning of the Green Fly Inn and Ownby's perching in a peach tree to contemplate the government tank (cf. *OK* 48–51). Neither editor objected to the tone of this passage, but Bensky was confused by it. He asked in his letter of October 9, 1962, "Is this a general piece of exposition about Rattner? If it's Ownby, when has he been in Brushy Mountain (which I presume this is) and why?" (list 1). In fact, as Erskine recognized, the passage began with the description of the inmates and the martial mowers at the state asylum, not the prison (see *OK* 223–24), and after a line break it continued with Ownby's affirmation of his memories of Red Branch: "I remember the mountain road . . . laced with lizard tracks, coming up through the peach-orchard . . . And I remember the . . . cadaver grin . . . in the murky waters . . . , slimegreen skull with newts coiled in the eyesockets ("Late Draft" 51–52).

Deeper into the "Late Draft" is another passage relating to Ownby's memory of the corpse in the pit. The page begins with young Ownby's declining to turn back with his friends to take a second look at a woman undressing at her window. That boyhood experience now seems to him like a dream, so that when he returns to the pesticide pit, it "was like going back for the second look" at that which frightens him. He thinks that he returned "to feel things again that needed this light, transforming the familiar and strange alike into the fantasy of memory" (93). So Ownby's overture, his lyrical memory of the mountain road and the corpse, seems to represent the emotional accommodation he achieves when he returns for his second look and decides to tend to the corpse for seven years. The novel explores several characters' memories, but this passage, like the interlude itself, specifically extends the hallucinated recollection motif to Ownby. It links the old man's return to the pesticide pit with John Wesley's return to it and with the younger man's eventual return to his old home and the cemetery. The implication is that the site of trauma must be revisited to reconstruct it in "the fantasy of memory" and thus to rid it of its power to inflict pain or fear. McCarthy did not carry the "fantasy of memory" line forward into the final draft, but he did keep the linkage between Ownby's calming second looks at the naked woman and at the corpse (cf. *OK* 89–90). And the "fantasy of memory" is restated in John Wesley's "hallucinated recollections" (*OK* 245).

McCarthy explained to Bensky that his idea had been to use Ownby's lyrical memory to introduce him in the peach orchard ([early Dec. 1962]: 5). But the conjunction of asylum and orchard material so early in the "Late Draft" was indeed confusing. Only if readers recognized that the mowers at the asylum relate to Ownby would they see as well that the memory comes from the old man's point of view. But this would not be possible on a first reading because the reader does not see him sent to the asylum until much later and because the passage precedes and foreshadows his discovery of Rattner's corpse. Furthermore, the passage's status as one of the lyrical retrospectives might have implied to one who has finished reading that it too originates in the voice of the *spiritus mundi* or the remembering and reconstructing John Wesley—or even that John Wesley invents Ownby's memory. Because the narrative frame implies that the whole of the novel derives from John Wesley's memory and imagination, to give *spiritus mundi* overtures to both characters would have needlessly confused the matter. To address these problems, McCarthy repositioned the passage to just before John Wesley's visit to Ownby in the asylum, added the clarifying reference to the "eldest" inmate, Ownby, and removed the "I remember" refrain that belonged to the *spiritus mundi* passages ("Final Draft" carbon 255/259; cf. *OK* 224).

A "Late Draft" version of John Wesley's thoughts after he has heard Sylder's confession to killing Rattner had also created a shift from John Wesley's literal thoughts about his newly gained freedom to a passage tonally similar to the overtures. He comes to an intuition that the "value of freedom, like love, was . . . proportional to the . . . suffering it engendered and that the long journey out of mire . . . was . . . less than that non-incremental breaking of light by which we see our way, not guided, but illumined." McCarthy had eased this abrupt shift into the mature narrator's voice with a penciled addition at the beginning of the paragraph, which indicated that the boy was groping toward something he could not yet grasp; and in the margin he identified John Wesley's insight as "an empheral [ephemeral] vision" (228B). The passage is further evidence that in McCarthy's conception, the *spiritus mundi* passages originated in the mature John Wesley's imaginative vision. But when the editors read the now-lost final-draft version of this passage, neither Bensky nor Erskine found the segue from the boy's tentative thoughts to the narrator's mature expression of them effective. Paraphrasing Erskine's reading notes closely, Bensky commented: "This tone is much too advanced for a semi-educated backwoods boy. If you want to say this kind of thing, you must use the narrative voice, not the interior monologue of the boy's vision" (list, Oct. 9, 1962, 3). In his December reply, McCarthy indicated that he had in fact intended the lines to represent the narrative voice (as his penciled transition in the "Late Draft" makes clear), but he expected to cut them, especially if he cut Sylder's revelation to John Wesley (10).

The interludes were a striking departure from the narrative stance of the rest of the novel, but they reinforced the implication that the novel is the product of the mature John Wesley's hallucinated recollections.[9] They broke the action of the novel periodically, taking a step back into the retrospective and meta-narrational mode established in the prologue and epilogue. At the same time, they provided tonal overtures to the seasonal changes that structured the main action of the novel. Perhaps most significant for McCarthy's strategies in later novels, is that the interludes comprise narrative commentary divorced from the logic of the plot and thus challenge the reader to do the work of integration. Perhaps they were too jarring as McCarthy first experimented with them in his drafts of *The Orchard Keeper*, but he would return to similar strategies in the epilogues to *Suttree, Blood Meridian,* and *The Road,* in which the time setting is wrenched out of the overall chronology of the novel and/or the identity of the figure described is ambiguous. Indeed, in *Suttree* and *The Road,* the figure may be dead, and in *Blood Meridian* he is purely emblematic. In all three, the epilogues function as tonal narrative commentary, and in *Blood Meridian, The Road,* and *Cities of the Plain* as well, the voices of the epilogues seem to derive from the *spiritus mundi*—the meditative narrator himself.

The revision for Bensky that called for the most substantive change was the reconception of the novel's resolution, which required that McCarthy rewrite the late scenes of the novel in which John Wesley visits his two incarcerated mentors. Despite his initial reluctance to do that much cutting, McCarthy took seriously Bensky's criticism that the resolution was too conventional. When he undertook these revisions, he did as much amplifying as cutting, especially in the asylum scene. The problems included how to move John Wesley to his mature vision of the events without directly revealing to him what had happened to his father and how to create some other means of closure for the boy's relationships with his mentors.

McCarthy's revision of Sylder's revelations to John Wesley appears on newly typed pages 243/245, 245A/246, and 245B/247 in the "Final Draft" carbon.

Here, as in the published novel (*OK* 212–15), Sylder does not reveal that he killed the boy's father, but he does ask John Wesley not to confront Gifford. When the boy remains stubborn, Sylder contrives the argument that he and Gifford are square because each earns a living by opposing the other. Then in desperation he accuses John Wesley of trying to be a hero and angrily sends him away. This resolution creates a more definite breach between the two friends, ensuring that John Wesley will not pursue vengeance against Gifford. But it makes the boy's liberation from his pledge to avenge his father far less explicit. In this revision, there is no account of John Wesley's new sense of freedom, nor of his dawning awareness, nor any hint yet that this encounter with Sylder will prompt him to return the hawk bounty, which McCarthy now placed after John Wesley's visit to Ownby instead of between the two. Now the scene in Sylder's jail cell was followed by the cat's being taken by an owl and Eller's hearing her cry—a scene that serves to separate the two episodes in which John Wesley visits his incarcerated mentors, while alluding metaphorically to the release of Rattner's spirit.

Like the Sylder scene, the Ownby scene no longer survives in the "Final Draft" carbon as it was before McCarthy revised it. Following up on Erskine's early reading notes, Bensky observed about the Ownby scene that "the disclosure of the body, and the subsequent attempt to identify it, destroy the mystery of the story. Must John Wesley be brought into it? Can't the sheriff and humane officer find out some other way?" (list Oct. 9, 1962, 5). The editors not only preferred a more ambiguous ending, but they disliked the idea that John Wesley would uncover his father's bones, hoping to recover something of the truth. So after McCarthy deleted Ownby's accidental revelations about the location of the corpse, he rewrote the paragraph about the recovery of the remains, so that John Wesley has left Red Branch by the time officials exhume the bones from the pit. This revision now implied his repudiation of any official investigation as well as his repudiation of the hawk bounty ("Final Draft" carbon 268/272). Deleting the revelations to John Wesley implied other resolutions for the boy's reluctant promise to avenge his father, emphasizing his grief at the loss of his two substitute fathers, his alienation from the progressive order in Red Branch, and his internalizing Sylder's warnings against vengeance and Ownby's conceptions of justice and peace.

McCarthy's revision of the Ownby conversation in the "Final Draft" carbon comprises fifteen new leaves—a significant expansion of the scene over the versions in both the "Late Draft" and the "Final Draft" the editors first saw, to judge from the scene's pagination in Bensky's revision suggestions. The addition of Ownby's italicized interior monologues accounts for much of the expansion. Some of these involved recasting thoughts Ownby had spoken to John Wesley in the "Late Draft," such as his regret that he had allowed the body to be burned ("Final Draft" carbon 260/264; cf. *OK* 227–28). But others were new ideas about Ownby's vandalizing the government installation and how he had not made the gesture of protest for his own benefit, developed in two underlined passages that helped to clarify his motivations ("Final Draft" carbon 261/265 – 262/266; cf. *OK* 228–29). In the second and longer of these passages, Ownby thinks, "I kept peace for seven year sake of a man I never knowed. . . . I seen them fellers that never had no business there and if I coudnt run em off I could anyway let em know they was one man would let on like he knowed what they was up to" ("Final Draft" carbon 262/266; cf. *OK* 229). In addition, an orderly's passing through the room prompts the old man's thought that this is not the doctor who had asked about his shotgun scars, which in turn prompts his memory of how his insistence on seeing Ellen resulted in his being shot ("Final Draft" 263/267; cf. *OK* 230–31), a passage comparable to Rattner and Sylder's memories of old injuries prompted by present-time pain. All these new passages of interior monologue and memory help to clarify Ownby's attitudes about Sylder's outlawry in the context of his own, and they address Bensky's specific questions about whether Ownby knows Sylder, and why he so hates the government tank (list, Oct. 9, 1962, 1–2). They also amplify the memory trope running through the novel, adding to the memories Ownby experiences while he talks to the young boys of Red Branch on a snowy afternoon, providing a little more of his and Ellen's backstory, and perhaps compensating somewhat for the deletion of the lyrical reminiscences from the narrative voice.

The revised resolution created greater ambiguity but also new sources of puzzlement for some reviewers. However, creating it may have taught McCarthy early lessons in the powers of undercutting genre conventions. The revision experience established a pattern in McCarthy's writing process during his Random House years. He accepted that his submitted drafts, usually labeled "Final" drafts in his archive, were not in fact final and that each book would receive editorial commentary to stimulate further revisions. In his letter of early December 1962, McCarthy had confided to Bensky that he disliked revising and found it slow going, but the correspondence reveals that from the beginning of his career he embraced revision as an opportunity to perfect his work in response to editorial challenges. Always he revised on his own timeline and on his own terms, rejecting any editorial suggestions he did not see as improvements.

Bensky acknowledged receiving the revised typescript on June 25, 1963. In his undated letter of transmittal, McCarthy wrote with modest understatement that he had addressed nearly all the editorial criticisms, especially those relating to time and the identity of characters. He reminded his editor that the book was largely chronological and reported that now he had italicized those sections that were not. He had also "christened" the "nameless." However, study of the typescripts shows that McCarthy's revision for Bensky was more thoughtful and substantial than his letter suggests, not the "slightly revised" version Daniel King infers (*Cormac McCarthy's Literary Evolution* 24). By this time, the manuscript had been under active consideration at Random House for over a year and undergoing McCarthy's revision for about half that time. When Bensky forwarded the revised typescript to Erskine on July 9, 1963, enthusiastically recommending its publication, he acknowledged how painstakingly McCarthy had revised to clarify without "sacrificing . . . the book's natural power." Appreciative that McCarthy had responded so conscientiously to his suggestions, he commented, "This is a writer of real talent with an unlimited future. Our correspondence indicates to me that this book is the first work of a dedicated writer of real ability."

On August 6, 1963, Bensky sent McCarthy the encouraging news that although the revision was still being looked at, an owner of the company had read and liked the book. This would have been either Bennett Cerf or Donald Klopfer—probably Cerf. Later that month, on August 22, Bensky reported a "happy ending": Random House would publish the novel and was finally offering McCarthy a contract with a $1,500 advance upon signing. Bensky explained to Josyph that Erskine would have advocated for the book with the owners, who made the financial decisions: "although Cormac was getting almost nothing, the almost nothing would go to him versus somebody else's almost nothing. It all had to be fit into a budget, and Albert couldn't just decide a contract. Even if it was pro-forma, Albert had to run it by Bennett (Josyph, "Damn Proud" 28). Bensky wrote McCarthy graciously on August 22 that "This resolution of our long correspondence is extremely gratifying to me." But he also conveyed his regret that in the future McCarthy would be working with a different editor since he would soon leave Random and move to England.

Both as an editor and as a private citizen, Bensky was politically engaged. During his years at Random, he was arrested for his participation in Civil Rights and anti-war demonstrations. He found Bennett Cerf—"the man who had published *Ulysses*"—a person "of wonderful, open spirit . . . [,] a reflexive New York Liberal who had lived through all of this anti-communist shit [of the House Un-American Activities hearings]." Cerf had approved Bensky's idea to publish *The Haunted Fifties* (1963), a collection of the work of I. F. Stone, who had been blocked from publishing from the Joseph McCarthy era on. However, even though Cerf and Erskine valued Bensky's work, and he got along well with them, Bensky increasingly felt that "it was going to be very hard for me to continue at Random House and still be politically active in the way that I wanted to be. They weren't going to give me two months off to go to Mississippi [to support the Civil Rights movement]. And they weren't going to be happy if I got arrested" (Josyph, "Damn Proud" 7). He wanted to leave the publisher and the United States, not only for these reasons, but also because he believed that Random had promoted him as high as it ever would even though in their attempts to keep him, they offered him a title and his own office. So in fall 1963, after seeing McCarthy's novel through its first revision for Random, Bensky moved to England. Then in 1964, after the editor of *Paris Review* simply disappeared, Bensky responded to his friend George Plimpton's pleas, first that he travel to Paris to sort out the chaos and then that he take over editing the *Review* (Josyph, "Damn Proud" 30–31).[10]

Bensky notified McCarthy that his new editor would be one of the two who had already read "and admired" the novel, that his successor would likely suggest further revisions, and that McCarthy might need to travel to New York "to discuss the book" (letter, Aug. 2, 1963). In a brief, undated reply, McCarthy thanked Bensky sincerely for his editing and added more lightly that he imagined Bensky must be "heartily sick" of his book and that he hoped this was not what had driven him away from Random House ([Aug./Sept. 1963]).

The acceptance and the promised contract must have placed McCarthy on firmer ground during the subsequent editorial work. However, the editorial hand-off delayed progress on the novel by another month or so. Although Erskine was familiar with the typescript and with Bensky's and McCarthy's work on it, when Bensky sent the contract for McCarthy's signature on September 13, 1963, it still had not been decided who would edit the book. McCarthy continued to correspond with Bensky and his secretary about contractual matters through September. He read the contract carefully, and although he had a few questions about its stipulations, he signed and returned the required copies later that month. In his undated transmittal letter, he queried Bensky about these business details, and Bensky replied in his final letter to McCarthy, dated October 3. McCarthy wondered if Random now needed a fresh carbon copy as called for in the contract, and he offered instead to send the "Final Draft" carbon on which he had worked out his revisions and which had a few further changes that he had not yet transferred to the revised typescript. Bensky replied that a carbon copy was not necessary since Random had a copier that "for an exorbitant fee, will make a semi-legible reproduction. . . . This extra copy is usually used for other editor's [sic] opinions and a preliminary look by the design department." McCarthy also wanted to know about a clause limiting the author's royalty payments in any given year. He assumed this was to limit his tax liability, but he wanted to understand the rationale. Bensky explained that the provision would benefit the author "by spreading his income over several years so that his bracket will not become prohibitive." He indicated that since the annual sum had been left blank in McCarthy's contract, he needn't worry about it. Implied was that a first novel by an unknown author was unlikely to generate enough income to push him into a high tax bracket. McCarthy also stipulated that his typescripts and proofs be sent back to him after publication, thus beginning to build the extensive collection of his papers that would eventually go to the Southwestern Writers Collection at Texas State University–San Marcos. Bensky assured him that after publication he would be asked if he wanted these documents and suggested that McCarthy mention his preference to his new editor.

Finally, McCarthy expressed interest in having an excerpt from the novel published in a periodical as Bensky had suggested in his long letter of October 9, 1962. McCarthy wondered if that was something Random would arrange for him. In his reply of October 3, 1963, Bensky indicated that if McCarthy wished to submit excerpts to magazines, he could do so, but that Random would also investigate the possibility, so he should keep them informed of his efforts. He suggested five periodicals McCarthy might approach: *Kenyon Review, Carlton Miscellany, Paris Review* (where Bensky would soon begin work), *Noble Savage* (edited by Saul Bellow) if it was still publishing, and *Esquire*. The editors of the first three—Robie Macauley, Reid Whittmore, and George Plimpton, respectively—were Bensky's "good friends," and Bensky recommended that McCarthy mention his name if he wrote them. Since none of these journals did, in fact, publish excerpts from *The Orchard Keeper,* and since no correspondence with periodicals survives in McCarthy's archive, we may infer that McCarthy chose to leave the negotiations to his new editor. It seems that since Random was willing to undertake such tasks for him, he decided even before the publication of his first novel to entrust them with selling excerpts in order to devote his time more fully to the writing of new novels.

# Working with Albert Erskine

O n October 10, 1963, Bensky sailed for England, but it was not until October 29 that Erskine wrote McCarthy to say he would undertake the remaining editorial work on the book. Although it may have been distressing to be assigned a new editor after meeting the demands of his first one, in many ways it was fortunate that McCarthy had so quickly become one of Erskine's authors. Erskine was not McCarthy's first editor, nor would he be his last, but he was arguably his most important one. Erskine worked with McCarthy in his most formative years, from 1963 through 1986, shepherding each novel from *The Orchard Keeper* through *Blood Meridian* to publication and doing at least one reading of *All the Pretty Horses*. Although their working relationship was sometimes awkward at first, they quickly learned to trust and like each other. In effect, they taught one another how to work together, and Erskine taught McCarthy much about editorial and publication processes. He promoted McCarthy's career steadfastly—although without the financial returns facilitated by McCarthy's first Knopf editor Gary Fisketjon and his International Creative Management agent Amanda Urban in the 1990s and 2000s.

As his correspondence with Bensky reveals, there is some truth to McCarthy's characterization of the process that delayed publication of *The Orchard Keeper* from its May 1962 submission to its May 1965 release as "arguing" with his editors. The debates continued and to some degree intensified with Erskine. But by the time he and Erskine completed their work on *Blood Meridian*, McCarthy would, in its front matter, "express his appreciation to Albert Erskine, his editor of twenty years" (iii). He knew that Erskine—then seventy-four—would not continue editing him. Erskine had been semi-retired and working from his home in Westport, Connecticut for several years. As early as 1979, in a letter postmarked November 5, McCarthy had complained to book dealer and bibliographer Howard Woolmer that without Erskine around, the Random House offices appeared to be run by "transients." He remarked that Erskine might be viewed as "a relic . . . by the functional illiterates" who were then in charge of the publishing house.[11] Erskine saw McCarthy's long-delayed *Blood Meridian* through publication, then confined his editing mostly to James Michener, "whose voluminous manuscripts" required a huge investment of time and labor, McCarthy wrote Woolmer in a letter postmarked June 28, 1985. But the severance of their relationship was entirely amicable. McCarthy warmly agreed with Woolmer, who had met Erskine earlier in the year, that the editor was "a good chap."

Erskine was a generation older than McCarthy, but he shared a background in Tennessee. He grew up in Memphis, where he attended Southwestern College (later renamed Rhodes College), then earned his master's degree at Vanderbilt under the direction of Southern Agrarian Donald Davidson in 1933, the year McCarthy was born (Blotner, "Albert Erskine" 142). Erskine followed his friend and teacher Robert Penn Warren to Louisiana State University, where Erskine served as an English instructor and as editorial assistant for the university press. Together with fellow editors Warren, Cleanth Brooks, and political scientist Charles Pipkin, he was involved with *Southern Review* from its inception (Cutrer, *Parnassus on the Mississippi* 51). Initially he bore the title of "business manager" and was responsible for contributors' payments, printing, subscriptions, and distribution (Montesi, *Historical Survey* 32). But in fact he functioned as a managing editor. Everyone on the editorial staff read every submission, and the decisions to publish or reject were made in collaboration (Cutrer, *Parnassus on the Mississippi* 63). Albert Montesi infers from the editors' correspondence that Erskine took the lead in evaluating the fiction submissions, while Warren specialized in poetry, Brooks in criticism, and Pipkin in political essays (93).

Through *Southern Review*, Erskine met and briefly was married to novelist Katherine Anne Porter. In that period, she saw him already as "a born editor, an acute and sensitive critic," and she found it "a shameful waste of gifts that he does not have a good authoritative editorial job" (Blotner, "Albert Erskine" 144–45), by which she may have meant an editorial position in the for-profit New York publishing world. In spring 1940, after only two years together, they agreed to separate (Givner, *Katherine Anne Porter* 314–15). That fall she moved to Saratoga Springs, New York, and the next year he joined New Directions in New York City, where he served as "editor and man-of-all-work" (Cutrer, *Parnassus on the Mississippi* 103, 259; Blotner, *Robert Penn Warren* 189).

Before settling with Random, Erskine worked sequentially for the *Saturday Review of Literature*, Doubleday Doran, and Reynal and Hitchcock by fall 1942 (Cutrer, *Parnassus on the Mississippi* 259; Grimshaw, "Robert Penn Warren" 117). He stayed with Reynal and Hitchcock for five years, but after a falling out over the merits of Malcolm Lowry's *Under the Volcano* (1947), which Eugene Reynal intensely disliked (Bowker, *Pursued by Furies* 397), Erskine and fellow executive and editor Frank Taylor left that firm for Random in 1947, taking with them authors Karl Shapiro and Ralph Ellison (Cerf, *At Random* 235). By 1950, Erskine had also drawn Robert Penn Warren to Random House (Erskine, "Editor's Note" xii).

Taylor left Random after only a few years to become a film producer at MGM, but Erskine stayed on for the rest of his career (Cerf, *At Random* 235). He became managing editor in 1955, and by 1959, three years before McCarthy submitted his first novel to Random, Erskine had become a vice president (Lambert, "Albert R. Erskine, 81"). Random House founder Bennett Cerf had offered to make him editor-in-chief, probably when editor Saxe Commins died in 1958, but Erskine turned him down. He "didn't want to be bothered with all the details involved; he already had his hands full working with a long list of authors," Cerf writes, "including some of our most famous" (Cerf, *At Random* 235; Margaret Becket, "Random House" 307). In addition to Ellison,[12] Michener, Shapiro, and Warren, Erskine edited Random House authors William Faulkner, Moss Hart, John O'Hara, and, starting in 1970, Eudora Welty, whom he had admired and befriended during his time at *Southern Review* (Kreyling, *Author and Agent* 208; Cutrer, *Parnassus on the Mississippi* 94). Erskine's experience with these writers and his steeping in the literature and culture of the South made him an appreciative reader of McCarthy's Tennessee novels, and his work with

Faulkner, especially, had schooled him in the structural and temporal disloca-
tions of modernist fiction.

To a remarkable degree, Erskine earned the loyalty and appreciation of
authors of varying temperaments. Cerf claimed that Faulkner once told him,
"Albert is the best book editor I know," but Faulkner had never told Erskine
this because "when I've got a horse that's running good, I don't stop him to
give him some sugar" (Cerf, *At Random* 133). This praise constituted oblique
criticism of Faulkner's previous editor, the comparatively uncritical Saxe Commins, who tended to see his role as propping up the egos of his authors. Faulkner's biographer Joseph Blotner writes: "For all Faulkner's appreciation of
Commins's solicitude, his response to ongoing work was sometimes fulsome
praise, but Faulkner valued precise and frank criticism far more highly" (Blotner, "Albert Erskine" 155). Michener had been so unhappy when Commins sent
the unfinished manuscript of *Sayonara* to the printer without editing it that his
agent Helen Strauss pushed against heavy resistance from Cerf for Michener's
reassignment to Erskine. She thought her persistence in making this happen
was "probably the best thing I did for [Michener's] career, because with Albert
and, later, Bert Krantz, his copyeditor, Jim got the editorial help he always
wanted" (quoted in Hayes, *James A. Michener* 117). Michener biographer Stephen J. May reports that with each successive book, Erskine's role "in focusing
and shaping the rough edges" of Michener's work was "increasingly essential"
(May, *Michener,* 157). Michener found Erskine "a brilliant man intellectually
and a perceptive one artistically. He points with devilish accuracy at points
where I have gone wrong, at interior contradictions, at sloppy motivations for
specific acts. Erskine is an educated man with one hell of a good eye, which is
all important" (quoted in May, *Michener* 157).

The more neurotic Malcolm Lowry eventually became emotionally dependent on Erskine for approval and took it personally when he was honest about
problems in his work, but early on, after working with Erskine on *Under the
Volcano,* Lowry had told his agent Harold Matson, "So complete was [Erskine's]
. . . creative sympathy with my work that psychologically and in every way
it seems to me unthinkable that I could ever have another editor" (quoted in
Bowker, *Pursued by Furies* 481). For years Lowry tried unsuccessfully to termi-
nate his contract with Reynal and Hitchcock so that he could resume working
with Erskine (Bowker, *Pursued by Furies* 444, 457, 481). Robert Penn Warren was
a close friend—he dedicated *Eleven Poems on the Same Theme* (1942) to Erskine
and Brooks (Cutrer, *Parnassus on the Mississippi* 163)—but Warren shared other
writers' deep appreciation for Erskine's editorial skills. In 1949, as they were
finishing their work on *World Enough and Time,* Warren wrote Erskine, "I'm
certain that no writer could ever hope for a better and more careful piece of editing. . . . I'm damned grateful to you" (quoted in Blotner, *Robert Penn Warren* 253).

In Cerf's opinion, Erskine would not "overwork": "When he thinks he's slaving, other people don't think so, but he has his own pace. Nobody would dream of telling him what to do" (Cerf, *At Random* 235). New York native Cerf attributed this to Erskine's being a Southerner, but Erskine conscientiously managed his workload so that he could do justice to each author and book. The correspondence reveals that he acted very promptly with nearly every task associated with McCarthy, usually replying to his letters and acting on his requests the day they came in, and often going well beyond what an editor today might do.

However, Erskine was not quick to take on McCarthy. When he agreed to assume the editorial work on *The Orchard Keeper* after Bensky left Random, he wrote McCarthy on October 29, 1963, that he would need to finish work on his projects for the spring 1964 Random House list before turning his attention back to McCarthy's book. This is one of a very few times he ever indicated that he was too busy with other authors to give anything less than full concentration to McCarthy's work and concerns. But he had not initially expected to work with this fledgling writer. He was, after all, a senior editor with several well-established writers in his stable. It seems likely that his willingness to edit McCarthy had much to do with his recognition of McCarthy's sheer talent and the astonishing virtuosity of his first novel, which Erskine had read by then in both its submitted and revised versions. Moreover, McCarthy had shown in his revision of the novel that he had the intelligence, persistence, and flexibility of mind to maximize that talent. For Erskine, it was probably a factor, too, that Faulkner had died in July 1962, just a few months after McCarthy submitted *The Orchard Keeper* and less than two years before Erskine became McCarthy's editor. It may have seemed providential that this extraordinary young fiction writer should come into the Random House fold so soon after Erskine had lost his best novelist.

Despite Erskine's need to postpone briefly his work on *The Orchard Keeper,* he planned to reread McCarthy's revision once the spring books were in production, and he hoped the further editing and production processes could be completed in time for publication in August 1964, which he considered "a very good month to publish a first novel." He anticipated having questions and suggestions but reassured McCarthy, "I do not believe that anything I might ask you to do on this manuscript can be extensive enough to cause you any grief" (letter, Oct. 29, 1963). His statement would prove overly optimistic.

Erskine sent the revised typescript and Bensky's correspondence with McCarthy to assistant editor Roger Jellinek, who recorded his assessment of it in a memo dated November 14 and signed with his initials.[13] Jellinek admired McCarthy's prose style. However, even in its revised version he found the novel's structure too "subtle" and difficult to follow although on backtracking he found that all the necessary clues were there. He did not see a solution for this aspect of the work's narrative difficulty. However, he recommended that McCarthy further clarify the tensions he had described in his letters to Bensky. Finally, he did not like McCarthy's use of italics to highlight breaks in the chronology and suggested that line breaks be used instead—the solution McCarthy had earlier employed.

By November 14, Erskine too had reread about fifty pages of the revised typescript, as well as the correspondence. He sent McCarthy a five-page letter outlining his concerns and forwarded a copy to Jellinek, with a note that they could discuss it when he returned to the office. Drawing from his experience with Faulkner's "apostrophical eccentricities," Erskine warned McCarthy that unconventional punctuation practices such as the omission of apostrophes and quotation marks led to increased compositors' and proofreaders' errors and thus inconsistencies in the published books. He worried, too, that such unconventionality might appear derivative without enhancing the quality of the novel. In McCarthy's case, he thought this would be a shame "because though I feel the influence [of Faulkner] is there I believe you have already developed, out of whatever influences there are, a style of your own (though critics might point out the similarity between Legwater's mania and that of Henry Armstid in *The Hamlet*)." However, if the issue was important to McCarthy, Erskine was willing to go along if McCarthy developed an "air-tight" system of punctuation that he could use consistently in future books and if he could explain his rationale for it. Erskine indicated that he was querying punctuation with hyphens and commas and making more substantive notes on a photocopy of the first portion of the revised typescript and sending that to McCarthy for his response (letter, 1–2). These notations comprised the first stage of editorial markings, in red pencil,[14] that Erskine inscribed on the editorial copy. Ordinarily, Erskine said, he would have house-styled the punctuation, "but since we don't know each other I think it well that we find out what areas of agreement and of conflict might exist in such matters before I proceed" (3).

Next Erskine addressed the chronology in the opening scenes, where Sylder and Kenneth Rattner were not "running on the same timetable" (letter, Nov. 14, 1963, 4). Although he had read the revised typescript in its entirety and now had reread its opening, it seems likely that he was still influenced by his impressions of the reading difficulties posed by the version McCarthy had originally submitted. Thus Erskine was especially vigilant about time disruptions in the narrative. On a page of holograph notes that outlines issues he wanted to address in his letter, Erskine observed that Rattner's narrative progressed across hours, whereas Sylder's advanced "in unspecified much longer intervals." Although in his letter he acknowledged that chronological order was not always best in a narrative, he felt that "if the scenes seem to have that kind of relationship and don't have it, the effect can be pretty troublesome." He found this feature more worrisome than the flashback to the porch collapse at the Green Fly Inn, which had been the focus of some of Bensky and McCarthy's interchanges, but which had always been identified as Rattner's memory and became even more clearly so in revision. But Erskine still disliked the shift forward in time for the burning of the inn in 1936, and unlike Bensky, who had admired the passage, he thought the scene "serves no purpose except to confuse and should be cut; it must be a leftover of some earlier draft" (letter, 4).

Although Erskine admitted that he wasn't sure the time disruption between the Rattner and Sylder scenes was a "serious flaw" or that he knew how to remedy it, he suggested that McCarthy might start the novel with Sylder and delay the introduction of Rattner until their alternating scenes could be synchronous. Sylder's three opening scenes could be made continuous, bringing Sylder up to "standard Rattner time"; then Rattner's first three scenes could be inserted on pages 30, 32, and 33 of the typescript (4). Erskine marked on the editorial copy exactly where these might be repositioned. The first Rattner scene, of his hitchhiking to Atlanta (see *OK* 7–10), would go between Sylder's turning twenty-one and his fight with Conatser on the following Friday (see *OK* 29–30). Rattner's next passage, when he examines the wallet of the driver he has assaulted and perhaps killed (see *OK* 15), could be placed after Sylder is fired and before he goes to Monk's to drink (see *OK* 31). The third, in which Rattner drinks at Jim's Hot Spot and remembers the porch collapse (see *OK* 22–27), would appear just before Sylder arrives at the Hot Spot, after the line, "The air came cool and damp under the windscreen" (see *OK* 32). Erskine thought that in the rest of the novel "the problems of sequence are not going to be so difficult after Rattner is disposed of" (letter, 4). So he had decided to write McCarthy the letter of November 14 to see if they could resolve the basic problems of punctuation and time before he read further. He was about to go on a ten-day vacation and wanted McCarthy to have something to work on in the interval (1). Erskine knew that McCarthy was then composing a new novel and did not lack for employment, but clearly this was a way of beginning their working relationship, a method for Erskine to learn how wedded McCarthy was to his design for the novel and to his nonstandard punctuation. He may have felt, too, that once he had received the writer's responses, he could more efficiently work through the rest of the editorial copy.

In the letter of November 14, Erskine also expressed his confidence in McCarthy's future as a writer. He was already convinced that McCarthy was a genuine talent, a writer whose opinions about the shape of his work were not to be discounted. Erskine would have found it easier to have the typescript copyedited and sent to the printer, he pointed out, but "what I see in this one makes me believe that you know what you are doing and can do more and better" (5). Hence Erskine's reluctance to claim authority over McCarthy's novel. If his plan to restructure the opening "horrifies you, don't hesitate to say so," he wrote (4); and he reiterated, "please feel free to reject any suggestion you think is wrong" (5).

In his long reply dated December 1963, McCarthy tested Erskine's sincerity. Rising to his challenge, he attempted to identify his principles of punctuation. Although he found apostrophes "superfluous . . . and an eyesore," he didn't care that much about them, so conventional usage was okay with him (1). He was more adamant about commas. They could be inserted to avoid "reason-able ambiguity," but otherwise he found them "impediments" to fluid reading. McCarthy felt that "overpunctuation" was often "the result of bad writing. If a sentence is properly built it wont need much punctuation" (2). The same held for quotation marks. He didn't like them, he thought there was a trend away from them, and no passage in his novel was ambiguous without them (2–3). McCarthy admitted that his use of hyphens and compound words had been rather haphazard, but he proceeded in a "half-jocular" way to articulate three rules that guided his usage. If the stressed syllable fell at the beginning of the second word ("half-dóllar"), he tended to hyphenate; if on the first word ("hálfpenny"), he did not. Secondly, hyphens were used to separate medial vowels because in the rare case when this convention is violated, such as "pineapple," it results in confusion about pronunciation ("pinneyapple"). Finally, when a combination creates a conjunction of consonants that obscures the boundaries between the words, a hyphen is used, as in "pot-hook" or "foot-rail" (5–6).

As for the opening of the novel, McCarthy asserted, "I doubt it is quite such a mess as everyone seems inclined to believe." This time he declined to lay out his rationale, except to say that his instinct was still to begin with Rattner. The time disparity was no accident but a considered choice (3). He preferred that his novel pique interest with its very challenges: "As a reader . . . I have no objection to anyone trying my understanding, my open-mindedness, even my stomach, but let them not try my patience" (4). McCarthy believed that his opening created interest by establishing an immediate conflict, and he defended his strategy by invoking Dostoyevsky (4). Perhaps McCarthy was thinking of the shocking opening of *Crime and Punishment* (1866) with Raskol-nikov's murder of the pawnbroker and her sister, followed by the gradual un-folding of his motives for the crime and the exploration of its aftermath.

In fact, although the restructuring Erskine suggested might have made for a less confusing opening, it would also have lessened the mystery and the prolonged suspense created by the Rattner material both in its placement and in his characterization. It would also have made less obvious the parallels be-tween John Wesley's return to Red Branch in the prologue and his father's return in the next section, obscuring the hint that the images of Rattner's return echo John Wesley's own recent experience, which informs his imaginative reconstruction of his father's (see Luce, "'They aint the thing'" 26–27). McCarthy's other, unstated, reasons might have included that juxtaposing all of Rattner's activities with Sylder's job loss may have implied too overtly that Sylder's anger calls Rattner forth as his ominous double and challenger. Additionally, it would have distorted McCarthy's overall plan to structure his novel through short scenes of the central characters presented in rotation. Shifting Rattner's scenes would have given him less prominence both structurally and thematically. McCarthy's design for the novel gave approximately equal weight to Rattner, Sylder, and Ownby until Rattner dies; then it introduced John Wesley in rotation with Sylder and Ownby for the remainder of the book, a structure that emphasizes how John Wesley's life is in many ways redeemed by Sylder's elimination of his father and by Sylder's and Ownby's mentoring, how Rattner's death allows the boy's sensitive, ethical, and courageous nature to emerge. As Jellinek observed, this was unusually subtle narrative structuring. But it was also effective. In his letter of December 1963, McCarthy suggested that if Erskine were to read the novel's opening with the simplified time structure he was recommending, he would not like it (4).

Erskine's response of December 27, 1963, was again lengthy but this time less patient and sometimes sarcastic. He seems to have interpreted McCarthy's disquisitions on punctuation as amateurish, defensive, and unreasonably resistant. Erskine refuted nearly all of those relating to commas and hyphens, citing precedents and *Webster's Collegiate Dictionary* (5), and pointing out specific sentences from the typescript in which the absence of a comma made for ambiguity. He argued that even for a writer of McCarthy's caliber, who did not need a great deal of punctuation, "there is an irreducible minimum, and when that is reached, where can the trend trend?" He observed further that "even without any prodding from me you use a lot more punctuation than is found in the Beowulf ms," so maybe the long-term trend was toward more punctuation (3–4). He also wrote that house-styling was standard publishers' practice and that in terms of the rigidity of its application, Random fell in a middle range (4). He argued that since editors often received the blame for errors and inconsistencies, they had a right to be concerned. Critics "assume that even if the writer made a mess the editor should have cleaned it up. It is a common assumption, shared indeed by most writers" (5). He may have had in mind such stories as those about Maxwell Perkins, whose grasp of spelling had been imperfect and who was criticized in print for allowing Fitzgerald's spelling errors in *This Side of Paradise* to remain uncorrected (Berg, *Max Perkins* 20).

But Erskine did not insist, and he hoped that while he was "trying to be flexible," McCarthy could "be reasonable" (5). McCarthy's minimal use of apostrophes and quotation marks could stand as written although Erskine hoped

McCarthy would omit apostrophes only in negative contractions and not in possessive nouns. He still thought the time disjunctions of the opening scenes might be a problem, but he would not lobby further for restructuring. In a holograph addition to this letter, he agreed with McCarthy, "They do read well." Yet he still thought that deleting the "anticipatory references to the burning of the Green Fly" would benefit the novel (6). He would continue to mark and mail batches of the novel, and they could work out solutions for specific passages that way. He promised to return the portion that he and McCarthy had already marked once, continuing their dialogue but in a different color—green as it turned out. Both correspondents expressed dwindling patience for the debates by mail, and in a typed note affixed to his "tedious document" on December 31, Erskine asked McCarthy to "forgive its sometimes rather testy tone." But he had already ended his letter dated December 27 on a cordial note: "I'm enjoying the rereading—which is something of a test, and it the third time. Enjoyed this exchange, too, but I've give out" (6). He marked the remainder of the editorial copy and mailed it to McCarthy in Sevierville on January 7, 1964, with a brief and friendly cover letter.

By mid-January, McCarthy had moved to Asheville, North Carolina, and he asked Erskine to send mail to him there in care of Gary Goodman, a friend from his university days who worked as a salesman (McCarthy, Letter to Erskine, received Jan. 13, 1964; Gibson, "Knoxville Gave Cormac McCarthy" 28). In an undated letter of late January or early February 1964, McCarthy informed Erskine that he had returned to Tennessee and picked up the editorial copy. He was working on it, and he asked Erskine to give him a deadline to help him pace his work. Erskine replied on February 11 that if the typescript had arrived three weeks earlier, that would have ensured a summer 1964 publication. They might still make it if McCarthy could finish revising that month, but Erskine did not want him to hurry the job: "Do it as soon as it can be done properly, and we will take over from there," he wrote.

However, by March 4 McCarthy's revisions had not yet reached Erskine, who wrote to check that McCarthy was all right, confessing that now he was "worried . . . I might have seemed over-insistent about apostrophes, hyphens, commas, etc. I hope you know that I meant it when I said for you to do what you wanted about these things." Erskine explained that he had been involved in trying to create a new text of Faulkner's *The Sound and the Fury* that would correct the errors and inconsistencies introduced by copyeditors and typesetters in the 1929 first edition and compounded by new typesetters' errors in the 1946 Modern Library edition. "It was against this background that I was making my perhaps too insistent plea for normalcy," he wrote. Erskine was now uncertain that McCarthy's novel could be published in 1964, especially because he needed lead time to send advance copies to "influential readers" who might provide endorsements for its jacket. Underlying this letter, one hears Erskine's anxiety that he may have alienated or discouraged McCarthy. He may have been relieved to find that his letter had crossed the newly revised typescript in the mail (Baskin, Letter to Cormac McCarthy, March 6, 1964).

In this round of revisions, McCarthy made fewer substantive changes than he had for Bensky. Wisely, he did not accept Erskine's recommendations that he delay the introduction of Rattner and that he eliminate the burning of the Green Fly Inn. In his cover letter that reached Random on March 6, he did not explain why he did not reposition or delete the fire scene, but clearly Mc-Carthy placed less value on strict chronology than on more aesthetic issues such as tone, pacing, juxtaposition, and balance in determining the sequence in which the reader would encounter his scenes. Even though it skips forward two years from the main action of Part I, the placement of the fire at the end of the opening section creates a sense of closure for that stage of Sylder's life as well as for the violence between him and Rattner, who are both associated with the inn, one as an integrated member of its community and the other as an interloper. In addition, the destruction of the inn closes down any implication that with the death of Rattner the community of Red Branch will be immune from further inroads from the new order. Indeed, it subtly reinforces the prohibitionist sentiment of some in the community that lies behind the corrupt, arrogant Gifford's persecution of the main characters. (That sentiment had been most explicit in the conversation between Mrs. Eller and Mildred Rattner after the porch collapse, which McCarthy had deleted when he revised for Bensky.) The burning of the inn, perhaps by arson, foreshadows the doom of the Red Branch community, and stylistically and tonally it anticipates and counterpoints the epilogue's "myth, legend, dust" passage: "It is there yet, the last remnant of that landmark, flowing down the sharp fold of the valley like some imponderable archaeological phenomenon" (*OK* 48). Performing so many functions within the novel, the scene is pivotal and could not be spared.

Erskine was similarly troubled by the delayed narration of Ownby's waking in the woods after he has been struck down by a tree split by lightning (see *OK* 172, 184). In the editorial copy, Erskine traced the relevant time references and wrote, "Old man waking on 210 makes it seem he's been lying there 5 or 6 days—which don't seem likely" (209 verso). He wondered if McCarthy might place the waking scene earlier, possibly between the description of the cat in the downpour and John Wesley's checking his traps on the third day of rain (see *OK* 176), or invent some other solution. McCarthy replied that he wanted the entire section of the spring rains (the first subsection of Part IV) to be framed by scenes of Ownby, as the sequence in his "Late Draft" confirms. So the best option he could devise would be to italicize the scene of the old man's waking, since in the novel italics consistently signaled "displacement in time" (Editorial Copy 209 verso). Even with italics, this placement has raised questions for some readers; but since Ownby experiences his injury as Valkyries' descending to carry him off, the delayed scene of awakening has the benefit of sustaining the reader's concern for the old man's survival (*OK* 172). Then it creates a hint of his metaphorical rebirth into the quiet and "*kind*" rainfall in the night woods, when he wakes to hear "*the rain mendicant-voiced, soft chanting in that dark gramarye that summons the earth to bridehood*" and marks the advent of spring (*OK* 184). The juxtaposition of this passage of praise and benediction with the next section, when officers come to arrest Ownby, wrenching him from his mystical union with his natural environment, makes for another profound and effective tonal shift.

The final issue of scene placement that Erskine raised had to do with the cat's being carried off by the owl. Bensky had wondered, "What does the cat's death contribute?" Although he did not object to the scene, he hoped McCarthy would reconsider "its place in the ms." (October 9, 1962, list 3). Bensky's advice was ambiguous, and he may have been more concerned about its function than its position within the structure of the novel. Before McCarthy's revisions for Bensky, the sequence of scenes had moved from John Wesley's meeting with Sylder in the jail, to his return of the hawk bounty, to the owl's taking the cat. When McCarthy rewrote his scenes of the incarcerated Sylder and Ownby to eliminate their revelations to the boy, he delayed the bounty scene until after John Wesley's visit to Ownby but left the cat-and-owl scene between John Wesley's two visits to his mentors, where it prepared for Ownby's explanation that the spirit of a dead person could transmigrate into a cat.

However, as he invented the first of Ownby's interior monologues when he revised the asylum scene for Bensky, McCarthy had introduced a new inconsistency relating to the cat's death. Ownby thinks that Rattner's spirit must be gone because "I heard him . . . high up and leavin out cat and all bound for hell most probably and it squalled twicet and that was the last I heard of it and I hope not to hear no more never." McCarthy was aware that this might contradict a minor detail he had established earlier. When Eller heard the cat, it had cried once, and McCarthy penciled a question mark above "twicet" in his new Ownby passage ("Final Draft" carbon 260/264). However, because Ownby's passage was a memory, it seems McCarthy had not foreseen the potential for confusion in his repeating the cat's demise in Eller and Ownby's differing time levels until Erskine queried the scene:

> why have you placed the cat where it is, after Ownby has been taken away, and made Eller the one to hear it?

Is Ownby supposed to be able to hear it wherever he happens to be? If so, that seems to be adding an unneeded dimension, plus some confusion. (Editorial Copy 260, verso)

McCarthy took this seriously. Beside Ownby's reference to hearing the cat in the "Final Draft" carbon, he noted the problem: "[Ownby] was already in pokey then?" (260/264), and on the page describing the cat's death he debated where he might reposition it: "Use just before finding of body/ or use just before Legwater digging/ Use before old man wakes in rain/ rewrite for rainy season" ("Final Draft" carbon 246/248?/250). In his revision notes for the page, McCarthy reminded himself, "Something must be done about cat. . . . shift cat scene." On another unpaginated leaf of the revision notes, he charted the dates of the relevant scenes and considered various repositioning options, but this led him to realize that placing the cat's death before Ownby's incarceration was not the solution: "Cat's death should trigger general decline of everybody. 7 years not up until August—Boy could hear cat and tell old man about it. & he could give his exp[lanation]./ but boy leave[s] in 'May or June'—so cat has to die before then." So he was thinking that the solution might be to place the cat's death and Rattner's release before John Wesley leaves Red Branch, while retaining Ownby's explanation of its connection to the corpse. The problem finally came down to having someone plausibly on hand to hear the cat's dying squall at the right time of year.

McCarthy drafted a few lines on the verso of page 2 of these notes, passages that emphasize Eller's hearing the cat's cry overhead. Then he rewrote the problematic paragraph on a new page for the editorial copy, deleting Ownby's hearing its scream and adding the old man's new thought during his final conversation with John Wesley, "that had to of been him Eller was supposed to of heard, wonderin what-all it could of been squallin thataway" (see *OK* 227–28). McCarthy penciled a note to Erskine below this revision: "This at least absolves the old man of 1st-hand-hearing the cat." McCarthy felt it was not necessary to explain how Ownby knew Eller had heard the cat's cry because the novel established that they knew one another (Editorial Copy 260A). With this solution McCarthy let go of his original idea that the cat would die in August, exactly seven years after Rattner's death. He remarked in his cover letter for the final revisions that he was uncertain about this revision but that it was the only solution he could devise. Probably referring to his aborted notes about the scene's problems, which may have been intended for Erskine, he wrote that he had composed "a long explanation" of its placement, but he had not sent it because the rationale was a bit too "involved and confused." He acknowledged the "wrench" in the chronology but added, "whenever anything is moved, something else falls over. It's all a sort of juggling act" (Letter to Erskine, received Mar. 6, 1964).

The tone of the interchanges on the editorial copy and in subsequent correspondence is cooperative, informative, and flexible, with moments of lightness and humor. For instance, McCarthy had written that it took a year to "deciduate" Ownby's cut cedars, and Erskine suggested changing this to "defoliate." "[S]ounds like the undoing of a virgin," McCarthy quipped, and he substituted the word "fret" (Editorial Copy 100; *OK* 90). And although the editor was usually businesslike when he questioned word choices, he used a light touch when he circled "bemaculate" in McCarthy's description of "clear water . . . bemaculate with greenery" and wrote, "Where you find this one? Pretty flossy?" (Editorial Copy 196). Indeed, "bemaculate" is not in the *Oxford English Dictionary* but seems to be McCarthy's coinage from "maculate" or "maculated," meaning spotted: the opposite of "immaculate." When his editor questioned it, McCarthy considered changing the word to "mackled or "macled" (Revision notes) before deleting the phrase (see *OK* 173).

In the first batch of marked pages of the editorial copy, Erskine had changed "grey" to "gray," and McCarthy questioned whether "grey," which looked better to him, was "too English" (19). Erskine explained in his letter of December 27, 1963, that both spellings occurred in McCarthy's typescript and that Random's house-styling usually converted British spellings to American. He related an anecdote he had heard from a copy editor about "one of our most Sensitive writers" and his "high-pitched, octave-above-girlish voice: 'But grey is so much <u>grey</u>-er than gray!'" Erskine continued, "So I could be grossly wrong—or wrongly gross—in not detecting the subtle difference" (5). The camaraderie of Erskine's story seems to have gone a long way toward appeasing McCarthy's own initial sensitivity about editorial changes (although Erskine's ridiculing such sensitivity as effeminate may also have had its effect). In the margin of the editorial copy next to the first instance of "grey," McCarthy wrote, "<u>Your little anecdote on grey being 'so much grey-er'</u> sold me. Gross <u>gray it is</u>" (9).

The other interchanges between author and editor in the editorial copy address relatively minor details, but they offer further intriguing insights into McCarthy's conception of his novel or his working practices as well as revealing aspects of Erskine's editorial role and of their relationship. Erskine's queries elicited explanations from McCarthy comparable in their candor to those he had offered Bensky in his undated letter of December 1962. For example, Erskine's questioning the misplaced modifier of the early line, "Going east from Knoxville Tennessee the mountains start," prompted McCarthy's reply that it was okay as written: "(<u>You</u> is understood. A borrowing from the jargon of travel guides) The purpose here was to continue the peripatetic impression of the first 4 pages. i.e.: 'As you go' east etc." (5). Nevertheless, he revised the line to the more standard syntax that appears in the published novel: "East of Knoxville Tennessee the mountains start" (*OK* 10). Erskine also flagged a sentence fragment listing the lunch foods Sylder eats in the café but admitted he didn't care too much about it. McCarthy's response hints at the rationale for his frequent use of fragments to represent narrators' or characters' sequential sensory perceptions: "Of what did the lunches consist? Beans & Fatmeat . . etc. (I dont see the need for a predicate—the items on the menu dont need to <u>do</u> anything" (Editorial Copy 29; see *OK* 29).

When his editor questioned word choices, McCarthy cited the dictionaries he consulted, *Webster's International* and the *Oxford English Dictionary* (Editorial Copy 33), and usually he declined to alter his diction. Occasionally Erskine failed to get a clear image from a phrase until McCarthy explained his conception. For example, the editor flagged the description of the molten glass left below the Green Fly Inn after it burns: "encysted with crisp and blackened rubble, murrhined with bottlecaps." He queried, "shd it be encysting crisp etc?/ encysted with seems to denote that rubble enclosed the glass while the glass enclosed bottlecaps. Is that the picture?" McCarthy explained that the glass is "<u>imbedded</u> with cysts of rubble—as a piece of pork might be with cysted . . . worms. . . . [I]f the worms were encysted in the meat couldnt the meat be encysted <u>with</u> the worms?" He acknowledged that his dictionaries did not cite that usage, but no word quite conveyed his meaning. He suggested another phrasing, "imbedded, with cysts of crisp and blackened rubble" that Erskine could substitute if he thought it an improvement (Editorial Copy 53; cf. *OK* 48). In another passage—"From a lightwire overhead, dangling head downward and hollowed to the weight of ashened feathers and fluted bones, a small owl hung in an attitude of forlorn exhortation"—Erskine circled the words "hollowed," "ashened," and "fluted"; and he noted on the verso, "This passage sounds great, but I can't connect with it—as a whole or in detail, esp. the circled words." McCarthy replied that he had taken the sentence through multiple revisions and that his description of the dead owl had not seemed unclear to him. "Should I maybe use the word <u>dead</u> at the beginning . . . ?" (Editorial Copy 161 and verso; *OK* 143). In both instances, McCarthy's explanations convinced his editor to accept the original phrasing.

Other cases in which Erskine questioned McCarthy's diction or the precision of his imagery resulted in changes. The editorial copy had described the mountain ridges "like lean burning hounds racing . . . to the land's end . . . at the firy mitre of earth and sky." Erskine commented, "This doesn't seem an accurate figure to me since a miter is not a junction but something done to both things joined to make the joining possible." McCarthy disagreed and quoted an unspecified dictionary to establish that "mitre" could denote a joint.

He pointed out that until the "beveled" surfaces are conjoined, no mitre exists. Yet he reconsidered his image of a mitre at the horizon since he realized that "the joint is imaginary, there being no < & no line of junction, and therefore not truly a mitre-joint" (Editorial Copy 214 verso). He sacrificed his sonorous image of the "firy mitre" between earth and sky and substituted "westward, hard upon the veering sun" (Editorial Copy 214; *OK* 189).

In the same paragraph, McCarthy had described how night shadows appear to Ownby as they fall on vine-covered banks, "drawing . . . shapes of creatures mythical or extinct, shades of tarriers shouldering hammers of grapevine." The passage was one of several in the novel in which the images move from the realistic to the fanciful or mystical, but Erskine wrote, "I can't connect with it. / hampers?" (Editorial Copy 214). McCarthy's tarriers may well allude to the Irish railroad workers in the American folk song, "Drill Ye Tarriers, Drill" (1888), with lyrics by Thomas Casey. The song was recorded by various folk groups, one of which took The Tarriers as its name. Their recording was released in 1957, just two years before McCarthy began *The Orchard Keeper.* With its references to blasting with dynamite, the railroad song was appropriate to Ownby's work experience, and for McCarthy the broader railroad context might have evoked an image of workers driving spikes with heavy hammers. However, if Erskine's query prompted him to research the word, he would have found that tarriers use augurs or drills rather than hammers, as Ownby would have known. The word tarrier may derive from the French for "drill," *teriére,* and the *Oxford English Dictionary* defines it as the augur itself. McCarthy simply struck through Ownby's fanciful vision of the ghosts of tarriers carrying hammers formed of vines (McCarthy, *The Orchard Keeper,* Editorial Copy 214; see *OK* 189).

The next paragraph was a description of a white cat Ownby comes across in the road. It springs to the top of the roadbank "vertically like a sudden puff of smoke . . . it's [*sic*] apparently mystical ascension betrayed only by the hysterical rattle of dead leaves" as it loses its footing, then bounds over the rise and disappears (McCarthy, *The Orchard Keeper,* Editorial Copy 214–15). Perhaps still a little frustrated by the tarrier image, Erskine wrote beside this passage, "now there's a gratuitous one" (214). However, the incident had several defensible functions in the novel. It contributed to the cat motif, either introducing the housecat associated with Rattner or adding a second one. Its ghostly ascension foreshadowed the cat's being lifted into the sky by the owl. And most important, his vision of the white cat conditioned Ownby's interpretation of that other ascension. Nevertheless, McCarthy simply deleted it rather than defend it, perhaps out of fatigue.

At several points Erskine questioned details and caught a few factual errors in the editorial copy, and McCarthy repaired the mistakes with minimal rewriting. Erskine pointed out that in the fight between Sylder and Rattner, Sylder has his opponent face down when Rattner suddenly sits up and spits. McCarthy substituted "twisted sideways" for "sat up" (McCarthy, *The Orchard Keeper,* Editorial Copy 41; *OK* 39). When Sylder opens the car trunk where he has hidden Rattner's corpse, "a . . . swarm of flies burst in his face like some palpable embodiment of the horrendous stench that followed" (Editorial Copy 49). Despite the effectiveness of the simile, Erskine wondered how the flies came to be there, whether they would fly up in the dark, and whether the offensive smell would have developed that soon. He added that the details might be fine, "but I want to be sure you're sure." McCarthy conceded that he had made a mistake: "they wouldnt fly up at night." But "If the car were parked in the sun all day the temp in the trunk would be in the 100's—it would smell." His revision eliminated the flies and retained the foul odor (Editorial Copy 49; *OK* 44). McCarthy had also referred to "borers and termites" that left traces of wood dust in the Rattners's log house. Erskine reminded him that "Perhaps the most sinister characteristic of termites is that they don't leave any evidence of this kind to betray their presence," and McCarthy changed them to "woodworms" (Editorial Copy 68; *OK* 63). In a later passage, the cat hears the "interstitial boring of termites," and Erskine pointed out that termites "eat wet, not dry." McCarthy changed these termites to "wood-beetles" and joked, "You must have had lots of trouble with termites" (Editorial Copy 246; *OK* 216). Erskine wondered too about the hood release on Sylder's car: "They have these that early? My '53 Studebaker doesn't." McCarthy replied that his '41 Ford had had one, "but I find the 39 didnt—which is what this is" (Editorial Copy 209), and he struck through the reference.

For a few details, the editor confessed his unfamiliarity with East Tennessee usage and realities and asked McCarthy to explain or verify. When Erskine sent McCarthy the final batch of pages from the marked editorial copy on January 7, 1964, he wrote that he had flagged the usage of "stit (apparently a local equivalent of still, which is unfamiliar to me)" and "kindly (which seems to stand for kind of, and is also unfamiliar to me. . . . I seem to remember seeing stit once before in my life, but I can't remember where. Kindly is entirely new to me, but if you are sure of it for the region I can see no harm in it—even though it pulls me up sharp every time I come to it." These queries about regional dialect were clearly meant to test the author's certainty of their authenticity rather than to push for eliminating them. Noting that he was a West Tennessean, Erskine asked for an explanation of splo whiskey, to which McCarthy replied that it was a term for "city-made moonshine" that routinely showed up in the local newspapers (McCarthy, *The Orchard Keeper,* Editorial Copy 30; *OK* 29).[15] Erskine also wondered what "the Hopper" was (Editorial Copy 16). McCarthy explained in his letter of December 1963 that this was "a geographical phenomenon, a steep road descending into a hollow where the old man lives." He noted that the novel included at least one further reference to it and asked if the first mention was unclear (3). Erskine replied on his second pass through the editorial copy: "if Hopper is local geog. name, it seems dangerous to use with no explanation. Later it is l.c. [lower case]. Let's hope for some readers outside of E. Tenn." McCarthy clarified by adding the identifier, "the steep Twin Fork Road" (Editorial Copy 16; cf. *OK* 19). The editor asked too if McCarthy was mistaken in writing of puffballs that erupted into "a poisonous verdant cloud": "I thought it was when they were dry and brown in late summer & fall." McCarthy informed him that "the green ones are only one of a variety—family Lyeoperdaceae—of fungi. The smoke is actually ripe spores" (Editorial Copy 228; see *OK* 200). Sometimes Erskine merely circled unfamiliar words or put question marks near them. McCarthy explained that "killy" was the "cry of a kestrel, or sparrowhawk specifically (also known as a killy-hawk)—generally a hawk's call—like a duck's quack" (Editorial Copy 97; *OK* 87). "Balds" were "mountain tops covered with laurel or heath and . . . devoid of timber" (Editorial Copy 225; *OK* 198). In the expression, "They Lord God, son," he explained, "They is used as an idiomatic expression." In this case, it was equivalent to "why" (Editorial Copy 168; *OK* 149). Erskine wondered if Ownby should tap down his cigarette paper rather than taping it, and McCarthy answered that although the usage was not in the dictionary, the word was "tape" (Editorial Copy 219; *OK* 193).

Other terms, while not local references or colloquialisms, were simply outside of Erskine's experience and/or too specialized to appear in his dictionary. McCarthy noted that a boat's "cutwater" was "the forward edge of the bow." Thus his description of the cutter's running lights "bobbing . . . in the black wash of the cutwater" referred to the parting waves made by the bow and the lights' unsteady reflection in them (McCarthy, *The Orchard Keeper,* Editorial Copy 183; cf. *OK* 161–62). "Lovejoys" were "a type of adjustable shock absorber used in . . . cars during the 40's," but McCarthy didn't think the word warranted an explanation within the novel (Editorial Copy 183; *OK* 161).

Significant about all these exchanges is that McCarthy was comfortable with readers' unfamiliarity with his fictional world and that Erskine usually did not insist that McCarthy's explanations be made explicit in the novel. The editor seems to have queried these details primarily to be certain that they were accurate. Both seem to have felt it was better not to talk down to the reader. And this became characteristic of McCarthy's work—that he trusted his readers to infer meaning from context or to remedy their unfamiliarity by investigating further. As Richard Marius observes about McCarthy's depiction of Knoxville in *Suttree,* he writes as if his reader is native to his fictional world, thereby inviting the reader to become acculturated (Marius, "*Suttree* as

Window" 118). Further evidence of Erskine's comfort with this aspect of Mc-Carthy's work is that he restored a line Bensky had earlier questioned. Bensky seems not to have caught the reference to the repeal of federal Prohibition in Sylder's thought that "Louisiana or anywhere else, his job went off the market December fifth 1933." In his revision suggestions of October 9, 1962, Bensky had written, "Why? What's Louisiana mean?" (list 1), failing to connect this line with the Coast Guard scene later in the book. McCarthy had struck through his reference at that stage, but on the editorial copy Erskine noted, "I don't see any harm in keeping this." McCarthy agreed, but left the final decision to his editor, who wrote "stet [let stand] this sentence" in the margin but changed "went" to "had gone" to clarify the time sequence (34; *OK* 32).

Once the major structural issues had been addressed, Erskine seems to have defined his editorial function as that of the thoughtful reader who raises questions for the author to consider but is unwilling to overturn the writer's decisions. He could be more insistent about syntax and punctuation that might confuse or be viewed as errors, but in more substantive matters his role was that of the challenging gadfly. An interesting example of this is his reaction to McCarthy's description of Sylder's shirt, "creased thrice across the back" (see *OK* 14). Erskine thought maybe it should read "down" instead of "across," and McCarthy responded that one could see it either way (McCarthy, *The Orchard Keeper*, Editorial Copy 9). Rather than simply changing the phrase since Mc-Carthy seemed amenable, Erskine questioned further: "I see what you mean—but doesn't the direction of the crease determine the choice[?]" And he drew vertical and horizontal arrows (9 verso). McCarthy answered with his own drawing of a shirt back with three vertical pleats. He wrote that although both expressions might be "ambiguous," he preferred "across because I wrote it that way instinctively; I cant think of any case in which a crease goes <u>across</u> an article of clothing . . . so I think it clearer that the <u>arrangement</u> of the creases is across." But he conceded that he wasn't certain (9 verso). Despite McCarthy's flexibility here, Erskine accepted his explanation and wrote "stet" beside the passage. In other cases, the editor raised questions but jotted "Not important" (Editorial Copy 2) or "I don't care" (Editorial Copy 19).

In McCarthy's letter of March 6, 1964, that accompanied the revised editorial copy, one in which his fatigue is evident, he deferred to his editor's judgment in several matters and addressed a half-dozen final issues. Line spacing was one concern. In the typescript, McCarthy had called for a one-line break between John Wesley's falling asleep on the porch on the last night of summer and his waking to chill and wood-smoke (McCarthy, *The Orchard Keeper*, Editorial Copy 71; see *OK* 65). McCarthy's intent seems to have been to highlight the hiatus in John Wesley's consciousness and the overnight change of seasons. However, Erskine noted on that page that if they used a line break there, "maybe we'd better have larger # [space] breaks for change of scene, character, time, etc.?" McCarthy pointed out two one-line breaks on another page that did not signal any more profound shift. He confessed that he had gone over the line breaks multiple times to attempt consistency (Editorial Copy 71). Indeed, one layer of his revision notes plans systematically for the page breaks and one- or two-line breaks throughout the typescript. In the March cover letter, he reiterated that he had done as well as he could with the type breaks, but he could find no rule to govern such practices. He may have lost patience with going over them, and he acknowledged that Erskine's experience with breaks to signal shifts in time and focus was deeper than his own, implying that the editor should make the final decisions. In this letter McCarthy also expressed his preference for the spelling "till" instead of "til" and "all right" rather than "alright," as well as his willingness for apostrophes to be used in negative contractions. He would leave the consistent application of these directives to his editors.

McCarthy's letter addressed two substantive issues as well. Erskine had circled a passage in which Warn's dog Rock was identified as a North Carolina Plott Hound, "a huge shuffling beast with ears too short for a hound, who carried his head low as if in perpetual shame—a posture that further exaggerated the mooselike hump of his shoulders." In the margin Erskine jotted, "Note on this," and McCarthy responded that the note was missing but that the passage did not contribute much, so Erskine could delete it (McCarthy, *The Orchard Keeper*, Editorial Copy 151). In his early March 1964 letter, McCarthy reiterated that he would accept whatever Erskine's note had recommended. Erskine replied on March 31 that he had forgotten to write the note. He now explained that Rock was first mentioned in the italicized flashback just before the passage in question (see *OK* 134), and he thought "it was illegal to make this reference to something in the flashback after you had returned to present time." The sentence could be moved to the next page, where Rock was present (see *OK* 135), but Erskine thought deleting it was "the better solution." The Plott Hound passage does not appear in the published novel, a sacrifice of a regionalism and one in a series of sharply envisioned canine companions of the East Tennessee men and boys. One wonders if McCarthy would have deleted the passage had he understood from the beginning that Erskine's objection was not to the unfamiliarity of the Plott Hound breed.

When he wrote on March 18, 1964, Erskine indicated that he would spend the next week going over McCarthy's final changes and preparing the setting copy. If McCarthy did not mean for apostrophes to appear in all the negative contractions (instead of just the two-syllable ones), he should make that clear very soon. Erskine hoped no more questions would arise although he doubted that would prove the case. "But maybe you can have a little peace now on #2," he wrote. McCarthy's reply, received March 31, 1964, reaffirmed what he had written earlier that month: that all the apostrophes should be restored. They adhered to this practice in the first three books, but in *Suttree* and the later novels, apostrophes are dropped in one-syllable contractions.

His work on the revisions completed, at least for the most part, McCarthy had moved for the second time in three months—this time to a new address at 20 Woodlink Road in Asheville, North Carolina. By that time Erskine had worked his way through about half of McCarthy's latest revisions. He wrote on March 31 that McCarthy had "done a fine job with the various corrections and prunings as far as I have gone. Hardly a change that is not an improvement" (2). But he raised more editorial questions, most of them concerning the insertion of italics and page breaks to clarify time relationships and structure. McCarthy again agreed to Erskine's suggestions about typography, deferring to his experience in such matters (McCarthy, Letter to Albert Erskine, received April 9, 1964). Gradually, the two had worked out a nuanced system of chapter, page, and line breaks and italics to flag the discontinuities between sections, a system that made the published novel easier to follow than the "Final Draft" had been.

By the time he received McCarthy's letter on April 9, Erskine had finished working through the revision, and on the same day he wrote with further queries and suggestions. And he inquired about McCarthy's next book: "You haven't mentioned the new book for some time, and I guess I know why. I hope I've left you some time to work on it" (2). He received McCarthy's reply in mid-late April 1964. There was not one new book but two he was working on "almost simultaneously." The long novel (*Suttree*) existed in about 250 pages at that point; the short one (*Outer Dark*) about 200. Both would require several revisions, but McCarthy thought he might finish the short novel in two more years, the long one in five or six.

As the intensive editorial work on *The Orchard Keeper* wound down, author and editor began exchanging friendly favors and gifts as a way of staying in touch and cementing their relationship. Erskine had hinted that the Easter bunny might deliver a much-needed new typewriter ribbon, and McCarthy replied in his letter received March 31, 1964, that his machine was a Royal Quiet Deluxe portable from about 1958.[16] In the same letter, McCarthy asked Erskine if he had encountered the cartoons of Fernando Krahn that were running in *The Reporter*.[17] Krahn was a Chilean-born artist who lived in New York City in the 1960s and published his cartoons not only in *The Reporter* but also *The New Yorker, Atlantic,* and *Esquire.* McCarthy especially recommended Krahn's "The Artist" and a series of four images entitled "The Hunt," and he wondered whether Random might be interested in publishing a collection of Krahn's work. Erskine replied on April 9 that he liked Krahn's cartoons, especially

"Secret Weapons," which had recently appeared; but he thought they might be more effective if seen intermittently rather than in a collection. A colleague at Random recalled that Krahn might have submitted a book to them, but Erskine had yet to uncover any record of it. (In fact, Dutton would publish *The Possible Worlds of Fernando Krahn,* a collection of his cartoons, the next year.) In May, McCarthy wrote to thank Erskine for the new typewriter ribbon and several newly published Random House books which Erskine had edited. These included Faulkner's *As I Lay Dying* (presumably the corrected 1964 Vintage edition); Robert Penn Warren's *Flood,* set in a Tennessee town about to be flooded by a government damming project; and Richard Bankowsky's *On a Dark Night.* By then McCarthy had read and liked Bankowsky's novel about characters struggling with the entanglements of flesh and spirit and destroyed by their passions, but he had just started on Warren's.

The setting copy of *The Orchard Keeper* does not document editorial back-and-forth as the editorial copy and the correspondence do, but it incorporates the end results of this process. That is, a copy of the revised typescript McCarthy submitted to Bensky had been kept clean during Erskine's editorial work so that it could be used as setting copy when all the decisions had been made and transferred to it, a practice that Erskine and McCarthy followed for later books as well. Preparing the setting copy was, of course, a near-final stage in the editing process, and it was performed partly by copy editor Bertha Krantz. She was so skilled at this that when she later became assistant managing editor (Cerf, *At Random* 239), her duties still included copy editing. Together with Erskine, she worked on all of McCarthy's novels through *Blood Meridian.*

On June 2, 1964, Erskine wrote with chagrin that as Krantz worked on the setting copy, she had still found many inconsistencies in hyphenation and in the punctuation that introduced dialogue. He included a list of hyphenation issues Krantz had compiled, and he suggested McCarthy let her regularize these matters: "She knows what she is doing, and she loves this book; I don't think she will do it any harm, but if she does come up with some form that does offend you, we can fix it in proof" (2). Erskine was eager to send the setting copy to the typesetter, and he hoped that McCarthy would give Krantz the green light. McCarthy could not just turn these decisions over, however, and he gave the issues careful study. On a single leaf of typed title possibilities, McCarthy penciled notes on the hyphenation he had used and began working out principles that had guided his practice. His own inconsistencies and the difficulty of resolving them seem to have prompted his notation at the top of this page: "mild horror, creeping bibliophobia, locomotor ataxia, /general lassitude and despondency" (*OK* revision notes). Two versions of McCarthy's reply to Erskine survive, an early draft among his own papers, heavily marked with holograph notes and revisions, and the version he mailed to Erskine among the editor's papers. The first draft of McCarthy's letter devolves into a complex disquisition on the use of hyphens in color designations depending on grammatical context. Marginal notations show that McCarthy himself debated some of these forms, and he apparently realized that his analysis was likely to frustrate Erskine, as his earlier letter about punctuation had.

The version Erskine received on June 8, 1964, preserves only seven lines of the draft, but it articulates a few principles that McCarthy's work on the first draft of the letter and his revision notes had helped him to formulate. He admitted he found it difficult to be consistent in hyphenation, but so did dictionaries. Nevertheless, he thought that except where it would place two vowels adjacent to one another as in "hugeeyed," it was all right to create compound words such as "grayhaired" and "lanterneyed" that referred "to physical characteristics, and specifically where they could conceivably have appellative forms" (1). McCarthy's penciled notes help amplify his meaning. He thought that a compound word with no hyphenation should be used for "a physical characteristic of an animate body <which might be a noun>. Ie: Hey there, Hooktooth" (*OK* revision notes). In his letter to Erskine, he added that colors with adjectival functions such as "limegreen" + noun should take compound forms, but color designations comprised of nouns with modifiers, for example, "metal-gray," could all be hyphenated. For automotive parts such as "dashlight" and "quarterpanel," he favored unhyphenated forms (letter 1).

McCarthy's letter also addressed the punctuation of dialogue. When introducing speech, he felt a colon "represents a pause—perhaps for emphasis, perhaps reflective—and as such draws stronger immediate attention to what follows" than does a comma (1). At the end of the letter, McCarthy added that he sometimes chose the internal punctuation of dialogue to reflect how the character's utterance would be delivered. An example is the line, "They all drinkin aint they?" On the editorial copy, Erskine had inserted a comma, but McCarthy had responded, "They all drinkin. Aint they? aint the same as: They all drinkin aint they? It is a retort. The inflections & stresses . . . are entirely different. . . . It seems to me that in dialogue . . . punctuation should indicate the way the thing is said." However, he conceded that such nuances might be too subtle to be worthwhile (McCarthy, *The Orchard Keeper*, Editorial Copy 10 and verso). Erskine had replied that the comma was normal usage to denote a shift from a declarative sentence to a question and pointed out that McCarthy had followed that convention just a few lines earlier, so McCarthy had agreed to use the comma in both these instances (Editorial Copy 10; *OK* 14). Nevertheless, his commentary in his letter implied that in general his punctuation of dialogue should be preserved since he considered it indicative of a character's speech and tone.

McCarthy was willing to leave the application of these rules to Krantz, with "admonitions to restraint. . . . As a general rule, when in doubt, do not punctuate, do not hyphenate" (letter to Erskine, received June 8, 1964, 3). Along with these instructions, he returned Erskine's letter of June 2 with his own light annotations, indicating his preferences and responding to a few queries. For example, Krantz had noticed that the bird John Wesley sells to the county as a chickenhawk was designated a sparrowhawk when he first found it. She and Erskine wondered whether this was a bit of deception on the boy's part or an instance of "authorial inadvertence." McCarthy jotted, "Chicanery. (I aint that inadvertent)" (2). Together with his and Erskine's letters, McCarthy returned Krantz's working list of hyphenated and compound words. Erskine may have sent the list only to document the dimensions of the problem, but McCarthy had briefly marked each item with his decision and relied on his letter to explain his principles.

Apparently, these missives gave Erskine and Krantz enough guidance to continue. On June 17, 1964, the setting copy went to the production department. Erskine had filled out the Manuscript Transmittal Data Sheet calling for a printing of 5,000 copies to be published in April 1965. On the same day, he wrote to Sidney Jacobs of the design department, explaining that his plan was "to make a paperbound edition to send out for comment long before we go to press with our jacket, in the hope of getting some authoritative support for it before the reviewers get their hands on it. . . . Accordingly, I would appreciate as fast composition as you can get—though it's got to be a good compositor, because though it is a clean manuscript it is a difficult one. Only instructions to compositor are: Follow copy as corrected"—that is, follow the setting copy exactly without regularizing its unconventional punctuation (Erskine, Letter to Sidney Jacobs, June 17, 1964). According to Erskine's later Publishing Summary, 4,250 copies of the 5,000 printed would be for sale, priced at $4.95.

The advance copy strategy added further delays to the publication of the book; but recognizing the challenging nature of the novel, Erskine wanted to create every chance of a positive reception for this first work by an unknown writer. "If I can get some good advance quotes from eminent or responsible or respectable or even notorious persons to put on the jacket, I think it might grease the books [*sic*] launching," Erskine wrote to McCarthy on June 30, 1964. The plan was also a measure of just how enthusiastic about McCarthy's novel and his talent Erskine had become. When Leon Rooke interviewed him about McCarthy in 1985, Erskine recalled that "Lowry's *Under the Volcano* in 1944, was the first novel I sent out advance bound galleys of to booksellers, reviewers and critics. I believed in it that strongly. *The Orchard Keeper,* 21 years later, was the second" (Rooke, "'Author! Author!'"9).[18]

On June 17, when the book went to production, Erskine wrote McCarthy alerting him to plan to read proofs early in August. If McCarthy wanted to include a dedication, he should provide it soon, and now they needed to revisit the question of the title. Fairly often McCarthy has sent a final typescript to his publisher with no title or has discarded his first thoughts and come up with his final title after discussing options with his editor. But in each case, it has been McCarthy who titled his works. The name of his first novel had been uncertain in its draft stages and remained so until the second set of galleys. The "Late Draft" was stored in a box McCarthy labeled "Red Mtn." When he submitted the untitled "Final Draft" to Random in May 1962, he explained in his cover letter that he still had only a "tentative" title, perhaps "Red Mountain," but when he sent his revised typescript to Bensky in June 1963, McCarthy tentatively suggested calling the novel "Toilers at the Kiln." He did not explicate this title, but it refers to the red clay soil of Red Branch that dusts the characters as if they were workers in a brick kiln (*OK* 10). It also alludes to the lime kiln of "Ethan Brand" as well as to the Ammonites whom their neighbor King David defeated, enslaved, and put to work in his brick kilns (2 Samuel 12:31). The biblical allusion comprises an implicit commentary on the Tennessee Valley Authority's transforming the life of East Tennessee and on the residents' sense of their subjugation to this new order. McCarthy considered this title "descriptive" but not overly "enigmatic or whimsical." His assertion may have been somewhat facetious, but Bensky did not question the choice, and "Toilers at the Kiln" became the novel's interim title in Random House communications.

However, McCarthy remained unsatisfied and asked Erskine several times what he thought. He raised the issue in the letter that accompanied the typescript pages revised for the editorial copy, which Erskine received on March 6, 1964. Erskine replied on March 18 that he too had never really liked the working title and suggested they both consider it further. On June 17 he wrote urging McCarthy to resolve the issue soon; but he also transmitted the edited manuscript to Sidney Jacobs under the title "Toilers at the Kiln," commenting that unless McCarthy settled on another shortly, that would be it. An undated leaf filed with McCarthy's revision notes and deleted pages bears the crossed out holograph title "Toilers at the Kiln" and several typed alternative titles. Given that this leaf also bears McCarthy's penciled notes on compound words, inscribed around and below the typed titles, the list of title options was probably created between March 18 and early June 1964, when Erskine wrote to raise questions about punctuating compound words. The vexing issue of compound words took precedence, but in a letter Erskine received on June 26, 1964, McCarthy reported that he had been working on titles and would soon send a list of possibilities, "none of which I am in love with." Erskine's reply of June 30 urged him on. Publication was still scheduled for the following April, but he wanted to have the "limited paperback advance promotion edition" available by Christmas at the latest. The editor had been brainstorming about the title himself, consulting Bartlett's *Familiar Quotations* and playing with such words as "hawk," "untamed," "untrammeled," even "The Wind Is Sotherly," which could be paired with a quote on the title page from Hamlet's asser- tion to Rosencrantz and Guildenstern that he knows a hawk from a handsaw (*Hamlet* 2.2). Erskine had thought this might "pluck several relevant strings, but maybe too many that are not," and he decided it would not do. Nothing more suitable had struck him yet.

In a letter Erskine received July 7, 1964, McCarthy replied that he liked Erskine's quotation, but surprisingly, since his novel alluded to *Hamlet,* he did not recognize it and asked its source. Now he narrowed his title options to two new ones of his own: "Such Hawks, Such Hounds" and "The Orchard Keeper." McCarthy recalled that the first of these came from the traditional seven- teenth-century Scottish ballad, "The Twa Corbies," but his phrase is closer to the related English version, "The Three Ravens," which ends: God send every gentleman / Such hounds, such hawks and such a leman" (ll. 19–20). At the same time, the tone and language of the end of the Scottish version adumbrate the "myth, legend, dust" passage at the end of *The Orchard Keeper.* McCarthy may well have had both versions of the ballad in mind since his father often read poems from *The Oxford Book of English Verse* to his sister Bobbie when she was a child, and this anthology prints both versions side by side (McCooe, Interview with Bryan Giemza and Dianne Luce; Quiller-Couch, ed. *The Ox- ford Book of English Verse, 1250–1918*).[19] Of the slain knight, "The Twa Corbies" sings:

> Mony a one for him maks mane,
> But nane sall ken where he is gane;
> O'er his white banes, when they are bare,
> The wind sall blaw for evermare. (ll. 17–20)

McCarthy's other option, "The Orchard Keeper," had come to him only a few days earlier. He thought it was straightforward but also apt in a "macabre" fashion—an indication that he thought of the corpse in the pit or even death itself as the primary keeper of the orchard, an idea that anticipates the "*et in Arcadia ego*" theme of *Blood Meridian.* This title appealed to him as much as any of his other ideas. He rather playfully noted that he had also thought of "Watchglass and Fiddle"—one of the titles on his typed list—but rejected it because it was both irrelevant and abstruse. He seems to have had in mind the hourglass used to measure sailors' time on watch, rather than the protec- tive glass on the front of a timepiece. If so, the title option may allude to the alternation of work and leisure. In addition, the shape of a watchglass echoes the shape of a fiddle. Thus, this title evokes a tenuous connection between art and the passage of time. It seems to conjoin the novel's themes of time and memory, linking Ownby's serving out his watch over Rattner's bones with John Wesley's artistic creation of his hallucinated recollection. Closing his letter, McCarthy added that the problem of titles was giving him "fidgets." He had recently run across a book titled *Mildred at Home,* which induced horrors of his "first love" coming before the public in similarly "unpromising garb" (letter to Erskine, received July 7, 1964). The drably titled *Mildred at Home,* book five in a late nineteenth-century children's series by Martha Finley, made its way into *Suttree* as one of the randomly acquired books Suttree and Wanda read as they wait out the persistent rain under the shale bluff on the banks of the French Broad River (*S* 358).

Erskine did not rush to settle on "The Orchard Keeper." He wrote on July 14, 1964, that he slightly preferred "Such Hawks, Such Hounds," and he prompted McCarthy to consider also "something with bones in it"—perhaps because he remembered or had then reread "The Twa Corbies." Meanwhile he was consulting others at Random House. On August 7 and 10 respectively, both editor Roger Jellinek, who had read McCarthy's revised typescript in 1963, and Erskine's secretary Suzanne Baskin submitted lists of phrases from the novel that might serve as titles. Both suggested "The Green Fly Inn," perhaps recognizing it as a metaphor for the doomed mountain community, but also perhaps simply because the name was so striking. The best of Jellinek's thirteen uninspired suggestions was "Traps"; but few of his ideas were relevant to the novel as a whole, and the worst, "Just Turn Me Loose," sounded absurdly like the rock song recorded by teen idol Fabian in 1959. Many of Jellinek's titles were short declarative sentences and thus did not conform to the convention of noun phrases for titles. Although his list reached the senior editor first, Erskine made no notes on it and probably set it aside.

Baskin's ten options were better, and Erskine crossed out the ones he didn't care for, leaving five. When he mailed the first galleys of this "variously titled as yet untitled" novel to McCarthy on August 13, Erskine conveyed the best of Baskin's suggestions, which included "All Through the Tree"; "Fiends and Warlocks"; "Watcher of the Seasons"; and "A Seventh Year"—as well as "Hawk Bounty," which would later become the title of an excerpt published in *Yale Review.* Erskine wasn't sure what he preferred, but he still liked the sound of McCarthy's "Such Hawks, Such Hounds." He urged the author, "Tell me what you think; ask your wife, your friends, your liquor dealer, the local bookseller." As McCarthy made no comment on Baskin's suggestions, apparently none appealed to him. He did not change the title "Toilers at the Kiln" on his set of the galley proofs; but once he finished correcting them, he promised in his letter of transmittal (received on September 2, 1964) to choose between his own two finalists soon. On September 10, perhaps hoping to elicit a final decision, Erskine wrote that although he liked the sound of "hawks and hounds" better, he now felt that McCarthy's other option was more relevant to the book. A week later, McCarthy settled on "The Orchard Keeper." This decision may have been reached or relayed by phone, since the evidence is not a letter from McCarthy but Baskin's memo of September 17, 1964, to managing editor C. [Charles] A. Wimpfheimer.[20] On one set of the first-pass galley proofs, "Toilers at the Kiln" is emended to "The Orchard Keeper" in a hand other than McCarthy's. The corrected galleys of September 23 printed the novel's final title.

When he sent the galley proofs to the author on August 13, 1964, Erskine requested that McCarthy "carefully read and judiciously correct" them, using any system of notation with which he was comfortable, and that he give special attention to the typographical division of sections and subsections. The marked galleys were to be returned by September 1. The Random House proofreader (Krantz) would then transfer McCarthy's corrections together with the in-house ones to the printer's copy. McCarthy mailed the proofs on September 2, asking that Erskine double-check the page break after "the old man slept" (see *OK* 195). The next paragraph begins Huffaker's conversation with the agent who has come to arrest Ownby. They had called for a line break in the setting copy, but replying on September 10, Erskine agreed that "there is a considerable time lapse as well as a change of scene between the two passages, and the new page and big initial letter help to signify this."

As she conflated McCarthy's corrections with her own, Krantz again found discrepancies that needed McCarthy's attention. On September 9, 1964, Erskine pulled the relevant galley sheets, recorded the queries on them, and sent them back to McCarthy, with the apologetic comment, "When you think you're through you aren't." Baskin made an undated note that further corrections would come from McCarthy and recorded the date when they arrived, on September 29. Erskine returned the proofs to Neil Van Dyne and Tere LoPrete in the production department the next day, with instructions that the printer could prepare the plates but that they did not want the books printed and bound until after the new year. He noted that the "About the Author" copy was still to come (Erskine, Memo to Neil Van Dyne/Tere LoPrete).

# Placing Excerpts
# in Periodicals

As part of his program to launch McCarthy's career, Erskine made considerable effort to place excerpts from *The Orchard Keeper* in periodicals. This had been on his and Bensky's minds from the beginning because exposure in a periodical might not only net the author some additional revenue from his work but also result in increased sales of the novel. In effect, it was an aspect of marketing that the editor could perform. Jotting "magazine" in his reading notes from 1962, Erskine had flagged the section in which John Wesley and his troubled relationship with his mother are introduced (3; see *OK* 61–73). Bensky did not convey Erskine's suggestion in his letter to McCarthy of October 9, 1962, but he nominated three other sections: the scene in which John Wesley buys his traps in the Knoxville hardware store (*OK* 77–85); the episode in which he rescues Sylder from his wrecked car and Sylder gives him a puppy (*OK* 98–112); and the section in which Ownby escapes arrest at his cabin and is later apprehended outside the store in the mountains (*OK* 185–205). Bensky felt that these scenes represented "some of the finest writing in the book" and could "stand alone," if not as short stories then as excerpts (Letter to McCarthy, Oct. 9, 1962, revision list 2–3).

After he finished his revisions for Erskine, McCarthy inquired again about placing excerpts, writing Erskine that he could not recall what Bensky had told him (letter, Mar. 31, 1964). Replying on April 9, Erskine assured McCarthy that he would pursue magazine sales and have extra galleys printed for submission to periodicals (2). When galleys became available, one of the first editors Erskine tried was John E. Palmer at *Yale Review*. Palmer had worked with Erskine as an editorial assistant at Louisiana State University Press and had succeeded him as managing editor of *Southern Review* (Cutrer, *Parnassus on the Mississippi* 26, 188–89, 84). On September 16, 1964, Baskin sent Palmer bound galleys of the novel still entitled "Toilers at the Kiln." But either Erskine had forgotten about the scenes he and Bensky had identified as potential excerpts a year and a half earlier, or he wanted to give Palmer free rein, and he did not recommend specific episodes. Palmer wrote Erskine on September 29 and noted that he did not identify a section that could stand alone as a short story. He found the novel "very much of a piece," and since it was so "understaged and spare in its narrative management," he felt that the difficulties for the reader would be compounded in an excerpt. He had considered the work at length because he recognized that McCarthy's writing was remarkable and believed that if *Yale Review* could publish something from the book, their issue eventually would be highly sought by collectors. He couldn't think of another contemporary writer whose work offered such a "total evocation of a physical scene, or this sense of absolute rightness of human behavior." And in a statement that adumbrates the perceptions of McCarthy's early and current admirers, Palmer pinpointed the merits of McCarthy's style, which he thought was as poetic as prose could be and maintain its function as prose. McCarthy had written no "fine phrase or figure . . . that doesn't have something more important to do than sound elegant," Palmer wrote.

The week after receiving Palmer's glowing rejection letter, on October 5, 1964, Erskine wrote McCarthy to share it and to update him on his lack of success. He noted that unfortunately Palmer's regretful refusal seemed "non-negotiable." Palmer's difficulty in finding an excerpt that would function as a self-contained piece of short fiction was typical of the magazine editors' responses so far, and Erskine had received several other rejections tempered with praise for McCarthy's talent. Erskine reported that he had approached not only small, prestigious literary journals, but also more lucrative popular magazines. The *Saturday Evening Post,* with its large circulation and generous payment to authors, had rejected the offer of an excerpt "with many nice complements [*sic*] rendered on the telephone." When the *Post*'s senior editor David McDowell returned the galleys to Erskine, he enclosed a brief letter explaining that the novel was "too broken up" with its narration distributed among three main characters. But he was impressed by the "ring of truth" in its dialogue (McDowell, Letter to Albert Erskine, [c. Sept. 10, 1964]).

Erskine had next tried *Esquire,* another high-paying magazine (Baskin, Memo to Natalie Bates, Sept. 11, 1964). Editor Robert Brown's undated note to Erskine expressed cautious interest in the beginning of the novel through the death of Rattner and asked for the benefit of Erskine's familiarity with the work in carving out a workable excerpt. "I confess that it stymies me," Brown wrote, because the book "is so intricately woven that the reader is forced to hold matters in abeyance until some later section offers clarification" (1). Although this was fine in the novel, which he deemed "excellent" (2), it would take quite an "editorial trick" (1) to carry off the pretense that an excerpt was a short story. A subtext of this note may have been that Brown lacked the time to shape stories from novels, even that the author or book editor should have done this already. Baskin's holograph notation on her memo to Natalie Bates that galleys 3–19 were resubmitted to *Esquire* on September 15 supports the inference that Erskine immediately turned his hand to at least a rudimentary paring of the Sylder and Rattner conflict in hopes of making a coherent piece of short fiction. But he could not have devoted much time to the editing since the resubmission followed the initial one by only four days. Perhaps he had simply rearranged the galleys to delay the introduction of Rattner until he and Sylder are on the same timeline, as he had once recommended to McCarthy. In his letter of October 5, Erskine informed McCarthy that *Esquire* was interested in the Sylder/Rattner confrontation or had been when they had last been in touch. He had given Brown permission to make whatever cuts he thought appropriate to help the excerpt function more like a short story. Erskine felt that the pages included material "that could be dispensed with for such a usage" and hoped McCarthy would approve such cutting. When he replied on October 15, McCarthy granted *Esquire* a free hand, but Erskine's next letter, on October 20, reported he had heard nothing further from Brown. *Esquire* did not publish the excerpt, and it seems that Brown either did not find it possible to reshape the material or set it aside for some weeks before finally deciding not to try.

With Palmer's refusal of an excerpt for *Yale Review, Saturday Evening Post* uninterested, and the Sylder/Rattner scenes of interest to *Esquire,* Erskine had Baskin send proofs of the novel on October 1 to both *Kenyon Review* and *Sewanee Review,* offering them excerpts but informing them that the novel's opening was not available (Erskine, Letter to Cormac McCarthy, Oct. 5, 1964; Baskin, Letter to Robie Macauley, Oct. 1, 1964; Baskin, Letter to Andrew Lytle, Oct. 1, 1964). *Kenyon Review* editor Robie Macauley was spending a year in England, however, and acting editor George Lanning responded only by providing Macauley's London address and offering to return the galleys (Postcard to Miss Baskin, Oct. 3, 1964). But it appears that Erskine then urged Lanning to read the proofs himself, perhaps by telephone since no letter from Erskine to Lanning survives. In such a conversation, Erskine probably would have made a case for McCarthy as an important new talent and stressed that with publication scheduled for spring, time would not permit him to mail the galleys to London. By October 22 Lanning had read the novel, but he wrote Erskine declining an excerpt. He explained that he had not found a stand-alone episode to print and that the journal was fully committed for fiction through its summer issue.

This refusal could not have surprised Erskine. When he summarized his efforts to place excerpts for McCarthy on October 5, 1964, he wrote that since all the editors they had heard from so far had expressed difficulty in identifying a "detachable" episode, he would suggest to *Sewanee Review*'s editor Andrew Lytle that he give special consideration to the trap-buying and hawk bounty material (*OK* 77–85), which Bensky had thought a likely excerpt, and the raccoon hunting scenes in which John Wesley saves Sylder's dog Lady from drowning (*OK* 119–27). Perhaps Erskine had found inspiration in his impression that the book largely featured hawks and hounds. The galleys had already been mailed, but since Lytle was another friend from his Nashville and *Southern Review* days, Erskine followed up with a personal letter on October 5. He implied that given its Tennessee setting, an excerpt from the novel might be particularly appropriate for the *Sewanee Review,* but he remarked that even if Lytle could not find an extract to publish, "it is my belief that you will enjoy reading this book anyway. Mr. McCarthy is thirty-one, and this is his first book—the best first book that I have encountered in many a day." Indeed, even though most editors were turning down excerpts from the book, Erskine's attempts were helping this first-time writer to become known within publishing circles.

Despite Erskine's warning that they were on a short time schedule, Lytle did not reply to Erskine until November 2, 1964. He did not think that the hawk bounty section constituted "an action," but he accepted the raccoon hunting episode for his April issue. "I think the boy is good," Lytle added tersely. Replying on November 6, Erskine reminded Lytle that the novel would be published early in May, so only if the spring number of *Sewanee Review* were issued in April would it precede the book's release. Adding that he thought McCarthy "deserves support," he asked if Lytle might have time to write something for the book jacket. However, he had received nothing from his friend by January 5, 1965, when he wrote to reiterate his request, and ultimately Lytle did not provide an endorsement.

On January 12, 1965, *Sewanee Review*'s managing editor Elizabeth Chitty wrote Erskine to say that the hunting excerpt was in the printer's hands and that the issue should be published "near April 1." She needed a title for the piece and McCarthy's address for the proofs, which she expected soon. Baskin sent her McCarthy's new address in New Orleans on January 15, and since he had been transient of late, she also supplied a copy of the biographical information that would appear on the book jacket. The same concern prompted Erskine on January 20 to send Chitty a list of his own "inspired" title options for the excerpt in case McCarthy could not be reached: "Lady," "A Hunt," and "Coon Hunt." On the same day he wrote McCarthy listing these titles and acknowledging that McCarthy might think of a more resonant one. Erskine wryly asserted his preference for "Lady" and added, "That would sure fool the reader." Reluctant to create delays, in both letters he opined that the title of an extract from a novel was of little significance. He received McCarthy's reply on January 29, which informed him that he had written to *Sewanee Review,* repeating Erskine's title options and adding one of his own. He was interested to know which one they preferred. When the excerpt appeared, it bore McCarthy's more evocative title "The Dark Waters."

When Erskine wrote the previous fall, on October 5, 1964, about his efforts to place excerpts, he had asked how McCarthy would feel about appearing in *Playboy,* which, he remarked, "in addition to its campaign for women's rights does try to publish some good fiction." McCarthy replied that he would not "mind" being published there, but he thought he should let Erskine know that in late July he had been approached by an agent in New York who wanted to try placing fiction for him. McCarthy had sent the agent a story, and he had submitted it to *Playboy*, but McCarthy had heard nothing more about it (McCarthy, Letter to Albert Erskine, received Oct. 15, 1964). It is unclear whether this "story" was an excerpt from *The Orchard Keeper*, as seems most likely, or from another novel-in-progress. No evidence in Erskine's files documents an attempt on his part to contact *Playboy* on McCarthy's behalf before 1971, and it seems likely Erskine let that idea go, trusting to McCarthy's new agent to follow through.

Nevertheless, Baskin continued to submit galleys to other magazines in late fall 1964, including ones with largely female readership. Possibly these periodicals were not ones whose editors had a personal relationship with Erskine, so he left corresponding with them to his capable assistant. In an internal Random House memo, Natalie Bates informed Baskin in early November that *Glamour Magazine* liked to publish extracts from promising first books and that they wanted to see *The Orchard Keeper*. Baskin jotted on Bates's memo that she had supplied one galley for Bates to forward to *Glamour*'s Lee Wright, but no record of a response survives in the Erskine or McCarthy papers. A list prepared by Baskin on November 12 indicates that in addition to *Glamour*, *Harper's Bazaar* and *Redbook* wanted to consider the novel and that galleys were sent to *Harper's* on November 16. Its literary editor Alice Morris declined on December 15, writing to Bates that they had given the book "serious consideration" but did not find it quite right for their audience (Morris, Letter to Natalie Bates, Dec. 15, 1964).

With Lytle's acceptance of the hunting story, "The Dark Waters," but no sales of excerpts to the high-paying commercial magazines, Erskine tried once more to interest John Palmer, whose initial reaction to the novel had been so positive. On January 8, 1965, Baskin wrote McCarthy that Palmer had phoned Erskine at home to report that he would, after all, publish an excerpt in his March 1965 issue of *Yale Review*, under the title "Bounty." She added that "this time it <u>was</u> salesmanship on Albert's part." When Erskine wrote McCarthy on January 20, he explained that he had pulled out the "hawk and traps" section, resubmitted it to Palmer as a stand-alone piece, and that this time he succeeded. Palmer had little lead time, and he moved quickly to have the excerpt set in type. Within three weeks of accepting the episode, he sent proofs to Erskine, and Baskin forwarded them to McCarthy in New Orleans on January 22.

Despite several rejections, Erskine's efforts to sell excerpts from *The Orchard Keeper* were more successful than for any other of McCarthy's Tennessee novels. Perhaps because of many journal editors' observation that the first novel was so intricately constructed that it was nearly impossible to find a section that would work as a story, Erskine and McCarthy did not attempt to sell excerpts from *Outer Dark* or *Child of God.* With the episodic *Suttree,* they made a concerted effort in 1970 and 1971, but only one piece eventually found a home, in 1979, with *Antaeus,* edited by poet Daniel Halpern, who would issue McCarthy's early novels as paperbacks in his "Neglected Books of the Twentieth Century" series and would publish some of McCarthy's dramatic works, all under his Ecco Press imprint.[21]

**With the difficult editing** on *The Orchard Keeper* completed, Erskine had proposed on November 4 that they correspond on a first-name basis, and McCarthy replied playfully that he regretted having stressed his editor with such "formality" since he did not know the conventions of interpersonal relations between publishers and writers. He wrote that he had several names or nicknames, including Doc, as he was affectionately called in his family,[22] but he asked Erskine to call him Mac (McCarthy, Letter to Albert Erskine, received Dec. 4, 1964).

Once McCarthy's proofreading on *The Orchard Keeper* was finished, he had planned a move from Asheville to New Orleans, a warmer place to spend the winter of 1964/65. New Orleans was also the setting for the novel that had been simmering in the back of his mind since he had heard the legend of Leon Roppolo in Chicago two or three years earlier. In early November 1964, he assured Erskine he would remain in Asheville for another week. Two weeks later, McCarthy wrote to provide his editor his new address: 808 St. Phillips, in the Vieux Carré,[23] which is only a short walk from where Faulkner had lived in 1925 (McCarthy, Letter to Albert Erskine, received Nov. 18, 1964). Bill Kidwell recalled visiting McCarthy in New Orleans and finding him writing on an overturned wooden packing crate bearing the slogan "World's Best." Gesturing to it, McCarthy quipped, "That's me," and Kidwell had the impression he was not entirely joking (Kidwell, Conversation with Arnold and Luce).

Anticipating the publication of *The Orchard Keeper,* McCarthy asked on December 4 whether Random might consider sending him another advance. He told Erskine that if the answer was no, that would be all right, but he would need to find employment. Erskine replied with four options: a new advance against the sales of *The Orchard Keeper*; a contract for the next book with a larger advance than Random had paid for *The Orchard Keeper*; a contract for two new books, with a yet more generous advance; or a contract for one or two new novels with advances to be drawn periodically and repaid out of the combined earnings of the new work(s) and *The Orchard Keeper.* Erskine thought the fourth arrangement might be best for McCarthy since if the first novel were to do well enough to repay its advances as well as the new ones, McCarthy could then receive further advances against the potential earnings of his subsequent book(s) (Letter to McCarthy, Dec. 16, 1964). McCarthy's reply reached Erskine on December 23. He concurred with Erskine's recommendation for the fourth option. He felt it was too soon to contract for the third novel (*Suttree*), for which he had composed four hundred rough-draft pages. But the first draft of the second novel (*Outer Dark*) was more-or-less complete and was then in a safe deposit box in Knoxville. If Random would contract for the second novel and advance him a thousand dollars, he thought he could complete a second draft by early summer 1965, when he expected some income "from another source."[24] There was a delay over the Christmas season, but when Erskine replied on December 30, 1964, he fleshed out the details of the advances for the next novel. He suggested that Random send McCarthy $1,000 when he signed, $500 each on the first of June and October 1965, and $500 more when he submitted the final draft. These dates were flexible, and he would have the contract drawn up once McCarthy made his wishes known.

More good news came in Erskine's letter of January 20, 1965: the English rights to *The Orchard Keeper* had been bought by André Deutsch in London, which had been publishing the books of John Updike and other young authors successfully. Erskine did not yet mention the possible sale of French translation rights to Robert Laffont, but he indicated that if more foreign sales came through, McCarthy's advances from Random for the first book would be repaid even before its publication date.

In his letter of December 30, 1964, Erskine had expressed his surprise and pleasure at learning that McCarthy had made such progress on the short second novel, perhaps not yet recognizing that McCarthy would not be satisfied with a second draft. As it turned out, McCarthy would not finish the second draft of *Outer Dark* before he left for Europe in August 1965, would conceive *Child of God* as he worked there on revising *Outer Dark,* and would continue to work on those two novels and *Suttree* until he sent the final draft of *Outer Dark* to Erskine in January 1967.

# Compiling the Jacket Copy

**E**rskine could begin writing the brief author's biography and book description for the jacket before the advance copies were printed, but the endorsements from readers would have to wait. He began drafting "About the Author" and sent it to McCarthy for feedback in October 1964.

As noted earlier, when McCarthy was working with Bensky in October or November 1962, he had written a first-person draft of his biographical material that was longer and more facetious than the version eventually printed on the book jacket. In this wry piece of creative nonfiction, he self-consciously adopted the persona of a starving artist whose lack of funds obstructed his path and whose narrative arc was a progression from government assistance to Thoreauvian self-sufficiency. He declared that during his first college semesters, "Most of my time was spent hustling pool for a living and carousing by night. At the end of the year I was asked not to return" (1). He enlisted in the Air Force because he was "broke" and had "no prospects." After his discharge and spending all his "mustering-out pay," he re-enrolled at the University of Tennessee "and wandered from one department to the next taking what courses I thought would please me, like a drunk in a supermarket." Upon the expiration of his GI benefits, he dropped out without earning a degree even though he had been offered graduate fellowships in three different disciplines (2). Although he held a job for a year in Chicago, he was unemployed and on welfare when he finished *The Orchard Keeper.* In this brief autobiography, McCarthy elided his temporarily moving with Lee into the home of his middle-class parents, writing only that at the time he was living rent-free in a farmhouse in the mountains (2). After this performance, he confessed to Bensky, "The person described here is not necessarily me; it is a brief outline of my activities to date" (3).[25]

To compose the author's note, Erskine worked from a photocopy of McCarthy's letter to Bensky, marking it for deletions and revisions. He omitted most of the information about McCarthy's life after leaving the university but quoted his account of his undergraduate and Air Force years. McCarthy's blithe chronicle of shiftlessness and financial distress became Erskine's economical statement, "Mr. McCarthy began work on The Orchard Keeper [*sic*] in 1959, but the necessities of life delayed its completion." In the typed version of his draft, Erskine left a blank in his sentence about the writer's present location and sent the document to McCarthy for revision on October 5, 1964.

Between writing his autobiographical sketch in fall 1962 and mailing a response to Erskine's draft on October 15, 1964, McCarthy had undergone a significant change of heart about revealing his personal information. He now told his editor that he would prefer "not [to] be quoted about myself" and that he hoped the author's note could be quite brief, but he did not supply a revision. Uncertain of McCarthy's location, Erskine replied to his Asheville address on October 20 with the request, "please forward." He urged McCarthy to submit a biographical sketch he would be happy with and to provide a photograph. He assured McCarthy that the sketch needn't be long and suggested "you could cut and recast in the third person the stuff I sent you. I thought it had a little more flavor as a quote, but maybe it has too much." No copy of McCarthy's revision survives in the archives, but it seems he sent a brief one in a letter Erskine received on November 5, in which McCarthy commented that he didn't much like the author's note but conceded that it was of little importance.

In late November 1964, "About the Author" was sent to the typesetter (Apicella, Letter to Joseph Levy). The published version is cast entirely in the third person and is rigorously objective in tone. It probably closely represents the revision Erskine received from McCarthy on November 5. It carries forward Erskine's evasive phrasing "the necessities of life" and omits any reference to Lee or McCarthy's son, or to his location. With the prospect of finally appearing in print, and with the trauma of his separation from Lee and Cullen, McCarthy seems to have decided to minimize personal revelations. He steadfastly maintained his reluctance to share personal information for decades, granting few interviews and then only to local newspapers in East Tennessee and Lexington, Kentucky[26] until Richard Woodward's full-length interview for the *New York Times Magazine* in 1992. By that time Cullen (who now goes by Chase) was thirty and capable of making his own assessment of his parents' relationship. McCarthy's sense of privacy has earned him a false reputation among journalists as a "recluse," a misjudgment belied by his outgoing, gregarious storytelling with Knoxville buddies (De Lisle, Conversations); his warm correspondence with editors, translators and friends; his more recent interviews; his cordial collaborations with artists, actors, and film-makers;[27] and his daily interactions with the scientists at the Santa Fe Institute. De Lisle observes that although he is private, he is not in the least shy, and the two seem to have made new friends easily everywhere they went (Conversations). Richard Woodward found McCarthy "a world-class talker, funny, opinionated, quick to laugh" (Woodward, "Venomous Fiction" 30); and editor Gary Fisketjon told Mick Brown, "Cormac's a terrifically personable and interesting fellow. . . He's not reclusive in the least" (Mick Brown, "On the Trail" 25). This sociable aspect of McCarthy is evident in the autobiographical sketch he wrote for Bensky. It seems likely that his reversing himself in 1964 about the kind of author's note he wanted to see on his books was an attempt to avoid offending Lee and to protect their privacy and Cullen's. It may also suggest that he experienced lingering embarrassment over his divorce. When Ecco press issued *The Orchard Keeper* in paperback in spring 1982, by which time his marriage to Anne De Lisle had also ended, Ecco reprinted the author's note; and when he saw the publication, McCarthy objected to the recirculation of a biographical note that was twenty years out of date (McCarthy, Letter to Ecco Press). Ecco's managing editor Megan Ratner offered to include an updated author's note in the next printing, but McCarthy reiterated that he preferred there be none (Ratner, Letter to Cormac McCarthy).[28]

Accompanying the revised biographical sketch Erskine received from Mc-Carthy on November 5, 1964, was a close-up snapshot of the author in half-profile, wearing a dark, open-collared polo shirt or sweater and standing before the rough-hewn, unpainted boards of a rustic building, his brooding, heavy-browed gaze avoiding engagement with the camera. It was a recent photo, dated October 1964. He chose this one, he wrote Erskine, because it was not fully in focus, which allowed him to feel somewhat "anonymous." Ironically, this photograph was more in keeping with the home-spun persona McCarthy had adopted in his autobiographical sketch for Bensky than was the more conventional image published on the dust jacket. And it was also more compatible with the subject of his first novel since it suggested his familiarity with rural life rather than the professional-class background of his birth family. McCarthy hoped the informal snapshot would suffice, but the publicity department found it too unfocused and perhaps too bleak. Publicity maven Tom Gervasi wrote Erskine on January 6, 1965, that Suzanne Baskin had tried protectively to discourage him from writing McCarthy to solicit a clearer picture, on the grounds that McCarthy preferred to stay "uninvolved" with the publicity for his book. Likely Erskine and McCarthy had candidly discussed McCarthy's desire for privacy. Not to be deterred, Gervasi went on to say that although he understood and sympathized with McCarthy's stance, he wondered if McCarthy might be less reluctant if he were made aware of the "disadvantage" he was placing himself in when competing with the other six hundred first novels to be published in 1965 by *Publishers Weekly* estimates. Gervasi preferred publishing without a photo if they could not get a better one. He asked whether Erskine thought it would be all right for him to contact McCarthy or if Erskine wanted to do it himself.

There is no record of who contacted McCarthy, but Gervasi or Erskine prevailed on him: the photo that appeared on the back flyleaf is a studio portrait of the author in a conservative jacket, white shirt, and narrow tie, with a faint smile and direct gaze into the camera, his deep-set eyes less obscured by his heavy, dark brows—handsome and genial, if reserved. McCarthy had made this concession, but he also made it clear to Gervasi, directly or through Baskin or Erskine, that he would not participate in publicizing his work (Gervasi, Memo to Jean Ennis, Albert Erskine, et al., Mar. 22, 1965).

Not long after settling the author's note and before the advance copies went out, Erskine turned his mind to writing the jacket description of the book, a task he confessed "I hate worse than poison" when he wrote McCarthy for help on December 16, 1964. He explained that although he had a strong sense of the book and found it easy to praise, he still found it difficult to capture its essence for others. He recognized that the book was too complex to be summarized economically, and he hesitated to write a description that might not match McCarthy's idea of it. He was especially puzzled by McCarthy's having described Ownby as an "anarchist" in a letter to Bensky; Erskine felt the term fit Rattner better. He continued, "To me, Ownby is an individualist who feels endangered by the encroachment of 'civilization' and the demands of law and order—especially when these are found in such hands as he finds them in." He thought all three protagonists were "resisters" whose code of ethics was more conscientious than that of the people who represented the new order. He hoped McCarthy would give him some guidance. Although he did not feel that book buyers were often swayed by the jacket description, he knew that reviewers were, and had even known some to repeat it verbatim.

On December 23, 1964, Erskine received an evasive reply. McCarthy agreed that Ownby was not a "bombthrowing malcontent" but more of an "amiable anarchist." He confirmed Erskine's understanding of the novel and thought that the difficulty of describing it lay with its interwoven plot lines. However, he did not have models of jacket descriptions at hand and did not have a feel for what was usual. So he suggested that Erskine rough out something to which he could respond. Because Erskine wished to have plentiful endorsements to quote, he was late in getting the jacket copy ready, and he did not send a draft of the book description to McCarthy until March 4, 1965. Erskine confessed that he was "not exactly in love with" his own words but thought that with quotations from John Palmer's letter to "back them up" they would do. He hoped that McCarthy would "find nothing here that makes you ill."

Reflecting his sense of inadequacy to describe the book, Erskine devoted only a short paragraph to the description, supplementing it with a brief statement of the book's forthcoming publications in England and France. Unfortunately, the description began with the erroneous assertion that the novel was set in the first quarter of the twentieth century (in fact it begins in 1934 and ends after World War II); and McCarthy did not catch this error. Although Erskine apparently felt it would do sales no good to highlight the poetic quality of McCarthy's prose, he quoted the rest of Palmer's summary of McCarthy's strengths, as well as his closing declaration that *The Orchard Keeper* was "a beautiful novel" (*The Orchard Keeper*, first edition, front flyleaf). McCarthy made only style changes on two successive drafts, the most significant of which was his revision of Erskine's "The plot is complex and compelling, but it is so bound up with and dependent upon the author's way of telling it that to summarize it would be to diminish it." He rewrote this as "The *story* is complex and compelling, *and its quality* is so bound up with and dependent upon the author's *style and narrative method* that to summarize it would be to diminish it" (changes italicized; Erskine, *The Orchard Keeper* front flap copy, drafts [A] and [B]). Erskine's statement echoes not only his and McCarthy's communication about it, but also Palmer's initial rationale for refusing an excerpt for *Yale Review*.

The last tasks for the book jacket were the gathering and selection of endorsements from readers of the advance copies. The advance copies were to be ready for mailing to roughly one hundred writers and literary scholars on January 4, 1965, according to the Revised Manufacturing Schedule, with the trade edition shipping on March 1 to meet the new publication date of May 1965. In the cover letter of January 15, 1965, that went to most recipients of the advance copies, Erskine was frank about his hope to gather quotes for the dust jacket from "people who I believe will value it," and he explained that although he had "great admiration for this book and a firm belief in Mr. McCarthy's ability to enlarge the talent he so clearly has," he felt that as a "complex first book by a new young writer," *The Orchard Keeper* "might be either overlooked or maltreated in the routine business of book-reviewing." A more personal letter went to Saul Bellow on January 21, beginning with Erskine's acknowledgment that he was asking quite a favor: "I don't think I've ever solicited you before like this." Erskine created a document to track the mailings and responses but seems to have ceased recording replies when it became clear that there would be relatively few (Erskine, Schedule of solicitations).

Of those who responded, not all offered praise suitable for the jacket. The reaction of writer and creative writing teacher Kay Boyle was the most negative. Although *The Orchard Keeper* gave evidence of "conscientious" work, she found its style flourishes without substance or meaning. Consequently, the book struck her as a Faulkner parody (Boyle, Letter to [Tom] Gervasi, Mar. 26, 1965). More encouragingly, Michael Millgate wrote that although he and his wife Jane, both literary scholars, could level some critical charges against *The Orchard Keeper*, they recognized McCarthy's talent and great promise (Millgate, Letter to Albert Erskine, Feb. 15, 1965). John Longley, of the University of Virginia, found the novel "beautiful" and declared he had been recommending it enthusiastically to everyone. Neither he nor Millgate, both Faulkner scholars, was reminded of Faulkner. Instead, Longley predicted that McCarthy would be compared with Knoxville writer James Agee although the only similarity was the setting in Knoxville. These observations were not substantive enough to appear on the jacket, but two of the readers with whom Longley had already shared the book had suggested that it might be a candidate for the William Faulkner Foundation award for Notable First Novel of 1965 (Longley, Letter to Albert Erskine, Feb. 17, 1965). Memphis novelist Shelby Foote was also highly enthusiastic about *The Orchard Keeper*, but his comments reached Random too late to appear on the jacket. He wrote to his editor Robert Loomis that he admired its evidence of writerly skill more than any inaugural novel he had read in recent years. He predicted that if McCarthy continued to develop, Random would soon have another powerhouse novelist in its list (Foote, Letter to Bob Loomis, April 12, 1965). Bellow and Foote's receipt of advance copies of

*The Orchard Keeper* resulted in their championing McCarthy's work for years to come (see my "Robert Coles and Cormac McCarthy").

Despite some dead ends, Erskine secured timely, appreciative, and usable endorsements from Ralph Ellison, James Michener, and Robert Penn Warren, as well as Warren Beck and Malcolm Cowley. Erskine edited the first three; the latter two were associated with the work of William Faulkner. Cowley, the editor of *The Portable Faulkner* (1946), noted some weaknesses in *The Orchard Keeper* such as echoes of Faulkner and unknotted plot strings, which may have struck editor and author as ironic given Bensky and Erskine's urging McCarthy to revise toward a less neatly tied up denouement. Nevertheless, Cowley congratulated Erskine on having discovered a young writer who "loves language" as Faulkner had. Erskine selected for the jacket Cowley's affirmation that McCarthy writes "with . . . baresark joy as he rushes into scenes of violence. He loves the countryside and makes us feel how a poor boy grew up loving it; everything comes alive" (Cowley, Letter to Albert Erskine, Jan. 26, 1965).

Warren Beck was a novelist in his own right and author of early and respected articles collected under the title *Faulkner* in 1976. He shared Erskine's concerns about the reception of McCarthy's novel since its complex design might be too challenging for many readers. He applauded Random's being undeterred by such commercial considerations. Beck predicted that McCarthy's subsequent work would be no less complicated in narrative technique, no less "subtle" in style, but he thought it possible that future books might hit on "less kaleidoscopic" narrative designs. For the jacket, Erskine drew excerpts from Beck's third paragraph, where he professed his admiration for the novel's "harmonious melding . . . of naturalistic detail, realistic . . . mountaineer dialogue, and evocatively poetic description and narration." Beck found that such a blending of authentic speechways with the narrator's lyricism made *The Orchard Keeper* "altogether oral." With Beck's permission, Erskine removed the clause about the novel's becoming "altogether oral," a deletion that slightly altered Beck's point while it retained his admiration for McCarthy's vigorous and flexible narrative voice. In his letter to Erskine, Beck indicated that he would like to review the book for the *Chicago Tribune* but that he was not certain this could happen because of changes at the newspaper (Beck, Letter to Albert Erskine, Feb. 19, 1965). However, on April 16, 1965, Beck wrote again with the news that the *Tribune* had agreed to his reviewing *The Orchard Keeper* after all.

James Michener found that McCarthy wrote within the tradition of Southern writers Truman Capote, William Faulkner, and Carson McCullers. Like others, he predicted that McCarthy's literary career would be one of high achievement. Erskine deleted Michener's reference to Faulkner and his citing of specific passages he admired and included only his assessment of McCarthy's strengths: his lyrical style, his unusual feel for the land, his striking originality (Michener, Letter to Albert Erskine, Feb. 12, 1965).

The last of the quotable testimonials to arrive were those that Erskine secured through sheer persistence. When he sent McCarthy the copy for the jacket endorsements on March 4, 1965, he wrote that he had "taken down the last of them" by telephone that morning. These were Ralph Ellison's and Robert Penn Warren's. On February 4, Baskin had heard from Ellison that he liked the book and would write something for the jacket (Baskin, Holograph note), but it appears that he had delayed doing so and eventually dictated his statement over the phone. A draft of his comments in Erskine's handwriting survives, jotted with a few shorthand abbreviations, most of which are expanded in his draft of the jacket copy. Ellison's appraisal was wholly positive, and on the jacket, Erskine quoted his statement in its entirety. Ellison declared that the novel powerfully held his interest and that he admired its "descriptive prose of great beauty and hallucinating vividness." The characters emerged from the writer's "insights" rather than lifeless outlines derived from "psychiatry textbks." He concluded resoundingly, "McCarthy is a writer to be read, to be admired, and quite honestly—envied." At the end of the year, Michener and Ellison would both place *The Orchard Keeper* at the top of their lists of the three books they had found most rewarding in 1965 ("A Gift Bag of Favorites," Dec. 5, 1965).

Ellison's statement for the jacket has the feel of a crafted statement, but Warren's appears more off-the-cuff, the kind of spur-of-the-moment assessment that Erskine could urge his friend to provide at the last minute. The document which preserves it is not a letter from Warren, but a typed page headed "RPW re THE ORCHARD KEEPER." The lines are exactly as they appear on the back of the jacket: "McCarthy is a born narrator, and his writing has, line by line, the stab of actuality. He is here to stay."

When McCarthy thanked Erskine for his copy of the printed jacket in late March, he remarked modestly, gratefully, "That's quite a collection of encomiums."

# Awards

As Erskine worked to launch McCarthy's career with as much fanfare as possible, awards for his promising new novelist were on his mind. Erskine was probably instrumental in McCarthy's receipt of that year's travel fellowship from the American Academy of Arts and Letters, but Erskine did not, as Daniel King asserts, apply on McCarthy's behalf (King, *Cormac McCarthy's Literary Evolution* 28). Nominations for the awards from the American Academy are put forward by its members, and the evidence suggests that John Hersey, who had been a member of the Academy since 1953 and its secretary since 1961, may have nominated McCarthy (Updike, "1938-1947" 129). Hersey then chaired the Academy's grant committee (Hersey, Letter to Gerald Freund, Apr. 7, 1966). He had been brought into the Random House fold when Knopf and Random merged in 1960 (Cerf, *At Random* 279, 282), and Erskine had provided him with an advance copy of *The Orchard Keeper* on January 11, 1965, according to his schedule of recipients. Other members of the Academy's literature department at that time who may have served on the selection committee or had informal input included Saul Bellow, Malcolm Cowley, Karl Shapiro, Robert Penn Warren, and Eudora Welty (Updike, "Appendix: Academy Members, Past and Present").

On February 19, 1965, three months before *The Orchard Keeper* was published, Erskine wrote McCarthy that Hersey had phoned him at home with the news that McCarthy would receive a prize of (he thought) about $2,000. Erskine explained that he had known the award was possible, but there had been questions about the eligibility of a book still in its production stages, and so he had not wanted to "set up possible anticlimaxes" for McCarthy. But the committee was impressed. Hersey later wrote to Gerald Freund of the Rockefeller Foundation that although no one on the Academy's selection committee had read anything by McCarthy before *The Orchard Keeper*, they unanimously agreed that he "should receive as much support and encouragement as possible." Hersey noted too that in his several terms on the committee, he had seldom known this kind of unanimity to occur (Hersey, Letter to Gerald Freund, Apr. 7, 1966). According to a quotation recorded by Baskin, the award was made "To Cormac McCarthy . . . who in a single short novel has already put a strong sense around his own vivid, personal literary territory." (One wonders if, gathering information by telephone, she might have misheard "fence" as "sense.") She also recorded that the Academy granted only one travel fellowship in any given year (Baskin, Notes on American Academy 1965).

When he gave McCarthy the good news about the travel award on February 19, Erskine indicated that McCarthy would receive formal notification from Hersey soon and that the Academy would issue an official announcement. McCarthy's award proved to be much larger than Erskine had estimated, perhaps because of the committee's unanimous desire to support McCarthy's work. On March 22, 1965, Random's Gervasi wrote an internal memo summarizing the preliminary publicity plan for *The Orchard Keeper*, which included the information that the Academy was awarding McCarthy $6,500 for his European travels.

The American Academy of Arts and Letters would follow McCarthy's accomplishments over his career, bestowing on him its $5,000 Jean Stein Award for Fiction in 1991[29] and its Award of Merit for novel writing in 2015 (American Academy of Arts and Letters). At some point its affiliated institute invited McCarthy to become a member, a common follow-up to the awards, which went only to nonmembers.[30] John Updike writes, "Election is first and foremost an honor, a tribute paid to outstanding work; secondarily it is an invitation to attend the year's four convivial events and to participate in the work of the institution, which primarily consists of the fostering of the arts through monetary awards and prizes and also by means of [art] exhibitions and [music] recordings." Although participation was not required of members, McCarthy declined membership (Updike, "Foreword" xi). The periodic gatherings with other literary figures, where he might have been pushed to discuss his writing, would have held no interest for him. Furthermore, traveling to New York for the events might well have added to his financial difficulties at least in the early decades of his career. Neither would participation in the gatherings or the institutional committee work have appealed to a writer who held to the principle that above all he must protect his work time. He may also have shared the reservations of other invitees over the decades, such as William James, who declined membership because he saw the institute as elitist, an exercise in vanity, having no genuine purpose except the honorary (Lewis, "1898–1907" 20–21). Until it established enough of an endowment to begin its financial support of individual artists in 1941,[31] the institute had been seen by some as "an otiose body" of "fossilized old jossers," in the words of Ezra Pound (Updike, "1938–1947" 118), and its origins among the brahmins of New York may have put off McCarthy even decades later.

*The Orchard Keeper* also won the William Faulkner Foundation Award for the most notable first novel by an American in 1965. When Faulkner established the prize, he had specified that the judges should be young educators, and for the 1965 cycle the selectors were three assistant professors of English: William R. Robinson of the University of Virginia, creative writer R. W. H. Dillard of Hollins College, and Richard A. Johnson of Mt. Holyoke College. John Longley, who had so appreciated the book when he read an advance copy, had proposed it to Robinson, who chaired the committee; and on February 17, Longley asked Erskine to provide copies for the judges to consider (Longley, Letter to Albert Erskine, Feb. 17, 1965). They read sixty-five novels in their deliberations, and in addition to *The Orchard Keeper,* they singled out as finalists C. D. B. Bryan's *P. S. Wilkinson,* Donald Harington's *The Cherry Pit,* Earl Rovit's *The Player King,* Stephen Schneck's *The Night Clerk,* and Mark Smith's *Toyland* (Wylie, List of William Faulkner Foundation Award finalists). But they judged *The Orchard Keeper* the best. According to the Random House publicity release, Robinson found the book "a cornucopia of literary delights . . . truly, and by any standard, an outstanding novel." Dillard asserted that "McCarthy is a young writer of dark vision who has been able in *The Orchard Keeper* to transmute that vision into an art which is strong and vital for all its darkness." For Johnson, "reading the novel was to discover a self-contained world of quiet verbal richness, and to be reminded of how rare it is that a novel can stand firmly on the virtues of its prose style." A much-abbreviated version of the press release appeared in the *New York Times* on March 17, 1966 ("Books–Authors").

# Reviews and Sales

The *Orchard Keeper* was published in the United States on May 5, 1965, and on that day Erskine sent a congratulatory telegram to McCarthy at his parents' home in Vestal. Random placed an advertisement for the book in the *New York Times Book Review* of May 9 (Random House, "Random House Congratulates Cormac McCarthy"). When McCarthy replied to Erskine's telegram, he noted that although he had not seen any reviews, he guessed some had appeared. He thanked his editor for the work he had devoted to the novel and expressed the wish that it would "eventually repay you in some part" (McCarthy, Letter to Albert Erskine, received May 10, 1965). In the back of his mind may have been some nervous doubts about the reception of the novel, despite the laudatory comments Erskine had secured for the jacket. Random had sent out 125 review copies to periodicals, and in March they were already expecting positive assessments from *Atlantic Monthly, Time, Newsweek*'s Saul Maloff, and the *Wall Street Journal*'s Edmund Fuller (Gervasi, Memo to Jean Ennis et al., Mar. 22, 1965). McCarthy may have been watching for these, but strangely none seems to have appeared.

Nevertheless, the novel garnered considerable notice and appreciation. Although many reviewers in the press were exasperated by its complex structure and uncertain about McCarthy's control of language, almost all recognized that here was a new novelist of "infinite promise," in the words of an unsigned notice in the *Virginia Quarterly Review* ("Notes on Recent Books" lxxx). This was possibly an early assessment by Walter Sullivan, who reviewed the book at greater length in *Sewanee Review*. (Sullivan was a Vanderbilt University graduate and professor who, like Erskine, had studied under Donald Davidson. Sullivan specialized in the work of the Agrarian and Fugitive writers and was a friend of Allen Tate, Andrew Lytle, and Robert Penn Warren and thus possibly of Erskine as well.)

Despite the diligent efforts McCarthy had made at his editors' behest to provide greater clarity, readers often expressed frustration with the novel's plot disjunctions, its calculated withholding of information, and the perceived obscurity of its scenes' settings in time and place (see, e.g., Bingham, "From the South"; Byerly, "Haunting Memory"; Hicks, "Six Firsts for Summer"; Murray, Review of *The Orchard Keeper*; and Orville Prescott, "Still Another Disciple"). But some of the most perceptive reviewers defended the novel's challenging narrative techniques and kaleidoscopic structure. *The National Observer*'s Arthur Edelstein praised its structure as "carefully complicated." Closer to home, the *Tennessean*'s Sara Sprott Morrow wrote that the novel's avoidance of a linear plot contributed to its "wonder—that McCarthy divulges, a bit at [a] time, the over-lapping lives of these tormented mountaineers . . . interwoven in complexity" (Morrow, Review of *The Orchard Keeper* 12D). Walter Sullivan recognized that the novel was partly structured by the intersections of the inhabitants of Red Branch (Sullivan, "Worlds Past" 721). Two years later, novelist David Madden reviewed it for *Masterplots*; his assessment, which was both lengthier than the typical review and composed at greater leisure, provided a more considered analysis of the novel's narrative techniques. He observed that McCarthy employs a strategy of juxtaposition akin to cinematic montage and thus the structure presents (and requires of the reader) "a process of unification" (218–19). He noted further that in this novel of crossing paths, chance and accident are represented as "agents of coherence" (Madden, Review of *The Orchard Keeper* 219), a structural and thematic device that McCarthy would return to in his road narratives and explore most strikingly in *No Country for Old Men* (2005) with the symbolic character Anton Chiguhr, whose coin tosses determine his actions and others' fates.

Another trend in the reviews was the complaint that McCarthy appeared reluctant to convey the inner experience of his characters (see Byerly, "Haunting Memory"; Craig, "Tanks, Trees")—a misapprehension of his methods of characterization that continued to surface as late as Vereen Bell's 1988 assertion that *Outer Dark*'s Rinthy is "virtually without thoughts" (Bell, *The Achievement of Cormac McCarthy* 8) and Denis Donoghue's still more extreme pronouncement ten years later that McCarthy's characters have no inner life (Donoghue, "Teaching *Blood Meridian*" 260). It may be that McCarthy's oblique methods of characterization contributed to the entirely negative reaction of A. M. Tibbetts, whose brief and dismissive assessment of the novel in *Southern Review* sniped that it focused on "unpleasant people" prone to "pointless violence": characters about whom no reader could care (Tibbetts, "A Fiction Chronicle" 192). The *New York Times*'s Orville Prescott observed that McCarthy's objective presentation of his characters resulted in his understating their motivations (O. Prescott, "Still Another Disciple"), an issue his editors had worried about and had asked McCarthy to address in his revisions.

However, more reviewers found McCarthy's subtle characterizations highly effective. In the Madison *Capital Times,* August Derleth, who praised the novel as "beautiful . . . in every sense—as form, as prose, as story," wrote that the novel's characters were "remarkably well realized" (Derleth, "Books of the Times" 8). Sullivan noted the author's lack of explicit attention to the psychology of his characters but defended it as a method that was in keeping with the reserved mountaineer temperament (Sullivan, "Worlds Past" 722), and if Sullivan is the anonymous writer of the piece in *Virginia Quarterly Review,* he made his position clear when he wrote there that like the Appalachian people, notable for their "unobtrusiveness," the book's "stylized" characters "emerge one by one to insinuate themselves in the reader's consciousness, so that presently he becomes aware of their intuitive distrust of strangers, their protective isolation, their solidarity, and, above all, their desperation" (Anonymous, "Notes on Recent Books" lxxx). *Saturday Review*'s Granville Hicks, too, cited McCarthy's talent for delineating characters that gradually "come alive" on the page so that "we eventually grasp the strange relationships that exist among them" ("Six Firsts for Summer" 36). The entirely enthusiastic reviewer for the *Cleveland Plain Dealer* admired the novel's "love and understanding of people and the way people behave" (Anonymous, Review of *The Orchard Keeper*). Writing for the *Montgomery Advertiser,* Alfred Alcorn detected an oblique characterizing technique in the novel's gothic scenes since "they evoke terror not so much in their vivid description as in their effect upon the characters"—in the way such scenes suggest the characters' inner lives (Alcorn, Review of *The Orchard Keeper* 4A). This strategy would become more prominent in successive novels.

In general, reviewers who were familiar with the southern Appalachian region tended to find McCarthy's characters authentic and sympathetic and to see them as integral to the landscape. The book page editor for the Louisville, Kentucky *Courier-Journal,* Mary Bingham, found the characters "graspable people inhabiting an unendingly beautiful countryside." She reported, "I have not for a long time read a book so full of lyricism, of sharp, inspired observation of woods and creeks and turning seasons" (Bingham, "From the South" D5). And in one of the most appreciative reviews, the Nashville *Tennessean*'s Morrow applauded McCarthy's "description of the natural world [and] his microscopic delineation of complex characterization." She admired the empathy with which McCarthy treated his mountain people: "You become aware of the dignity, honesty and love of these poor, uneducated, and, in many instances, criminal characters" (Morrow, Review of *The Orchard Keeper* 12D). Madden, who, like McCarthy, was born in 1933, grew up in Knoxville, and attended the university there, considered McCarthy especially good at rendering dialogue and admired both his authentic dialect and the evocative descriptions of his characters as they move against the backdrop of the East Tennessee landscape (Review of *The Orchard Keeper* 220). In the *Greensboro Daily News,* Mary Frances Hazelman praised McCarthy's physical descriptions of his characters and of the mountains they dwell in as "equally . . . good," and she too was especially impressed with the "accuracy of his ear and the authenticity with which he handles the Southern mountain dialect" (Hazelman, "McCarthy's Mountain Tale").

Novelist and popular historian Wilma Dykeman, whose study *The French Broad* was one of McCarthy's sources for *The Orchard Keeper* and *Outer Dark* (Luce, *Reading the World,* 5–7, 131–33), reviewed his book for the Knoxville *News-Sentinel.* She found "some of his scenes in the hills, along the river banks, . . . clear and sharp as etched glass" (Dykeman, "Cormac McCarthy's Book Impressive" F2). Reviewers in the national periodicals and newspapers from other regions, such as Mary Byerly, Granville Hicks, and Katherine Gauss Jackson, also praised McCarthy's depictions of the landscape, even when they were uncertain of his success in other areas. Stanley Trachtenberg found faults with the book but ended his assessment for *Yale Review* with high appreciation for its treatment of the land and natural processes: "Lyric, evocative, . . . *The Orchard Keeper* detaches itself from its specific locale in the very process of naturalistic description, observing the organic unity possible in nature, . . . perhaps . . . only in imaginative recreation" ("Black Humor, Pale Fiction" 149). In uniformly positive reviews, the *Chicago Daily News*'s Thane Ritalin praised McCarthy's "exquisitely wrought synthesis of nature and humanity" (Ritalin, "A Brilliant, Vital First Novel"), and the *Cleveland Plain Dealer*'s reviewer declared that McCarthy was possessed of "an awareness of nature that is without parallel in contemporary American writing" (Anonymous, Review of *The Orchard Keeper*).

Several reviewers commented on McCarthy's minimalist punctuation practices, as Erskine had feared, although most recognized that this did not matter much. Finally, there was the issue of McCarthy's poetic prose or stylistic excesses, depending on the taste and temperament of the reviewer. Interestingly, his fellow Appalachian writers Wilma Dykeman and David Madden were among the most critical of his lyrical prose style, either because they found it derivative of Faulkner or perhaps because they found it incompatible with the rusticity of his characters and setting. To Dykeman McCarthy's language was "more tortuous than clear," and she warned that McCarthy might become a "coterie writer" of "abstruse prose" (rather than an accessible popular writer, like herself; Dykeman, "Cormac McCarthy's Book Impressive" F2). Madden pronounced McCarthy the most talented of the many "Faulkner mimic[s]" to appear in the mid-twentieth century, but he thought his "buckshot style" was not entirely under control. Although it sometimes hit the mark, it "tends to give everything equal value" and thus "often claims an importance which the experience being depicted cannot justify" (Madden, Review of *The Orchard Keeper* 220). James G. Murray identified three styles in the novel, the realistic dialect of the characters, the naturalistic descriptions, and the poetic passages, which he found uneven and sometimes overwritten. For Murray, instead of narrative flexibility, these three modes created a "confusion of styles" (Murray, Review of *The Orchard Keeper* 866). Further, he felt McCarthy's wordplay obscured his poetic observations more than it revealed them.

Other reviewers experienced mixed reactions to McCarthy's prose style. In a review titled "Still Another Disciple of William Faulkner," Orville Prescott complained that McCarthy somewhat "submerges his . . . talents beneath a flood of imitation." While he conceded that McCarthy did not mimic Faulkner's "marathon sentences," he objected to other Faulknerian characteristics: "the . . . pronouns with no visible antecedents; the recondite vocabulary and coined words; the dense prose packed with elaborate figures of speech; the deliberate ambiguity." Yet he felt the novel was written with "torrential power." McCarthy excelled at "generating an emotional climate, . . . suggesting instead of . . . stating, . . . creating a long succession of brief, dramatic scenes described with flashing visual impact" (M49).

In general, those who appreciated McCarthy's stylistic daring wrote the most glowing reviews overall. Ritalin lauded his "masterly subtle shifts in style, his disciplined control of the rhythm of sentences which never confuse poetic prose with poetry." Ritalin stressed, as Foote had in his letter to Loomis, that in this novel McCarthy succeeded as a *writer* (Ritalin, "A Brilliant, Vital First Novel"). Sullivan found agrarian influence in the novel, but not in its "magnificent" prose, which was "full of energy and sharp detail." With his deep familiarity with Faulkner and the agrarians, Sullivan declared that impressions of the influence of these writers ultimately proved false (Sullivan, "Worlds Past" 721). (It seems that throughout the decades of McCarthy's reception, the principle holds true that the better a reader knows Faulkner's and McCarthy's work, the less imitative of the bard of Yoknapatawpha he or she finds McCarthy.) The *Cleveland Plain Dealer* observed that "For a first novel, it is astonishingly free of influences. McCarthy . . . writes with a Southerner's love of the highblown phrase, but he has developed his own voice and it rings true and clear and lovely" (Anonymous, Review of *The Orchard Keeper*). Edelstein was the only reviewer to recognize that McCarthy achieved the "haunting, spectral quality" of his language through his "fusion of concreteness and metaphorical suggestiveness" (Edelstein, "In the South, Two Good Stories" 17).

Despite some reviewers' uncertainty, the American response was remarkably favorable to this first novel by an unknown writer. A few placed *The Orchard Keeper* among the best first novels they had ever read. Many reviewers expressed frustration with the challenges of the reading experience or some ambiguity of response, but all of them (with the exception of A. M. Tibbetts) recognized McCarthy's talent and the success of his work on many levels. Several anticipated a brilliant writing career, although perhaps Edelstein stated it most emphatically: "If Mr. McCarthy's future work is of equal caliber, he is sure to join the first rank of American writers. He may, in fact, already be there" (Edelstein, "In the South, Two Good Stories" 17).

As the reviews came to their attention, Erskine and McCarthy shared them with one another. On May 12, 1965, Erskine sent copies of the first two. He wrote that "Little Orvie" Prescott's mixed review in the *Times,* was "for him . . . as good as I'd hoped for—and a hell of a lot better than a deadly silence." The other was a brief rave by Theodore O'Leary in the *Kansas City Star,* one that was so admiring that Erskine wished it had appeared in New York. O'Leary wrote that *The Orchard Keeper* was one of those first novels like Alan Paton's *Cry, the Beloved Country* or Ken Kesey's *One Flew Over the Cuckoo's Nest* that, arriving without warning, "gives fresh hope and zest to a man whose job is to read books and who . . . more often is disappointed than enamored." McCarthy's was a "much needed new voice in American fiction, one that can speak to the world and find a response everywhere" (O'Leary, "Once in a Long, Long While").[32] When McCarthy replied to Erskine, he acknowledged that Prescott seemed "exasperated," but he found the O'Leary review and Warren Beck's brief notice in the *Chicago Tribune Books Today* section quite "generous" (McCarthy, Letter to Albert Erskine, received May 20, 1965). Beck acclaimed the novel as "rich with life's substance, intriguingly patterned, quickly modulent of mood, brilliant in style, and engagingly fresh as well as authentic" (Review of *The Orchard Keeper, Books Today* sec.:7). On May 21, Baskin sent McCarthy a copy of the wholly admiring review from the *Cleveland Plain Dealer,* remarking, "If the reviews continue in this vein . . . we will soon have the makings of a good quote ad." She and/or Erskine prepared an ad with brief quotations from eight of the best reviews, and in 1968 it appeared on the back of the first edition of *Outer Dark* (Erskine, "Back ad" draft).

Among the reviews that came out later, McCarthy was especially pleased (as he should have been) with Ritalin's in the *Chicago Daily News* and Edelstein's in the *National Observer.* The latter was "one of the most enthusiastic" of the reviews he had encountered (McCarthy, Letter to Albert Erskine, received June 4, 1965; McCarthy, Letter to Albert Erskine, received Aug. 11, 1965). Clearly McCarthy read the reviews; but with the exception of Prescott's, he made no comment about the criticisms.[33]

With the attention it was getting in the press, the first printing sold moderately well by the standards of the day. On August 3, 1965, when the reviews had slowed, Erskine wrote McCarthy, "sales though not big have been steady and I am hopeful that they will continue." Between 1965 and 1969, when a second printing was issued, the book sold 3,926 copies (Lane, Letter to J. Howard Woolmer). Since the publishing summary for the book prepared in October 1964 had projected that the publisher would break even if 3,155 copies sold, this was a modest success for the publisher of a first novel. McCarthy was to receive $2,105 in royalties or advances, whichever was larger. But the novel was more successful by the measure of critical esteem than it was financially. And this may not have surprised the publishers. Cerf, who had purchased the Modern Library imprint from Horace Liveright in 1925, recalled, "When I started publishing, fiction outsold nonfiction four-to-one. Now that ratio is . . . reversed, [and] . . . the bulk of new fiction doesn't sell at all. It's heartbreaking to bring out a good first novel and watch it die virtually at birth" (Cerf, *At Random*, 203–204). Partly to keep his hopes realistic, Scribner had informed F. Scott Fitzgerald that a good sales performance for a first novel would be 5,000 copies; but *This Side of Paradise* (1920) proved dramatically more successful, with 35,000 sold in the seven months after publication; and Hemingway's *The Sun Also Rises* (1926) had initial sales of 20,000 (Berg, *Max Perkins* 20, 41, 100). Both had been edited by Scribner's legendary Maxwell Perkins, who energetically promoted his writers and who had an uncanny instinct both for talent and for what would sell. On the other hand, Boni and Liveright had less confidence in Faulkner's first novel, *Soldiers' Pay* (1926), and had printed only 2,500 copies. By the end of the depression year of 1930, Faulkner's *The Sound and the Fury* and *As I Lay Dying* together had sold fewer than 4,000 copies (Blotner, *Faulkner* I 494, 685). Random House editors and staff had invested a great deal of time and energy in *The Orchard Keeper,* but the publisher did not gamble on a large first printing. If Erskine did not expect blockbuster sales, he knew that McCarthy's talent and the attention he had attracted with his first novel had launched his career in such a way that they might hope for increasing respect (and sales) with each subsequent book.

# Part Two
## *Outer Dark,*
## 1962–1968

# Biographical Context and the Novel's Genesis

**W**hen *The Orchard Keeper* was published in 1965, the author's note on the back flyleaf revealed that McCarthy was "at present working on two more novels." These were *Suttree,* begun in 1961 or 1962, and *Outer Dark,* begun in late 1962. Richard Woodward's highly informative 1992 interview with McCarthy is one of our most important biographical resources, yet Woodward seems to have misunderstood McCarthy when he reports that *Outer Dark* was written in Ibiza, a misleading oversimplification (Woodward, "Venomous Fiction" 31). In 1968 McCarthy told a Knoxville journalist that he had been "living up in Sevier County at the time I began writing my second novel" and that he had composed it "over a period of several years, some time in Asheville, and finished it in Spain" ("Author Lives in Blount" F5). Correspondence with editors and dates in the "Rough/First Draft" of the novel confirm McCarthy's early statement and show as well that he completed the initial draft in Asheville and New Orleans in 1964. He composed his "Early" (second) draft in Knoxville and then Europe, where he also produced "Middle" and Final" drafts during his courtship of Anne De Lisle and the first year and a half of their marriage.

When McCarthy mailed Erskine his "Final Draft" of *Outer Dark* from Ibiza in January 1967, he referred to it as "this bloody book which I began in December of 1962"—which places its genesis only seven months after he submitted *The Orchard Keeper* to Random and about three years after he had begun drafting the first novel in 1959 (McCarthy, Letter to Albert Erskine, received Jan. 23, 1967). The first page of *Outer Dark*'s "Rough/ First Draft [A]" provides the specific day on which he began, December 16, and the year 1962 appears in the middle of page 15. This reliable dating situates the genesis of *Outer Dark* at the juncture of stressful events in McCarthy's professional work and his emotional life: his first revision of *The Orchard Keeper* to meet the demands of his editors, the failure of his marriage to Lee Holleman McCarthy, and the resulting loss of a parental role with his infant son Cullen. Archival evidence reveals how *Outer Dark* stands at the threshold between the subjective and the objective, deriving both from McCarthy's emotional challenges and from his efforts to hone and defend his craft.

As mentioned in Part One, Bensky's request for substantial revision of *The Orchard Keeper* in October 1962 came when Cormac and Lee's relationship was troubled and their finances were dwindling. It seems likely he had quit his job in Chicago by February 1962 to devote his full attention to finishing *The Orchard Keeper*. When he and Lee left Chicago around May 1, 1962, she too had given up her employment, and although Lee sought Tennessee teaching certification in June (Wesley Morgan, Email to the author, Apr. 25, 2018), they likely had little or no income until McCarthy finally received an advance for the book in September 1963 (Bensky, Letter to Cormac McCarthy, Sept. 13, 1963). In her poem "It's in the Cards," Lee recalls that their relationship was tenuous as early as 1961, their first year together. The "wallflower amputations" of buildings undergoing demolition between Division Street and North Avenue in Chicago's Old Town told her the "marriage wouldn't last" (ll. 6–7). Still, about two months pregnant, she returned to Tennessee with Cormac. Before McCarthy received Bensky's revision suggestions, the couple had moved to the rent-free house in Sevier County, where Cormac lived for a little more than a year (McCarthy, Letter to Lawrence M. Bensky, [late Oct.–Nov. 1962]). In Paris in 1966, when McCarthy reconstructed the locations and costs of all his Thanksgiving meals since 1960 on a page of his second draft of *Outer Dark*, he recalled that in 1962 he had spent the November holiday at home in Walden Creek, Sevier County ("Early Draft [A]" 126). That week, the baby was born in Knoxville's Presbyterian Hospital on November 30 ("McCarthy, Cormac," *Who's Who*).[1]

Under these circumstances, an advance and a 1963 publication date for *The Orchard Keeper* would have given the couple much-needed reassurance. But on December 13, 1962, when Bensky briefly acknowledged McCarthy's letter defending the novel, he gave no indication that Random would accept the work without revision. Faced with indefinite delays in the publication of his first novel, McCarthy started *Outer Dark* three days later. He may well have begun this new, shorter novel out of urgency for money, knowing that his other novel-in-progress, *Suttree,* would take much longer to finish, but his conception for *Outer Dark* had much to do with the dissolution of his marriage and his impending separation from Cullen so soon after his birth. Read with caution, Lee McCarthy's self-avowedly autobiographical poems published in three collections between 1991 and 2002 provide primary evidence about the period from early winter 1962 through August 1963, by which time she had left Cormac. (Lee filed for divorce only after moving to Wyoming ["Lee McCarthy"].) She writes that she gained her independence in winter and "declared it in July." After she left "the union," she seceded "from the state" (Lee McCarthy, "Only Child" ll. 12–16). That is, their emotional separation occurred in winter 1962/63, but she did not leave until July 1963. A news article reports that both Cormac and Lee attended the marriage of McCarthy's youngest sister Maryellen in Knoxville in June 1963 and that they lived in Sevierville ("Miss McCarthy" 10). They may still have been living together because they did not have the money to separate and/or because Cormac wanted time with his son, but if Lee is not fictionalizing in her poem "Mother Outlaw," in July she moved into a hotel room "in East Tennessee" (Lee McCarthy, "Mother Outlaw" l. 1), when Cullen was just beginning to crawl and teethe (ll. 7–11). Then reluctantly she reached out to McCarthy's mother (Lee McCarthy, "Mother Outlaw" ll. 26–27), who took in Lee and Cullen for the brief time before Lee moved to Wyoming to take a job teaching. Lee recalls taking a train from Cheyenne to Chugwater, Wyoming, in August 1963 (Lee McCarthy, "It's in the Cards" l. 9).

Given that McCarthy started writing *Outer Dark* on December 16, 1962, it seems possible the couple's decision to separate was at least partly triggered by Bensky's terse letter of December 13 that implied McCarthy's defense of his submitted draft of *The Orchard Keeper* would not absolve him of revision. Lee's 2009 obituary claims that when she was "caring for the baby and tending to the chores of the house," Cormac urged her to secure a job "so he could focus on his novel writing" ("Lee McCarthy"). This suggests that lack of income and the editorial demands for revision, together with differing views of gender roles, were serious challenges to their marriage. Lee's reluctance to leave her newborn and go to work is certainly understandable. She may have been nursing Cullen. She may still have been recovering from the physical stresses of childbirth. She may even have suffered from postnatal depression. And if she already saw herself as an aspiring writer, she may have been reluctant to give up her own writing time. If she was writing this early (we do not know that she was), she might have felt McCarthy's suggestion that she take a job devalued her creative work. Ironically, however, her becoming a single parent responsible for her child's support may itself have postponed her writing. Although she received a prestigious Stegner Fellowship in prose writing at Stanford University in 1974–1975, her first book, *Desire's Door*, was not published until 1991. By then she had published verse and prose in *High Plains Literary Review*, *Intro*, and *Raccoon* and was drafting a novel ("About the Author"), but this would not see publication.[2]

Yet Lee's obituary also suggests that McCarthy may have been looking for practical solutions to their problems. He may have been willing to be the exception in the early 1960s: the stay-at-home father who would revise the novel which had secured interest from Random while caring for his son Cullen—a strategy that many families in the decades since have adopted. This seems plausible in light of McCarthy's close relationship with his second son John Francis and his participation in John's childcare, although it is also possible that his involvement with John has been motivated at least partly by a desire to atone for his absence from Cullen's childhood, as Woodward surmises in his 2005 interview for *Vanity Fair* (Woodward, "Cormac Country" 104).

McCarthy's suggestion that Lee seek employment was perhaps also a level-headed plan for effecting the separation they had agreed to. We do not know whether Lee went to work when McCarthy asked her to, but if she did, it would have allowed her time to secure a teaching job out of state and to earn the money she would need to relocate and file for divorce. And if she was teaching during the last months that she stayed with McCarthy, this too might explain why she did not leave their house until summer 1963, after the school year had ended.

# The Drafting Process

For a *Kingsport* (Tennessee) *Times-News* story of December 1973, McCarthy talked candidly to interviewer Martha Byrd about his writing process. She was struck by the differences between the research processes of the historian and McCarthy's preparation as a fiction writer. He spoke as if he were the crucible in which all his experiences and reading steeped and melded until he was ready to write. Then "the words come easily and quickly. 'I go into a state of mind. . . . My hands do the thinking. . . . It is not a conscious process'" (Martha Byrd, "East Tennessee Author" 9C). He seems to be describing the highly enjoyable experience of *flow* common to creative people, in which the artist is fully absorbed in the creative process, free of self-consciousness, and so completely focused that distractions and anxieties are shut out (Csikszentmihalyi, *Creativity* 110–13). "In one sense, those 'in flow' are not conscious of the experience at the moment; on reflection, however, such people feel that they have been fully alive, totally realized, and involved in a 'peak experience'" (Howard Gardner, *Creating Minds* 25–26).

When McCarthy considered where his creativity comes from, he observed memorably: "It's like jazz." Jazz musicians "create as they play," he said, "and maybe only those who can do it can understand it" (Martha Byrd, "East Tennessee Author"). This is a revealing statement of the sources and nature of his creativity. While most highly creative people experience flow, many fiction writers outline their plots on paper before drafting and/or take extensive notes from their focused reading for their works; and in fact the archives hold many of McCarthy's source materials for *The Gardener's Son* and his reading notes for his historical novel, *Blood Meridian.* But McCarthy seems gifted with a phenomenal memory for everything he reads and hears. His sister Bobbie reports that he once told her that if he saw the first line on any page of a book he had read, he could recall the rest of what was on the page (McCooe, Interview with Bryan Giemza and Dianne Luce). Like the jazz musician who has so mastered his instrument and the principles of musical composition that he can improvise from what he has deeply internalized, McCarthy creates his art out of a wellspring of inner resources attentively accumulated. As he told Oprah Winfrey years later, he does not outline his novels before he begins writing, and the absence of outlines among his papers bears this out. Preplotting a work, he told Winfrey, "would be death." Instead, "You just have to trust where it comes from." And he remarked to David Kushner, "I just sit down and write whatever is interesting. . . . The best things just sort of come out of the blue. It's a subconscious process" (Kushner, "Cormac McCarthy's Apocalypse" 48, 52).

McCarthy's drafts of *Outer Dark* are especially rich in revelations about his working processes in the early stages of a novel's composition, and they largely corroborate what he has told interviewers. Although the scarcity of true first drafts among his papers makes it difficult to determine how the structure of most of his novels has evolved, the case is different with *Outer Dark.* Because McCarthy preserved most of its first or discovery draft, with this novel we can see the subconscious process at work and gradually giving way to the more conscious aspects of artistic control in revision. Moreover, because he quite consistently dated his first-draft work sessions for *Outer Dark,* it is possible to trace the evolution of his thinking about the novel—his embarking on new directions—especially when he rearranged leaves within "Rough/First Draft [A]" or moved them to other draft folders.

A passage of first-draft material composed on May 5, [1963] and saved among the unused leaves in the second draft, "Early Draft [B]," seems especially likely to have been generated out of McCarthy's melancholy over his failed relationship with Lee. Culla encounters a man who has abandoned his family and who speaks with bitterness about his home life. The man explains that he has a wife and five children in the next county whom he has not seen for years. Interested in this parallel to his own situation, Culla presses him to explain why he left, and the man says, "I caint hardly say. Mostly just sick and tired of em. Tired of it all." The man confesses that he remarried, but he abandoned his second wife as well, having decided that when a man marries, he goes "out of his way to screw himself." Culla vaguely agrees that this may be true, but he asks if the man does not miss his children, a question derived from

Culla's barely acknowledged sense of loss and one that comments ironically on the bitter deprivation he has inflicted on Rinthy. But the man rejects the idea of a parental bond between a father and his children, partly because a man cannot be certain his offspring are his own and partly because he cannot love his children if he does not love his home. The man declares that his own father wasted no love on him, hinting at the origin of his own inability to love, and he thinks that there is no more "natural love" between a man and his children than between a bull and its calf ("Early Draft [B]," 89/202). The passage ends on this dubious assertion, and McCarthy discarded the scene in his second-draft stage. There are other unhappy marriages in *Outer Dark,* the turnip farmer and the butter-maker who have lost all their children, and the "crone" who rejected her husband; and it may be that McCarthy initially thought of including a more prominent pattern of failed marriages and lost or sacrificed children. But the man who speaks disparagingly of marriage and dismisses the idea of a father's bonding with his child gives voice to this bitterness most directly and in its most extreme form. An intensely private individual, McCarthy may have deleted the scene because it touched too directly on his own disappointments in the final months of his life with Lee. However, in general his revisions also moved away from direct revelations of the inner lives of his characters.

As much as the impulse to write a new novel may have been derived partly from McCarthy's grief for and guilt over his son, its content was also influenced by his living near Sevierville in the Great Smoky Mountains and by his thinking about certain stereotypes of Appalachian culture: incest and feuding. Of the two, he explored incest most centrally and for its tragic aspects rather than to contribute to the clichéd popular view of the mountain South. The dating of his work on various scenes reveals that as he began composing, he had not yet settled on the novel's structure except that it would begin in Culla and Rinthy's shared cabin and establish the central problem of the birth of the baby who is palpable evidence of Culla's sins of rape and incest. As in the published novel, the first-draft scenes follow the siblings' separate paths in alternation. In addition, given the resentments, alienation, and plain meanness of many of its secondary characters, especially those Culla encounters, it seems that from the beginning McCarthy was working with the idea of an appalling Appalachia as a kind of Dantean or Yeatsian purgatory for its various characters. However, the scourging triune and Culla's terrifying dream of the eclipse did not emerge until McCarthy had written about half of the first draft.

McCarthy composed material as it came to him or as he felt interested in working on a scene, and he numbered his pages in order of their composition. Later he renumbered as he arranged and completed the scenes. His initial pagination confirms that on May 16, 1963, he had composed typescript pages 100 and 101, as he informed Bensky in a letter of that day ("Rough/First

Draft [A]). But between then and June 23, when he was busy revising *The Orchard Keeper*, McCarthy drafted only a dozen more pages of *Outer Dark*, some that remain in the "Rough/ First Draft" and some which survive only in the typescript of photocopied leaves labeled "Early Draft [B]." In late June 1963, McCarthy turned back to *Outer Dark*. Lee moved out in July, and by July 29 McCarthy estimated that he was about half done with the first draft, with about 32,000 words written ("Rough/ First Draft [A]" 121/116). On September 16, with 158 pages composed, he noted that he had been at work on the novel for nine months and projected "3 mos to go, 72 pp = 230" ("Rough/ First Draft [A]" 158/162). Thus he planned to finish the draft before Christmas 1963, for a short novel of about 230 typescript pages. That would require him to increase his pace to about twenty-four pages per month as opposed to the sixteen he had averaged so far. With *The Orchard Keeper* revised and resubmitted, his goal probably seemed achievable, but further delays arose when Erskine requested yet more revisions to the first novel, as detailed in Part One.

McCarthy's apparently moving in with Gary Goodman in Asheville after the first of the year no doubt caused Erskine to wonder about his marriage; however, McCarthy did not mention that he and Lee had parted, perhaps because it was still too personal and sensitive an issue, but likely too because the editorial demands had introduced insurmountable stress into their already frail relationship. As late as August 13, 1964, a year after Lee had moved to Wyoming,[3] Erskine was unaware that they had separated; with the galleys of the first novel printed but its title still undecided, the editor sent McCarthy a list of title suggestions and urged him to "Tell me what you think; ask your wife." Indeed, none of McCarthy's letters to Erskine mentions his separation from Lee although he refers several times, if laconically, to his courtship of Anne De Lisle in Europe. It may be that Erskine's allusion to Lee in the August 13 letter and later to their marriage in his draft of the author's biography for *The Orchard Keeper* prompted McCarthy finally to reveal their separation in a phone conversation ("About the Author" draft). There is a hint that Erskine was aware of his circumstances at least by fall 1964, when McCarthy was in transit to New Orleans with little certainty about where he would stay (McCarthy, Letter to Albert Erskine, Oct. 15, 1964). On October 20, Erskine wrote him at the Asheville address, with the directive "please forward." In this letter he quipped, "You will have to get an address pretty soon, because it will be too cold in the park."

McCarthy's 1966 list of his recent Thanksgivings suggests the loneliness he had experienced as he continued to draft *Outer Dark* in the years immediately following his separation from Lee and Cullen. He could not remember where or with whom he had dined on Thanksgiving in 1963, when he was living alone in Walden Creek. Likely there had been no shared festivities even with his birth family in nearby Vestal. The next year he ate at a Walgreen's Drugstore on Thanksgiving, possibly in Knoxville but more likely in New Orleans (see note 11 below), and it seems that his separation from family was especially disturbing on holidays (*OD* "Early Draft [A]" 126). One thinks of the poignancy and frequency with which McCarthy writes of young men who find themselves far from home on days traditionally celebrated with family—John Grady Cole, Billy Parham, and particularly the lonely and alienated Suttree, who eats a solitary Thanksgiving meal at Walgreen's in Knoxville (*S* 171–73). Nevertheless, on that Thanksgiving Day of 1964, nearly two years after the genesis of *Outer Dark* and his breach with Lee, McCarthy noted on a page of his first draft: "$7.97 in poke/ prospects dim/ writing = happy" ("Rough/ First Draft [B]" 198/26/191).

The date and pagination reveal he was then returning to the novel, having made no progress on it since April, when he wrote Erskine that he had composed about 200 pages, or indeed since beginning his second-round revisions of *The Orchard Keeper* in January 1963. At the bottom of that leaf he also wrote in holograph: "On Camus/ –Because the highest aspirations of man are spiritual & therefore it demeans him to say that his highest purpose is simply to eliminate pain" ("Rough/ First Draft [B]" 198/26/191). If this line is borrowed from Camus, neither Michael Crews (*Books Are Made out of Books* 28) nor I have been able to identify it. Neither is it a direct quotation from Faulkner's essay "Albert Camus," which had appeared in *Transatlantic Review* in Spring 1961, although the idea is compatible with Faulkner's thoughts on existentialist Camus's rejection of suicide, on his spirit that constantly searches and demands of itself (Faulkner, *Essays, Speeches and Public Letters* 113–14). I am inclined to agree with Crews that here McCarthy inscribed his own idea formulated through reading Camus and perhaps Faulkner's essay as well (Crews, *Books Are Made out of Books*). Decades later, McCarthy's defeated Billy Parham would express the sentiment McCarthy finds demeaning, telling John Grady, "When you're a kid you have these notions about how things are goin to be. . . . You get a little older and you pull back some on that. I think you wind up just tryin to minimize the pain" (McCarthy, *Cities of the Plain* 78). And the suicidal Professor White confesses that his life is nothing but the attempt to minimize pain (McCarthy, *The Sunset Limited* 123). So while it is possible that when McCarthy inscribed his note about Camus, he was thinking of its relevance to the themes of *Outer Dark,* it is also possible that this holiday notation was more personal, arising from his grief, loneliness, and his pursuing higher aspirations and hence finding consolation and purpose through his writing. It suggests that his embrace of the writing vocation above all else was a considered choice from early in his career, one that he reaffirmed many times over.

The December 16, 1962, date for the genesis of *Outer Dark* places it not only around the most likely time for his break with Lee but also during the time when he was doing his most intensive thinking about Bensky's long initial critique of *The Orchard Keeper*. One by-product of McCarthy's efforts to defend, explain, and clarify his first novel was his evolving conception of some of the strategies and features of his second. Bensky had objected to the interspersed but initially asynchronous movements of Sylder and Rattner in the opening of *The Orchard Keeper* and the way this structure invited readers to conflate the two. Now McCarthy conceived a new novel prominently structured around two characters' parallel journeys traced in alternating sections. But this time they would be the estranged parents of an abandoned infant. As with Sylder and Ownby, McCarthy would raise expectations for Culla and Rinthy's convergence, as well as for Rinthy's reunion with her baby, but defer them indefinitely. However, unlike with Rattner and Sylder, the interspersing of the siblings' respective scenes in *Outer Dark* would pose no potential for confusion not only because he could refer to them with different gender pronouns, but also because he usually named them. Culla speaks Rinthy's name for the first time on page 10 of the first draft, in the birth scene. Although Culla begins as "the man" on page one, on page 5 Rinthy calls him by name ("Rough/First Draft [A]"). Indeed, Culla's name became a recurring motif in the novel, with various characters asking it and reacting to it. It seems McCarthy was again pointedly overresponding to his editors' requiring names. Furthermore, as Jay Ellis suggests, Culla's name, emphasized throughout the novel, may have resonated for McCarthy with that of his son Cullen, becoming a private mantra of grief (Ellis, *No Place for Home* 123). However, although McCarthy acceded to his editors' recommendation by naming *Outer Dark*'s primary characters, the novel would also include more unnamed characters than *The Orchard Keeper* had, figures identified only by their roles in the narrative or simply their occupations, consistent with their status as strangers to Culla and Rinthy.

Initially as McCarthy drafted *Outer Dark,* he situated and coordinated the characters' movements in time, heading off editorial objections. For example, to establish the pattern of near-misses in which Culla and Rinthy's paths cross, he jotted a reminder at the bottom of a first-draft page about Rinthy in the woods: "[Culla] takes the same route, talks to the man, walks all night" ("Rough/ First Draft [A]" 109). Two pages later, McCarthy drafted a passage describing Culla's approach to the snake hunter's cabin that makes the overlapping of the siblings' movements explicit: "It was three weeks since she had followed [the same] road if he could have known it and now he too came from the last of the kept land and into the sunless woods" ("Rough/ First Draft [A]" 111/108). McCarthy made this subtler in subsequent drafts, where the time reference is omitted and the detail that each passes the last of the "cleared" or "kept" land is all that implies Culla follows in Rinthy's footsteps ("Early Draft [A]" 122; "Middle Draft" 109, 119; *OD* 108, 117). Yet in the second-draft stage, McCarthy was still working to establish a clear timeline, at least in his own mind. In the margin of the scene in which the turnip farmer pressures Clark to remove the hanged men from his property, McCarthy jotted notes that work out the chronology for several scenes: Rinthy's conversation with the old woman who kills snakes with a hoe, Culla's arrival in Wells Station, the turnip farmer's ruining his wife's butter, Salter's death, and another murder, probably Clark's ("Early Draft [A]" 143).

Traces of these calculations remain in the published novel, but in general as he revised further, McCarthy relaxed his efforts to maintain strict chronology. In the novel as published, Culla and Rinthy's travels are more truly asynchronous and less frequently fixed in time than are the movements of *The Orchard Keeper*'s characters. For example, the horse who careens off the ferry (*OD* 166) seems to be the crazed creature Rinthy has heard pounding over a bridge seventy pages earlier (*OD* 97)—a notable time disruption. In the first draft McCarthy had already composed several versions of the early scene in which Rinthy hears the horse, and a marginal note in the next draft reveals that when he conceived the horse in the ferry disaster, he thought of them as the same creature: "The riderless horse passes Rinthy later" ("Early Draft [A]" 172). But rather than shifting the scene of Rinthy and the horse to a point after the ferry episode, he loosened his chronology in favor of amorphous dreamtime. In the published novel, Rinthy encounters the horse twice: in its original position before she meets the gardening grandmother (97) and again when she leaves the farmer she has lived with (212). The repetition suggests that for Rinthy the loose horse's function is symbolic, an eruption of her brother's chaotic influence, his uncurbed passions, into her serene sphere or, alternatively, her own emotional upheaval in scenes where the absence of her baby drives her to leave those who might offer her work and/or shelter. Erskine challenged McCarthy about only one chronological disruption when he read the editorial copy of *Outer Dark*; indeed, he had acknowledged when editing *The Orchard Keeper* that maintaining a strict timeline was not necessary in every novel (Erskine, Letter to Cormac McCarthy, Nov. 14, 1963).

# Culla's
# Monologues

**A**mong the most revealing passages in the first draft are those in which McCarthy explored Culla's motives and haunted inner life more explicitly than in the published novel. Richard Pearce, director of *The Gardener's Son,* writes that one characteristic of McCarthy's third novel, *Child of God,* that had attracted him was that "By never presuming an author's license to enter the mind of his protagonist, McCarthy had been able to insure the almost complete inscrutability of his subject matter, while at the same time thoroughly investigating it" ("Foreword" v). This "Negative Capability" is also evident in *Outer Dark* as published, but it was a method to which McCarthy worked his way in successive drafts. Perhaps when he wrote the first draft, he was anticipating the kind of editorial queries about character motivation that *The Orchard Keeper* had elicited, or perhaps at this drafting stage he was simply defining Culla's character for himself, even exorcizing some of his own demons through him. Early in the process, McCarthy invented circumstances in which Culla vocalizes his emotions. When he abandons his newborn son in the woods, he expresses through word and gesture his shame, guilt, and will to self-punish when he tells the baby that it is not being abandoned in punishment for its incestuous birth: "It's jest that I caint be your daddy. We'd be double kin." Culla emits a single sob, curses himself, and walks away "with the jerky aimlessnes[s] of a blind animal." He stumbles on, "making no effort . . . to fend or clear his way" ("Rough/ First Draft [A]" 14).[4]

Later in the same scene, McCarthy narrated Culla's inner experience omnisciently, establishing his guilty flight from his repudiated son as a template for his habitual state of mind and spirit. Disoriented in the woods, Culla hears without surprise the baby's wail coming from behind him in "corroboration of what he had expected to hear all his life and dreaded." Then McCarthy reinforced Culla's anguish at his transgression through objectively narrated gesture before resuming the exposition of his inner life. Culla does not change pace or direction but "screamed, once, loud and piercing." When he reaches the cabin where Rinthy sleeps, he pauses briefly before moving "toward the bed, not wanting to sleep next to her but not having any choice and too tired to forego sleep" ("Rough/ First Draft [A]" 16). The two passages of omniscient commentary directly communicate Culla's sense of the fatedness of his sin, his recognition of his evil impulses and his lack of will to combat them.

Yet another strategy that McCarthy employed in his first draft—if sparingly—was direct reportage of the impression Culla makes on the narrator or other characters. On November 19, [1963], he composed a scene in which Culla cradles wheat with a scythe and which is fraught with Culla's potential for violence, a scene that anticipates the triune's murder of the squire, which McCarthy would compose later. As Culla labors, he hears the panicky squeaking of fleeing field mice. When he finishes, he falls asleep in the field until the man who has hired him wakes him for breakfast. Culla starts toward the house, then returns to pick up the scythe. As he runs to catch up to his employer, he balances it on his shoulder so that he appears to be "overtaking him with foul intent." At breakfast, when the man remarks that Culla is "a good hand with a cradle," inadvertently reminding Culla of the baby, he sees Culla's "eyes go to points until they were so nearly all blue as a blind man's. He saw his jaw muscles jump and then something happened else and then he was all right" ("Early Draft [B]" 194/187). These four narrative strategies for exploring a character's psyche—vocalization, omniscient narration, gesture, and characters' impressions of one another—had been interspersed judiciously in *The Orchard Keeper* and would be deployed liberally in *Suttree,* but in drafting *Outer Dark* McCarthy progressively pared down and finally eliminated direct access to Culla's inner life, creating space for the reader to experience the mystery of his torment and to infer its sources.

Eight months after drafting the scene in which Culla speaks to his ill-fated baby, McCarthy composed the first of several passages in which Culla hides from his pursuers in a hollow live oak tree he has climbed, trapped there when the rotted wood gives way under him, trapped in his guilt and violence. In this captivity, he considers the nature of God and speaks to Him—sometimes in despair, sometimes in anger. Evidence of McCarthy's prior planning for Culla's rebellion against God appears in a holograph note on a leaf saved in "Early Draft [B]," a document comprised of photocopied, dated pages from the first draft that McCarthy deleted or superseded as he wrote the second draft. The typed portion of the leaf describes a rainy night on which Culla addresses the moon reflected in the waters of the creek: "You go ahead and watch. Aint nothin here for you to see." At the top of the leaf, McCarthy inscribed "But first/ He should utter a threat of defiance—hence his freedom" (99). Although it is undated, the pagination of this leaf suggests that it is first-draft material composed some thirty pages before the scenes of Culla's captivity in the tree, where his defiance of God, personified in the moon, is apparent. In one of these scenes, on his third night in the tree, a dehydrated and delirious Culla utters his rebellious prayer to the moon and mouths his tongue "like a piece of indigestible meat." If the moon were "your eye you couldnt see me better," he admits to God. But he refuses to acknowledge his guilt, to deny it, or to abase himself. Echoing Camus and the ancient gnostics, he asserts that the God of guilt is alien to him: "Whatever part of me you get hold of is a stranger to me so I'll not concern myself with it." Still, once the lunar eye of God goes down, Culla feels relief to be free of its accusing gaze. The passage establishes his resentful sense of religious guilt and his alienation both from the watchful one-eyed God of judgment and from self. A holograph revision on the leaf reinforced these feelings. Culla addresses the tree in which he is captive: "You a tough old tree," but then he wishes it would "blow down" ("Rough/First Draft [A]" 134)—faintly suicidal, but also a wish for liberation from both his captivity and his guilt. Indeed, "Early Draft [B]" includes a scene in which Culla tries to dig out from the tree, one of several from *Outer Dark* that McCarthy discarded and later revisited for *Child of God*—this one for Lester Ballard's captivity in the cave where he has eluded his persecutors (*OD* "Early Draft [B]" 93–99; *CoG* 188–90).

On September 2, McCarthy wrote another of Culla's meditations in the hollow tree, one in which he admits to breaking the laws of God and man but rationalizes his acts, paraphrasing the gnostic idea that the human spirit is trapped by the demiurge in his fleshly body: "If I done sin it's because I'm evilnatured and I caint help that if I am" ("Rough/ First Draft [A]" 146). These lines reinforce Culla's agony over his acts and give him an explicitly Christian consciousness of sin that is nowhere apparent in the published novel, while also exploring his gnostic resentment of the Christian and legal prohibitions he has violated, his sense of being trapped between his guilt over incest and his guilt over leaving the child to die. Significantly for the evolution of McCarthy's strategies to reveal Culla's interior life, this meditation also introduces the biblical idea that the sins of the father are visited on the child: "It would of been cursed on account of the sins . . . is visited," he thinks. "So maybe I spared that, the visitin" ("Rough/ First Draft [A]" 146). McCarthy considered reinforcing this King David parallel two pages later through a reference to Uriah, Bathsheba's husband; and biblical references to the sins of the father and to child sacrifice would inform the dialogue, action, and imagery of Culla's two confrontations with the triune. But at some point, McCarthy scribbled "Awful" in large letters across the "visitin" passage, deleting it.

A related passage among the photocopied leaves in "Early Draft [B]" further develops Culla's conception of God. He thinks of the "dim and apocalyptic" God who watches as "a Being dimly remembered out of his youth in a dark and frangible dream," One who monitors his acts "with a sleepless and inappeasable eye." Culla does not view this Deity as omnipotent. "Omniscience was godhead enough. It made the outside inside" (207/196). Such explicit revelations of Culla's despair, resignation, and intermittent defiance were rare even in the first-draft stage, and McCarthy abandoned them in favor of conveying interiority in Culla's dream of the eclipse and through the triune's violent acts and confrontations with Culla. Significantly, however, this passage hints that Culla's argument with the omniscient God who spies on his deeds occurs in a dream. And if the Deity's omniscience makes "the outside inside"—creates inner consciousness of sin by inducing Culla to view his acts from the judging Deity's point of view—then the passage anticipates the triune, who are outside Culla yet inside him, who are interior impulses projected like Macbeth's witches/wishes into the world around him.

In November [1963], just after he composed the leaf on which Culla scythes wheat and his violent urges are conveyed through the impressions of the narrator and Culla's employer, McCarthy drafted Culla's final approach to the triune, when he feels indifferent to his fate because "he was no longer a man but a point moving . . . over the mapless surfaces of the earth with neither destination nor will" ("Rough/ First Draft [B]" 195/188). Again McCarthy rejected this direct reporting of Culla's feelings, writing "Terrible" in the margin. Then at the top of inserted page 195A, one of several drafts of the scene in which the triune kill Culla's son, McCarthy reminded himself that for the novel to work "the <u>events</u> must assume the shape of a character & . . . become . . . mere manifestations of the . . . coherent, logical, and immutable <u>deformation</u> of evolving fate" ("Rough/ First Draft [B]"). This affirmation about his handling of character and his tragic plot—this movement away from overt psychological delving and toward representation of character through action, making the inside outside, emerged almost a year into his drafting of *Outer Dark*.[5] He had largely followed this practice in *The Orchard Keeper,* but here he articulated it as an artistic principle. In late February 1980, he would write to Robert Coles and paraphrase the argument of Spanish philosopher José Ortega y Gasset in "Notes on the Novel" that a "first class novel could commit its characters to a completely different series of episodes and make an equally successful book" (2). McCarthy thought this was the case even though Ortega y Gasset "ignore[s] the paradox that to a large extent the characters in a novel are created and defined out of what they do and say"—a comment that reflects his own practice of presenting his characters through dramatic or objective point of view, rarely entering their inner lives except in their dreams. If in *Outer Dark* he had initially tried out reporting Culla's motivations in hopes of satisfying his editors, he now trusted his own instincts for indirection, for a Shakespearean "strategic opacity" that would foreground the enigma of human behavior (Greenblatt, *Will in the World* 324). But McCarthy's conception of the triune and his composition of Culla's dream of the eclipse in September 1963 had already been crucial moves in that direction.

# Sins of
# the Father
## The Triune Surfaces

The mysterious triune, whose path intersects Culla's in a violent eruption of his inner corruption, owes much to McCarthy's early and revised conceptions of Kenneth Rattner, the symbolic character who functions obliquely as Sylder's alter ego, a violent persona that the young whiskey runner expunges from Red Branch, from John Wesley's life, and from his own psyche. In *Outer Dark,* the triune are more consistently if subtly identified with Culla's psyche as embodied projections of his murderous and self-punishing impulses, evidence of his blindness to his own motivations and deeds. Despite their similar roles, Rattner is a more realistically drawn character than the triune.

It seems likely that McCarthy's reluctant naming of Rattner for Bensky and the compensatory revision of the porch scene to introduce his shadowy double in the early months of 1963 influenced the genesis of the triune for his new novel in the months that followed. On July 22, [1963], he drafted a version of the snake hunter scene that anticipates and glosses Culla's conversations with the triune and shows that their inception derived from McCarthy's thinking about ways to externalize Culla's inner voices. In this unused passage, the snake hunter muses that the solitary life does not make one lonely because "you aint jest one person." A man who lives alone starts talking to himself, but this is not a sign of craziness, he thinks. Both the speaker and the listener are the self. "And then a third somethin likely as not will butt in with his own opinion" ("Early Draft [B]" 113/110; cf. *OD* 119). Thus the idea of three voices or selves in one emerged quite early in McCarthy's drafting. At this stage, it seems he had in mind Freud's concept of the tripartite human psyche. But a page dated Thursday, June 12, [1964], after he had conceived the triune, begins with an isolated and unused passage that reveals more of McCarthy's multifaceted thinking: his linking the three aspects of human psychology with the three-in-one God: "He speaks to me of the Trinity of the Godhead but how am I to be astonished who find in myself the selfsame triune, the three persons neither sacred nor profane but simply warring" ("Rough/First Draft [A]" 297/213). Although such passages indicate that McCarthy primarily conceived of the externalized figures of Culla's psyche as male, he also briefly considered that they might "need a female quadrator—a mother?" which he noted in the margin of a half-sheet of notes and isolated passages, clearly after he had invented the triune ("Early Draft [B]" 207/196). However, no draft of a scene with a female fourth aspect exists in his typescripts, and he seems to have recognized that such an addition would have diminished the psychological and religious resonances of three.

Although the triune are vitally important to the structure, action, and effect of *Outer Dark* as published, they did not surface as physical presences until McCarthy drafted the campfire scene by the river in September 1963,[6] and it may have been around this time that McCarthy went back to the scene in front of Clark's store that he had composed in April and jotted an important statement of their role: "THEME: The triune <(tribunal?)> Kill all that Holme wants to kill—ending w/ child. ?" ("Rough/ First Draft [A]" 73). The two words he debated to designate them collectively reflect their essences as a consubstantial three-in-one trinity (Father/Son/Holy Ghost; Superego/Ego/Id) and as those who sit in judgment on Culla's acts and desires, like the deity or the conscience. His choice of *triune* over *tribunal* left their symbolic implications more widely resonant and flexible. Their accusatory, judgmental role would become evident in their interactions with Culla.

It seems that when he drafted the rainy night-time convergence of Culla and the three at their campfire in the dark woods, McCarthy also had in mind Macbeth's similar meeting in "A desert place" (1.1.1) or on "A heath near Forres" (1.3.1) with the three weird sisters who tempt him to his doom, stirring his ambition and his murderous impulses. In Shakespeare's witches, McCarthy found a model of eerie characters who could walk the stage but who functioned also as outward manifestations of the protagonist's corruption and madness. His adapting the psychology of *Macbeth* influenced the newly evolving structure of *Outer Dark* most markedly in the introduction of the two confrontations between Culla and his projected selves and in the sequence of ambiguous murders committed by Culla/ the triune. But while Macbeth's tormented conscience is externalized in his guilt-induced dreams rather than through the witches' accusations, Culla's alter egos represent both his profound guilt and self-punishment and his evil intentions and acts. Consistent with the ideas of Jacobean England and with James I's obsession with witches, Shakespeare invites the interpretation of the weird sisters as literal demons who brew a "hell-broth" and intend to tempt Macbeth to evil (4.1.19), while also suggesting his protagonist's ready susceptibility to their temptations and the possibility that they are phantasms of his diseased soul, ambiguities Shakespeare explores in the ghost of Hamlet's father as well. Indeed, Banquo, wiser than Macbeth, asks the witches, "Are ye fantastical, or that indeed/ Which outwardly ye show?" (1.3.53–54). On the leaf on which Culla challenges God to watch him, McCarthy at some point jotted a statement that captures his conception of the triune as walking evil and adumbrates Holden in *Blood Meridian* and Chiguhr in *No Country for Old Men* as well: "That evil is no longer generally held in belief by the people seems neither to have arrested its prevalence nor tempered it's [*sic*] malignancy" ("Early Draft [B]" 207/196). Yet compared with *Macbeth, Outer Dark*'s ambulatory evil is presented less literally as demons, more symbolically and psychologically as outer manifestations of Culla's sick soul and inner torment.

Shakespeare and McCarthy's protagonists differ in motivations for their evil acts as well: while Macbeth is driven primarily by his ambition for power and the desire to prove his manliness to his wife and to himself, the more craven Culla is governed by sexual desire, envy, resentment, shame, and fear. The displacement of Macbeth's temptation into the witches' prophecies allows him intermittently and imperfectly to repress acknowledgment of his evil: "Let not light see my black and deep desires:/ The eye wink at the hand; yet let that be,/ Which the eye fears, when it is done, to see" (1.4.51–53). Macbeth foresees quite clearly that his conscience will inflict self-punishment, and he wishes to be unconscious of his deeds: "To know my deed, 'twere best not know myself" (2.2.73–74). But with the goading of Lady Macbeth, he acts repeatedly to promote his ruthless advancement in power and fails to achieve that comforting repression. As Monteith says of him, "all that is within him does condemn/ Itself for being there" (5.2.24–25). Since Culla's awareness of his guilt is externalized in the triune, his self-blindedness is more pervasive than Macbeth's, and his rejoinders to the triune's accusations are usually stubborn denials. Indeed, in the novel as published, Culla's acts are predominantly evasions of self-knowledge, culminating with his dim wonderment at the physically blind man who serenely and securely travels a road which for Culla leads to a desolate swamp. Yet the triune's accusations are manifestations of Culla's troubling inner awareness, which he struggles to repress.

Like Rattner in the early pages of *The Orchard Keeper* as McCarthy first submitted it, two of the symbolic triune's figures are unnamed, identified through their attributes alone: the bearded leader, the mute. But early in his composition of the triune's sections, possibly recalling how much Bensky disliked unidentified characters, McCarthy briefly considered providing the mute a name. On his draft of Culla's first encounter with the triune, he jotted the notation: "Uriah, Harmon, & the <u>Beehiver</u>?" ("Rough/First Draft [A]" 148/ 153/ 152),[7] and on a later page in the same scene, he penciled "Uriah 'the <u>Hittite</u>'" ("Rough/ First Draft [A]"156/161). The Uriah notes refer to Bathsheba's husband, whom King David cuckolded and sent to his death in battle to hide his sexual guilt (2 Samuel 11–12). Reminding the reader of David's transgressions, the name Uriah would have evoked an inexact biblical parallel not only to Culla's sexual

sin but also to his desire to murder the baby to conceal it. The wrongfully conceived son of David and Bathsheba died for the sins of his father, as foretold by
the prophet Nathan when he rebuked the wealthy king David for taking Uriah's "one sheep" (2 Samuel 12.14). McCarthy had already introduced the trope
of the sins of the father in one of Culla's meditations inside the hollow tree,
and as he composed two versions of the first campfire scene on September 12,
[1963], invoking the names of both David and Uriah, this motif was a primary
emphasis.

The name Uriah in *Outer Dark*'s draft is the second literary reference to the
sins of King David that McCarthy considered deploying in his first two novels
but rejected before publication. As discussed in Part One, the tentative title for
McCarthy's first novel, "Toilers at the Kiln," refers to David's political tyranny,
while "Uriah" refers indirectly to David's sexual offenses. Clearly McCarthy
had been thinking about the ruthlessness of the Hebrew singer king favored
by God, and we might speculate that in summer 1963 he had been reading or
rereading both 2 Samuel and William Faulkner's reworking of David's story in
*Absalom, Absalom!* (1936). Faulkner described his novel as the story of a man
who wanted a son but got too many so that they ended up destroying one another and thus his own hopes to found a dynasty (Gwynn and Blotner, *Faulkner in the University* 35, 71, 73, 76); and *Absalom* revisits the fratricide between
David's grown sons, which further fulfilled the terrible fate that his children
would suffer for his sins. David's son Amnon raped his half-sister Tamar (2
Samuel 13.14–15), and her brother Absalom killed Amnon in turn (2 Samuel
13.28–29), acts of incest and revenge Faulkner reimagines in Judith Sutpen's
engagement to her unacknowledged half-brother Charles Bon and her brother
Henry's killing Bon to prevent the marriage. However, *Outer Dark* seems little
indebted to Faulkner's novel in its quite different deployment of the Davidic
themes of sexual sin, incest, and suffering children. McCarthy does not make
the sinner's son an adult actor in his novel but keeps him in the role of the
child victim. And while Faulkner's David-figure, Thomas Sutpen, appears little
troubled by his sins, Culla is "Tore up with guilt" (*OD* 222). To the extent that
*Outer Dark* is McCarthy's answer to *Absalom, Absalom!,* this profound sense
of repressed guilt for sinning against one's children is the primary focus of his
departure from Faulkner.

Although he considered it, McCarthy never applied the name Uriah to the
mute. Instead, the bearded leader declines to name him yet lectures Culla on
his refusal to name or claim his own child.[8] McCarthy would have recognized
that as son figures the mute and Culla's baby are closer analogues to David and
Bathsheba's child, fated to an early death, than to the wronged husband Uriah.
Further, although Culla's sexual assault of Rinthy is analogous to the powerful
king David's taking of Bathsheba, the fact that Rinthy is Culla's sister makes

him a closer parallel to the rapist Amnon. The intersecting references to the sins of the father remain suggestive, however. It seems plausible that McCarthy's meditation on David during summer 1963 speaks to a deep concern with guilt and forgiveness that may have been rooted in his personal experiences, not only his inherited complicity with the Tennessee Valley Authority and a sense that he must somehow atone for his father's role in helping the agency seize the property of East Tennesseans by asserting eminent domain, but also his guilt over what his absence would mean for his son. He continued to explore Culla's guilt as parallel to David's, expressing it through the triune's accusations.

The two consecutive versions of the campfire scene at the river, which McCarthy drafted in rapid succession on September 12, do not remain in the first draft, but photocopies appear in the second of the two typescripts labeled "Early Draft." While some of the first-draft leaves included in this "Early Draft [B]" duplicate originals that remain in the first draft, others fill gaps in the first draft's sequence and are the only surviving copies of these discarded passages or scenes. This is the case with the two versions of the campfire scene in which McCarthy tried out material related to David and Uriah ("Early Draft [B]" 153, 154–56).

The first version of the Uriah material begins with the triune's leader asking Culla abruptly whether he thinks "that Uriah forgave David?" On the preceding page he had challenged Culla about his fine boots. But the note connecting Uriah with the mute, the unnamed son figure, suggests that for McCarthy the leader's question also addresses Culla's guilt for the abandoned and later murdered baby. Is there forgiveness for the murderer, for the father who abandons his child? The leader claims that after death Uriah, the victim, would not forgive David because "mortal mind . . . seethes with vindication." He argues that the murderer "usurps the power of God," so he wonders, "how [c]ould Uriah usurp the prerogative of forgiveness when no God . . . forgives." The leader's questions extend Culla's own dread of a watchful and vengeful God expressed as he hides in the hollow tree, but in rhetoric more consistent with that of the sinister preachers and false prophets that eventually came to people the book. Through a strange association of ideas, the leader concludes that because Uriah like God could not forgive, Uriah was saved "because his heart was foul with loathing for . . . David" ("Early Draft [B]" 153/158). Then he demands the boots Culla has stolen from the squire, a demand that hints at the conflicts Culla himself feels between his desires and his guilt and between his self-punishment and his desire paradoxically to be saved through his recognition and judgment of his misdeeds.

McCarthy added another reference to Uriah, partly typed above the line and partly hand-written in the margin, to emphasize the leader's vengeance and his embodiment of Culla's guilt: "Uriah, that's my name, and every man that has something I want . . . is David to me & I'm sick with revenge it eats on me inside." Here McCarthy still associates the wronged Uriah with the triune, but now he identifies not the mute but the accusing leader with the biblical man who was robbed of his only sheep, Bathsheba, taken by David who had so much. His words express not only Culla's resentment for his poverty but also Culla's self-judgment. It seems McCarthy considered having Culla counterargue the leader's Old Testament vengeance, since lower on the page he typed three New Testament lines that suggest God's care: "He provideth for the birds of the air [Matthew 6:26–27]./ What you do for the least of these you do for me [Matthew 25:40]./ He was a stranger and I took him in [Matthew 25:35]" ("Early Draft [B]"153/158). But McCarthy developed concepts of divine providence and Christian charity neither on this page nor on those that followed except in Culla's meek suggestion that Uriah might have forgiven David ("Early Draft [B]"154/159).

The first, one-page draft of the Uriah material demonstrates McCarthy's early exploration of the triune as Culla's adversaries yet also as manifestations of his inner houndedness, his inability to forgive himself even as he persistently denies his sin. But with its shifting associations of Uriah with the baby, the squire (whose murder and stolen boots had yet to be committed to paper), and the bearded leader, this version was puzzling even as it experimented with a new method of projecting Culla's guilt. Moreover, it assumed both the reader's and Culla's familiarity with the biblical story. In the next version ("Early Draft [B]" 154–56), also drafted on September 12, the leader introduces himself as Uriah Westray (the surname suggestive of human sinfulness—we-stray—that McCarthy would decades later assign to an American drug dealer in *The Counselor*). After Culla introduces himself in turn, the leader says he thought his name might be David, and then he recounts the story of David and Uriah ("Early Draft [B]" 154/159). He relates that as king, David had everything—sheep, women, and fancy boots—again alluding to Culla's sins. But this version makes it clearer that the leader demands the boots both as an expression of his alter ego Culla's own lust for what he does not have, and as Culla's self-punishment. In the first version of the scene, Culla eats the triune's meat and wonders what kind it is, but in this version McCarthy more clearly identifies the intractable meat with Culla's guilt. As he agrees with the leader about the sins of David, he chokes down the meat, which sits "weighty and tru[cu]lent in the pit of his stomach" ("Early Draft [B]" 154/159). Thus the passage develops further the implication of the scene in the live oak composed three weeks earlier, in which Culla mouths his tongue "like a piece of indigestible meat" while he contemplates God's judgment. In the early drafts of the second confrontation between Culla and the triune, McCarthy would identify the meat retrospectively as the slain child's body, cannibalized not only by the triune but also, unknowingly, by Culla.

The leader continues relating the story, and as in the first version he asks, "What do you think now, a good man like Uriah was. Did he forgive David for doin him that way?" ("Early Draft [B]" 154/159). However, here the leader does not comment on God's vengefulness. Instead he shifts his attention to Culla's boots, and the scene builds in suspense as it leads to the coerced trade. As the leader persists in prodding Culla's sense of guilt, Culla struggles with the unyielding meat in his mouth until he surreptitiously throws the last piece into the weeds. When the leader urges him to take more, Culla replies, "I've got about all I can hold" ("Early Draft [B]" 155/160). The surfeit of guilt leads directly into Culla's surrendering the boots in response to the leader's simple challenge, "Well?" ("Early Draft [B]" 156/161).

This second version evolves closer to the expanded scene that appears in the published novel, but the boots are not yet traded round-robin among the three. The triune take Culla's boat (which does not appear in the published version), and in the morning Culla walks away barefoot, an image McCarthy later used only in the trespassing scene (*OD* 198). As he subsequently completed the A version of the "Early Draft," McCarthy eliminated the David and Uriah material, allowing the leader's subtle accusations to prick Culla's sense of guilt for the ferryman's death as well as the squire's, his desire for the horse as well as the boots, guilt which is expressed again in his hopeless chewing on the nameless mass, which "tasted of sulphur" and is so hard to swallow ("Early Draft [A]" 179; *OD* 172).

McCarthy had conceived the Uriah material as a strategy for projecting Culla's guilt and reinforcing the important theme of the sins of the father in his confrontations with the triune. But this method of externalizing Culla's inner turmoil, voicing his self-judgments through the leader's lectures on David and Uriah, did not satisfy McCarthy's growing preference for implication. He continued to work with the triune as manifestations of Culla's psyche, and he briefly considered their referring as well to Abraham's intended sacrifice of Isaac. McCarthy would draw parallels to biblical child sacrifice through his imagery of the child's murder, and the theme remains implicit throughout the novel, yet in its published version there is little to suggest that the characters themselves are inheritors of the Christian religion.

# The Ferry Scene and Culla's Psychotic Break

**M**cCarthy's invention of the triune influenced his sequential revisions of the ferry scene, through which he transformed it from a realistic incident of East Tennessee life into an episode of Culla's profound psychological trauma. In the earliest draft of the scene, composed in late August [1963], before McCarthy drafted Culla's first meeting with the triune, the ferryman and his passengers safely reach the other side of the river, where Culla and the ferryman help the rider steady the horse up the steep and muddy bank. As in the published novel, a horseman hails the ferry, watches until it has crossed more than halfway to him, and then rides away. This places the ferryman together with Culla on the bank so that they can talk while waiting for another horse and rider. The ferryman tells Culla that the deceptive horseman and his brother both make a habit of inconveniencing him this way because they blame him for a third brother's arrest. The ferryman had been transporting the fugitive brother across the river when his pursuers started shooting, demanding that they turn back. The wanted man held a pistol on the ferryman and insisted that he continue across. But when the fugitive received a shot to the head, the ferryman believed he was dead, reversed the ferry, and delivered him to his pursuers. The man lived to be imprisoned. The ferryman says that the horsemen "think I was supposed to get shot on account of their brother" ("Rough/First Draft [A]" 138/143).

The ferryman's story contributed to the narratives of vengeance that characterize many of the people Culla and Rinthy encounter, the realm of hostility through which the siblings travel. Other scenes in this pattern include the snake hunter's implying that he killed the mink hunter because that man poisoned his dogs (*OD* 120), the old woman's implying that she ran off her husband (*OD* 110), and the fight between the farmer and the butter-maker, whose grief for their dead children has congealed into bitterness and abuse toward one another (*OD* 107–108). In addition, the illogic of the brothers' blaming the ferryman in the first draft of the scene is matched by the ferryman's own illogic in insisting that he cannot afford to make a crossing until a horse and rider come along, potentially condemning Culla and himself to days of waiting by the river although operating his current-driven ferry costs nothing but his time ("Rough/First Draft [A]" 138/143). Such absurdity recurs in other episodes involving Culla, such as his trial for trespassing (*OD* 200–208; see Luce, *Reading the World* 127–30) and the drovers' blaming him for the death of their brother by hog stampede (*OD* 220ff). Thus, initially the primary function of the ferry scene was to contribute to the pattern of blame, vengeance, feuding, scapegoating, and sheer perversity in the secondary characters' dealings with others. But the ferryman's story had been rather confusingly drafted and would have required amplification and clarification before it could be used; instead, when McCarthy revised the ferry scene roughly ten pages after he drafted the first campfire scene, he eliminated the ferryman's story and reduced the motivation for the first horseman's vindictive ruse to "a little argument" ("Early Draft [A]" 164).

When McCarthy first worked on the ferry scene, from August 21 to September 1, 1963, neither Culla nor the triune had yet murdered anyone. But when McCarthy composed the first campfire scene in early September, he had the leader accuse Culla of coveting the horse he had crossed the river with, and this idea led to a series of plot revisions to the ferry scene that culminated with the deaths of the ferryman and the rider in the "Middle Draft," deaths in which Culla and the triune are implicated. In the second draft of the scene, the ferry's cable breaks, manifesting the risk of running in high water that the ferryman has explained to Culla. The ferry drifts in a dark, undifferentiated bowl of water and sky, newly suggesting the sheering away of Culla's psychological grounding that now prepares for his encounter with the triune. Still, the men and the horse survive the crossing ("Early Draft [A]" 170). However, on the following page, McCarthy started anew on the aftermath of the broken cable, and this time Culla sees that the ferryman has vanished. He strokes the horse, perhaps for comfort, perhaps in unacknowledged desire for it, and the rider orders him not to touch it ("Early Draft [A]" 171). As the ferry drifts closer to land, the rider prepares to swim the horse to the bank, and Culla asks if the horse will "haul two." Again, he is rebuffed: "Mister I dont much like your company" (173). The rider's rudeness, possessiveness, and refusing aid are the kind of offenses that eventually lead to the triune's or Culla's committing murder, but the potential for the rider's death did not yet reach fulfillment. In "Early Draft [A]," when the rider swims his horse to the bank, Culla is left alone in a deep fog, spinning away down the river, "no more adept than a blind man . . . praying silently and godless in his heart" until he sees the light from the triune's campfire as if they are the terrifying answer to his impious prayer (174). As he considered the scene further, McCarthy marked as "N/U" (not used) the paragraph about the rider's swimming the horse ashore and leaving Culla behind, and he jotted in the margin, "Both men [the ferryman and the rider] taken. He is alone w/ mad horse" ("Early Draft [A]" 172). In the "Middle Draft" McCarthy incorporated this new concept, with the rider disappearing overboard and the maddened horse charging Culla repeatedly before it too plunges into the river (171–72).

From the second version of the ferry scene onward, McCarthy consistently placed the river crossing just before Culla's first encounter with the triune, as if the river were a psychic Rubicon, a fragile barrier between one mode of consciousness and another. With the deaths or murders of the ferryman and the rider in the "Middle Draft," the episode more strikingly suggests that this is a scene of Culla's psychotic rupture, in which his unacknowledged violence breaks through his restraint. Culla's madness takes external form in the deranged horse, an adaptation of Duncan's wild cannibalistic horses representing the general disorder that follows on Macbeth's murder of the king (*Macbeth* 2.4.14–20), as well as Freud's concept of the id as a horse only intermittently controlled by the ego/rider in *The Ego and the Id* (1923) and Plato's antecedent metaphor of the wayward horse of nonrational appetites in the *Phaedrus*. In the next scene, Culla's madness is manifest in the surfacing of the triune, who embody his malign impulses as the bearded witches do Macbeth's and who come into overt communication with him as his internal voices for the first time.[9]

McCarthy alluded to Culla's madness in a holograph note on an undated page filed with the superseded material in "Rough/First Draft [B]." On this leaf he labeled "Last Page," he drafted the scene of Rinthy in the glade where she sees the corpse of the tinker but does "not know what to make of it." At the bottom of the leaf, McCarthy jotted "Richard Harris/Diary of a Madman," a reference to the Irish actor's one-man performance of the 1835 short story by Nikolai Gogol. Adapted from Gogol by Harris and Lindsay Anderson, the play opened at London's Royal Court Theater on March 7, 1963, and ran for twenty-eight performances. After a rocky opening, it was well received and was reviewed in England in spring 1963, when McCarthy was working on his first draft of *Outer Dark*.

Gogol's story of a clerk in the reign of Tsar Nicholas I is told as the clerk's journal entries, and it gradually reveals his insanity through his increasingly nonsensical perceptions. Like Culla, Poprischin is obsessed with grievances against others, especially those with whom he works in the bureaucracy of the councillors' offices, where he performs such lowly tasks as sharpening the director's pens. He suffers frustrated desires for validation by the nobility and for the love of the director's daughter. When he learns (or imagines) through letters written by her dog that she is engaged to a handsome young aristocrat, his jealousy and resentments devolve into a deeper psychotic break with reality in which he "discovers" that he himself is the king of Spain. Naturally, others do not share his delusion, and he is incarcerated in an asylum, where he is beaten and subjected to water torture (or imagines himself to be). At the end of the story, he calls on his dead mother to "Press the poor orphan to your bosom!

He has no rest in this world; they hunt him from place to place," a line that resonates with Culla's huntedness, with Rinthy's curse on the tinker that he will find no rest because he refuses to return her child, and with the blind man's concern for the man who bears the guilt for the false faith healer's departure: "If somebody don't tell him he never will have no rest" (Gogol, "Memoirs" 140; *OD* 194, 241).

While Gogol's story narrates Poprischin's experiences across time and in various places, the reviewer for the London *Times* noted that Harris's adaptation was set entirely in Poprischin's room, where "he engages with duologues with himself as a substitute for contact with the outer world" ("Solo Actor" 15). The concept of the duologue would have caught McCarthy's attention as he worked his way toward dramatizing his own mad character's inner torment. (Perhaps the idea also informed his later work on *The Sunset Limited,* a play in which two characters locked in Black's tenement room debate competing points of view about life, death, and God.) It is possible that McCarthy knew of Gogol's story only through news and reviews of its theatrical adaptation, but it also seems possible that the account(s) McCarthy saw prompted him to read "Memoirs of a Madman" if he was not already familiar with it.

McCarthy was well into composing his first draft of *Outer Dark* when Harris's production was reviewed in spring 1963, but he had not yet conceived the triune and the extremity of Culla's madness. It seems likely that Gogol's story joined *Macbeth* in McCarthy's thinking that year about how to project Culla's inner life. McCarthy did not care for the kind of first-person verbal expression that Gogol had given Poprischin in diary mode, but in Gogol's unmediated representation of the madman's felt experience, McCarthy found another adaptable model for his treatment of Culla. If Poprischin is revealed through the dog's letters (fantastical projections of his diseased imagination), and Macbeth's inner promptings are manifest in the prophecies of the weird sisters, Culla's could be explored through the chaos of the river, the maddened horse, and the actions of the triune, who would become projections of his psychosis not only in his dialogues with them but also in the world at large.

# Culla's Dreams

**M**cCarthy first thought of giving Culla a nightmare of guilt and retribution at about the same time as he conceived the Uriah and David parallels that he explored in the triune's accusations by the campfire, that is, at about the same time as he decided to adapt Shakespeare's strategies for projecting Macbeth's inner life, in September 1963. It seems likely that McCarthy's growing dissatisfaction with the scenes in which Culla speaks his feelings led him to the subtler strategy of conveying them through dream imagery. The monologue he deemed "awful" appears on page 146 of the first-draft A version. On the verso of page 149, where Culla escapes from the river and approaches the triune's fire, McCarthy jotted three notes that suggest Culla's tenuous hold on reality, his deep denial, and the surfacing of his repressed guilt in his dream-life: "In reality he has abandoned the child/In his mind he remembers <u>handing it</u> to <u>the tinker</u>/Christ dream—eclipse" ("Rough/ First Draft [A]" 149/154). On September 12, McCarthy finished the scene at the campsite with its variations on the theme of David's guilt; then he turned to Culla's nightmare of the eclipse. The passage begins with the line, "That night he had the first of several dreams" ("Rough/ First Draft [A]" 157/2). An unpaginated revision of the dream exists among disconnected fragments in the "Rough/ First Draft [B]" folder. As he worked on the novel's second draft, McCarthy may have been uncertain about whether to use the dream or where to place it, as no version appears in "Early Draft [A]," and a photocopy of the revised first-draft page is filed in "Early Draft [B]" as if it were discarded material. When he created the "Middle Draft," well after he had decided to add scenes of the triune independent of their interactions with Culla and to open the novel with one of these triune passages,[10] McCarthy inserted a third version of the eclipse dream as page 2, where it functions as a second prologue to Culla's story, as in the published novel. By then he had settled on this single nightmare to reveal Culla's desperate sense of guilt and impending punishment, rather than a series of dreams identified as such.

Yet McCarthy's holograph query to himself, "Present tense for all dreams & overtures?" on an undated, unnumbered leaf among the fragments in "Rough/ First Draft [B]," suggests that he thought of all the triune's sections as parallel manifestations of Culla's nightmarish dreamlife. That is, the triune's scenes, which serve as overtures to Culla's, were to be read as his "dreams" or as projections of his terrifying inner life. Casting them in present tense would have highlighted their difference from the action of the novel proper and linked the triune sections with Culla's dreamlife, but by the time McCarthy created "Early Draft [A]," in which the triune are presented as autonomous actors within the world of the novel, he had decided instead to employ past tense for the dream and triune sections and italic type for the triune when they appear to function separately from Culla. This linked them less obviously with Culla's experiences and placed them more firmly in an alternate realm of being until they intrude into Culla's "waking" life later in the novel.

In addition to the three drafts of Culla's eclipse dream, a related dream narrative exists that probably precedes them all. Among the fragments at the end of "Rough/First Draft [B]" appears a remarkable version of the eclipse dream narrated by a persona whose vocabulary is far more literate than Culla's and whose concerns, sophistication, and ability to gloss his own nightmare resemble those of the educated and troubled Suttree or the semi-autobiographical father of *The Road*—indeed of McCarthy himself. It begins, "I did not fully understand the dream then. But . . . in not understanding it I came gradually to understand . . . at least my inability to understand." Then the narrator recounts his dream, which is much like Culla's in sequence. However, in this version it is Christ rather than a faith healer who promises to cure the supplicants. When the sun does not reappear, the mob, described memorably as "a ragged horde of bodies, bonebags in rags and tatters," turns its fury on the dreamer. In holograph, McCarthy added retrospective commentary: "The . . . ambiguity . . . is really only an intolerance for the inconsistency which is truth." Or, he says, perhaps the intensity of his desire to interpret the dream had led him to overcomplicate it. He adds that then he was less fully "Agnostic" than he now is ("Rough/First Draft [B]" 8/1; photocopy in "Early Draft [B]").

It is not likely that this first-person dream was composed as part of *Outer Dark*. Its personal significance is attested by McCarthy's note to himself that he had saved a version in Park National Bank, likely the bank on Gay Street in Knoxville ("Rough/First Draft [B]" 8/1).[11] He inscribed this notation on November 27, 1964, but he did not date the dream's composition. Furthermore, the initial numbering of the leaf, 8, does not mesh with the pagination of the first, early or middle drafts; and except for anticipating the events of Culla's dream, the first-person narrative does not cohere with *Outer Dark*. Possibly the number was added later, when McCarthy drafted a series of dream passages and numbered them sequentially. In that case, the initial figure on the first-person leaf is sequence number 8, and McCarthy later renumbered it 1 to indicate that it would be revised as the first of Culla's dreams and/or would appear on page 1 of the novel.

The first-person dream and the drafts from Culla's point of view were composed without reference to one another: there is little traceable evolution of language from one to the next. Yet we do see an evolution in narrative details from the first-person dream through the three successive dreams from Culla's point of view, which further supports the conclusion that McCarthy composed the first-person dream first. McCarthy's terse note to himself in the novel's first draft—"Christ dream—eclipse"—might well refer to this already-existing dream narrative in which Christ addresses the supplicants. Perhaps the dream was one McCarthy had experienced before he began *Outer Dark*. If so, the first-person dream may be one creative germ of the novel, one that lay dormant until, frustrated with his attempts to narrate Culla's emotional states and his vexed relationship to the God who watches, McCarthy recast his own nightmare as Culla's. Culla's sense of a Deity "dimly remembered out of his youth in a dark and frangible dream" ("Early Draft [B]" 207/196) may have been a private allusion to McCarthy's eclipse dream, one that reflected his adult skepticism about his childhood religious teaching.

Alternatively, the first-person dream may recount a nightmare McCarthy experienced while he worked on the first draft, one that provided a solution to his problems with projecting Culla's interiority. If so, the dream too may have been influenced or reinforced by *Macbeth*, in which the protagonist observes an eclipse and wonders if it is a cosmic reflection of his guilt:

> 'tis day,
> And yet dark night strangles the travelling lamp:
> Is't night's predominance, or the day's shame,
> That darkness does the face of earth entomb,
> When living light should kiss it? [2.4.6–10]

Either way, it supports the inference that important aspects of *Outer Dark* derived from McCarthy's unconscious, his inchoate feelings of remorse and dread, even a crisis of belief that the failure of his marriage exacerbated. McCarthy has repeatedly acknowledged the ways in which dreams and the unconscious fuel the creative life: in his statements to Martha Byrd, David Kushner, and Oprah Winfrey about the subconscious origins of his writing, and in his cartoon self-portrait for Bert Britton,[12] in which he drew himself working at his manual typewriter, his brain wired up, his irises weirdly slanted to suggest an altered mental state, above the caption, "Them old dreams are only in your head" (Britton, *Self-Portrait* 33). In his 2017 nonfiction essay, "The Kekulé Problem," McCarthy elaborates on a comment he made to Winfrey about scientists' solving work problems in their dreams, and he considers the relationship of the prelinguistic unconscious to the language-using conscious mind: "Problems . . . are often well posed in terms of language . . . , a handy tool for explaining them. But the actual process of thinking . . . is largely . . . unconscious." Readers have disputed the scientific basis for this assertion, but it seems a valid statement of his own creative process, especially in the state of flow. McCarthy returns to these ideas about the role the unconscious plays in thought in *Stella Maris* (99–100, 129, 174–75).

The earliest version of the eclipse dream from Culla's point of view follows immediately after his encounter with the triune at the river. Thus, McCarthy initially thought of the dream as resulting from the triune's judgment or even as another manifestation of it. However, in a holograph addition at the end of the passage, McCarthy resituated the nightmare as another of Culla's tormented experiences while he lies captive in the hollow live oak: "He woke flailing out at the darkness, his hands striking the shell of the tree" ("Rough/ First Draft [A]" 157). This line retroactively identifies the whole sequence of the leader's accusations, his demanding the boots, and the dream of the eclipse as nightmares generated by Culla's subconscious while he is imprisoned in the tree, an idea McCarthy did not pursue.

In its imagery of the setting, the crowd, and the eclipse, this version is more fully fleshed out than the first-person dream, and its pacing and style are more characteristic of a developed fictional scene. The supplicants are "dressed in curious costumes, ragged and barefoot," and they stand "in a square of an ancient city with the sunn [*sic*] beating down upon them" ("Rough/First Draft [A]" 157). In the first-person dream, the gathered people are blind, but here they suffer from diverse "ailments." In both, the dreamer presses forward, asking to be cured. While the first-person dream asserts unequivocally that the "figure in white" who addresses the crowd is "Jesus Christ" ("Rough/First Draft [B]" 8/1), in Culla's dream the supplicants address "a bearded man in a white robe whom . . . [Culla] perceived to be Jesus." Later in his dream, Culla thinks of him as "The Man in White" ("Rough/First Draft [A]" 157). Nothing in Culla's dream indicates that the figure in white causes the eclipse, but the first-person version establishes Christ's agency: "he raised his arms . . . and the sun diminished, failed" ("Rough/First Draft [B]" 8/1). This terse statement of the eclipse's appearance is elaborated with realistic and poetic imagery in Culla's dream, where the supplicants observe "the wirethin rim of the sun where it crouched behind the moons [*sic*] shadow and the lacelike aureole of almost stellar pale light that emanated from it." They wait, muttering begins, and then they let out "shrieks of anger and despair and . . . they began to . . . fall upon him" ("Rough/ First Draft [A]" 157).

The next version from Culla's perspective, filed among the fragments in the "Rough/ First Draft [B]" folder, is considerably closer to the published version. Here Rinthy's shaking Culla from sleep frames the dream: "You kept hollerin out, she said. Me. What about me." The leaf is not numbered, but Rinthy's waking Culla now places the dream among the opening scenes of the siblings in their cabin and reflects McCarthy's decisions to abandon Culla's distress in the hollow tree. Culla's talking in his sleep, like Lady Macbeth's, is evidence of his disordered mind, consumed with guilt. The crowd now is comprised of the "Lame halt and blind and himself." The ancient, cobbled city becomes here simply a "square," more appropriate to Culla's experience; and the Christ figure of the earlier versions becomes first "the man in the square" and then the "prophet"—a reconception that diminishes his authority and divinity, potentially situates him among the novel's false prophets and preachers, and obliquely evokes the manipulative prophecies of *Macbeth*'s witches. In accordance with the increased ambiguity of the figure but to opposite effect, this draft restores the hint that the prophet causes the eclipse, that he is an agent not of righteousness but of darkness: "He raised his arms and dark fell." Although McCarthy further honed the language of the dream in his "Middle Draft," the essential transformation from what seems to have been his own nightmare to Culla's was accomplished.

As McCarthy's reference to Culla's experiencing "several" dreams suggests, he drafted or partially drafted others, all filed in the "Early Draft [B]" folder. Many of these dreams establish scenes in the novel as projections of Culla's emotional life. The Macbeths' guilt-ridden visions and dreams may have suggested the dream strategy, but the idea that the triune's objectively presented murders would arise from Culla's "dreams" was McCarthy's innovation from Shakespeare's model.

A reference to Culla's waking from a dream in a barn, composed on December 13, may represent McCarthy's earliest attempt to follow through on the idea of multiple dreams that he first formulated in September 1963. Here the dream's content is not narrated, but if the barn in which Culla awakens is Squire Salter's, then by implication the dream would be of the squire's murder, and its status as merely a dream rather than a literal act of violence Culla commits in a fugue state would be called into question ("Early Draft [B]" 176/209).

Two other unused passages are identified explicitly as dreams. One, an anomaly among the dream passages, is Culla's vision of Rinthy in "the twilight jade" of a glade, where "she stands out of mist . . . all slender and trembling like a reed in the river. So . . . will he see her stand in all dreams henceforth both waking and sleeping" ("Early Draft [B]" 216/3). The references to jade light and the glade suggest that this is a version of Rinthy's entering the clearing where her baby and the tinker have been murdered (*OD* 237–38), but its identification as one of Culla's recurrent dreams also ambiguously circles back to the clearing in which he first abandons the baby as well as to the clearing in which he has dug its mock grave. The dream's recurrence is another instance of Culla's compulsive circling and repetition, manifest not only in his physical movements but also in his guilt-ridden psyche. And his image of the bereft Rinthy standing alone in the glade where her baby has died functions as a correlative of his deep sense of having wronged her.

The green light of the glade recurs with different emotional shading when Culla dreams of the triune at their campfire, the passage in which the influence of *Macbeth* is most explicit. The three sit in a thunderstorm about their "cook-kettle" with its "outrageous fare." Lightning strikes, and the triune appear "in a wreath of green flame in the center of which the kettle glowed and quivered" until it explodes "in pyrotechnic splendor," scorching them to "homomorphs in ash identical in attitude until one tilted forward soundlessly." This, then, is a dream not only of horror but also of wish fulfillment: of the death of the triune, of the end of their tormenting Culla with their/his guilt. The image of the three gathered around their kettle with its "outrageous" meal evokes the witches of *Macbeth* and through that analogy emphasizes that the triune are aspects of Culla's psyche. Their disintegration by lightning bolt hints at Culla's wish for divine intervention, even retribution. But a concluding line forecloses his hope for respite: "He dreamt this, but it never happened" ("Early Draft [B]" 200). As manifestations of Culla's murderous impulses and relentless guilt, the triune do not die; they simply fade away after they have killed the child, as Shakespeare's witches vanish from the sphere of action when Macbeth is brought to his final doom.

McCarthy's strategies for representing Culla's inner turmoil evolved from his monologues and arguments with God in the hollow tree, to his first campfire confrontation with the triune as his alter ego/id/super-ego, to his suffering nightmares of the eclipse and of the trio, and finally to the triune's apparent autonomy within the external world of the novel in scenes when Culla is present only by implication—as if *Macbeth*'s witches were dramatized killing Duncan. Several additional dream passages with discontinuous pagination are grouped together in "Early Draft [B]" just after a photocopy of the page that announces Culla's several dreams (157/2). These bear sequence numbers 3 through 7 in addition to their page numbers, and probably they were all composed at the same stage.[13] Even though these passages are less explicitly established as products of Culla's inner torment, their clustering and sequencing constitutes circumstantial evidence that McCarthy conceived them as manifestations of Culla's dreamlife. Several narrate the triune's murders of Culla or the squire. All focus on the triune's violence, and some of these dream passages eventually evolved into objectively presented scenes of the triune.

The leaf given sequence number 3 bears both Culla's recurring dream of Rinthy in the glade and a scene of the triune gathering on a bluff, a passage which emphasizes their predatory quality. They cluster there, "shifting as wild animals . . . might coming upon some strange scent, but when they fanned and deployed down the bluff toward the river they looked more like trained warriors, assassins" ("Early Draft [B]" 216/3). With so little context, it is not possible to determine whether this sentence is Culla's dream or is objectively narrated, but some of its phrasing is recalled in the fourth passage, which seems to be Culla's nightmare of his own murder at the hands of the triune. Dream passage 4 also deploys incidents and language that appear in the published novel in Culla's headlong flight from the villagers, drinking from a stream and vomiting, falling, and skidding through the pine straw (*OD* 93–94)—a scene that replaced his hiding from them in the hollow tree. The nightmare passage narrates the triune's pursuing and knifing the dreamer. They come upon their victim drinking from the stream, and he sees their reflections in the water like his own mirror image, "three wistful and viscious [*sic*] anthroparians, homunculi about his shoulders" (cf. *OD* [51]). When they charge down the embankment at him, Culla runs until he throws up "and is still running when he sees the . . . blood spew out and . . . feels the knife . . . grinding against his shoulderblade." Finally, he collapses limply, becoming "only flesh." In holograph, McCarthy added that Culla's skidding fall "bare[s] the ground . . . as if to say: here is the earth again and here is what you have made of me" ("Early Draft [B]" 293/4/214). In the published novel, Culla's flight from the villagers is a reconfiguring and extension of his dreamed assault by the crowd angered at the eclipse. And his accusatory address to his murderer(s) in passage 4 is directed to both the triune and the unforgiving God he has argued with as he hides from his pursuers in the hollow tree. Indeed, a crossed-through passage on another page that seems to belong to a scene of his entrapment in the live oak resembles this resentful address. Culla turns his face to the heavens: "Youve done for me aint Ye . . . I knowed You would" ("Early Draft [B]" 106/208).

McCarthy dated a fifth passage in the dream series June 12, which he identified as a Friday. It follows logically after the barn scene composed on Thursday, June 12, and actually may have been composed on Friday, June 13. It seems to be the squire's own account of the triune's invading his house, cutting his throat, and robbing him. Thus, it departs from the focus on Culla's experience; yet it may develop the content of Culla's dream in the barn, and it introduces the idea of a victim assaulted with his own farm implements. The three do not speak as they cross his veranda "like a slapstick farce . . . grimly transpiring into travesty and horror as they advance upon him with . . . mindless fixation, purpose." One lifts him "by the forelock" and cuts his throat with a stock blade. Then they pass through his house "in a swath of aimless desecration and pillage and out the other side." ("Early Draft [B]" 298/210/5]). References to the veranda, the stock knife, and householder's possessions suggest that the victim here is Salter, as does the triune's single-minded passage through the house and out the back, which revisits the description of their sweeping through his barn in "unswerving and near maniacal progress" composed on the same or preceding day ("Rough/First Draft [A]" 297/213; cf. *OD* [35]). The scythe does not come into play in dream passage 5, but it appears in a different context McCarthy later jotted on dream passage 4: "Scythe-blade sticks out of his chest, he wants it away" ("Early Draft [B]" 293/214/4).

Passage 5's narration of a secondary character's account of the triune's acts is quite different from anything McCarthy eventually included in his novel, and the incident is plausible only if the squire has survived his injuries or has dreamt them. Indeed, the episode includes the victim's desperate clasping his slashed throat at a hospital, a detail that seems jarringly contemporary and urban in comparison with the period and rural setting of the published work (although it anticipates the transitional world of Sevier County in *Child of God*). But the proximity of these two dream passages in pagination and time of composition suggests that McCarthy was then trying out a range of methods to establish that Culla is not only the victim of the triune but also the selfsame perpetrator of their violence, that the triune is in and of him. Here McCarthy had yet to commit himself fully to granting the triune autonomy within the external world of the novel. Perhaps in this early scene of Salter's murder, he was experimenting with the idea that Culla's dreamlife somehow invades Salter's, much as the crazed horse invades Rinthy's experience.

The next dream passage is composed entirely in holograph. Although drafted several months later and dated January 17, 1965, it is continuous with the dream scene in the fourth passage, where the triune murder Culla as he drinks from the stream. Yet now the bluff overlooks a river, which suggests that McCarthy was then reconceiving the dream-killing of Culla as a scene that might follow the hog drovers' turning on him after their charges stampede over the river bluff (cf. *OD* 220–27). If so, in both discarded dream episodes 4 and 6, McCarthy associates the triune with Culla's human pursuers in the novel, as Culla's subconscious accommodates and transforms these human pursuits in his recurring dreams of the triune. Culla's nightmare of the eclipse does not narrate the crowd's attacking him in detailed visual imagery, and in the novel as published, Culla consistently if narrowly evades his human pursuers. But in these unused nightmare narratives he does not escape, and in passage 6 he dreams not only his death, but also his gutting like a hunted animal. The triune, "ragged . . . surgeons," cut open his torso, pull out his entrails, and fling them into the river ("Early Draft [B]" 206/127/6). Thus, the unused passage experiments with an alternative resolution to Culla's plotline, one that is more similar to Macbeth's and Poprischin's, which respectively depict or hint at their deaths. McCarthy's passage also lies behind Lester Ballard's autopsy, in which his "entrails were hauled forth and delineated" (*CoG* 194) and anticipates or echoes an incident McCarthy deleted from the "Final Draft" of *Suttree,* in which Suttree as implied narrator imagines his own autopsy in medical detail (see Luce, "Tall Tales" 244–47).

Suttree's autopsy immediately precedes his leaving Knoxville, and Culla's dream of his body's rude disposal also ends with an ambiguous leave-taking. The triune fill his body cavity with rocks, push him off the bluff, and "watched him go face upwards . . . through the water . . . with his arms in a farewell gesture of embrace to their peering faces and the sky beyond" ("Early Draft [B]" 206/6/127). Culla's "farewell gesture of embrace" implies both his reluctance to leave his life and his acceptance of his death, and it also reinforces his intimacy with the triune who have murdered him. It suggests that his death is a rending of the connection between self and darker self, but with no meaningful liberation. In this sense, the passage fulfills the function of the discarded scene of Culla in the imprisoning tree he wishes would blow down, either to kill him or to free him. And his suicidal impulses appear also in a marginal notation in "Early Draft [A]," where a year after the mob pursues him, Culla is "indifferent" to his fate. There McCarthy considered writing a scene in which a man tells Culla, "You fixin to get killed," and he responds, "I caint get killed. I aint never goin to die but I wisht I was" (193/200/233A).

# The Triune Walk

The leaf McCarthy created as the seventh in this sequence is not a continuous narrative but a gathering of paragraphs and notes in which he formulated the nature of the triune and took further steps toward defining their autonomy. Indeed, it may be that he wrote these passages soon after he decided to grant the three full autonomy and to eliminate references to Culla's dreaming them. In one passage McCarthy introduced the idea of their being set mobile in the landscape as walking manifestations of the darkness in Culla's soul: "figures [who] . . . created in their passage an isocline of bloodshed and ravage, a mobile gehenna fused . . . borne with inappeasable violence out of the night of soul upon an inane . . . track of death." In the margin McCarthy noted that Gehenna is the site "where children were sac[rificed]. to Moloch (hence: hell)" ("Early Draft [B]" 215/7). In biblical tradition, as a god of the pagan Ammonites, Moloch was a false god sometimes identified with Baal. Gehenna was the desert wasteland near Jerusalem on which Moloch's idol Topheth was situated and where parents burned their children in sacrifice. Among many references to Gehenna and Moloch in the Old and New Testaments is the passage in Leviticus 18.21, where God proclaims to Moses that the worship of Moloch is prohibited: "You shall not give any of your children to devote them by fire to Molech [sic], and so profane the name of your God: I am the Lord" (see also Jeremiah 7.30–34). As a mobile Gehenna, then, the triune are manifestations of Culla's evil and torment and specifically the agents of the death of Culla's child.

The technical word "isocline"—literally "same slope"—reinforces the identity between the triune's malignity and Culla's. As a geological concept, it is associated with the bluff down which the triune sweep to assault Culla in some of the dream passages, but the term is also used in ecological studies to refer to the graphed ratio of predators to prey, which if out of balance leads to excessive death or extinction. McCarthy refers to the "isocline of death" in *The Road,* where skeletons of fish graph the tideline and the extinction of all life seems imminent (222). But in the right margin of the *Outer Dark* page, McCarthy also listed other words with the prefix iso-: "isobar/ isoseismic/ an isoscism" ("Early Draft [B]" 215/7), evidence that the principle of sameness was foremost in his mind as he considered how to define the triune's relationship to Culla. Indeed, the subsequent pagination (215) of passage 7 suggests that it was written in close temporal proximity to the first-draft passage about the existence of an embattled "selfsame triune" in human nature, "neither sacred nor profane" ("Rough/First Draft [A]" 297/213).

As the paragraph treating the triune as a mobile Gehenna continues, it emphasizes their self-sameness not only to Culla but to one another as well, consubstantial and melded in their common intent. They are "wedded together in an unholy triumvirate, webbed in a net of common evil almost palpable which gave only enough to change the shape of the perimeter they made" ("Early Draft [B]" 215/7). Their web of "palpable" evil recalls the flies that burst from Sylder's trunk "like some palpable embodiment of the horrendous stench" of Rattner's corpse, which McCarthy deleted during the final editorial stage (*OK Editorial Copy* 49). It recalls as well Macbeth's tormenting vision of a dagger "in form . . . palpable" (*Macbeth* 2.1.40).

The important image of the triune as an evil born of Culla's guilt and despair swooping down to murder either Culla or those he has encountered recurs in the early dream/triune narratives. Although none of this material reappears untransformed in the published novel, there the opening image of the triune's emergence at sunset at the top of the bluff and descent into darkness is one that coalesces many of their symbolic nuances explored in the unused pages of "Early Draft [B]." The image introduces the world of the novel as that psychic terrain in which they roam at large and charge down with murderous intent. McCarthy also carries forward the triune's compositional origin in Culla's dream of the first campfire scene in the published opening's description of their making and breaking camp, which establishes their nature as mobile and nondomestic (*OD* 3). So in the published work, the juxtaposition of the opening triune scene with Culla's waking from his dream of eclipse and pursuit suggests that the triune overture too originates in Culla's tormented dreamlife: that the triune's stalking him is also a dreamed manifestation of his sense of guilt and houndedness throughout the novel.

Also appearing in the seventh of the dream/triune segments is an anomalous first-person paragraph from Culla's voice and point of view. It bears some resemblance to his musings in the tree, where he addresses God about his guilt, but here his monologue is addressed as much to himself as to God: "I said Lord . . . I dont know no more what is right because I didnt do what was right. . . . There is in me another me that does for me and I dont know if it is me in God or me in Satan" ("Early Draft [B]" 215/7). Here Culla explicitly acknowledges his moral confusion and his sense that his actions are determined by some force or alter ego in him that remains a mystery. Earlier on the page, McCarthy identified the triune with Gehenna, hell, and evil, but here Culla wonders whether God or Satan is the inner agent of his actions, a confusion that makes sense when one considers that he is driven not only by lust, greed, envy, and seething resentment, but also by guilt, desire for punishment, and even a sense of justice: that he dreams not only of killing through the triune all those who thwart or threaten him, but also of being murdered by the triune.

Clearly these passages that represent the transition from Culla's dreams to more objectively presented triune scenes are the labor of a craftsman hammering out a set of effective strategies for his novel, ways of presenting Culla's tortured inner life without resorting to interior monologue or direct address to the child or to the God who torments him, methods of implying that the triune who judge Culla and who kill in his place are projected manifestations of the dark night of his mad soul. While *Outer Dark* seems to have had its genesis in McCarthy's pain over the loss of his infant son and in his own dream of eclipse, perhaps even in a spiritual crisis, the drafts he accomplished from 1962 to 1965 were also the product of much creative thought and objective judgment about how best to manage his materials, including his thoughtful adapting of ideas and strategies he found in the Bible, Dante, *Macbeth,* and Gogol's "Memoirs of a Madman." They reveal his considered movement from the subjective genesis of the novel to objective control.

All but one of the dream scenes date from late 1963 or spring 1964. Overlapping with these dates, McCarthy began drafting scenes in which the triune act in apparent independence from Culla, as if he had not yet decided whether he would include these episodes of their autonomy instead of Culla's dreams or in conjunction with them. In the third week of November [1963], he drafted the scene in which the triune murder the child. On November 30, he wrote a scene in which the bearded leader incites the mob to violence against the itinerant millworkers ("Rough/First Draft [B]" 201/36; *OD* [95]). He revised the child's death scene in early December ("Early Draft [B]" 202/194–203/195), and then there was a hiatus of five months during which McCarthy did nothing further with the triune episodes. On May 11 [1964], he composed their opening prologue ("Rough/First Draft [B]" 272/212), and he followed this on May 13 with a draft of their second scene, in which they course through Salter's barn collecting his farming implements ("Rough/First Draft [B]" 274/212 [?]; *OD* [35]). Another version of this barn scene is dated June 12 [1964] ("Rough/First Draft [A]" 297/213). On June 26, [1964], McCarthy wrote his second version of the tinker's death, newly making the triune's presence explicit ("Early Draft [B]" 183/189). He recorded that he transferred the triune's murder of the squire into the first draft on July 17 ("Rough/First Draft [A]" 324/209), and its late pagination there suggests that it too was composed in 1964, eight months after he drafted the scene of Culla's temptation to assault his unnamed employer with the scythe. These scenes established the pattern that McCarthy had noted to himself, that the triune would murder all those that Culla wished dead. Revised versions of their violent acts appear in the "Early Draft," except for their murder of the snake hunter, which does not emerge until the "Middle Draft" (131; *OD* [129]).

In the published novel, McCarthy represents Culla's dreamlife explicitly only in his archetypal dream of the eclipse, and he italicizes the episodes of the triune's "autonomy" to stress their origin in Culla's subconscious. The italics cease once Culla meets them face to face, reluctantly confronting their evil and accusations, a strategy that conveys their nature obliquely.

# Rinthy's Evolution

As the wronged and bereaved sister and mother, Rinthy functions in the novel as an object of Culla's guilt, as does their child. Yet she has her own goals and narrative arc, and McCarthy treats her with great sympathy. Except for her final scene, which receives only a brief mention, all of Rinthy's sections emerged in some form in the first-draft stage, and they comprise more than one third of the novel's structure. It seems that with his second novel, as spare as it is, McCarthy undertook to imagine a female character more fully than he had in his first, where Mrs. Sylder's sketchy character had led Bensky to confuse her with Mildred Rattner in one scene (Bensky to McCarthy, Oct. 9, 1962, list 2). McCarthy's tendency to embody his narrative concerns in male protagonists has remained consistent across his career,[14] but in *Outer Dark* he created a major female character—almost a dual protagonist—whose path would parallel, complement, and comment on her brother's. The distortion of her fate by grief would be the crucial counterpoint to Culla's by guilt, and both suffer emotional derangement. Both are relatively static figures, repeatedly enacting their fates. Yet paradoxically McCarthy grants both Rinthy and Culla ample scope for choice and action and by implication tremendous depth of feeling. Although he defines Rinthy in broad strokes by her undiminished bereavement and yearning, her steadfast quest to recover her son, and her weeping breasts, she is a deeply suffering and emotionally affecting character.

McCarthy sometimes handled Rinthy's emotions more explicitly in the first draft, as he did her brother's, but he never presented her inner life in soliloquies. He drafted only one dream for her, a recurring nightmare of her lost child and his too-brief life, composed in the first-draft stage and deleted in the second-draft stage. She dreams of "The cold amniotic wetness. Then the cold and colorless beestings that oozed from her breasts in dreams where she heard a child cry." After an intervening passage on the same leaf, in which Culla addresses God from his hollow tree, McCarthy resumed Rinthy's distressing dream in mid-sentence. She hears "cries of execration or blind disavowal of the worlds [sic] darkness or perhaps of creatures [too] short lived . . . to sorrow the sun's passing" ("Early Draft [B]" 106/208).

In his earliest drafts, McCarthy more frequently included explicit impressions of Rinthy from those who meet her. For example, in her scene with the compassionate doctor that McCarthy first drafted in August [1963], Rinthy weeps, and the doctor intuits "that it was the first time she had cried over it and that this soundless grief was of seven months duration and accretion" ("Early Draft [B]" 131/125). When he asks what happened to her baby, her expression strikes him as "wild," and he thinks that "she might be going to spring up and run from the room" (132/126). These lines do not appear in the published scene; however, a hint of the second passage remains when "something half wild in her look" prevents the doctor from saying what he knows as scientific truth, and instead he tells her the comforting lie that her milk-flow might mean her baby is still alive (*OD* 155). In the finished novel, the reactions of others to Rinthy still comprise one of McCarthy's most important strategies for conveying her character, but their responses to her are illustrated through their actions and dialogue, seldom through narration of their internal perspectives.

Among the assessments of Rinthy that McCarthy deleted, the most striking occur in scenes of the farmer she briefly lives with and then abandons. Culla's refusal to claim and love his son derives from his deep shame and self-loathing because of the baby's origin in incest. Rinthy suffers no such feelings of guilt, but she too exhibits an inability to love when she departs the "loveless house" of the man who desires her affection, to continue her fruitless search for her lost child in the "outer dark." This is her own version of derangement, her own dark night of the soul. A two-page scene with the farmer, dated July 3 and 15, [1963] and carried forward into "Early Draft [A]," is the first draft of the scene we know from the published novel, in which Rinthy silently prepares the man's cold supper and he fails to secure her attention (191/184–192; *OD* 209–210). The narrator identifies her depressed mood as "unfeigned lassitude" (191/184), a label McCarthy later eliminated in favor of more objective representation of her state of mind.

In November [1963], McCarthy tried out a brief, related scene of the farmer's watching Rinthy hoe her garden beds. The man ponders how Rinthy has seemed to be "drawn by a certain gravity toward homes and the . . . useless flowers about them" ("Early Draft [B]" 193/186). And indeed, we see her attraction to and flight from the home of the gardening grandmother, which McCarthy had drafted on May 15, [1963] ("Rough/First Draft [A]" 99; *OD* 98–100). But now the farmer struggles "to understand her saying that if there were no homes there would be no people because that is where people live." To him Rinthy has seemed domestic by nature (the very opposite of the man Culla meets who has twice abandoned his home and family). But after the interval in which she lives with him, the farmer has sorrowfully concluded that she must have mistakenly thought even a humble farmhouse such as theirs "spawned unaided and of itself whole systems of human flesh to tend it" ("Early Draft [B]" 193/186). Her depression prevents her from developing intimacy. She is willing to nurture flowers but not her relationship with the farmer because her ability to love either him or their potential children has been stunted by her grief for her first child and her denial that he is lost. In the discarded passage, the farmer's recognition of her inability to love him emphasizes Rinthy's compulsion and articulates her psychology more explicitly than in the novel as published. The farmer's insights might have satisfied an editor's desire for clearly motivated characters. But McCarthy's evolving strategy for this novel was fully to embrace the intriguing opacity that he could achieve through a consistently objective point of view. Rinthy abandons three homes because of her desperation to recover her baby: the cabin she and Culla inhabit (she is the first to leave), the gardener's home where Rinthy hears the grandbaby crying, and the home of the farmer who longs for her love and attention. Her repeated acts reveal her motivation.

Yet another deletion from the scene with the farmer reduced the reader's access to Rinthy's inner life. In these unused lines, McCarthy wrote that "She turned west with no more purpose than to give her whatever infinitesmal [*sic*] bit more of night to be gained by going from the sun." The line unnecessarily reinforced the earlier statement that her going was unconscious, but it newly suggested she was by now a fugitive from light ("Early Draft [A]" 217–4). Although a few of the narrator's assessments of Rinthy remain in the episode of her departure from the farmer's home, such as the comment that "She did not even know that she was leaving" ("Early Draft [A]" 217–4; cf. *OD* 211), McCarthy's revisions to these scenes with the farmer allowed her compulsion to be conveyed obliquely.

In addition to eliminating Rinthy's dream of the crying baby and including instead the scene of her flight from the grandmother's crying grandchild, McCarthy reduced passages that reported Rinthy's waking thoughts in favor of revealing her character almost entirely through her actions, dialogue, and sensory perceptions of the external world. This transformation is especially striking in his drafts of the negotiation between Rinthy and the tinker, the

Rinthy scene that McCarthy revised most heavily. In the first-draft stage, Mc-Carthy created complementary scenes in which the tinker successfully extorts Culla for money and Rinthy for sex and then reneges on his implied bargains with each to relinquish the child. McCarthy emphasizes the tinker's shifty ma-neuvers to keep the child in these scenes. In Culla's first scene of negotiations for the baby, composed on September 5, [1963], the tinker inquires how much money Culla has and then asks for twenty-five dollars more, postponing the return of the child ("Early Draft [B]" 147/152). Another sequence of first-draft pages, dated October 15 and December 12 [1963], has Culla paying him one hundred dollars and the tinker demanding yet more ransom, whereupon Culla moves to assault him ("Early Draft [B]," 168/171–175/172). McCarthy discarded this treatment of Culla's violence against the tinker and instead resolved the tinker's plotline with his murder by the triune, only obliquely implicating Culla in his death. In the novel as published, Culla makes no overt effort to recover his son, remaining committed to his intention to disown him. He half-heartedly suggests to the triune that his sister would take the child, even as he kills him through his triune avatars (*OD* 236).

In an unused first-draft version of Rinthy's conversation with the snake-hating "crone," she tells the old woman that she had been working for money to ransom her child from the tinker, but that she had needed to spend her earn-ings to survive ("Early Draft [A]" 120). In versions of her scene with the tinker, she offers to "work it out," but the two never agree that she can repay him financially. Rather, in the earliest drafts, the tinker's aim is to keep the baby while extorting her for sex. Readers sometimes compare Rinthy to Faulkner's Lena Grove, who wanders serenely searching for the father of her unborn baby in *Light in August* (1932), but in her potential cheating by the tinker, Rinthy also counterpoints Dewey Dell Bundren, who is desperate to abort her illegitimate baby in *As I Lay Dying* (1930). The first draft of Rinthy's encounter with the tinker, composed two weeks after the scene of Culla and the tinker's first negotiations for the baby, recalls Dewey Dell's experience with the callow drugstore assistant Skeet MacGowan, who "treats" her for her unwanted preg-nancy by giving her a dose of turpentine and coercing sex with her. Dewey Dell suspects his dishonesty, but her extreme need leads her to submit (*As I Lay Dying* 236–38).

In McCarthy's first draft, the tinker initially denies having the child, but he soon sees that he might manipulate Rinthy into sex if he allows her to think he has the baby and will return it. On September 19, [1963], McCarthy drafted a passage in which the tinker asks Rinthy for a kiss, and she tells him, "I'll do what you want. . . . But I aint much for kissin" ("Rough/First Draft [A]" 162/166). His sexual innuendo is obvious, and Rinthy clearly recognizes what he is after. In the work McCarthy did on October 11, she submits to the tinker and then refuses him assertively when he tries to touch her again: "I done what all you wanted." When he suggests that he may not yet be "done," she says, "Get done then . . . if you aint" and turns onto her back. But either the old tinker, who has been drinking steadily, is finished for the night, or he is discouraged by her passivity. He lies back, saying that *she* might feel "more peart" in the morning ("Rough/First Draft [A]" 166/169). This too appears to be a ruse, however, because Rinthy hears the tinker "leave the bed . . . before there was enough light to have even seen him had he not been naked" ("Rough/ First Draft [A]" 165/168). She feigns sleep, allowing him to sneak away from the cabin, and then she runs to catch up with him, which suggests that she has avoided morning sex but still hopes to recover her child. Problematically, this version of the scene left unresolved for her the question of whether he would return the baby, which might have required that McCarthy write another scene of more definitive refusal.

In her dealings with the tinker, Rinthy is tougher and more pragmatic in this initial draft than in later versions, sharing more of Dewey Dell's hard edge than in her other scenes with men, where she is serenely untouchable. One focus of McCarthy's revisions was to place greater emphasis on her reluctance and vulnerability with the tinker. On December 27, [1963], he composed a holograph passage for the scene that made Rinthy's despair explicit and that paralleled Culla's early, discarded suicidal wish: "A dark & noisesome [*sic*] swamp wind came through the paneless windows and she turned her face to it. She said: if they's a poison to a wind such as that I'd breathe big of it till I was done w/ breath and never fret no more" ("Rough/First Draft [B]" 204/ 209/ 212; cf. *OD* 188).[15]

McCarthy reworked the scene extensively in the second-draft stage, and in early drafts A and B are several discontinuous versions, more than I discuss here. In the earliest of these versions, one with holograph pagination, Rinthy steps "trembling" into the abandoned cabin. McCarthy describes her inhaling the stale wind after the tinker hands her a broom and instructs her to sweep the debris off the bed, which suggests her revulsion at what she may have to do to recover her child. But here McCarthy has already eliminated the explicit reporting of her suicidal thought, as well as the reference to the origins of the wind in a noisome swamp. These revisions achieved the final form of the sentence, in which the "faint stale wind" serves as a correlative for Rinthy's unspoken reaction to her situation ("Early Draft [A]" 194; *OD* 188). Toward the same end, McCarthy added other portentous imagery to a later and more complete version of the scene, which bears mostly typed pagination. Soon after breathing the stagnant wind, and after the tinker confesses that her son is not at the cabin, Rinthy goes to the window, where she sees a "gross" hornets' nest in the bare outhouse framework and dark birds flying "across the fields to the west like heralds of some coming dread." In the margin McCarthy jotted "portending/advent/dolor," words that reveal the emotional coloring he was working toward in the scene ("Early Draft [A]" 197; cf. *OD* 188). Further, when Rinthy sees two beds at one end of the deserted cabin, she crosses to the door, where she finds a dead bird and the grub that feasts on it. Despite these fearsome or disgusting images, she finds inner resolution, and closing the door, she takes the flower from her hair and holds it before her like a bride as she turns to face the old man ("Early Draft [A]" 198).

However, during the second-draft stage, McCarthy began to think better of the derivative incident of Rinthy's submitting to sex with the tinker only to be betrayed. He now worked to devise a scene of conflict between the two that would avoid her sexual compromise but still have the tinker reneging on a perceived promise. McCarthy developed this by honing dialogue in which the tinker gradually learns that the baby is a child of incest, a factor of which he is unaware in the first-draft material. His anger and revulsion finally lead him to abandon his intention to finagle sex from Rinthy and instead to refuse self-righteously to return her child. The potential for coerced sex and the potential for the baby's return had to be sustained through most of the scene, which would trace a dramatic arc through the dialogue of the two principles, in which each tries to persuade and/or manipulate the other until they reach a stalemate, neither achieving his or her desired outcome. There are lies and evasions on both sides, but also unexpected revelations.

On a leaf with holograph designation "A," Rinthy negotiates with the tinker while they eat a cold supper, and the old man remarks that he has never seen a healthy child left lying in the woods, adding "That's untimely rest. . . . They wont nourish out of the earth like a stalk of corn." However, McCarthy found this too judgmental. In the margin, he cautioned himself, "He is an old roué, not a moralist." Still, he added holograph lines in which Rinthy replies to the tinker's implicit accusation: "I didnt/he did/what you want with me?" ("Early Draft [A]" page A). A later version in "Early Draft [A]" softens the tinker's moralizing and adds Rinthy's shock at his revelation that Culla abandoned the baby to die in the woods: "Was he not give to ye?" she asks (201). In subsequent drafts and the novel as published, Rinthy tells him she knows he has her baby because her brother gave the child to him ("Midde Draft" 193; "Late Draft" 207; *OD* 185). But in fact, she has no evidence for this other than perhaps a preconception that tinkers will take on the children of others and her recognition early on that Culla has lied about the baby's death. It is a belief driven by her need.

On the same leaf as the tinker's moralizing, the next typed paragraph makes it clear that he is curious about the origins of the child and believes Rinthy can tell him what he wants to know since she has convinced him that she is the baby's mother. The tinker compares himself to a man who has acquired a horse cheaply, not knowing its breeding. If such a man came across the owner of the horse's dam, he would want to ask questions about its sire ("Early Draft [A]" page A). But in the subsequent version in "Early Draft [A]," McCarthy dropped the tinker's horse-breeding analogy and had him ask Rinthy directly about the baby's father: "Is he your brother sure enough?" (201), a question that recurs in several of the scene's early drafts. Rinthy is reluctant to admit this, and when finally she does, the tinker curses her (203). As he leaves the cabin, he admits, "I brought you up here to screw but I done changed my mind" (204B).

*Outer Dark* as published only delicately hints that if she must, Rinthy will trade sex for the return of her child, and the tinker's revulsion at the child's incestuous conception reprieves her from that degradation. Here she possesses the unwavering purity and self-composure that belie her victimhood and her desperate circumstances. McCarthy refined her character, then, to make her less pragmatic and more emotionally consistent, essentially unsullied by Culla's or the tinker's sexual abuse, immune to the attempts at seduction of Luther's callow son, but also to the farmer's attempt to form a relationship with her.

If Culla was initially conceived as an objective correlative of McCarthy's guilt over failing his child, Rinthy may be the objective correlative of his parental grief and longing for the son who was largely lost to him. If this speculation is near the truth, then in creating Rinthy McCarthy drew on the innocent, nurturing, and bereaved aspects of his own psyche.[16] A photocopied page of first-draft Rinthy material dated October 15, [1963] bears the lines, "The pain of our past lies within us, [b]ears . . . the yieldless gravity of iron. Not love itself compensates its own agony" ("Early Draft [B]" 167/170). Still, McCarthy did not think of Rinthy as fully sharing the protagonist's role in the novel. He wrote me in 1980 that he considered Culla the novel's primary character.[17] And his creation of the triune as nightmarish projections of that guilt-hounded, self-punishing psyche ultimately gave nearly two thirds of the novel to Culla.

# The Murder of the Tinker

**D**uring the first-draft stage, McCarthy anticipated that *Outer Dark* would end not with Culla's meeting the blind man on the road, but with Rinthy's discovering the bones of the tinker in the glade, which would bring her together with the old man once more and provide closure to his story arc and stasis to hers. This would later become the novel's penultimate scene. As mentioned above, McCarthy briefly drafted Rinthy's final scene in the glade on an undated and unpaginated leaf he labeled "Last Page" and filed with the superseded material in "Rough/First Draft [B]." At a later point, he added his handwritten note about Harris's stageplay "Diary of a Madman," evidence that the Rinthy passage alluding to the death of the tinker had been sketched no later than spring 1963, when the play was being reviewed. Over the course of a year, McCarthy wrote several drafts of the tinker's murder in which he tried out differing ways to represent the agent(s) and means of his death. On November 25, [1963], he composed a passage that begins, "The tinker made himself at home in the glade," and ends with the narrator's speculation that the tinker may have heard the swish of an axe descending ("Rough/First Draft [B]" 190/197). McCarthy had invented the triune that September, but they do not have a role in this passage, and the wielder of the axe is not identified. Nevertheless, the axe implied Culla's agency in the murder, given that in other draft material from 1963 he is linked with the tool when he takes an axe to a blacksmith for sharpening, a scene that McCarthy later deleted and rewrote for *Child of God*. In the absence of the triune, the tinker's death by axe blow would have invited the reader to visualize Culla as the murderer and thus would have demystified his ambiguous nature, making more explicit here than in later drafts that he means to kill the tinker and recover the child to fulfill his persistent intention to do away with his son, to hide away his guilt. Indeed, a crucial plot function of the tinker's murder in all drafts is to place the doomed child in the hands of Culla/the triune.

In the second draft, before he changed the weapon that kills the tinker, McCarthy planned to have the triune gather an axe as well as a pick and a brush hook from Salter's barn, which would have implicated them in the tinker's murder ("Early Draft [A]" 34). A new version of the murder scene, dated June 26, alludes to the triune's recent presence in the glade, which places its composition in summer 1964—after their 1963 genesis. The tinker approaches the pecan grove warily, sees the matted vegetation where the triune have slept, and intuits danger. "Standing there above their recent abod[e] with shotgun against his chest . . . [the tinker] looked like a worn assa[s]sin . . . minutes behind his quarry. But for the fear that danced in his pale eyes" ("Early Draft [B]" 183/189). This version anticipates that the triune will kill him, then, but does not narrate their reappearance or his murder. Perhaps McCarthy felt at this point that he might imply the tinker's death through his dread and his proximity to the triune, especially since he already had planned that Rinthy would come upon the tinker's remains. Or perhaps McCarthy intended to complete the scene by describing the murder, as he did in the next version. But clearly at this stage he had decided that the agents of the murder would be the triune, acting for Culla.

The undated third stage of McCarthy's work on the tinker's death is a revised and expanded draft filed with the unused material in "Rough/First Draft [B]." Its leaves are numbered 1–3, as if McCarthy composed them as a discrete entity and did not feel satisfied enough to assign them a position within his draft before further revision. Again the tinker sees the shapes of the triune where they slept, "the grass already brown and poisoned," but they do not appear until the tinker and the child are asleep (1–2). In this draft their presence is explicit, and when the tinker wakes, he sees them, as have other secondary characters throughout the novel, in keeping with McCarthy's primary strategy for complicating their symbolic nature by providing witnesses to their physical solidity. When they materialize, seeming to have "risen up out of the ground," the tinker cannot "account for them." He greets them, but the leader immediately calls on Harmon, who shoots the old man in the chest, perhaps with his own shotgun. As the tinker dies, Culla's son cries in grief or fear (3). Harmon's shooting the tinker makes Culla's agency in the murder oblique, and it prepares for the second scene between Culla and the triune, in which the triune have the child and murder him. Yet page 4/186 of that scene in "Rough/First Draft [B]" ends with the bearded leader's making the veiled accusation that Culla has killed the tinker, and it is likely that McCarthy composed this page immediately after pages 1–3, with the idea of identifying Culla with the triune's murderous acts. The leader abruptly asks Culla where he thinks the tinker might be, and when Culla does not reply, the leader disingenuously remarks that he must have "goneon [*sic*]." In a holograph addition at the end of the page, Culla denies knowledge, claiming that he "aint studied it." But the leader replies knowingly, "Yes. Youve studied it" ("Rough/First Draft [B]" 4/186).

The version McCarthy settled on for "Early Draft [A]" is more concise, suspenseful, and polished. The tinker enters the clearing and eyes the remains of the campfire. He is wary yet unaware, listening to the night sounds with "<u>deaf ears</u>" and treading through the impress of the triune's bodies in the grass. McCarthy conveys the approach of the deadly triune to the reader, but not to the tinker, by the sudden suspension of a fox's barking and the bats' hunting. In this stillness, the tinker nods off, wakes to find the triune in the glade, greets them, and begins to bargain for his life before Harmon shoots him. In this and subsequent versions, nothing directly connects Culla to the murder ("Early Draft [A]" 234). McCarthy leaves his readers to infer that the will to kill is Culla's as they become aware that the triune are externalized aspects of his psyche.

McCarthy remained unsatisfied with the scene, however, and he penciled in the margin, "delete the tinker's words save O God?" ("Early Draft [A]" 234). The version in the "Middle Draft," more compressed still, describes the tinker in the grove and the return of the triune in two paragraphs and eliminates all dialogue and action after his friendly salute to them, "Howdy." However, here McCarthy introduced the narrator's telling commentary that compares the central characters to ghosts forever wandering their purgatorial realm, hounded by their respective fates of guilt (Culla), grief (Rinthy), or malediction (the tinker). As in the earlier draft and the published novel, rather than narrating the tinker's death, McCarthy implies his murder through two scenes: the passage in which the tinker wakes to find the triune at his campfire, which now concludes with his greeting ("Middle Draft" 242; *OD* [229]), and the later scene of Rinthy's finding her baby's "little calcined ribcage" lying in the ashes of the burned-out fire and the remains of the tinker hanging in his "burial tree," weathered to a "bone birdcage" ("Middle Draft" 250–51; *OD* 238). The drafting progression for this scene is another instance of McCarthy's reduction of the explicit, his working toward pregnant opacity by obscuring Culla's agency in the murders through successive iterations, manifesting his violence only through the triune. Moreover, the increased compression and understaging of the tinker's resolution creates emotional space for the shocking murder of the baby, augmenting its impact.

# The Child Sacrifice

U nlike the off-stage murder of the tinker, the sacrifice of the child is narrated in all its horror; and while the trio are the dramatized agents of the boy's death, Culla is present and fully implicated in their enactment of his barely repressed desire. The child is the contested linchpin of the novel; thus the logic of the plot requires his death so that Culla's desperate need to deny his sin/son and Rinthy's desperate need to deny his death and recover her child can both reach a tragic point of rest. The most plausible alternative resolution would have been Culla's death, as in the unused dream scenes in which the triune murder him, and the baby's restoration to Rinthy.[18] A relevant literary precedent for such a denouement is the death of Macbeth, betrayed by the demonic witches, and the consequent restoration of civic and political order typical of Shakespearean tragedy. But it seems McCarthy saw quite early that Culla's death would too neatly and artificially wrap up his dilemma: how to live with excoriating guilt and the psychological denial it promotes; how to escape from his purgatory.

The murder of the baby was necessary to complete the "perfect, logical, and immutable <u>deformation</u> of evolving fate" initiated with his incestuous conception, as McCarthy had jotted on a draft page of the child's death scene ("Rough/ First Draft [B]" 195A), and he drafted no other resolution for the boy. Neither did he draft a version in which he dramatized Culla as the direct agent of his son's murder, an act unthinkable for the man who has so deeply repressed his shame, rage, and violence and whose psychological evasion has been manifest since his initial attempt to kill the baby without claiming his deed by deserting him in the woods. McCarthy first drafted the triune's murder of the child on November 21–22, [1963], two months after he had composed their initial confrontation with Culla and three days before he backtracked to draft the tinker's implied death by axe. In the November passage, when Culla comes into the sphere of the triune's campfire for the second time and sees his son crawling on the ground, he feels "ready for *them* to do what *they* would [italics added]" because by now, he has convinced himself, he is merely wandering "with neither destination nor will." But his passivity too is evasion and self-delusion, a passive giving in to what are after all his own rapacious instincts—as if he has nothing to do with the looming death of his son. McCarthy crossed through this too-direct revelation of Culla's emotional life, marking it "terrible," and later reformulated the idea of Culla's aimlessness in one of the leader's accusations. But at the bottom of the page, McCarthy abruptly forecast the cannibalizing of the child with the leader's advice to Culla, "Don't fret none about that young'n. We fixin to eat him here in just a minute" ("Rough/ First Draft [B]" 195/188).

McCarthy drafted the next page of the scene, dated November 22, concurrently but filed it in "Early Draft [B]." Again he composed more statements of Culla's inner reactions than he would retain for the finished novel. Watching Harmon and the mute guffaw at the leader's remark about eating the child, Culla stands "transfixed in a kind of horror and he thought that he had fooled himself, that he was not ready for this, could not have been ready," a direct acknowledgment that he has been lying to himself, yet ironically a thought which may itself be further denial of his readiness to sacrifice his son. McCarthy placed the sentence in angle brackets and marked it "BAD," noting too that the passage "sounds like 'this' is the cannibalism & not the eye" (196/189). So his objections were not only that he wanted to avoid explicit reportage of Culla's thoughts but also that the placement of the lines obscured a point he was working toward, that the son's ruined eye echoes the father's self-blindedness. In later drafts Culla would challenge the triune about the child's eye, an alternative strategy for introducing the ironic parallel between father and son, both half-blind. And McCarthy would further explore Culla's moral and spiritual blindness in his conversation with the blind traveler, which he had yet to compose.

Crucial to the scene, despite Culla's denial, is his recognition that this is his own abandoned son and not some other hapless crawling baby. When he touches the boy, he fully comprehends that the child has survived his attempt to kill him on the day of his birth, "that it was the child, and no revenant . . . trailing earthstained winding sheets and orts of its own decaying flesh could have visited its murderer with such limboid gravity" ("Early Draft [B]" 196/189). The unused passage sounds the purgatorial theme of the novel, again linking Culla's haunted inner life with Macbeth's, both self-deluded but guilt-haunted murderers. McCarthy rejected the lines, but the trope of the purgatorial ghost would resurface in his "Middle Draft" passage comparing Culla, Rinthy, and the tinker to "exiles who divorced of corporeality and enjoined of ingress of heaven or hell wander forever the middle warrens spoorless increate and anathema" ("Middle Draft" 242; cf. *OD* [229]).[19]

In the early draft of the child's murder scene, Culla's responses to the leader's brutal commands that he "Kick" or "Thow" the child to him reinforce his evasion of responsibility for his son. When Culla remains inert, the leader orders Harmon to "thow me that young'n over here," then says to Culla, "Unless you'd rather hand it here." The sequence of violent and then more benign verbs—kick, throw, hand—allows Culla to delude himself that he somehow spares the burn-scarred and half-blind child worse mistreatment when he hands him over. However, it softens Culla's implication in the child's death too effectively perhaps, and in later versions the verb sequence does not appear. Yet even in this version, when the leader in turn hands the corpse of the child to Harmon, Culla listens passively as the leader instructs Harmon to "Dress this meat and put it on the fire" ("Early Draft [B]" 196/189). Culla's conscience may induce hesitation, but he wants to have it both ways.

As McCarthy worked on this scene, he wrote and discarded passages that implied the nature of the trio's relationship to Culla, recognizing that the less access he gave readers to his protagonist's inner life, the more difficult they would find it to comprehend the triune. One abandoned strategy was to allow the leader, a psychopathic super-ego, to speak Culla's conflicted mind, as the triune enact his violent wishes. Usually the leader does this in his voiced accusations, which articulate Culla's guilt and self-judgment, but in the November 1963 version, McCarthy experimented with an anomalous passage from the leader's point of view, a summation of his unvoiced thoughts that constitutes a unique departure from McCarthy's strategy of narrating the triune objectively. Here the leader "watched Holme's face with inflexible solicitude. If he [the leader] were the actor . . . [Culla's face] was where the performance would be mirrored and there was no part of that in which he was not interested" ("Early Draft [B]" 196/189). Perhaps the image of the leader and Culla as mirrors spoke to their self-sameness too explicitly for McCarthy's taste. He did not strike through the passage with disgust, but neither did he carry it forward into subsequent drafts.

On undated holograph pages 195A and 195B/188B, McCarthy revisited the material he had composed on pages 195 and 196. He reworked the scene of Culla's approach to the campsite and honed his recognition of the tinker's abandoned traps and the mutilated child. The violence already enacted against the tinker is hinted when Culla hears "no sound save a dull moaning that was not the wind" ("Rough/ First Draft [B]" 195B/188B). Yet Culla has utterly repressed his role in that violence. In the antecedent version of the child's death scene, Culla sees the tinker's cart "with the hung pans catching the light like baleful and huge eyes and he knew" ("Rough/ First Draft [B]" 195/188). The concluding phrase is typical of those McCarthy rejected in revision, but it conveys Culla's understanding that the tinker is dead or dying, that the child is his own, abandoned months earlier, and that further disaster is in the offing. McCarthy's revision on page 195B/188B retains the image of the pans' "baleful" eyes but replaces the bald assertion that Culla "knew" with figurative language that establishes this is a scene of judgment: Culla perceives the tinker's pans "like baleful eyes of some outsized jury of the mute and mindless assembled there hurriedly against his coming." In the first version, when Culla sees that the burn-scarred child is missing an eye, he sympathetically touches his own, and even though he feels it "roll smooth and oiled under the lid," he imagines himself half-blinded—which in moral and psychological senses he is ("Rough/ First Draft [B]" 195/188). But in revision McCarthy reduced Culla's overt reaction to the child's maiming and implied it through the images that Culla sees: the baby's burn-scarred body and empty eye socket ("Rough/ First Draft [B]" 195B/188B). The structure of the passage in both versions, however, effectively conveys that this is a scene of merely illusory recognition and reckoning as Culla comes face to face with his own deeds, his own will to murder his son, yet paradoxically persists in displacing his guilt onto the triune.

When McCarthy worked on the scene again in two continuous leaves on December 6 and 13, [1963], he composed a vivid passage of implicating imagery in which Culla brutally hands his son to the murderous leader. Culla does not cradle the child as a father or even a disinterested person would; instead he grasps him by the neck in one hand, letting him dangle "like a skinned rabbit, . . . <an eldritch> doll . . . with ricket sprung legs and one eye opening and closing softly like a naked owl's," pitiful images that yet reveal Culla's appalling depersonalizing of his son ("Rough/First Draft [B] 202/194; "Early Draft [B]" 202/194; cf. *OD* 235). In the margin, McCarthy questioned his idea that the child seems to Culla like a fairyland doll. He recalled that he had already used the word "eldritch" in a draft of "opus III," where Suttree rows to the French Broad River feeling that because "the city had marked him," "no eldritch daemon would speak him secrets in this wood" (*S* 316). Yet McCarthy decided that it was worthwhile after all to deploy the image of an eldritch entity in *Outer Dark* as well as *Suttree,* one a de-animated doll, the other a wisdom-imparting daemon. The phrase lends an aura of unreality to Culla's consigning the child to death, tempers the otherwise grotesque imagery in which Culla perceives the abject child, yet further emphasizes Culla's denial of his son's humanity and of his own intentions. Similarly, in a deleted passage from "Early Draft [A]," Culla avoids looking at the "hominoid <homunculus>" who sits at the leader's feet (237). And of course, Culla refers to the baby as "it" throughout the novel and its drafts.

As he receives the sacrificial child from Culla's strangling hand, the leader draws a stiletto from the top of his boot. Ironically and too late, Culla says "Dont handle him thataway," as if in self-admonishment ("Rough/First Draft [B]" 202/194; "Early Draft [B]" 202/194). But the leader cuts the baby's throat; and instead of instructing Harmon to put the little body on the cookfire, in this December version the leader himself casts it into the flames. In these and subsequent drafts, the references to the triune's fire subtly allude to the sacrifice of children as burnt offerings to the pagan god Moloch in the fires at Gehenna, which McCarthy noted in his seventh dream passage. Indeed, McCarthy's wish to invoke the paternal sacrifice of children in fire to Moloch may have been one origin of his horrifying and persistent idea that the child would be subject to cannibalism as sacrificial lamb, as burnt offering to an unappeasable god.

Culla continues defensively to dissociate himself from his violent impulses; he watches the murder, "but he still couldnt credit what he was seeing" ("Rough/First Draft [B]" 202/194; "Early Draft [B]" 202/194). After the child is committed to the fire, Harmon studies Culla's face in a hint of their mirroring, and because Harmon sees insufficient evidence of grief or guilt, he challenges the leader, saying he should have made Culla eat the child because it is his. But the leader reminds Harmon that "They aint no need to do somethin already been done oncet." He refers to the first encounter between them, when Culla has eaten chokingly of their charred meat, here retrospectively identified with the son's flesh. Harmon, as one aspect of Culla's conflicted mind, continues to object to Culla's unnatural passivity while "the dollshaped corpse blister[s] and pop[s] in the flames," saying, "He aint even goin to try and reach it out is he?" The leader replies that Culla is "reached out." When Culla asks permission to leave, the leader assents. Then he orders Culla back and makes him wait while he monitors the progress of the fire. Finally he allows Culla to depart, presumably after his son's body is reduced to ash and bone, the fleshly evidence of Culla's sin destroyed ("Early Draft [B]" 203/195). McCarthy did not carry these interchanges into subsequent drafts, but they are interesting for their emphasis on Culla's having been a self-blinded actor in the horror of cannibalism and for their suggestion that the child's murder recurs in Culla's wish-fulfilling nightmares: that he revisits this harrowing scene of transgression and judgment multiple times, as the child has been burned and eaten before. Thus the evidence of this version suggests that in December 1963 McCarthy was still drafting fairly explicit indications that the triune and their actions are projections of Culla's vicious dreams, a feature that in the printed novel is more fully subordinated to their externalized aspect as his walking evil.

In the earliest versions of the scene, McCarthy's primary focus was on inventing the implicative action: the murder of the child and its potential cannibalizing. To emphasize that the baby's death is a profane act of paternal child-sacrifice, as he revised again for "Early Draft [A]," McCarthy made significant changes to that action, taking further cues from biblical and mythological prototypes of fathers' sacrificing their children to Moloch at Gehenna and Carthage, as well as Abraham's near-sacrifice of Isaac, and Cronos/Saturn's devouring of his sons. Indeed, in the physical handling of Culla's son, his slashed throat, the consuming fire, and the cannibalism, McCarthy deploys cultural imagery of child sacrifice to implicate Culla in his son's death and reinforce the idea that this particularly ruthless father, Godless in his heart, visits his own sins on his innocent child.

One Old Testament analogue to Culla's sacrifice of his child is made explicit in a marginal query in "Early Draft [A]," where McCarthy wondered if he might draft a "biblical story" for this scene, as he had for Culla's first meeting with the triune, when the leader lectures him about David and Uriah. Now McCarthy thought he might invoke the best-known exploration of child sacrifice in the Christian tradition, the story of Abraham and Isaac, often interpreted, as he noted, as a "precursor of sac.[rifice] of J.[esus C.[hrist]" (239). However, even though his early-drafted accounts of David had developed the key idea that the sins of the father are visited on the child, McCarthy ultimately decided against giving the triune's spokesman an explicit discussion of David. And the archived drafts of the baby's murder scene offer no evidence that McCarthy composed the contemplated parallel passage in which the leader recounts Abraham willingness to sacrifice Isaac.

Instead, the leader's cutting the child's throat with a stiletto and consigning him to the fire visually alludes to the impending blood sacrifice of Isaac depicted in Genesis 22, in paintings based on it by Titian, Caravaggio, and Rembrandt and in the bronze door panels created for Florence's Baptistery by Lorenzo Ghiberti and Fillippo Brunelleschi, in whose panel Abraham grasps Isaac by the throat as does Culla in the superseded passage ("Rough/First Draft [B]" 202/194; "Early Draft [B]" 202/194). In pious obedience to God's instruction, Abraham fully intends to cut his son Isaac's throat, and the blade in the father's hand figures prominently in all five artists' renderings of the scene, where Abraham's hand is arrested by an angel, the faithful father having proven his obedience to God. Furthermore, Isaac is meant for a burnt offering: when he accompanies his father into the mountains, he carries the wood that will fuel the fire and innocently wonders aloud where the sacrificial lamb is. When God relents, He provides a ram for the burnt offering in Isaac's stead. But there is no such divine intervention on behalf of the doomed son of the faithless Culla. Nor does Culla himself reach to stay the leader's hand. He does not allow himself to know what the leader intends to do.

When McCarthy wrote successive drafts of the tinker's death scene, he had assigned the murder to differing agents of Culla's will; and he did similar experimenting for the cannibalistic consumption of the child. In "Early Draft [A]," McCarthy explicitly gave the id-like mute the role of cannibal, which he had obliquely attributed to Culla in the first campfire scene. The horrific cannibalizing is not gratuitous. In Jeremiah, God declares that in punishment for child sacrifices to Moloch, He will destroy Jerusalem and "cause them to eat the flesh of their sons and their daughters" (19.9), one of several biblical passages McCarthy seems to have had in mind as he developed the idea that Culla's punishment for visiting his sins upon his son would be that he must consume its flesh.[20] On a single leaf, McCarthy composed three successive descriptions of the mute's cannibalizing the boy, in which he refined the scene's associations with child sacrifice to the ravenous god Moloch. Now when the leader cuts the boy's throat, the mute stretches his hands over the fire in inarticulate plea for the corpse ("Early Draft [A]" 240; *OD* 236). The reaching gesture is significant. In the previous version of the scene, Harmon observes with disapproval that Culla will not reach his son out of the fire, and the leader opines that Culla is "all reached out." This somewhat mysterious assertion, as well as the mute's reaching for the child, alludes to Moloch. In descriptions and visual representations, the monstrous bronze idol of Moloch at Gehenna, called Topheth, is depicted with arms outstretched to receive sacrificial children from the hands of their fathers. We might consider, for example, Dutch painter Rombout van Troyen's *King Ahaz Sacrifices His Son to Moloch* (1626), based on 2 Chronicles 28.1–5.[21] And in his classic cross-cultural study, *The Golden Bough*, Sir James Frazer describes the related ancient Carthaginian sacrifice to Baal or Moloch: "The children were laid on the hands of a calf-headed image of bronze, from which they slid into a fiery oven, while the people danced to the music of flutes and timbrels to drown the shrieks of the burning victims" (327). As the unmoved, sacrificing father, Culla hands over his son for death and burning, and then is "all reached out."

However, in "Early Draft [A]" the mute, the most primitive aspect of Culla's psyche, does reach out for the murdered child. Unlike Culla's grasping his son by the throat, when the mute receives the bloody body in the second and third of the draft passages on the page, he cradles the little head in nurturing posture. But the mute's impulse is neither to feed the child nor to rock him; rather, he "burie[s] his moaning face in . . . <its> throat," feeding on him—a shocking and provoking reversal of the reader's hopes. This effect is softened in the published version, where the mute's gesture of outstretched hands, echoing Topheth, is not followed by his momentarily cradling the boy's head ("Early Draft [A]" 240; cf. *OD* 236).

Ancient authors such as Plutarch, in "On Superstition," identified Carthage's Moloch with the primary god of the city, the Titan Cronos or Saturn, who devoured his own sons soon after their birth to prevent their overthrowing him (section 13). Peter Paul Rubens's *Saturn Devouring His Son* is a well-known depiction of this child-cannibalizing, in which bearded Saturn bites viciously at his living child's upper chest. Rubens may have inspired Francisco Goya's quite different painting of the same subject, *Saturn Devouring His Son*, in which the child's head and right arm are already consumed, his left arm disappears into his father's gaping mouth, and his blood runs profusely down his shoulders and back. Both paintings are in the Museo Nacionel del Prado, which Cormac and Anne De Lisle McCarthy visited over several days in Madrid in 1967. De Lisle tentatively recalls seeing these paintings.[22] She remarks that McCarthy would typically study artworks with an almost trancelike focus but usually said little about them (Conversations). However, although he would have been especially interested in the Prado's paintings of Saturn devouring his son, McCarthy had already drafted his child-sacrifice scene with its visual allusions to Moloch and Cronos/Saturn by 1964 or 1965, when he was working on the later portions of "Early Draft [A]."

McCarthy's depicting the child's sacrifice through iconography and the triune's acts, while Culla remains ignorant of his own intentions, created a pregnant opacity of motive, allowing McCarthy to sustain the illusion of dramatic opposition between the triune and Culla through his feeble attempts to save his son, and thus to dramatize Culla's psychological denial of his deepest desires. He appears to be horrified at what has befallen the child, at what victimizes him anew, but the culturally evocative imagery conveys that the triune act *in loco parentis*. Their deeds reenact Cronos/Saturn's devouring of his sons and the archetypal fathers' handing over their sacrificial children to Moloch or to God. In McCarthy's novel, Culla is no loving Abraham, and there is no salvific act of God's providence for this faithless father. Nor is there any hint that Culla's sacrificed child prefigures Christ's redemption of humankind, much less of Culla.

In a marginal note in "Early Draft [A]," McCarthy also considered two rather pragmatic plot problems: how would Culla know that the tinker had taken the infant, and how would he recognize the baby at the campfire as his own? McCarthy jotted the idea that "Early in book perhaps he hears of her [Rinthy's] seeking tinker/Does he find tinkers tracks day after the abandon-ment[?]" Making him aware of connections between the tinker and the child would have explained Culla's inference that the crawling baby at the camp-site is his son. Alternatively, McCarthy considered giving the child an iden-tifying birthmark, but he felt that device had been overused. A less clichéd solution would be that the child was missing the fingers of his left hand. (One might think of the bitten-off arm of Saturn's son in Goya's painting.) McCar-thy drafted in the margin: "S'thin's done gnawed off its fangers./It never had none." Here Culla seems to challenge the triune about the injuries to the child's hand, and the leader's prevaricating response implies either that the baby was born without fingers, a denial that this is Culla's son, or that he evades ad-mitting that it has been partially cannibalized in an earlier iteration of the nightmare encounter. Both options suggest that the leader voices Culla's psy-chological denial. On the same leaf, McCarthy briefly drafted another version of Culla's accusing the triune of the child's mutilation. He jotted in the margin, "What happent to his hand," new phrasing that is parallel to Culla's blaming the triune for the child's half-blinding ("Early Draft [A]" 236/2). (That a stiletto is often used to make eyelets in fabric is a cringe-worthy hint that the leader has used it to gouge out the baby's eye.) These references to the child's missing eye and fingers echo Matthew's metaphorical admonishment that if your eye or hand offends you or causes you to sin, you should pluck it out or cut it off, for it is better to cast off one part of the self than for your whole self to go into Gehenna or hell (Matthew 5. 29–30; see also Mark 9. 43–47).[23] Yet in Culla's hell, the child himself is cast away as the evidence or personification of his sin that offends Culla.

However relevant it was to Culla's experience of Gehenna, this train of thought recorded in the margins had drawn McCarthy away from his initial goal of giving Culla a plausible means of recognizing and potentially claiming the maimed boy as his son. In fact, however, Culla has already acted on his recognition of his son when, through the agency of the triune, he murders the tinker who has preserved the child's life, while remaining in denial of his own rapacious will. Instead of developing any of his ideas for identifying the boy, McCarthy apparently decided to let Culla's unexplained intuition that the damaged child is his son pique the reader's sense that Culla's encounter in the woods should be read as his deranged nightmare and/or inner dialogue. In-deed, when he speaks to the leader, Culla appears to be "addressing something in the night," much like Rattner's communing with his dark self in *The Orchard Keeper* (*OD* "Early Draft [A]" 237).

In "Early Draft [A]," McCarthy expanded the dialogue of the scene to make it parallel to Culla's first arraignment by the triune and to develop the tension between the leader and Culla that is resolved with the murder of the child. Although he decided against the leader's telling the story of Abraham and Isaac, McCarthy added more of the leader's riddling accusations and Culla's feebly voiced attempts to dissuade the leader from killing the baby after he has handed him over. At moments, Culla is sullen and resistant, marshalling his own accusations, and he tries intermittently and unsuccessfully to hold his own against the leader, a reflection of the growing futility of his inner struggle. Moreover, the dynamic and often absurd interchange between the two dramatizes both Culla's internal conflictedness and the chaotic nature of his thought processes.

The dialogue in "Early Draft [A]" appears mostly on pages 236–40, but there is also an unnumbered leaf that McCarthy probably composed first in the same drafting session but left unpaginated because he had already marked most of the material for deletion. On this leaf, the leader declares Culla "a pitiful mess . . . washed up out of the night like a wet dog. From nowheres nowhere bound."[24] Culla does not directly defend himself from this (self)-accusation; rather, he pointedly challenges the leader, "What are you?" ("Early Draft [A]" np; cf. *OD* 234). In the published version, Culla instead deflects the leader's assessment of his lack of direction when he asks him, "Where are *you* bound?" His query sets up the leader's provocative response, "I ain't . . . By nothin" (*OD* 233; italics added). His reply asserts his lawlessness and Culla's, who is, as the leader declares in the unused draft passage, "nowhere bound." But shortly after, Culla futilely distances himself further from the leader's accusations and intentions, asserting with a telling double negative, "You ain't nothin to me" (*OD* 234).

"Early Draft [A]" page 236 is continuous with this unnumbered leaf and was originally numbered 2. On this page, Culla challenges the leader about the child's missing eye, which elicits the evasive counteraccusation that some people have eyes yet are blind, while others manage with no eyes. This is a more obvious foreshadowing of the scene in which Culla meets the blind man than appears in the published version, where the leader makes no reference to the paradoxical ability of the blind to see (2/236; *OD* 232). The leader next accuses Culla of giving his son to the tinker and adds that Culla might have wanted the tinker to keep the child hidden away. Again Culla defends himself paradoxically in double negatives, saying he never figured "nothin," never gave the tinker "nothin"—simultaneous admissions and evasions of his guilt. Initially this passage led to the leader's mocking denigration—"Never figured nothin, never had nothin, never was nothin. . . . You a hardtime kind of feller aint ye?"—and to Culla's more affirmative but irrelevant excuse that nothing is his fault because "They run us off her and me. . . . We never had chance one in this world" ("Early Draft [A]" 2/236–237; cf. *OD* 233). But in the lower right margin McCarthy drafted another self-justification for Culla: he didn't give the baby to the tinker; he just told his sister he had—Culla's rather pointless lie about a lie, further evidence of his chaotic thinking ("Early Draft [A]" 2/236; cf. *OD* 233).

In a deleted section of the scene, Culla continues floundering, claiming that everything would have been fine if Rinthy had not "gone digging around the way she done" to uncover the baby's false grave ("Early Draft [A]" 237). The line meshes with his deflecting blame onto her at the mock gravesite, when he accuses her, "Now you really went and done it" (*OD* 33). In both instances Culla's thought is irrational since the baby exists regardless of Rinthy's actions. But in creating a false grave for his son, he has buried him psychologically, and Rinthy's resurrecting the truth is for Culla a return of the repressed that provokes him to deny the child in other, more bloody ways. In the "Early Draft" of the baby's murder, Culla's desires that everything be all right and that he appear blameless lead to the leader's ruthless assessment that Culla could have achieved these goals if he had "gone on and killed it." Culla hears this as another accusation, and he defensively claims that he "aint never killed nobody," lying to himself since he has killed multiple adversaries through the agency of the triune, at least in his nightmares. The leader agrees that Culla has killed no one, and then, capitulating to the leader's implication that the child should now be sacrificed, Culla claims, "I never had no choice," unintentionally admitting that he has always had a choice ("Early Draft [A]" 237).

As if Culla and the leader have reached a fateful alignment, Culla immediately obeys the leader's demand that he hand over the child, but McCarthy added and then deleted further dialogue before describing the baby's murder, noting to himself that the scene needed at least two or three more pages ("Early Draft [A]" 238). On an undated and unpaginated leaf, he sketched out a passage in which the leader accuses Culla of dooming the supplicants during the eclipse. McCarthy probably composed and revised the leaf at the same time as the "Early Draft [A]" scene and then discarded and filed it in "Rough/First Draft [B]." In this passage, when Culla claims to have killed no one, the leader replies, "What about all them people standin around in the dark. They had some chance till you hollered out but that never kept you from hollerin." And the leader repeats "Did it?" until Culla reluctantly replies, "No." Then Culla adds, "When youre among strangers . . . they aint no one to turn yourself in to"—as if he longs for penance, atonement, but also as if acknowledging his aim to dissociate from himself. And the leader seems to agree, remarking that such circumstances make it "take longer."

McCarthy expanded this passage in the "Early Draft [A]" scene, where he added it to other accusations and refined its effects. In the scene of their first confrontation, the triune's leader probes Culla's unacknowledged guilt for the deaths of the ferryman and the horseman, which establishes the principle that the triune know Culla's experiences and speak more of his violent motives and deeds than he will acknowledge or allow himself to know. In the "Early Draft [A]" version of their second encounter is an unused passage in which the leader levels the parallel accusation that Culla has had something to do with the dead hogs in the river the day before. "[T]hey was somebody not takin care," the leader asserts, and Culla denies that it was he—a true enough statement of his subjective experience. Then the leader launches abruptly into the accusation which takes us back to the novel's opening dream: that Culla called out and left the others standing lost in the eclipse. In this version, Culla is thrown off guard by the leader's unanticipated access to his nightmare. He blinks in confusion, then claims he had as much right to ask for a cure as the others did. But the leader counters that only Culla cried out, as if his asking for personal salvation doomed the collective.[25] Culla cannot deny that he alone hollered, so he retreats into his habitual not knowing, claiming that he can't remember it and that he "didnt know where it was even." When the leader counters that the others did not either, the non-sequitur leaves Culla stymied for a reply until he sees the leader turn his attention to the child between his feet. Then Culla offers the excuse that he has only lived around strangers, implicitly acknowledging that he has taken no responsibility for the others at the eclipse: "When you're amongst strangers all the time, . . . you dont know yourself any more." The leader does not dispute this and agrees that Culla has never been with anyone but strangers ("Early Draft [A]" 239).[26] There would seem to be no causal relationship between living without family and friends and lacking self-knowledge except for the principle that one learns self-identity through others' mirroring and validation of the self—a psychological concept with which Culla would not be familiar. Nevertheless, Culla's admission that he does not know himself is very much to the point. He lives in futile denial of his sins, which is manifested in the splitting out of his psyche into the three who execute his violent wishes and speak his self-judgments. And as if their agreement that Culla has no family brings them into better integration, the leader immediately draws his stiletto and cuts the child's throat.

However, at some point, McCarthy considered altering the wording of Culla's line to change its implication significantly. Instead of "you dont know yourself,'" McCarthy penciled in "how to act?" ("Early Draft [A]" 239). On first blush, the revision sounds like the admonishment a parent might make to a child who misbehaves around others, Culla's acknowledgment that he has been at fault in putting his needs ahead of others' during the eclipse. But it also suggests that Culla doesn't know how to act on his murderous desires, so he defaults to allowing the triune to act in his stead. The leader does so when he kills the child as if Culla has just asked him to. McCarthy did not choose between these equally good passages with their differing implications. In fact, he marked the whole interchange for deletion, perhaps because linking the triune to Culla's dream of the eclipse would have implied too blatantly that the triune are dreamed as well. Instead, he had the blind man recount the faith-healing scene in the final pages of the novel, but with more benign intent than the bearded leader does.

In the drafts of the child's murder, we see McCarthy working toward absurd dialogue that externalizes the characters' motives and dramatizes their conflicts through their evasive shifting of subjects, rhetorical manipulations, and illogic. Nothing like this appears in *The Orchard Keeper*, except for brief adumbrations in John Wesley and Sylder's negotiations in the county jail scene and the interchange at cross-purposes between Ownby and the county social worker. In *Outer Dark*, dialogue as dynamic speech acts reaches perfection in Culla's discourse with the triune and in Rinthy's negotiations with the tinker, dialogic scenes that underwent multiple painstaking revisions. Furthermore, in the conflicts between Culla and the triune, McCarthy deploys their tortured dialogue to externalize Culla's fractured psyche, achieving the strategic opacity that makes the novel endlessly fascinating while deceptively simple. Reviews of his early novels often praised McCarthy for the authenticity of his dialect rendering and the liveliness of his dialogue, but his adroit embodiment of evolving dramatic tensions within and between characters in their dialogue has less often been remarked. It is a skill he would deploy for comic effect in *Suttree* and to bewildering or horrific effect in the evasive, jockeying rhetorical performances of Judge Holden in *Blood Meridian*. Nowhere does McCarthy deploy spoken illogic to better effect than in *Outer Dark* and *Blood Meridian*, and few writers do it as well as he. In *Blood Meridian*, he would also return to the implication that interior argument is externalized in the late interchanges between the kid/man and the judge. And the skill of conveying conflict and character motivation through dialogue would be essential to McCarthy's development as a dramatist in the mid-1970s and later, when he would write filmscripts and stageplays in which he dared to embed even deeply philosophical arguments and challenging intellectual concepts in his characters' dialogue, especially in the conflicting metaphysics of Black and White in *The Sunset Limited*.

# Culla and the Blind Man

**E**arly in his construction of *Outer Dark,* McCarthy was uncertain that Culla would survive. His life is threatened in several scenes, and as late as January 1965, McCarthy drafted the second of two unused scenes in which the triune murder him, or he dreams that they do. If Culla were to die, then ending the novel with Rinthy's discovery of the bones of her child and the tinker would be appropriate. But having Culla live on with the persistent burden of his sin, the psychological necessity of endless denial, is more in keeping with the central dilemma of the novel. So it was more effective to close with the scene that exemplifies his indeterminate yet fated future, his circling on in a resolution without closure and without redemption. Not until McCarthy was deep into writing his second draft did he invent the scene in which Culla encounters the sightless man and then wanders blindly into the swamp; but McCarthy's thinking about the child's half-blinding and Culla's moral blindness had led naturally to his conception of the blind man, the first of several blind characters in his novels. As he drafted the closing scenes of *Outer Dark,* he undertook three primary tasks: to develop pertinent dialogue for the two differently blind characters who meet on the road; to create in the blind man a foil not only for Culla but also for the novel's earlier claimants to religious authority, especially the dreamed faith healer; and to delineate the swamp into which Culla wanders, in which he perpetually wanders, as a correlative of his moral and psychological state of being, his endless, benighted despair after the murder of his son.

The earliest draft describing the swamp is dated March 5, 1965, and is filed in "Rough/First Draft [B]" as superseded work (208/197), as is one page from an early attempt at the dialogue between Culla and the blind man (8). Leaves that represent McCarthy's subsequent work on the scene are filed in "Early Draft [A]" (242, 244, 252), and a complete, revised version appears in the "Middle Draft" (252–56). The approximately continuous, high pagination of the leaves in the early and middle drafts suggests that McCarthy may have composed them in one sustained work period after he had settled on the rest of the novel's structure. Among these leaves are alternate versions of Culla's meeting with the blind man and their ensuing conversation. The first in "Early Draft [A]" begins with a rather prosaic interchange about the weather that quickly becomes freighted with implication. As in the published version, the blind man remarks how good it is to "see" the sun again, "After so long a time," as if the eclipse of Culla's opening dream has ended at last (242; *OD* 239). Here Culla is not startled as he is by the bearded leader's more obvious reference to his nightmare of the eclipse in "Early Draft [A]," but some of the blind man's comments in this version faintly reprise the triune's guilt-inducing stance. In an unused line, the old man observes that "When the sun shines it shines for everbody" (242), a paraphrase of the apostle Matthew's admonishment that one should love his enemies in emulation of God, who "makes his sun rise on the evil and on the good, and sends rain on the just and on the unjust" (5.45). McCarthy had earlier tried out this biblical reference in the fragment that he saved near the end of "Rough/First Draft [B]," where the blind man says, "when the sun shines it shines over the whole world, dont it? . . . [E]ven if its [*sic*] rainin someplace the sun is still there aint it? . . . Not like at night" (8). In both the fragment and "Early Draft [A]," Culla agrees politely, blandly, but the reader sees that if he were to recognize the biblical context of the old man's words, they would probe his conscience for the injustices he has inflicted on Rinthy, his son, and so many who have thwarted or slighted him. At the same time, these words invoke the impartiality of divine blessings, the potential for forgiveness. The blind man's next utterance to Culla reworks and reverses the triune's accusatory reference to his eclipse dream. "You wadnt there. . . . Durin the darkenin," he says, and Culla agrees, once more denying his own acts ("Rough/First Draft [B]" 8; "Early Draft [A]" 242). The interchange maintains Culla's defensiveness, his hypersensitivity to what he perceives as others' criticism, and it reveals that he has gained neither wisdom nor serenity in later years.

However, the intermittent parallels between the triune's judgmental spokes-man and the blind man might have made him seem less benign than McCarthy wished. As he revised, McCarthy worked to differentiate the blind man not only from the triune, but also from the preacher/prophet in the eclipse scene by conveying his philosophy of self-guidance through simple faith and charity, an alternative to Culla's frenzied sense of aggrievement. A step in this direc-tion appears in a two-paragraph treatment in "Early Draft [A]" that addresses physical versus metaphysical sight. Culla wonders how the blind man makes his way, and the narrator observes that Culla "did not know that there are blind newts in the constant dark of caves who keep the days and seasons in disavowal of the world's darkness" ("Early Draft [A]" 252). Earlier McCarthy had written the similar, disconnected fragment that appears to derive from Rinthy's dream, in which she hears "cries of execration or blind disavowal of the worlds [*sic*] darkness" ("Early Draft [B]" 106/208). But the emphasis there was on the denial of evil as a kind of willed blindness. When he repurposed the phrase for the blind man's scene, it became more affirmative. The metaphor of the blind cave creatures who yet perceive diurnal rhythms implies that there are other ways of seeing, alternate senses that allow one to navigate darkness, and it adumbrates the more extended dialogue about blindness and vision in the "Middle Draft" pages of the scene.[27]

The "Middle Draft" version is quite similar to the published version, which suggests that the pages on which McCarthy first worked out the rest of the dialogue for the scene have not survived. In the "Middle Draft," the blind man does not ask if Culla witnessed the eclipse but rather whether he needs anything, and he offers to pray for him. He denies that he is a preacher, yet he claims he does the Lord's work, in effect by praying for beneficence for all, the just and the unjust. When Culla asks why he does not pray to have his vision restored, the old man replies that he would have eyes if he needed them, implying that the kind of vision he values has nothing to do with eyesight. In a passage that later underwent revision, the blind man adds that the person who believes only in the visible is disoriented if he loses his eyesight. He would then have to search: "if you hunt hard enough you might be pitied and showed. Salvation takes ye in the heart and that's too dark a place for even a blind man to see in lessen he's showed" ("Middle Draft" 253–54).

In the "Middle Draft," after the blind man's statement of belief comes a near-final version of his story of witnessing the healing preacher, which he recounts in apparent unawareness of Culla's similar experience before the eclipse. Here instead of stirring Culla's guilty conscience as the triune's account of the eclipse had done, the blind man's interpretation of the events absolves Culla. His story does not mention the eclipse since for the blind man no eclipse has occurred. His friends took him to the gathering because the preacher was reputedly able to make the blind see. When a man whose crippling was not obvious called out to be cured (as does Culla in his eclipse dream), the crowd assumed this caused the preacher to go away. However, the blind man is not only skeptical of the human desire for the redress of losses, but also doubtful of the faith healer, whose reputation is based on empirical evidence of visible ailments healed. So the blind man concludes that the healing preacher is "no true preacher," and he worries about the man blamed for the preacher's disappearance "Because he might not know about the Lord's ways and I could tell him. If somebody dont tell him he never will have no rest" ("Middle Draft" 254; cf. *OD* 241). He intuits that the man is crippled by guilt, and the blind man hopes to give this man what he most needs, respite from that guilt. Culla has denied needing anything, however, and he turns away from the old man's potentially healing message and follows the road that leads to the swamp.

In the "Late Draft," the blind man replies to Culla's query about praying for eyesight somewhat differently, but the emphasis on being shown or led to salvation rather than seeing one's way by empirical means is still central to the old man's philosophy: a believer has "no business astin to see too. . . . Besides salvation . . . takes ye in the heart and there's too dark a place for even a blind man to . . . [navigate] less he's showed (271).

The blind man's scene had come together quickly compared to the other scenes of resolution, so it is not surprising that McCarthy continued to revise it. On December 22, 1967, after he had sent Erskine his revisions in response to editorial feedback, McCarthy again reworked the blind man's commentary on faith. On a fresh page 271X he typed an abbreviated version of the passage from which to begin rebuilding it. One significant deletion was the blind man's bleak observation that the human heart is too dark to fathom, which McCarthy would later give to the hermit slave-killer in *Blood Meridian* (19). He had penciled some new lines in the margin of his "Late Draft" version: "What needs a man to see his way when he's drove there anyhow?/ It makes the way straighter when you caint look off to one side" (271). He typed these sentences in reverse order on his new version of the passage ("Late Draft" 271X), now beginning with the distraction of the visible world and moving to the truer, spiritual insight that comes unbidden. Then McCarthy inscribed angle brackets around the blind man's assertion that one's path is more direct if one is not misled by the visible world. He did not carry it forward into *Outer Dark* as published, but he would return to the idea in the blind revolutionary's section of *The Crossing* (283, 294). On the other hand, to reinforce his decision to keep the eloquent conclusion of the passage, McCarthy drew a bracket beside it, jotted in the margin that it was "an . . . inversion of Job," and reminded himself to tell Erskine ("Late Draft" 271X). And he did mention it to Erskine when he wrote him in May 1968 that the dust jacket might quote the blind man's statement, which inverts Job's "Why is light given to a man whose way is hid?" (However, the dust jacket of the first edition would not include that statement.) Unlike Job, *Outer Dark*'s uncomplaining blind man neither demands answers from God nor hopes for restoration of what he has lost. He is content with what he has, and his faith leads him serenely on. Throughout these revisions of the blind man's lines, McCarthy seems to have been seeking a concise and resounding way for the old man to declare his belief, a philosophy that Culla needs. The final version penciled into the galley proof achieves this (78–A; *OD* 241).

In "Early Draft [A]," the page preceding the description of the swamp is missing, but it probably included the first draft of the "shadeless burn" through which Culla travels toward the swamp. The paragraph appears in its final form in the "Middle Draft," where it contrasts and prepares for the swamp mire. The dry, burned land through which Culla wanders is a scorched earth, a "dead land" of drifting ash and "blackened corridors" of "charred . . . trees" ("Middle

Draft" 255; *OD* 242). The sequential, contrasting wastelands, the burn and the swamp, recapitulate Culla's movement in the final pages of the novel from the Gehenna of the burned, sacrificed son to the other-hell of punishment for his originating sexual sin. Culla backs away from the pull of the "vulvate" swamp, but with no understanding of how his road has "come to such a place" ("Middle Draft" 255; *OD* 42). And the hellish allusions in the swamp scene imply that Culla's destination can never be evaded, which is the darker implication of the blind man's assertion that a man is "sent" or guided—or fated.

McCarthy had written an exploratory description of the swamp as well as disconnected notes for the scene on March 5, 1965, lines that reveal his feeling his way to the diction and tone he wanted. This version establishes the analogy between the drowned trees and figures in hell as well as other salient details that remain in the more concise published version. The dead trees are "forked trunks" which appear like "wrecked torsos," and this vista of "gross figures" stretches to the horizon. In the margin McCarthy inscribed two other phrases that might apply to the limitless realm of the dead: "Apparently w/ out termination" and "perished from." Culla sees the tracks of a muskrat that has wandered into the swamp and more purposefully returned, and then he takes a tentative step into the mire: "the mud came up in a vulvate welt . . . and seized his shoe and clung slaggy <dict? sleeched?> and sucking."[28] The leaf also includes a slightly longer description of the stale wind blowing through the swamp, where nothing lives and the "reeds dipped with rasping slide and collision like . . . things chained and fearful" ("Rough/First Draft [B]" 208/197; cf. *OD* 242).

In the margin of the first paragraph, as if he were considering the English word "gruesome" or a related form, McCarthy inscribed "grue = crane in French." Reaching further, he jotted "brumous," a rare synonym for foggy, which might have evoked Stygian mist. Other marginal jottings recorded ideas for the images and diction of his next version ("Rough/First Draft [B]" 208/197). Of these, he incorporated in "Early Draft [A]" "black ferns," "spoorless waste," and "tortuous and dimly anthropoid," which he then revised to "dimly hominoid"; and in the holograph notes at the bottom of the page he repeated "brumous," "garden of grief," and "grue" in the compound form "grue-cramp," a shudder of fear ("Early Draft [A]" 244). (The striking phrase "death indigenous" from "Rough/ First Draft [B]" would not appear in *Outer Dark*, but it is rhymed in *Blood Meridian*'s "death hilarious [53]".)

McCarthy's diction and imagery of the swamp in "Early Draft [A]" emphasize Culla's inner landscape as a realm of death, devoid of the Edenic associations or the fecundity sometimes associated with swamps in American literature and painting, and more consistent with John Bunyan's allegorical Slough of Despond in *The Pilgrim's Progress*, itself a dream narrative (1678).

Indeed, the swamp Culla comes to in the novel's ending contrasts tellingly with the fertile, wooded wetlands—full of color, the sounds of water and birds, and lush life-forms—in which he abandons his baby (*OD* 16–17). In his "Early Draft [A]" passage, McCarthy composed several roughly continuous, somewhat overlapping sentences in which the imagery gradually accreted the implications he sought. In the first iteration on the page, Culla comes upon a stretch of "gray mire faintly steaming and sparse dead trees naked and tortuous." McCarthy initially conveyed the lifelessness of the scene through the absence of color and sound imagery. But then he made its sterility more explicit, announcing that it is a "dead gray world," before coming to the single touch of life, "the tracks of a marshrat [that] ventured forth . . . and circled . . . back"—an analogue for Culla's own directionless circling throughout the novel. Here McCarthy paused and typed the single word "achromatic" in the center of the next line, as if dissatisfied with the simple word "gray," or seeking alternatives, or reminding himself of the image pattern he wanted to maintain in the scene. The first several lines on the page reiterated that the mire was "steaming" or "smoking," and in the margin he jotted "tourmaline," the gem whose translucent, often blue or green tinting might be compared to mist over swamp waters (244). But perhaps because the word could also evoke attractive color, he did not deploy it in the scene.

Also in the margin, McCarthy picked up the anthropomorphic associations of the bare trees, jotting "torsos?" ("Early Draft [A]" 244), which had first appeared in the "Rough/First Draft [B] version (208/197). With great economy, his third description of the swamp scene on the page made the analogy between the contorted trees and writing human forms suggestive of hell: "a dead and spoorless waste populated with ruined shapes of trees naked and tortuous and dimly . . . <hominoid>" ("Early Draft [A]" 244). Again the imagery of the scene works by evoking traditional cultural associations. Christian-themed artwork is replete with depictions of figures in hell writhing in agony, and one might think specifically of Dante's Forest of Suicides in Canto 13 of the *Inferno* and Gustave Doré's engraved illustration of it (1861), in which the dead are partially entombed in oak trees and tormented by harpies. Perhaps McCarthy had also had Doré's engraving in mind when he drafted the unused scenes of Culla trapped in a hollowed live oak tree and tormented by his conscience and the watching moon, a personification of God.

The sterility of this swampland also takes us back to Culla's act of infanticide that brings him to this "spoorless waste," this childless land. At the bottom of the "Early Draft [A]" page, McCarthy penciled several possible designations for Culla's wasted inner landscape (244), and in the "Middle Draft," Culla's swamp becomes the "landscape of the damned" and a "garden of the dead" (255; *OD* 242), which makes its hellish associations explicit. Culla retreats from the mire, but he does not escape it since his moral confusion and spiritual death are forever his fate.

Although he drafted Culla's resolution scenes rather late in his composition of *Outer Dark,* McCarthy's crafting the blind man's serene, blessed path to contrast with Culla's recursive wandering from ashen burn to stale swamp, ever self-blinded and uncomprehending, created a poignant final commentary on his lost protagonist and intensified the tragic aspects of ungrieving, unrepentant Culla's evil by demonstrating that the alternative of forgiveness and benediction was always there for the seeking.

# New Orleans to Knoxville to Europe, 1964–1967

When McCarthy signed and returned his contract for the second novel in early January 1965, he was still in New Orleans. On January 29 he posted a letter informing Erskine that he had moved from St. Phillips Street to 937 Dumaine Street, only a few blocks away in the French Quarter,[29] and that he planned to be there for two more months before returning to Knoxville. But in February he learned that he had won the travel fellowship from the American Academy of Arts and Letters, and that added a new factor to his writing plans. Now he would use the award for a long sojourn in Europe, where he would continue his work on *Outer Dark* and *Suttree.* On February 19, when Erskine informed McCarthy confidentially that he would receive the award, he concluded with an invitation: "Maybe with all this unexpected wealth you'll feel like coming up to receive the award in person and making us a visit?"

Erskine was probably hoping to see a draft of the new novel then. He preferred to work with an author when a book was in its draft stages rather than encounter it first in its final draft, as had been the case with *The Orchard Keeper.* As early as April 30, 1949, after reading the first two chapters of *World Enough and Time,* he had acknowledged to Robert Penn Warren the risk that he might not clearly see the finished work if he had read preliminary drafts and discussed it with the author while it was in development; but he added, "I wonder if I'd be of any editorial use whatever . . . if I waited around until something was finished, and done in absolute secrecy for fear I might get some hint of it, and then read it for the 'pure' reaction. Maybe it is better to be fully implicated" (letter, quoted in Grimshaw, "Robert Penn Warren" 121). When he encouraged McCarthy to meet with him in New York, Erskine may have been hoping to spare them both another painful revision process such as *The Orchard Keeper* had undergone at Bensky's and his behest, and his preference was to hold face-to-face work sessions with his authors rather than to edit via mail.

Erskine was persistent in asking to see the draft of the new novel. On March 23, 1965, when he sent McCarthy a copy of *The Orchard Keeper*'s newly printed book jacket to fold around his advance copy, Erskine asked for an update on his writing and travel plans in hopes that they could "exchange all of our notes on the manuscript before your departure." Replying later that month, McCarthy reiterated that he would be back in Knoxville on April 1 to revise the novel. He could not predict how long the rewriting might take except that since the work was still in its initial draft, it would be a lengthy process involving more than one revision. He hoped to finish the second draft before sailing for Europe. However, he doubted that they could complete the editorial back-and-forth before his departure, since their work on *The Orchard Keeper* had taken a couple of years. It seems that Erskine had in mind that he would see and respond to a first or second draft before McCarthy revised yet again, while McCarthy felt that he would not be ready to share his disconnected work with his editor. But some time that spring Erskine's wishes became clearer to McCarthy, and he agreed to them.

The work was slower than McCarthy had anticipated, and his departure date was pushed back more than once. On May 19 a local journalist reported that McCarthy thought he would depart for Europe in June ("Knox Author Going"). If this was reported accurately, it may be that the interview had taken place much earlier than its printing because more than a week prior McCarthy had written Erskine that he had finished only about a quarter of his work on the "Early Draft" (between April and early May) and then expected to complete it in July. It would require considerable further revision, but he felt that at least then it would be in good enough shape for him to take to Europe. He promised to send a copy of the draft to Erskine (letter, received May 10, 1965). His actual departure occurred on August 19, and that month he was only about half finished with the revision, he confessed in a letter Erskine had received on August 11. McCarthy hoped that moving to a new location might be beneficial, a hint that he had not found Knoxville conducive to his work.[30]

Baskin replied for Erskine on the same day, telling McCarthy that the editor was then on vacation at his home in Connecticut and that he hoped McCarthy would be in New York long enough to meet with him. She provided Erskine's telephone number and suggested that McCarthy call to make plans. Indirect evidence that they did meet comes from Faulkner's biographer Joseph Blotner, who recalled forty years later that he had met McCarthy in Erskine's Random House office. Blotner thought that this had occurred before *The Orchard Keeper* was published ("Albert Erskine" 153), but the correspondence makes it clear that the earliest McCarthy and Erskine's first meeting could have taken place was in August 1965—several months after *The Orchard Keeper*'s May publication. Erskine wrote to Gerald Freund on March 24, 1966, that by then he had spent only "one very pleasant day talking with [McCarthy] about his work and the work of others." So he and McCarthy had little time to go over the half-finished second draft of *Outer Dark* line by line, and there is no evidence of an editorial hand on either of the two "Early Draft" documents in the McCarthy papers. But during their day together, McCarthy likely would have articulated his conception for this novel and for *Suttree* and received Erskine's reactions to his ideas for their structures and narrative strategies. If McCarthy sent Erskine a copy of the incomplete "Early Draft" in advance of their meeting, their discussion would also have been enriched by the editor's first reading, but no such copy survives in the editor's papers.

The events of McCarthy's European trip slowed his work on *Outer Dark* further. McCarthy met and fell in love with English dancer Anne De Lisle on his trans-Atlantic voyage on the Sylvania, where she was employed as an entertainer, half of the duo The Healey Sisters. She spotted him on the dance floor, asked him to dance with her, and they quickly bonded, spending their spare time together. Anne recalls that his trip terminated in Ireland, while she sailed on to Southampton, England. But they stayed in touch, and he accompanied her on part of her scheduled performance tours in Britain for several months (De Lisle, Conversations; Williams, "Annie DeLisle" E1). It was in a guest house there that he proposed to her. Later in the year, however, he settled in to revise his novel in Paris. On November 12, 1965, McCarthy posted a letter to Erskine, informing him that he was more than half finished and now thought his revision would be accomplished by February; and on January 27, 1966, he mailed Erskine the news that he was within thirty or forty pages of finishing. He planned to travel to England in the next week for a month's stay, he reported, drawn there by an "attractive" English woman (McCarthy, Letter to Albert Erskine, postmarked Jan. 27, 1966; Williams, "Annie DeLisle" E1). This letter is composed on stationery from the Hotel Mont-Joli on Rue Fromentin near the Moulin Rouge and Sacré-Coeur Basilica. Anne had introduced him to the hotel, and it became their usual place to stay in Paris (De Lisle, Conversations). In *The Passenger,* Western stays at the Mont Joli and McCarthy describes it as "favored by traveling entertainers and any morning there would be jugglers and hypnotists and exotic dancers and trained dogs in the lobby coffeeshop" (198). Since McCarthy was in transit, Erskine directed his reply of January 31, 1966, to McCarthy at André Deutsch, his publisher in London.

McCarthy's professional activities and his personal life both were going well. If his plans did not change again, he would have been in England by February 16, 1966, when Erskine wrote him in strict confidentiality that he would receive the William Faulkner Foundation Award but that he should say nothing about it before the official announcement. Random prepared a publicity release about the award from materials supplied by the Faulkner Foundation, supplemented, it seems likely, with information about McCarthy supplied by Erskine. In mid-March, when the announcement was made, McCarthy was in London for the publication of the British edition of *The Orchard Keeper* ("Books–Authors"; "McCarthy Wins Award"). He usually resisted publicizing his books, but he had personal reasons for wanting to be in England. He had written to Erskine in February 1966 that his "English campaign" was progressing perhaps too well. He had now finished working through the shorter novel, but he planned to let it sit for a month before doing another round of revisions on parts that still needed polishing. He thought he might mail a third draft by mid-summer unless Erskine needed it sooner.

When McCarthy replied to Erskine's news about the Faulkner Foundation award, he indicated that he had just been invited to apply to the Rockefeller Foundation. He had started drafting the required application essay but did not feel confident about it (letter, received Feb. 25, 1966). McCarthy was one of one hundred preliminary nominees for a grant from the Rockefeller Foundation's experimental new program to nurture highly promising individuals in literature and the humanities, and one of only forty invited to apply that year (Freund, Letter to potential Rockefeller Advisory Committee [1967]; Freund, Letter to Albert Erskine, Mar. 22, 1966; "Literature Program" enclosure). According to Gerald Freund, an officer of Rockefeller's Imaginative Writing and Literary Scholarship Program, the Rockefeller selection committee convened every eight to ten weeks year-round "to discuss the work of writers proposed by an annually changing group of nominators selected by them and the staff." In the beginning of the program's five-year duration, the selection committee included Saul Bellow, Robert Lowell, and Stanley Kunitz. Robert Penn Warren, John Hersey, Walker Percy, and James Dickey were added later, and finally the committee expanded to include Jean Valentine, Frank Conroy, and Robert Coles, who would become one of McCarthy's most influential supporters and friends (Freund, *Narcissism and Philanthropy* 94). Of these individuals, Bellow, Warren, and Hersey had received advance copies of *The Orchard Keeper* and were asked to write appreciations for the book jacket, but perhaps only Bellow was a selector at the time McCarthy was nominated.

Because the Rockefeller program did not have a fixed grant cycle, there may have been no deadline for McCarthy to respond. Still, the application was among the distractions from his creative work. He confessed in the letter

Erskine received on February 25, 1966, that he had slowed down on his writing recently but that he was still working and was anxious to finish "#2" so that he could revise "#3" before he let it get any lengthier. Replying on March 3, Erskine urged McCarthy to find the time to complete the Rockefeller application even if he found it "tedious." The grants were "negotiable, and usually ample" and he thought McCarthy might as well be one of the recipients—unless the award would require him to teach and thus take time away from his writing. This last bit of advice may simply have reinforced an inclination McCarthy already possessed, or it may have been a protective strategy he had already discussed with his editor, but it shows that Erskine endorsed McCarthy's intention to dedicate himself exclusively to his creative work no matter how pinched he was financially. Erskine's advice provides revealing context for McCarthy's remark to Woodward in 1992 that he thought the teaching of writing was "a hustle" (Woodward, "Venomous Fiction" 30). McCarthy seems to have found instruction unnecessary for the budding writer of talent and a harmful distraction for the teacher, who could be writing instead. At any rate, De Lisle has said that during the years of their marriage, he always found the money they needed (De Lisle, Conversations).

McCarthy's application packet, dated March 15, 1966, requested from Rockefeller a modest $4,000 in support, not for *Outer Dark,* which he then expected to finish in two more months, but for *Suttree,* which had grown to seven hundred pages of draft material requiring substantial revision. He estimated it would take him a year and a half or two to complete. He considered *Suttree* his masterwork so far, his most consuming project since he had begun it five years earlier, he wrote in his "Statement of Proposed Work." The rest of his eight-page packet combined the required essay with sample passages from the seventy pages of *Suttree* he had with him in Europe. First he set forth the aim of the book: through the actions of the characters, Knoxville would be presented as "a living organism. The overall effect aims not at total knowledge of life in this city but at an understanding of what life here would mean to a person who was totally aware. In a sense then, these characters . . . [embody] a single soul" (2). Then McCarthy introduced Michael, Suttree, Harrogate, and Ab Jones, quoting passages about them from his draft. Finally, identifying Knoxville as the novel's "cohesive force" (7), he closed with paragraphs describing the city.

After mailing off the proposal, McCarthy wrote Erskine that he had completed it but could not predict how the Rockefeller Foundation would respond. He hoped that the William Faulkner Award would console Deutsch and elicit more positive press in Great Britain since the reviews of the British edition of *The Orchard Keeper* had been unfavorable (letter, postmarked Mar. 15, 1966). Indeed, they were few and brief and more critical than admiring. No English reviewer commented on the novel's complex narrative strategies or demon-strated comprehension of its thematic tensions. All acknowledged McCarthy's sharp imagery yet found the novel derivative. The reviewer for the *Times Literary Supplement* dismissed it as too indebted to Faulkner while granting that McCarthy's talent for delineations of the natural world showed prom-ise ("Americans in Debt" 185). Norman Shrapnel, in the Manchester *Guard-ian Weekly,* found it impressive for a first novel, but deplored its mannered writing, which to him verged on parody (Shrapnel, "Echoes from the Corri-dors" 10).[31] And in the *New Statesman,* David Craig praised the novel's "sheer sense-perception" but disliked McCarthy's Joycean "insistence on external de-tail" stripped of direct exposition of the characters' emotions, and his "cult of the prose medium" (Craig, "Tanks, Trees" 348). With the English publication issued to disappointing reviews but with the encouraging announcement of the William Faulkner award, McCarthy planned to head back to Paris in the following week and stay about a month. He was unable to predict his return to the United States, but he thought it might be in the autumn (McCarthy, Letter to Albert Erskine, postmarked Mar. 15, 1966).

McCarthy's application reached the Rockefeller Foundation by March 22, 1966, when Freund wrote Erskine to ask him to review the proposal and assess McCarthy's capacity as a writer and the likelihood that he would complete the work. Erskine replied on March 24 with a glowing recommendation in which he affirmed that he had never worked with a more promising young writer and detailed the acclaim McCarthy had received for *The Orchard Keeper.* Erskine noted that even before it received any reviews or honors, both André Deutsch in London and Robert Laffont in Paris had accepted the first novel for publi-cation. Although he did not review McCarthy's application in any specificity,  · Erskine asserted that it was "one of the best of its kind I have ever seen" and was "additional evidence that this young man knows what he is doing and knows how to do it." He enclosed copies of *The Orchard Keeper* and some of its reviews.

Other letters of support came from Random House authors Ralph Ellison and John Hersey, who probably was not yet a member of the Rockefeller se-lection committee. Writing to Freund on April 5, 1966, Ellison repeated the endorsement he had composed for the jacket of *The Orchard Keeper* and ex-pressed his admiration for the excerpts from *Suttree* that McCarthy had included in his application, asserting "there is magic even in these bits of char-acterization and description." Hersey's endorsement of April 7 referred to the unanimous agreement of the American Academy of Arts and Letters that Mc-Carthy's "rare talent" deserved support, and while Hersey did not specifically address the excerpts from *Suttree,* he added that McCarthy "writes with fierce assurance in a style which is vivid yet does not seem mannered"—perhaps an implicit rebuttal of those reviewers of *The Orchard Keeper* who had complained about McCarthy's style.

As Rockefeller deliberated, Cormac and Anne married in the old Norman St. Andrews Episcopal Church of Hamble (c. 1100) on May 14, 1966. Since none of his family attended, Anne's younger brother Richard stood as Cormac's best man. Her performing partner, singer Nicky Banks, was her maid of honor, and some one hundred friends and members of Anne's family attended the wedding and the reception at her father's sports club. The couple rented a car and honeymooned for two weeks in Devon and Cornwall on England's southwestern coast. They stayed in Mousehole Village and toured the thirteenth-century Tintagel Castle (constructed on the birth site of King Arthur, according to the twelfth-century legend that had originated with Geoffrey of Monmouth). On their honeymoon, they attended the Bugatti races in Cornwall, when Anne first discovered Cormac's love of race cars, and later that summer they took a train from Paris to see Le Mans, sleeping in the open air (De Lisle, Conversations).

Although *The Orchard Keeper* had not received positive reviews in England, the Faulkner Award provoked new interest in publishing it in translation. While Cormac and Anne were enjoying their honeymoon, Erskine corresponded with staff at Mondadori Publishing Company in Italy, who were now considering doing an Italian translation of *The Orchard Keeper,* on which they had earlier passed (Erskine, Letter to Enzo Angelucci, May 19, 1966). And the next month, the publisher Diogenes Verlag in Zurich inquired about German-language rights (Diogenes, Postcard to Miss Currey, postmarked June 4, 1966), rights that would eventually be sold to the Swiss Roman Catholic publisher RCL Benziger at the end of January 1967 (Erskine, Letter to Cormac McCarthy, Aug. 8, 1967).

On June 2, 1966, about two weeks after the wedding, Freund wrote McCarthy in care of Random to inform him that Rockefeller's committee had approved him for support. The foundation would award him $5,000 for his living and working expenses for a two-year period beginning on July 1. McCarthy was one of twenty-three recipients out of the forty who had been invited to apply (Freund, Letter to potential Rockefeller Advisory Committee [1967]). The award was for $1,000 more than McCarthy had requested, but it was modest compared to others Rockefeller made in 1966/67 to writers of similar age and productivity. For instance, poet Fred Chappell and novelist Philip Roth were awarded $8,000 each; poet Thomas Gunn received $7,500; and novelist Donald Harington, who had also been in the running for the 1965 William Faulkner Foundation Award, received $7,200 ("Rockefeller Foundation Proposed Grantees 1966–1967 Literature Program," enclosed in Freund, Letter to Albert Erskine, July 5, 1966). Of the novelists, Harington, like McCarthy, had published only his first novel, *The Cherry Pit* (1965), while Roth had published three volumes of fiction: *Goodbye Columbus and Five Short Stories* (1959), *Portnoy's Complaint* (1959), and *Letting Go* (1962). When Erskine forwarded McCarthy the list of the Rockefeller grant recipients on January 16, 1967, he commented, "Please note how many people got more money by asking for it."

Freund would later write that the Rockefeller Foundation's systematic search for talented individuals often involved the officers' visiting candidates in their work places and developing relationships with them: "Systematic inquiry, friendly relationships . . . make it possible . . . to distinguish the exceptional from the very good, discovering in the process the trajectory of potential recipients' career paths, what senior people think of them, what their needs are to continue their work, and whether they are innovative and original or merely interesting" (Freund, *Narcissism and Philanthropy* 84). However, when McCarthy was nominated for the Rockefeller award early in 1966, he was living in Europe and often traveling. It seems unlikely that Rockefeller staff would have interviewed him there, although conversations could have taken place by telephone. But no archived correspondence substantiates personal contact between the Rockefeller staff and McCarthy either before or after he received the award. It may be that the Rockefeller selectors had based their decision entirely on the evidence of his application and the support of his editor and fellow writers. Nevertheless, the process had brought McCarthy to the attention of Freund, who would influence his receiving financial support from the Guggenheim and MacArthur foundations in the years to follow (see Luce, "Coles and McCarthy" 224).

With McCarthy newly married and assured of financial support through the end of June 1968, Erskine queried him about his work plans in a letter or telegram that does not survive. He received McCarthy's reply on June 15, 1966: he now had completed a second draft of *Outer Dark,* and he wanted to spend the summer rewriting it. This was essentially the same status he had reported to Erskine in the spring. If all went well with the revisions, he would send the novel to Erskine in late summer or early autumn. When Erskine replied to him that day in care of his French publisher, Robert Laffont, he already knew that Cormac and Anne meant to spend extended time in the Balearic Islands off the coast of Spain, but he did not yet have an address for them. De Lisle recalls that in Paris they had met writer Clifford Irving and that he encouraged them to spend some time in Ibiza, where he himself had lived since 1953 (De Lisle, Conversations).

On July 14, Erskine wrote McCarthy in care of Laffont again, asking where he could send royalties of $792.71 from the British and French editions of *The Orchard Keeper.* He feared that McCarthy would be traveling, and the check would miss him. And in fact, the couple took a twelve-day automobile trip in a used gold Jaguar XK-120 convertible that Cormac had bought and repaired. The car had a torn black ragtop, and when he first saw it, chickens were roosting inside it, as in one of the junkyard cars of *Child of God* (De Lisle, Conversations). Their tour began in Paris and wended through France to Geneva, across Italy and back along the southern coast of France to Barcelona, where they stayed a few days before they took the car ferry to Ibiza in early August 1966. There they settled in a *finca* on the outskirts of town (Williams, "Annie DeLisle" E1–2; De Lisle, Conversations).

On August 12 Erskine received McCarthy's letter assuring him that he was back at work, presumably crafting his "Middle Draft" of *Outer Dark,* but it was already clear that he would need longer to revise than he had most recently estimated. He and Anne stayed in Ibiza for a year instead of returning to the United States in fall 1966 as he had earlier thought they would. There they met Philadelphia writer Leslie Garrett, whose first novel *The Beasts* (1966) had just won the Maxwell Perkins award, and who would remain a friend until his death in 1993.[32] They also socialized with Clifford Irving and his fiancée Edith Sommer, who hosted them several times at their *finca*. Their electricity was unreliable, so they often baked potatoes in foil in the fireplace. Irving was then in the process of interviewing Hungarian artist/art forger Elmyr de Hory for the biography *Fake!—Adventures of the Greatest Art Forger of Our Time* (1969), and Anne recalls that she and Cormac met de Hory socially as well.[33] She remembers that their circle of friends would meet for morning coffee at a bodega while they waited for the mail to come in, and the drinking would start in the afternoon (De Lisle, Conversations).

After the announcement of the Faulkner Award, Erskine apparently had alerted McCarthy that *The Orchard Keeper* might eventually go into a second printing, and on May 10, 1966, he received McCarthy's note of three punctuation and spacing corrections to be made. A Random House Royalty Statement for *The Orchard Keeper* indicates that in the six months ending on September 30, 1966, the first printing had sold modestly, netting McCarthy a cumulative royalty of less than $100 for the preceding twelve months. On August 17, Erskine had written McCarthy that although there was no urgent need for a new printing, an inconsistency existed in the first printing concerning which of Sylder's feet was missing the big toe. Also, Erskine now recognized that he had made a mistake in preparing the jacket copy when he wrote that the novel's time setting was the first quarter of the twentieth century rather than the second. They would need to correct both errors in the next printing, and he wanted McCarthy to make the decision about Sylder's foot. In his reply, McCarthy recalled that although he had tried to be vigilant about such matters, a similar error in Ownby's speculations about the significance of the social worker's birth date had nearly escaped him even in the final draft. He thought he must have a "selfdefeating mechanism" that resulted in such oversights. He asked that the next printing change the reference on page 161 from Sylder's right boot to the left and reiterated from his note in the spring that the word "patch" on page 216 should be "path" (letter to Erskine, received Aug. 29, 1966). It was not until 1969 that a second printing was issued. In this and subsequent printings, Sylder's left foot is injured; however, the second of the corrections was never made, so that the cat still comes "down the patch obscure with parched weeds" (*OK* 216).

There is no surviving correspondence between McCarthy and Erskine for the rest of 1966, when McCarthy continued revising *Outer Dark,* completing the "Final Draft" by December 20. Because he could not afford the thirty dollars for airmail postage, he informed Erskine that he was sending the typescript to New York by ship (McCarthy, Letter to Albert Erskine, received Jan. 8, 1967). It reached the editor on January 23, accompanied by a letter in which McCarthy expressed his awareness of the many delays it had undergone. But in fact he had finished the third and fourth drafts quite quickly, from late summer 1966 to January 1967, a feat made possible by the facts that he had painstakingly solved all of the problems of structure and narrative technique in his first two drafts and that the submitted draft was substantially similar to the "Middle Draft."

In Ibiza, in addition to socializing with Irving and Garrett and enjoying a visit from Anne's performance partner Nicky, who had by then married their pianist Allen Tirrell (De Lisle, Conversations), McCarthy probably continued to work on *Suttree* as well as *Child of God,* which he had conceived by early 1966. It is possible that he needed more time with these novels before he could think of returning to the United States, and the Rockefeller award had enabled him to extend his time in Europe. Late in summer 1967, he and Anne finally left Ibiza and traveled back to her family home in Hamble via Madrid and the mountain hamlet, Burgete, in Navarre, where Hemingway's Jake Barnes enjoys fishing in *The Sun also Rises.* McCarthy too did some trout fishing there. Then they drove back to Paris, where McCarthy sold the Jaguar (De Lisle, Interview with Bryan Giemza and Dianne Luce).

As he left his friend Leslie Garrett, who later developed serious addictions, McCarthy advised him to give up the drinking and partying life in Ibiza for fear it would kill his work (Williams, "An Interview with Leslie Garrett" 54), and concerns about drinking and over-socializing may have been one reason for his own return to the United States. "If there is an occupational hazard to writing, it's drinking," he later told Woodward (Woodward, "Venomous Fiction" 36). De Lisle recalls that McCarthy drank, but never so much that it could affect his writing ability—only his discipline (Conversations). A more certain factor behind their removal was that Anne was excited to go to the United States to see where McCarthy had come from (Williams, "Annie DeLisle" E2).

She wanted to meet his family and friends. Furthermore, with *Outer Dark* completed, McCarthy may have wished to have a face-to-face editorial conference, as Erskine had persistently recommended. Finally, he may well have felt the need to be in East Tennessee to continue his work on *Suttree*, his big Knoxville novel.

On August 7, 1967, Erskine received McCarthy's request that the editor explain Random's financial accounting to him. McCarthy had just received a royalty check, and he wondered if that meant that the sales revenues from *The Orchard Keeper* had finally exceeded his advances. He asked, too, if he should by now have received an advance for the second novel. Erskine replied on August 8 that McCarthy's advances had indeed been repaid out of revenue from publication rights for his foreign translations. And the advance for the new novel was forthcoming; it had slipped Erskine's mind. Since the contract for *Outer Dark* had specified that Random would pay the advances in installments, this correspondence refers to the payment which had been due on McCarthy's submission of the final draft in January (Random House, Contract [for *Outer Dark*], Jan. 4, 1965).

In his August letter, McCarthy explained that he and Anne were back in England and had been to London to apply for her visa to the United States. However, Anne was encountering red tape. Erskine tried to facilitate through his friend Cleanth Brooks, who had served as Cultural Attaché at the American Embassy in London from 1964 through 1966. But despite their efforts, the visa was not issued until October. When it finally came through, McCarthy took a break from his and Anne's rushed packing to write Erskine that they would sail on the Queen Elizabeth on October 12 and reach New York on October 17 (McCarthy, Letter to Albert Erskine, received Oct. 11, 1967).

# The Editing Stage

When McCarthy met with his editor in the northeast for one day on his way to Europe in August 1965, he had carried with him the unfinished "Early Draft" of *Outer Dark*. There was little time for Erskine to read it, but presumably he gave McCarthy wholistic feedback to consider as he revised further. After he received the final draft of the novel early in 1967, Erskine inquired on March 15 whether McCarthy had rethought his stand on punctuation or wanted to follow the same principles they had agreed to for *The Orchard Keeper*. On April 10, Erskine received McCarthy's reply that he had not changed his mind. Erskine had read and made notes on the new typescript by May 23, and that spring he repeatedly suggested that they meet to go over the final draft when McCarthy returned to the United States. He felt that they could "save no end of letter writing if we can sit down and look at it together." He gave no indication that he had found significant problems in the typescript. "I have a number of questions that I am sure you can answer," he wrote, "and there are a lot of little details" (Erskine, Letter to Cormac McCarthy, May 23, 1967). They did meet to work on the draft when McCarthy returned from Europe in October, and through such visits to New York or Connecticut, McCarthy developed a more personal relationship with the Erskines. De Lisle recalls that after a brief stay in New York, they visited Erskine in Westport for about a week and a half (Interview with Bryan Giemza and Dianne Luce).

Erskine's meetings with his authors typically combined hospitality, friendship, and intensive work with their typescripts. Eudora Welty recalled, "I remember on my novel 'Losing Battles,' [Erskine] had me out to his house as a guest, eating wonderful food and having a lovely time, and every day we went to his desk and went over this long manuscript, line by line" (quoted in Lambert, "Albert R. Erskine, 81"). Further sense of the working sessions may be gleaned from the memories of scholar Matthew Bruccoli, whose *The O'Hara Concern: A Biography of John O'Hara* Erskine edited: "He had pages of notes on my work: he queried words; he identified clumsy sentences; he required me to recheck facts. . . . [H]e . . . was well and widely read. The vetting sessions were punctuated with Albert's anecdotes about working with Faulkner, O'Hara, Welty, and Warren." Bruccoli felt he "had been inducted into the most exclusive literary club in America" (quoted in Blotner, "Albert Erskine" 152). Bensky describes Erskine's geniality at a lunch meeting they once had with Faulkner during which no work could be accomplished because Faulkner had been drinking: "Albert would tell stories about . . . how he partied with Robert Penn Warren ... how he had a girlfriend in Oxford, Mississippi . . . Albert was this great Southern mouth. He'd wave his hands and smile" (Josyph, "Damn Proud" 14). It is not hard to see why over time Erskine and McCarthy, two southern storytellers, developed such rapport.

During his face-to-face editorial sessions with Erskine in mid-October, McCarthy made notes in red on his carbon copy of the final draft, the carbon typescript he has labeled "Late Draft" in his archive. The two agreed to some changes right away and Erskine marked them on his copy, as revealed in McCarthy's marginal notations of the revisions the editor had already recorded (see "Late Draft" 61; 68, for examples). Erskine's copy of the final draft became the setting copy, which shows several layers of minor changes. Erskine's markings in red pencil seem to be the earliest ones and to address some of the questions he had formulated for McCarthy to deal with. Most are queries about wording and plot details. Diction issues included Erskine's question mark at the phrase "an almost palpable amnion of propriety," but McCarthy penciled "OK" next to it when he met with his editor in the northeast ("Setting Copy" 166; *OD* 151). The editor had also flagged the phrase "awned storefronts" and jotted "awninged? Awned has different meaning" ("Setting Copy" 146). McCarthy revised the phrase to "store awnings" on the "Setting Copy" (cf. *OD* 134). Still other changes came out of their reading the typescript together and were recorded right away. They agreed that "arching" was not the right word for the fireplace opening in the cabin where Culla trespasses, and both changed it to "lintel" in red on their respective copies ("Late Draft" and "Setting Copy" 222; *OD* 196). They also caught a sentence that inadvertently created a rhyme: "the boat began to quiver and to move very slowly out into the river" ("Late Draft" and "Setting Copy" 181–82; cf. *OD* 164), and in the "Setting Copy" the final phrase is crossed out.

Erskine flagged a jolting gap in chronology between the scene of Culla's digging the graves for Clark in late spring and the following scene when the lawyer and doctor meet Rinthy in the fall, and she tells the doctor that the baby was born in March ("Setting Copy," 165; cf. *OD* 153). But since these scenes are focused on different characters, the asynchrony was intentional, as was Rinthy's seeing the maddened horse in a startling recurrence. Time ruptures were among the strategies McCarthy had deployed to undercut realism in this novel. The editorial query may have led to a productive conversation about the roles of chronology and phantasmagoria in *Outer Dark,* and McCarthy did not eliminate or mediate the abrupt temporal shift between these scenes. Neither is there evidence that Erskine tracked every time reference in the novel as Bensky had for *The Orchard Keeper,* which suggests that Erskine recognized McCarthy's strategy and queried the most obvious time disruption primarily in order to confirm his intentions.

Few substantive editorial comments are recorded on the "Setting Copy," and no separate list of queries survives in Erskine's papers. But he raised his other concerns as he and McCarthy went through the typescript line by line, some of which McCarthy noted on the "Late Draft." Back in Tennessee with his notes to guide him, McCarthy revised some of these passages in pencil on the "Late Draft," and on December 22, 1967, his editor received McCarthy's eight-page list of changes, keyed to the pagination of the final draft copies on which he and Erskine were working. McCarthy's notes and revisions support the conclusion to be drawn from Erskine's red penciling on the "Setting Copy": the editor did not ask for the degree of substantive change he and Bensky had thought the final draft of *The Orchard Keeper* needed—but he did question details and phrasing. So the editing of *Outer Dark* was more similar to that Erskine had done on the revised final draft of *The Orchard Keeper.* But their interchanges for the first novel had been carried out in writing back and forth on the typescript itself, while for *Outer Dark,* much of the discussion occurred during their work sessions, and some probably occurred in subsequent telephone conversations, leaving us to infer the process from McCarthy's notes on his "Late Draft" and his revision list.

In the cover letter for his revision list, McCarthy addressed his usage of three words that Erskine had asked him to verify, and in each case the word remains in the published novel. Adrift on the river, Culla sees the "gradied imprecision of the silhouetted trees" (*OD* 167). McCarthy explained that "Gradied" derived from "Grady," which the *OED* defined as "a heraldic term signifying stepped." He offered to delete it if Erskine thought it "too far-fetched or fanciful" (McCarthy to Erskine, Dec. 22, 1967). In one description of the triune on the "Setting Copy," Erskine had queried "anthroparian," a being possessed of human traits; but in their meeting together McCarthy had not been able to recall where he had found the word (50; *OD* [51]). When he submitted his revision list and cover letter in December, he still had not located a cite for it, but he offered to do so when he could get to the library; and eventually he must have satisfied his editor that the word was apt. The Greek noun "anthroparion," with a similar meaning to "homunculus," appears in the *Visions* of the third-century alchemist Zosimos of Panopolis. Carl Jung and his editor Aniela Jaffé briefly mention the word, its synonym and its ancient source in *Memories, Dreams, Reflections,* which McCarthy could have read in English as early as 1963 (Jung, *Memories* 185 and n 5). McCarthy refers to *Memories* in his *Suttree* papers (Crews, *Books Are Made* 97-98), and it appears to have influenced his treatments of the unconscious in *Outer Dark, The Passenger,* and *Stella Maris.*[34] Also addressed in his revision letter was McCarthy's unusual use of "camarine," defined as "a fetid marsh or swamp" in the *Oxford English Dictionary.* In the "Late Draft," a passage about the baby's wailing reads: "[Culla] lay there in his terror half witless and gibbering with palsied jawhasps while it rent the camarine night with wail on wail, as if some paraclete had finally stove a hole in hell," and a note in McCarthy's hand indicates "Albert likes up to here" (17). Possibly this was a reminder that for Erskine the sentence was the first false note, and McCarthy restructured it, making "paraclete" refer to Culla less ambiguously and "camarine" refer not to the night but to the "world of [the baby's] nativity" (cf. *OD* 18). But he also reconsidered his use of "camarine." In his revision list, McCarthy initially replaced it with "palustrine," then restored it (1). In his cover letter, he noted that "Camarine . . . is a noun, according to the OED, but I dont see why the adjective form shouldnt be camarine as well. Do you? Or do you?" Possibly Erskine also objected to McCarthy's indeterminate "as if some" in these lines, which emphasized the imaginative or counterfactual nature of his simile; but McCarthy did not revise it. When he edited *Child of God,* Erskine recommended that McCarthy avoid the usage, yet it has remained a feature of his style.

Other editorial queries addressed plot details, continuity, and clarity, and most interesting are those passages that McCarthy did not revise. For example, he chose not to identify more fully the farmer Rinthy stays with. At the beginning of that scene, he recorded in the margin, "Albert says who is it?" ("Late Draft" 238). But having already discarded draft material that fleshed out the farmer's character, he did not name the farmer or attempt to provide more backstory for him (see *OD* 209–211). Like Mrs. Sylder in *The Orchard Keeper,* the farmer was significant only for his relationship to Rinthy, and their scene economically illustrates her inability to form new bonds while she grieves for her lost child. The man's hard life and longing for connection evoke reader empathy, but he remains one of the mysterious elements of the novel, unexplored because Rinthy does not allow herself fully to know him, and more poignant for it.

Erskine may also have suggested more imagery of the triune's departure from their riverside campsite. During their work session McCarthy wrote in the margin, "perhaps he [Culla] should watch them go?" But as he considered this further, he crossed out his note in pencil ("Late Draft" 205), thus retaining the emphasis on the triune's dream nature when Harmon simply "turned and was gone," and Culla "listened for their voices but he could hear nothing" (*OD* 182–83).

A more puzzling editorial query appears in the scene in Cheatham when the mob chases Culla, where a marginal note asks, "Where is the sheriff?" ("Late Draft" 104). A brief reference to the sheriff occurs in the scene, and the question seems to be why he does not try to control the angry townspeople or investigate the grave robbing (see *OD* 88). When McCarthy responded to the query some time after his meeting with Erskine, he may not have remembered the issue Erskine had raised. Below the marginal note McCarthy inscribed an answer: "out of town - see p 150 or so," and he did not revise the scene ("Late Draft" 104). But the passage McCarthy refers to is the one in which the store owner Clark tells the irate turnip farmer that he was out of town when the men were hanged in the farmer's field (*OD* 140). Clark appears to function as the squire for his town, but it is not established that he is also the sheriff. Neither is this the same town as Cheatham. But McCarthy's slip suggests that he thought of Clark as one of the novel's agents of law and order. We cannot know whether he later realized he had confused the two scenes. If he did not, then he left the Cheatham scene unresolved because he thought it was not an issue; if he did, then he chose not to revise the Cheatham scene because he wanted the sheriff's inaction to be part of the scene's effect, a strategy he would employ in *Child of God*'s auction and lynching scenes.

Apparently, Erskine questioned whether "cranked" was the right word to use for the action of a pump handle, and McCarthy recorded the reminder to himself: "See TOK & car jacks?"—a reference to the scene in which Rattner dreams up a new kind of jack that is cranked sideways rather than up and down ("Late Draft" 129). In his revision list, he wrote "I think <u>cranked</u> is OK (the handle itself describes part of an arc in its descent" (4; *OD* 118).

Other queries demonstrably or probably Erskine's resulted in revision. In the "Late Draft," at the end of the scene at the baby's false grave, Culla raises his hands in threat or supplication to the "gray and windy heavens" (34). But earlier in the scene is a reference to "windy sunlight," and McCarthy considered substitutes for "gray" to make the weather consistent throughout. In the margin he jotted "blue?" and below it "bland," which he crossed through. "Blue and windy" would have been consistent with the sunlit day, but McCarthy may have found the phrase bland. Or he may have thought of "bland" to replace "gray" and to suggest the indifference of the heavens. But finally he hit on the inspired "mute and windy heavens"—a phrase that conveys Culla's sense that his challenges to heaven go unanswered, which McCarthy had made very understated when he removed Culla's direct addresses to God in his early drafts (*OD*: Revision list 1; *OD* 33).

As McCarthy and Erskine went through the final draft together, they also had spotted ineffective word repetition in a description of the mute, who "stood with long arms hanging at his sides, . . . his jaw hanging." In the margin of his "Late Draft" McCarthy jotted a question mark in red and tried out the revision "his jaw slung in his cheeks." Later he crossed out this revision in pencil but reminded himself that the problem was repetition: "2 hanging." Ultimately, he replaced the first "hanging" with "dangling" (188) and listed the change in his letter to Erskine (cf. *OD* 169).

It may have been Erskine's idea that McCarthy "break up" a description of Rinthy's following the tinker to the cabin that read: "When they came to the top of the hill the track turned and they went on through high meadow out of which sprang small fowl to wheel away with indignant cries over the sedgetops blueing with crept dusk" ("Late Draft" 210), but McCarthy's revision simply arranged the phrases more felicitously (*OD*: Revision list 5; see *OD* 187). Erskine questioned "The floor's fierce declination," and McCarthy revised this to "incline" ("Late Draft" 222; *OD* 196). It seems that Erskine objected to a reference to an "auditorium" because it was inconsistent with the setting of the novel, and McCarthy replaced it with "hall" ("Late Draft" 241; *OD* 212). And it may be that Erskine found the phrase "snaked off the limbs" too colloquial; McCarthy changed it to "dressed off the limbs" (*OD*: Revision list 1; "Late Draft" 42; *OD* 44).

In his earliest markings of the setting copy, Erskine had red-penciled angle brackets in the margin next to McCarthy's usage of "yander" (62). In his "Late Draft," beside the phrase "Right yonder in the box," McCarthy recorded this query about consistency of dialect usage, and he penciled the explanation: "yander is outdoors/ yonder is in (or close)" (90; *OD* 84). The editorial query prompted him to double-check his draft for consistency: in his list of revisions McCarthy calls for the correction of "yander" to "yonder" in the line, "Ast them fellers on the porch yonder"—a reference to the men gathered just outside the store ("Late Draft" 92; *OD* 85). At some point McCarthy must have explained his distinction to his editor and copy editor. The published text includes twenty-two instances of "yonder" and four of "yander."

At this late stage, McCarthy made more revisions to the scene between Rinthy and the tinker than to any other, perhaps because his most pressing challenges throughout his drafting had concerned Culla and the triune. Some of McCarthy's changes may have resulted from his and Erskine's conversations about the dynamics between the two at the cabin. One deletion made the tinker's sexual innuendo even less obvious. Before this late-stage revision, when the tinker questions whether Rinthy would do much to get a child and she replies that she would for this child, he asks suggestively, "Say you would?" She responds, "Yes. . . . I want him back." In the margin McCarthy recorded "No" in red, and then penciled a question mark as he considered further ("Late Draft" 208). Finally, he called for the deletion of these lines (*OD*: Revision list 5; cf. *OD* 186). In another passage Rinthy asks the tinker if they might reach her son "tomorrow," and the tinker chews on and does not answer. However, McCarthy decided that he needed to imply more emphatically that the tinker is changing his mind about returning the child. In pencil he wrote "up to here there is no indication that he is reneging" ("Late Draft" 215). In his revision letter, he added two more lines of dialogue to make the tinker's evasion more apparent:

Tomorrow?
Will we? (letter, Dec. 22, 1967: 6; *OD* 191)

When Rinthy says she will make up to the tinker whatever he gave for her son, in the "Late Draft" his response is "Ha"—as if he is still thinking he can extort sex from her or at least is judging her promiscuous (216). But the revision list changes this to "Will ye now," which gives more emphasis to his skepticism that anyone can repay him for the misery of his life (6; *OD* 192). Having made these changes, McCarthy deleted an explicit reference to the tinker's changing his mind about having sex with Rinthy once he learns that the child resulted from incest. In the "Late Draft" when he finally tells her angrily that she will see him dead before she sees her child, she asks, "What did ye bring me here for then." He replies, "It dont make no difference about that. Because I changed my mind about that even" (219). In his December 1967 revision list, McCarthy replaced this interchange with a new one. Here Rinthy keens in the line adapted from Gogol, "You wont never have no rest. . . . Not never," and the tinker replies bitterly, "Nor any human soul" (6; *OD* 194). The revision does not appear on the "Late Draft," where McCarthy had penciled a different response from the tinker to Rinthy's "never": "Never is now. Tomorrow is never." This reply would have emphasized the tinker's current misery, but the version McCarthy chose for the published novel turns Rinthy's prediction that the tinker will find no rest back on herself yet ironically resonates with the novel's end, where she sleeps.

As he revised, McCarthy also rewrote some stylistically challenging passages such as the one about the baby's wailing in the "camarine dark," working to make his language sharper and more concise. Perhaps Erskine had recommended that he take another look at any passage that might be accused of overwriting, especially considering the responses to *The Orchard Keeper* by Boyle, Dykeman, Madden and Murray. But it was also typical of McCarthy's revising practice that he would continually hone his language for poetic effect. His description of the hanged men in the field at dawn had read "these eyeless dead seemed alien and dreamlike, as of things come uninvited from the night to outrage the waking world with their grisly and improbable existence." In his concise penciled revision, the dead men "come alien and unreal like figures wandered from a dream" ("Late Draft" 160; cf. *OD* 146). His revised description of Rinthy's keening as the tinker leaves her behind is more rhythmic and elegiac in tone, while it retains the same imagery and diction. In the "Late Draft" the tinker can hear her keening across the fields, "his pans knelling in the night like buoys on some dim and barren coast, her sorrow lonely as seabirds' cries fending back in the night the vast and salt black solitudes they keep." McCarthy first tried out more parallel phrasing, "his pans knelling . . ., her sorrow fading" but the revised sentence compared the tinker's solitude to the ocean's, and perhaps he felt this was too inexact since the ocean does not feel its own solitude. He crossed out this attempt. Then he penciled in the new version that restored the solitude to the seabirds, ". . . his pans knelling . . . like buoys on some . . . barren coast, and he could hear it [Rinthy's keening] fading . . . lost as the cry of seabirds in the vast and salt black solitudes they keep" (220; cf. *OD* 194). (The vast, salt black solitude of the ocean would recur in key images in *Blood Meridian* [304] and *The Road* [215; 234].) McCarthy transmitted neither of these changes in his revision letter, and he communicated them to Erskine in some other way.

McCarthy worked on these final revisions mostly in transient living situations. He had bought a Continental convertible in New York, and on the way to Tennessee he and Anne visited his sister Barbara's family in Ridgewood, New Jersey, and McCarthy's parents, who had just relocated to Falls Church, Virginia, near Washington, DC. When the young couple reached Tennessee in late November 1967, they stayed with Gary Goodman for a time before finding their own place. Before McCarthy sent his long revision letter to Erskine in late December, Goodman read the "Late Draft" McCarthy was revising, and he jotted suggestions, which McCarthy identifies as "Gary's." Goodman's corrections addressed typographical errors and small dialect inconsistencies in the use of "ye" and "ary," and McCarthy accepted most of them. But where the "Late Draft" describes the noseless grandmother breaking off a twig of spicewood and fraying its end "to make herself a snuff stick," Goodman wrote in the margin: "Too much fuckin folklore/put her snuffstick in later" (69). McCarthy simply took out the explanation that the twig would become a snuff stick, while he retained other references to her using snuff (*OD*: Revision list 2; *OD* 67). It seems unlikely he would have agreed with Goodman that he included too much folklore in his Tennessee novels. One of McCarthy's originating conceptions for the novel was that its Appalachian locale would be treated as a purgatory or hell in an overarching metaphor, and the references to Tennessee folkways anchored his phantasmagorical narrative in the cultural realities of the region. However, McCarthy initially may have explained the twig's purpose as a snuff stick because it was the kind of regionalism Erskine had queried when he edited *The Orchard Keeper*. McCarthy's revision allowed the folklore reference to stand without the cumbersome explication.

When Erskine received McCarthy's revision letter and list on December 22, 1967, he recorded the briefer changes on the "Setting Copy" in red ink. He had a few longer new passages cut from a copy of McCarthy's list or retyped from it and taped in place on leaves corresponding to pages 54, 131, and 172 in the Vintage edition.

With the final revisions in Erskine's hands, McCarthy planned to spend the holidays with his youngest brother Dennis, then a ranger at Soco Gap in North Carolina's Balsam Mountains (McCarthy, Letter to Albert Erskine, received Dec. 22, 1967). Anne had found living with Goodman and his girlfriend uncomfortable, although he was well-read and affable. By mid-February, McCarthy rented a small, four-room place on Self Hollow Road in Rockford, south of Knoxville. The recently refurbished house sat on one hundred acres of land (McCarthy, Letter to Albert Erskine, Feb. 15, 1968). Pat Fields, who interviewed them there, described it as a "tidy little house on a secluded farm" (Fields, "Knox Native" A8). But De Lisle remembered it as a house situated on "a little pig farm. Just outrageous" (Williams, "Annie DeLisle" E2). And she meant this literally. There was a pig sty at the bottom of the garden, and one Sunday when McCarthy's father and petite mother, elegantly dressed in her Chanel suit, came to visit after church, they were greeted by a litter of squealing piglets running up the drive (De Lisle, Conversations).

When McCarthy sent Erskine his finished draft of *Outer Dark* from Ibiza, he had still been mulling over a title for it (letter, received Jan. 23, 1967). Although they discussed possibilities in their October work sessions, the issue remained unsettled. In a letter or phone call to Erskine after he reached Tennessee in late November 1967, McCarthy had apparently suggested a tentative title, perhaps in jest, provoking Erskine to respond on November 28, "I am sure that I can think of several titles . . . that are less attractive than the one you suggest, but it will take me a little time to dredge them up. Please keep trying." The novel remained untitled when it went to the designer on February 5, 1968 (Erskine, Memo to Sidney Jacobs). During their conversations, Erskine suggested "The Harrow," and in a letter the editor received on February 15, 1968, McCarthy responded that it was "not bad," and it might do if they did not come up with anything better. He thought that some titles seemed "right . . . because of sheer habituation." On the other hand, a title such as *The Glass Menagerie* was inherently intriguing. In any case, he was still thinking.

Erskine was pushing to publish the book in August, and he wrote on February 17, 1968, that they would need a title within another month. He was reluctant to insist on "The Harrow" because he had "doubts that it conforms with your conception of the book; it derives from my rather vague conception, which may, as I've indicated, be a misconception, or an over- or underconception of what the novel says, is about. Our conversations on this didn't get very far, and I still shudder at the thought of writing the description on the jacket. . . . I don't mean that the book doesn't say a lot to me, but that what it says or seems to say is beyond my powers of communication." He added that for him "The Harrow" resonated not only with "The Harrowing of Hell" but also with "In Tenebris" by Thomas Hardy. Hardy's poem uncannily captures the "bereavement-pain" (line 2) McCarthy was experiencing as he began writing *Outer Dark,* and Erskine may have recognized this. Likely the two had talked at least briefly about his divorce when they met just before McCarthy embarked for Europe in 1965, if not earlier when Erskine was drafting the author's biography for *The Orchard Keeper.* Erskine may have felt that Hardy's poem would not only provide an apt title but also might resonate for McCarthy with the circumstances under which he conceived *Outer Dark.*

The speaker of "In Tenebris" notes the advent of autumn and attempts to find limited consolation in the idea that the dark season cannot deepen his sorrow:

Flower-petals flee;
But, since it once hath been,
No more that severing scene
Can harrow me. (ll. 5–8)

However, the poem ends with no compensatory affirmation but with hopeless resignation to loss:

Black is night's cope;
But death will not appal
One who, past doubtings all,
Waits in unhope. (ll 21–24)

On March 11, Erskine received McCarthy's reply: he had read Hardy's "black poem" and thought that to some degree it anticipated "the tone of <u>untitled novel</u>" (1). But McCarthy did not take to Erskine's suggestion of "The Harrow." He claimed to worry that because the word evoked the farm implement, attaching it to his second book after a first novel titled *The Orchard Keeper* might give the impression that he was "an authority on . . . husbandry" (1). (Possibly the subtext of this largely facetious comment was that he was concerned that he would be limited as a writer if he were to be too insistently identified with the Southern Agrarians, with whom his editor was associated.) Still, he did not have a better title to suggest although he made some notations toward a title. His ideas included "Among Supplicants"; "Dark and Mortal Wood"; and "Blue Widow" (1). He also noted that a story told in the Grand Inquisitor section of Dostoyevsky's *The Brothers Karamazov* bears the title "The Wanderings of Our Lady through Hell," which he thought might be apt. But he added that if his title referred to another work, it needed to be relevant to his novel.

Two weeks later, on March 22, 1968, Erskine communicated through Baskin that the title must be firmed up by the end of the month. He suggested "Place of Darkness" from Job 38.19–20, as well as two minor variations, and invited McCarthy to call him collect so they could discuss the title further if one of these did not meet his approval. Several leaves of notes in Erskine's hand represent his own work on possible titles—many of them references to the Bible or to Dante's *Inferno*, in which he picked up on McCarthy's "Dark and Mortal Wood." Since one of these leaves, the back of an envelope, is headed with McCarthy's name and number, they may have made the final decision over the phone. Above McCarthy's name is inscribed "Outer Dark"—likely recorded during their conversation (Erskine, Notes on titles). Rather than selecting a title that alluded to Dante or Dostoyevsky, Shakespeare or Gogol, McCarthy settled on one that referred not only to the Bible and to two passages in his new novel (*OD* [129]; 211), but also to his first novel, specifically the paragraph he had added about Kenneth Rattner's silent communing with a figure in the "outer dark." Because *Outer Dark* had in effect partly grown out of his thinking about narrative strategies to convey Rattner's mysterious role, because the triune fulfill functions similar to Rattner's dark double, because Culla experiences the dark night of the soul, and because Rinthy too travels in "outer dark" when she compulsively resumes her futile search for her son, the title stood by itself. It was confirmed at Random House by April 9 (Baskin, Memo to [C.A.] Wimpfheimer, Apr. 9, 1968).

Early on, Erskine and McCarthy had agreed that they would follow the same punctuation practices for *Outer Dark* as they had for *The Orchard Keeper*. However, for a variety of reasons this did not happen consistently. In the transmittal letter Erskine received with the typescript on January 23, 1967, McCarthy alerted Erskine that the final draft had been prepared by multiple typists who spoke different native languages, and he repeated the warning in April, especially about the typists' varying practices with apostrophes (letter received Apr. 10, 1967). This would not have been an insurmountable problem, but copy editor Bertha Krantz was ill with pneumonia when McCarthy's revisions reached Erskine before Christmas of 1967, and she remained ill at least through mid-February (Erskine to McCarthy, Jan. 11, 1968; Feb. 1, 1968). Because Erskine wanted to publish the book quickly, he recorded McCarthy's changes on the setting copy and sent it on to designer Sidney Jacobs on February 5 with instructions that the printer should follow the punctuation and dialect spelling of the setting copy "faithfully." Erskine had promised McCarthy that Krantz would read the proofs and, presumably, do her copy-editing at that stage, but the process remained rushed. The galleys reached Erskine and Krantz on April 8, and before they mailed them to McCarthy on the next day, she flagged a few "inconsistencies" for him to resolve. The plan was for all of them to proofread over the next two weeks (Erskine, Letter to Cormac McCarthy, Apr. 9, 1968). Nevertheless, it seems that *Outer Dark* did not finally receive the same kind of rigorous copyediting and proofreading that McCarthy's earlier and later books did.

Now that McCarthy was back in the United States, Erskine's time-sensitive business with him was conducted by telephone, contributing further to the decrease in correspondence between them. As a result, little further documentation of the editorial and production processes for *Outer Dark* survives in the Erskine or McCarthy papers. The setting copy for the copyright page was approved on May 9, 1968. On May 27, 1968, Erskine received McCarthy's suggestion that the author's note should emphasize the period of his life after *The Orchard Keeper*. Accordingly, the "About the Author" section of the dust jacket stresses the critical success of McCarthy's first novel and the awards he had garnered. This time, McCarthy allowed Erskine to include the personal information about his marriage to "an English girl" and their home in Rockford, Tennessee. But there was no mention of Lee or Cullen. About his first marriage, McCarthy was still protecting his and their privacy.

The photograph reproduced on the back flyleaf of *Outer Dark* might be one taken during the same formal sitting as that on *The Orchard Keeper,* but no photo credit appears on the *Outer Dark* jacket to support this. McCarthy may have selected from photos he had on hand one that he thought would suffice. He wrote Erskine that although it was small, it was "sharp" and suitable for enlarging (McCarthy, Letter to Albert Erskine, received May 27, 1968). In this photo, again McCarthy wears a conservative dark jacket and tie over a white shirt. Thus it appears somewhat dated for the late 1960s: nothing here suggests his unconventional lifestyle or hints, as the pictures for *Child of God* and *Suttree* would, that he had adopted the informal dress of the youth culture. But this photo was a genial and animated shot. Instead of the brooding eyes and barely perceptible smile of the portrait selected for *The Orchard Keeper,* this more relaxed shot captures McCarthy in smiling conversation, his eyes sparkling, in cordial engagement with the viewer. The dark shadow of his beard in the photo for *The Orchard Keeper* does not appear in this second photo, which is lit better or retouched. Ironically, each photograph is better suited to the tone of the novel on which it did not appear, but they may reflect McCarthy's states of mind at the time he selected each, his relative ease with himself both personally and as a writer. Since *Outer Dark*'s portrait shows him in the more attractive light, it is also possible that Anne influenced this choice. For the browser in a bookstore, the photo might have looked a bit conservative for such a young man, but as one aspect of the book's marketing, McCarthy's expression may have conveyed a more positive subliminal message.

Erskine had confessed that he felt unequal to the task of describing *Outer Dark* for the book jacket, and in March he had sent McCarthy a typed draft and solicited his input. On this leaf, McCarthy made several revisions. The most significant is McCarthy's rewording of his editor's plot description. Erskine's prosaic "The wanderings of brother and sister about the countryside are related in alternating scenes which, though highly realistic in action and dialogue, have a[b]out them an eerie larger-than-life quality which increases as the story unfolds" becomes McCarthy's "Alternating scenes relate the separate wanderings of . . . [Culla and Rinthy] through a countryside . . . scourged by three ruthless men whom the inhabitants do not know and seldom see. Though highly realistic in action and dialogue, the episodes have . . . an eerie larger-than-life quality which increases as the story approaches its apocalyptic ending" (Draft of jackct copy for "The Harrow"). McCarthy's revision appears on the front flyleaf of the first edition with one further change: the substitution of "terrifying" for "ruthless."[35]

# Publication and Reception

**M**cCarthy and Erskine no doubt recognized that *Outer Dark,* with its disconnected structure of short, discrete sections, was not likely to interest periodical editors, and Erskine did not make a sustained effort to place excerpts as he had for *The Orchard Keeper.* He did, however, send the galleys to John Palmer, who had published "Bounty" in the *Yale Review.* Palmer replied on April 10, 1968, that he was overwhelmed with a backlog of manuscripts to review and could not, at any rate, publish an excerpt until the October issue. If Erskine thought the novel would come out after that, Palmer would read any sections Erskine might suggest to gauge "their integrity as independent works of fiction." Since the timing would not work, it appears that Erskine dropped the idea.

Erskine also made a subtle attempt to interest Willie Morris, who had become editor-in-chief of *Harper's Magazine* in 1967. Erskine sent him galleys of *Outer Dark* along with a copy of *The Orchard Keeper* and mentioned the awards McCarthy had won (Erskine, Letter to Willie Morris, Apr. 10, 1968). He had not submitted an excerpt from the first novel to *Harper's,* although Baskin had. But it seems Erskine was now laying some groundwork for the future by making Morris aware of McCarthy's talent. Morris would be the first editor to whom Erskine submitted an excerpt from *Suttree,* in 1970.

When *Outer Dark* was published in August or September 1968,[36] more than three years had passed since the publication of *The Orchard Keeper,* time enough for any excitement it generated to have died down, even though it had won the Faulkner Foundation award in 1966. So sales of *Outer Dark* were somewhat weaker than for the first novel. According to the sales figures Sharon Lane sent to Woolmer in 1983, the first edition of *The Orchard Keeper* had sold 3,926 copies, while the first edition of *Outer Dark* sold 3,471 copies, a performance Erskine would later characterize as "modest but adequate" (Erskine, Letter to Robie Macauley, May 11, 1971). Reviews were slightly fewer as well. Nevertheless, they were predominantly appreciative: in a letter Erskine received on November 8, 1968, McCarthy pretended wryly to be disappointed that there were no disparaging assessments of *Outer Dark* among the early ones his editor had sent him, since he found such reviews the most amusing.

*Outer Dark* brought child psychiatrist Robert Coles and poetry/fiction/ essay writer Guy Davenport into the public conversation about McCarthy's merits for the first time. Arguably the most important review for its writer's long-term impact on McCarthy's writing career was Coles's "The Empty Road," published in the *New Yorker.* Coles had already published the first of five volumes of his *Children of Crisis,* based on his field work with at-risk youngsters, and he was by then at work on the second volume, *Migrants, Sharecroppers, Mountaineers* (1971), focused on the children of Appalachia. His working method privileged listening to children's oral narratives for understanding, while avoiding the clinical labels and diagnoses more mainstream within his profession. It is likely that he read McCarthy's *Outer Dark* for its relevance to his own research among Appalachian families, but he appreciated it not only for its compassionate treatment of poverty and homelessness, but also for its literary quality—that is, he read it not as a sociological tract but as a work of literature. Coles recognized that although the characters' speech resembled that of the Appalachian region, they seemed "meant to represent . . . something that stretches beyond the limits of space and time." He admired the novel's irreducible strangeness, its subordinating plot details to a "mood of darkness and hopelessness that no technological progress, no refinement of psychological analysis, can explain away or . . . resolve." Far from desiring psychological delving in a work of fiction, Coles saw that McCarthy's novel was essentially universal, religious, and moral: "McCarthy's 'outer dark' is not that by now cozy unconscious whose wild and irreverent and banal tricks continue to amuse our fashionable novelists. Nor is he interested in becoming a gilded version of the American social scientist, who has . . . a label for everything and wants at all costs to be *concerned* and *involved*" ("Empty Road" 120). The timeless universality of the novel harkened back, Coles thought, to the classical Greek concern with fatedness: "Necessarily, says McCarthy, the dark is out there, waiting for each of us. Necessarily, our lot is assigned; we have to contend with our flaws, live with them, and all too often be destroyed by them" (124). Yet in Coles's view the book's tragic vision was relieved by the virtuosity and range of its language, "slow-paced and heavy or delightfully light, relaxed or intense, perfectly plain or thoroughly intricate. Eternal principles mix company with the details of everyday, pastoral life—always under some apocalyptic cloud" (125).

Since McCarthy and Erskine shared reviews, McCarthy may have seen Coles's laudatory assessment in 1969, and it may have reinforced his inclination to avoid overt psychologizing in his work. Certainly, Coles's recognition of the fatedness of the characters resonated with McCarthy's aim to allow the distortion of their fates to unfold through their actions. Coles's review was the first of three he would write of McCarthy's novels set in the mountain South. Eventually, his reviewing would lead to important correspondence and friendship between the two men, as well as to Coles's promoting McCarthy's receipt of grants from the Guggenheim, Lyndhurst, and MacArthur foundations (Luce, "Robert Coles and Cormac McCarthy").

Guy Davenport was a professor at the University of Kentucky and a neighbor of McCarthy's friends Frank and Carolyn Hare. In her freshman year, Carolyn had been Lee Holleman's roommate at the University of Tennessee, and she and Frank maintained their friendship with McCarthy after he and Lee separated, eventually becoming friends of Anne De Lisle McCarthy as well. Before Cormac and Anne returned from Europe, the Hares had moved to Frank's family home in Lexington, where they later hosted the McCarthys.[37] In a letter Suzanne Baskin Beves received on December 7, 1968, McCarthy mentioned that they had been to visit friends in Lexington for a week. This may be when Frank Hare introduced them to Davenport, but more likely their first meeting had occurred even earlier, possibly during a May visit when the Hares and the McCarthys, including Anne's mother, went to the Keeneland horseraces together (Hare; De Lisle, Conversations). With *Outer Dark* completed, it seems plausible that McCarthy was willing to talk with fellow writer Davenport about his work. It seems likely, too, that during McCarthy's fall visit to Lexington the gregarious Frank Hare, who made it his business to know everyone, according to Carolyn, also introduced McCarthy to local reporters and reviewers (Hare, Conversations with the author). McCarthy reported to Beves in his December letter that there might be some "funny" pieces in the Lexington newspapers, and in fact a favorable review by Tom Buckner, who seems to have met McCarthy, appeared that month in the *Lexington Herald*.[38]

Davenport's review appeared in late September, not locally but in the influential *New York Times*. It was highly appreciative of McCarthy's treatment of his locale if denigrating of Appalachia itself, which Davenport declared America's Balkans. (Davenport had been raised in the Piedmont of South Carolina and could cast an insider's critical eye on the region.) He observed that McCarthy had artfully exploited the features of East Tennessee, where the region's "speechways . . . put at [his] disposal a timeless epic diction; and the wildness of Appalachia exhibits for him a range of . . . depravities the ancient universality of which allows a tragic terror more sobering than any the portrayer of sophisticated agonies can hope for." In McCarthy, he declared, the region had found a novelist "to depict the darkness of . . . [its] heart and its futile defiance" of its fate. He considered *Outer Dark* better than *The Orchard Keeper* and somewhat Faulknerian in rhetoric and imagery, but sparer than Faulkner and without his "sociological dimension." Davenport recognized McCarthy's allegorical bent and his and his characters' belief in the reality of evil. The movement of the novel's taut tragic plot is, he wrote, as if "a malevolent hand [has discovered] the thread that knits the world; page by page it plucks the stitches loose until the fabric parts in a [horrifying] catastrophe. . . ." Like many reviewers, Davenport had high praise for McCarthy's vigorous, style(s), which he found thoroughly unpretentious: Appalachian diction complemented by "that rich store of English . . . in the dictionary to be used by those who can."

However, such features proved challenging for readers impatient with literary fiction, and at the other end of the spectrum was Patrick Cruttwell's disengaged review in the *Washington Post Book World.* He objected to the novel's "murky Gothic horror" and its "pointless erudite vocabulary." He blamed the latter on the influence of Faulkner, inaccurately charging McCarthy with imitating Faulkner's "interminable shapeless sentence" (Cruttwell, "Plumbless Recrements" 18). It seems that the combination of southern setting and poetic language led Cruttwell to fall back on the lazy complaint that McCarthy was trying to be Faulkner and failing. Most of all, he seemed to object to McCarthy's objective narration, the primary challenge for the reader's interpretive faculties.

Perhaps because of the book's originality of vision and method, reviewers in both the national and regional periodicals struggled to place *Outer Dark* within familiar genres and took their cues from its various features. Cruttwell considered it merely gothic. *Time*'s reviewer classified the novel as a morality tale blended with elements of gothic horror, and likewise James Powers, in the *Hollywood Reporter,* described it as a gothic morality tale. Less dismissively, in the *Masterplots 1969 Annual,* Jack Matthews treated the novel as a horror piece that yet serves as necessary catharsis for our worst nightmares (258), and he too recognized its indebtedness to biblical and Greek tragic traditions (Matthews, Review of *Outer Dark* 259). Jonathan Yardley also came to more nuanced conclusions for the *Partisan Review*; he found the novel "a picaresque horror story," but noted as well its mythic quality and the universality of its themes (292).

Taking his cue from the novel's narrative structure, Walter Sullivan identified it as a "double picaresque but complained that its world was not unified and that its unlikely characters and incidents "remain separate features of the surrealist landscape" (Sullivan, "'Where Have all the Flowers Gone'" 661-662). On the other hand, in the *Nashville Banner,* Howell Pearre noted the novel's construction as a "double quest," but he found the plot entirely satisfying: "At first glance, the pieces seem too disparately arranged to have any logical order; but the moving about of persons and events is so arranged . . . that the denouement is quite logical, giving a sense of . . . rightness" (Pearre, "About New Books"). Kay Morgan, writing for the *Memphis Press-Scimitar,* considered *Outer Dark* "a quest with heavy moral overtones" (Morgan, "Tennessean's

Novel Explores Rural Morals"). Grace Comans in the *Hartford Courant* also identified *Outer Dark* as a quest, but one that takes place "beyond time and space." "One of the amazing achievements of this book," she wrote, closely paraphrasing the dust jacket, "lies in the fact that the individual scenes are realistic in events and dialogue. . . . Yet [they] have a supernatural quality to them that expands as the tale approaches its terrifying end" (Comans, "Beyond Time and Space," 21). Similarly, Ruth Ann McKinney, writing for the *Fort Worth Star-Telegram,* pointed out that the novel's "evocative prose," combined with its "precise characterization," establishes a mood that is "at once eerie and realistic" (McKinney, "McCarthy Measures Up" 7F).

Focusing on one of McCarthy's realistic threads, G. R. Pouder of the Baltimore *Morning Sun* described the novel as an "authentic and frightening study of American folklore," while he or she also recognized the "infinite pathos and a kind of Greek tragedy in the telling and in the ultimate ending" (Pouder, "A Folklore Study"). Davenport found *Outer Dark* not only tragic but allegorical (Davenport, "Appalachian Gothic"), and the latter classification was echoed by novelist John William Corrington in the *National Observer* (Corrington, "Cormac McCarthy's Novel" 23), Dot Jackson in the *Charlotte Observer* (Jackson, "Cast into 'Outer Dark'"), and Minnie Hite Moody in the Columbus [OH] *Dispatch* (Moody, "Novels of the South"). Observing how the incidents suggest more than is apparent on the surface, the *Kirkus* reviewer acknowledged the novel's parabolic quality (Anonymous, Review of *Outer Dark*). And the *Lexington Herald*'s Tom Buckner, perhaps aided by his conversation with McCarthy, astutely recognized it as a dreamlike parable with existential overtones (Buckner, "Allegorical Narrative Set in Faulkner Land").

In general, those reviewers like Coles and Davenport who found in *Outer Dark* biblical or Attic resonances tended to assess it more thoughtfully and appreciatively. Although in *Life* Melvin Maddocks praised it as "a minor classic of American gothic" and deplored its "comparatively uncelebrated publication" (Maddocks, "A Few Fine Fish" 6), in general those who placed the novel in the gothic or horror genre tended to view it less favorably. This may be due in part to their low expectations of the genre, but it may also reflect their revulsion at McCarthy's unflinching depiction of the baby's maiming and death. While Paddy Gough of the *Greensboro News* admired McCarthy's "brilliance of style" and his "rare feeling for nature," she found the novel "sordid." She asserted that the book presented "such a perverted ideology that many would question the author's sanity" (Gough, "Darkness Inside as Well"). When Beves sent this review to McCarthy on December 13, 1968, she softened the blow by saying that it struck her as "pretty funny."

As examination of the drafts makes clear, McCarthy strove throughout the composition process to create a work of near-total narrative objectivity, projecting the inner lives of his main characters, especially Culla, into the exterior world, presenting them dramatically and leaving their motivations unexplained, their actions unjudged by the narrator, allowing the reader to ponder them in the opacity of their strange choices and experiences. He may have wanted to prove to his editor and to himself what effects could be achieved through understatement of motivation and ambiguity of action. Erskine understood and accepted his strategies for *Outer Dark,* but both editor and author may have wondered what reviewers would make of the novel and especially of the triune, the outward manifestation of Culla's inner madness. Appropriately, the description on the book jacket did not explicate, saying only that the triune are "terrifying men whom the inhabitants do not know and seldom see." Except for the *Publishers Weekly* reviewer, who mentioned the "secret inner life" of the characters (Anonymous, Review of *Outer Dark* 53), only those who were literary writers commented on McCarthy's objective narrative technique, and they wholly admired it. Corrington wrote, "Perhaps Mr. McCarthy's greatest success is that . . . he has managed to do what many experimentalists have tried without much luck: He has minimized narrative content in its rather dull role of conveying ethical and moral platitudes" (Corrington, "Cormac McCarthy's Novel" 23).[39] Davenport admired McCarthy's quick-paced movement from scene to scene of revelatory incident without "wast[ing] a single word on his characters' thoughts. . . . Such discipline comes not only from mastery over words but from an understanding wise . . . and compassionate enough to dare tell so . . . dark a story" (Davenport, "Appalachian Gothic" 4).

Reviewers who ventured to interpret the nature of the triune tended to read them simply as demons or avatars of evil, rather unconnected with Culla's psyche (Davenport, "Appalachian Gothic"; Hicks, "Literary Horizons"; Jackson, "Cast into 'Outer Dark'"; Matthews, Review of *Outer Dark*; Pearre, "About New Books"), and this was also true of many early scholarly readings of the novel. However, some saw them as personifications of fate as well. Buckner loosely identified them as three "horsemen (death, pestilence, famine?)" (Buckner, "Allegorical Narrative Set in Faulkner Land"). In his wholly positive review for the *New York Times,* Thomas Lask, who considered *Outer Dark* a "perfectly executed work of the imagination," saw the "unholy trio" not only as exemplars of "mindless evil," but also as horsemen of the apocalypse or the "unnameable threat [that] hangs over" the characters in the "doom-haunted" world (Lask, "Southern Gothic" 33). Pouder similarly perceived the three as "a sort of pursuing fate" (Pouder, "A Folklore Study"). And *Time*'s reviewer found them as "relentlessly hounding as the furies" and perceived, too, that the triune were like "dream figures," an observation that gets quite close to their compositional origin in Culla's nightmares (Anonymous, "A Southern Parable" E5).

The writer for the *Virginia Quarterly Review* saw the triune as "embodiments of evil" who "cast their malignant shadows" over the world of the novel, and he may have detected their affinity with the weird sisters of *Macbeth* when he characterized *Outer Dark* as "a witch's brew." At the same time, he felt the novel lacked philosophical depth, "quite apart from its merits as a bravura piece" (Anonymous, "Notes on Current Books" viii)—a critique that is compatible with Sullivan's assessment in *Sewanee Review*, in which he expresses dissatisfaction with McCarthy's theme that "we go blindly through the world and therefore the gods have been unjust to us." Sullivan considered this a "confusion of the physical with the metaphysical, of fate with the solid realities of flesh and stone," missing the point of McCarthy's strategically representing the metaphysical through the physical (Sullivan, "'Where Have all the Flowers Gone'" 662). In a short review for the *Rocky Mount (NC) Telegram*, Walter Spearman also expressed frustration with the book's themes: "Searching for the author's meaning is less rewarding than applauding his abilities," he wrote (Spearman, Review of *Outer Dark* 7D). While Matthews concluded that McCarthy was "richly talented" and that *Outer Dark* was "more than the work of a horror hack," like Sullivan he found problematic the novel's "lack of idea, or a mythic need in the writing, or a 'larger vision'" (Matthews, Review of *Outer Dark* 260). Interestingly, it may have been McCarthy's very pushing to the limit Faulkner's strategy of only partially revealing his characters that prevented Faulknerians Sullivan and Matthews from fully appreciating McCarthy's achievement in *Outer Dark*. But as has been discussed, in projecting Culla's interiority into the external world, he created an extraordinarily rich expression of the character's subjectivity.

Every reviewer who commented on McCarthy's language applauded the authentic dialect and vibrant dialogue of *Outer Dark*. For example, in her review for the *Charlotte Observer*, Dot Jackson declared its dialogue "perfection to the Southern ear" (Jackson, "Cast into 'Outer Dark'" 6G), and McKinney observed that McCarthy's dialect writing itself was "marvelously poetic" (McKinney, "McCarthy Measure up" 7F). While some, such as Cruttwell, deplored McCarthy's inaccessible vocabulary or his more baroque passages (Cruttwell, "Plumbless Recrements"), which *Saturday Review*'s Granville Hicks denigrated as "gaudy prose" (Hicks, "Literary Horizons" 22), in general those reviewers who most appreciated the book had high and unmixed praise for McCarthy as a stylist. The *Time* review lauded his "Irish singing voice imbued with Southern Biblical intonations" (Anonymous, "A Southern Parable" E5). Maddocks praised his "superbly crafted prose—Faulkner whittled in hard hickory" (Maddocks, "A Few Fine Fish" 6), while Corrington found his style unique to McCarthy: "In terms . . . of sheer ability to make the English language do things it is not expected to do, Mr. McCarthy needs no lessons from anyone"

(Corrington, "Cormac McCarthy's Novel" 23). Others commented on the larger purposes his styles served. Kay Morgan appreciated the unsettling effects McCarthy achieved by juxtaposing the triune's horrific deeds against the poetic language in which they are rendered (Morgan, "Tennessean's Novel Explores Rural Morals"). Similarly, Powers commented on McCarthy's unusual pairing of his "poetic style and fantasy setting," on the one hand, with his realistic and suspenseful plot, on the other (Powers, "Book Reviews"). Pearre, too, noted McCarthy's unique melding of disparate features, colloquialism interspersed with passages of brilliant prose, the realistic depiction of characters placed in a surrealistic setting, and he praised "the . . . awareness McCarthy keeps before you of his prose being his work, refined, influenced and refined again, creating a kind of lone original who is positively his own man" (Pearre, "About New Books"). It seems that with the highly inventive *Outer Dark*, through his daring allegiance to his own vision and his persistent refining of his prose, McCarthy achieved a firmer critical reputation as a master prose stylist.

# Subsidiary Rights and Awards

By the time *Outer Dark* was published, McCarthy's two-year award from the Rockefeller Foundation had run out. When he replied on September 23, 1968, to Freund's September 17 request for an assessment of the foundation's support program, McCarthy emphasized that Rockefeller had been his only source of income during the fiscal years 1966–1968. Although this was not strictly true, it was nearly so, and he clearly had little hope that *Outer Dark* would net much in royalties. He wrote Freund that he did not think he could have accomplished as much with his writing if he had not had some financial backing during those years. He added that he had "no trade or profession, and receive next to nothing for my writings, so . . . assistance must come from somewhere." So it must have been welcome news the previous month when Howard Kaminsky of Random's subsidiary rights department received an offer from Parallel Productions for film rights to *The Orchard Keeper* and *Outer Dark*. For a one-year option, Parallel offered $250 for *The Orchard Keeper,* $500 for *Outer Dark,* and $500 each for a second year's option. If films were made, Parallel would pay $12,500 for the first novel and $17,500 for the second, sums far beyond any income McCarthy had yet received for his creative work (Kaminsky, Memo to Albert Erskine, Aug. 22, 1968). On August 23, Erskine sent McCarthy a copy of Kaminsky's memo, saying that one of them would phone in a few days for his decision. A note jotted on Kaminsky's memo indicates that McCarthy approved the offer in a telephone call on August 29. Erskine received a letter from McCarthy on October 11, saying that he had not received payment and wondering whether Parallel had followed through. Erskine reassured him that contracts were being drawn up and examined by the lawyers (letter, Oct. 17, 1968).

On October 16, Kaminsky sent Erskine a memo informing him that he had secured an offer from Ballentine Books for the mass-market paperback rights to McCarthy's two novels for $7,500 combined. (Ballentine would become a Random House affiliate in 1973.) The rights were for a five-year period. McCarthy would receive an 8 percent royalty for *Outer Dark*; for *The Orchard Keeper*, the royalty would be 6 percent for the first 150,000 copies and 8 percent after that (Random House Reprint Rights Data Sheet). Cerf recalls that early in his career the standard royalty rate for paperbacks was 4–6 percent, but that soon the Authors League joined with agents to raise the rate to a new standard of 10–15 percent (199). Ballentine's offer was modest, then, but considering that there had been no previous bid to publish paperback versions of the novels (and Random did not plan to do so), Erskine thought the offer was fair. As if to guide McCarthy to his decision, he commented, "I don't need to tell you that these are not mass market novels, and I believe the Ballentine people are primarily adventurously gambling on your future: they want to have a foot in the door as your public acceptance becomes wider. Meantime, this is hard cash and will also have the effect of widening your audience" (letter, Oct. 17, 1968). McCarthy mailed a terse postcard of consent on November 2, and on November 8 Erskine received his explanation that the offer seemed all right even though it was not generous. The following spring, on May 23, 1969, Beves mailed McCarthy his copies of the Ballentine issue of *The Orchard Keeper*. Ballentine's *Outer Dark* followed in December 1970. As predicted by Erskine's acknowledgment that the book was not the typical mass-market novel, this paperback sold a modest 2,558 copies (Lane, Letter to J. Howard Woolmer). When the five-year contract for the two novels expired, Ballentine did not renew it, so McCarthy earned little from these paperback reissues of his novels, as he explained in a letter to Robert Coles in February or March 1979.

The publication of *The Orchard Keeper* had led to McCarthy's awards from the William Faulkner Foundation, the American Academy of Arts and Letters, and the Rockefeller Foundation, but the prize money had run out, and with *Outer Dark* in print in 1968, but with little royalty income to show for his work, McCarthy applied for a fellowship in creative arts from the John Simon Guggenheim Memorial Foundation. These awards are made to individuals who have already reached a high level of achievement in their fields, and with two published novels and multiple awards, McCarthy was now eligible. Freund had left the Rockefeller Foundation when it discontinued his program, and then he had joined Guggenheim. He writes that the Guggenheim Foundation was unusual in that it did not rely on nominators, and it accepted unsolicited applications. Its "careful staff procedures . . . took care of . . . directing the selection committee's attention to those most qualified. . . . In this way, the working numbers were drastically reduced to a manageable total . . . [even though] any selection committee member could initiate full consideration of any applicant" (Freund, *Narcissism and Philanthropy*, 95).

In the "Statement of Proposed Work" portion of his Guggenheim application, McCarthy wrote that he would use an award to support his work on *Suttree*, which he had been composing for the past six years and which then existed in 1,800 draft pages. This was a cumulative figure for all the "drafts and revisions," as McCarthy explained in his letter to Freund of September 23, 1968. In the application, McCarthy estimated that he needed another two years to restructure and rewrite this material. He included a brief description of the novel that drew heavily from his earlier proposal to the Rockefeller Foundation, but without the quoted passages from the draft (McCarthy, Application for Guggenheim award). We may speculate that he omitted them either because these passages had been revised and would be revised yet again or because of length constraints on the proposal.

As usual, Erskine helped. On October 1, 1968, he wrote McCarthy that he had recruited Warren, Ellison, and Hersey by phone to sponsor McCarthy's application. All three had been members of the literature department of the American Academy of Arts and Letters when it honored McCarthy with a travel award, and Ellison and Hersey had endorsed his application to the Rockefeller Foundation. Hersey and Warren had later served together on Rockefeller's Advisory Committee, strengthening their relationship with Freund. By fall 1968 Warren and Hersey had also been added to the Guggenheim selection committee, although it is uncertain whether Erskine was aware of this before he called them (Freund, Letter to Robert Coles, Nov. 27, 1968). Although none of these highly respected Random House authors had yet read *Outer Dark*, all readily agreed to write in support of McCarthy's application. Apparently doing so did not conflict with Hersey and Warren's role as selectors, especially since any member of the committee could ask for full consideration of any candidate. In his letter to McCarthy, Erskine expressed hesitation to serve as a fourth sponsor himself because he did not feel he had a strong success record for previous Guggenheim applicants. He also warned McCarthy that he had known few applicants to succeed on a first try. But the October 15 deadline was not far away, and on October 11 Erskine received McCarthy's last-minute reply that he would list the editor as his fourth sponsor. After conveying thanks to all four sponsors and to Bennett Cerf, who had sent him a note praising *Outer Dark*, McCarthy indicated that he was "muddling along" as usual. He hoped to take a vacation in the following week.

On November 8, 1968, Erskine received McCarthy's update that he and Anne had had a good trip to Virginia, where they visited his parents in Falls Church. They had spent several days in Washington, DC "looking at pictures." Indeed, a letter McCarthy mailed to Bill Kidwell on November 6, reports that he and Anne had devoted five hours to looking at the impressionist paintings in the National Gallery of Art. They had driven through the Outer Banks of North Carolina on their way home, taking in Kitty Hawk, Cape Hatteras, and Ocracoke Island. De Lisle recalls that they cooked their dinner over a campfire on the beach, and they slept in sleeping bags in their car before driving northwest to Tennessee. They were startled awake that night by the sounds of creatures scrabbling in the remains of their dinner. McCarthy would draw on this experience for the father's memory of his dead wife in *The Road* (219). McCarthy wrote Kidwell that they passed the next night in the jail in Goldsboro, North Carolina, because they were stopped for speeding and did not have enough cash to pay their fine. The police did not treat them like criminals but gave them an unlocked cell to sleep in together until Western Union opened in the morning. More than fifty years later, De Lisle does not remember the incident clearly, but she thinks McCarthy's story is probably true (Letter to Bill Kidwell, postmarked Nov. 6, 1968; De Lisle, Conversations).

Back in Tennessee, McCarthy planned to settle in for a winter's work on his third novel. In late November, the Guggenheim Foundation asked his sponsors to assess McCarthy's proposal. In his "Confidential Report" Erskine wrote that McCarthy's first novel had impressed him, his second had heightened his admiration, and the excerpts he had seen from the *Suttree* draft (the passages McCarthy had included in his Rockefeller application and perhaps others as well) made him confident that this would be his best book yet. Unlike many writers of his generation, McCarthy wrote not of his miserable childhood but from his imagination, Erskine wrote. He offered to supply the selectors with copies of the "extraordinarily enthusiastic" reviews McCarthy's first two novels had received. Erskine's endorsement was neither as long nor as carefully constructed as the one he had written for the Rockefeller Foundation, but together with those from the other sponsors it was sufficient. Contrary to Erskine's less than sanguine prediction, McCarthy received the Guggenheim award in spring 1969 ("Two from Area" 21).[40]

LEFT: The Healey Sisters: Anne De Lisle and Nicky Banks in performance, circa 1965. Photo courtesy Anne De Lisle.

Anne De Lisle and Cormac McCarthy at a seaside venue in Wales, 1965. Photo courtesy Anne De Lisle.

Cormac and Anne McCarthy, just married, Saint Andrews Church, Hamble England, May 14, 1966. Photo courtesy Anne De Lisle.

The McCarthy and Hare families at Keeneland races in Lexington, Kentucky, 1968. Back row from left: Vandy Hare, Frank Hare, Frank's cousin Dickie Cole, Cormac McCarthy. Front row: Anne McCarthy, Carolyn Hare, Anne's mother Irene De Lisle. Photo courtesy Anne De Lisle.

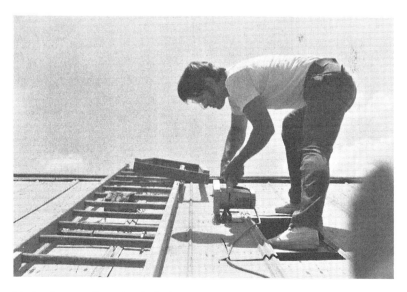

McCarthy installing the skylight in the bathroom roof at his home in Louisville, Tennessee. Photo courtesy Anne De Lisle.

The kitchen McCarthy designed and built at his home in Louisville, Tennessee. Photo courtesy Anne De Lisle.

Looking through the passageway to the living room, antiques, and McCarthy's writing desk in his refurbished dairy barn. Photo courtesy Anne De Lisle.

ABOVE: "Tennessee Gothic, 1973."
Cormac, Anne, and Blackie
at their home in Louisville,
Tennessee. Photographed by
David Owen Styles.

Anne McCarthy as the
Sugar Plum Fairy in *The Nut-
cracker,* 1973. Photo courtesy
Anne De Lisle.

Cormac McCarthy, 1973, photo for dust jacket of *Child of God*.
Photographed by David Owen Styles.

# Part Three
## *Child of God,*
## 1966–1973

# Genesis

In the few interviews he has granted, McCarthy has never pinned down just when he began writing *Child of God* or how the idea came to him. In her December 1973 interview with him, Martha Byrd reported that *Child of God* "began ten years ago, when McCarthy lived in Sevier County." But it had a long gestation period before he began to compose it. McCarthy told Byrd that he did not write until he was fairly confident about what he would do with an idea: "When you write something down you pretty well kill it. . . . Leave it loose and knocking around up there and you never know—it might turn into something" (Martha Byrd, "East Tennessee Author" 9C).

Many of *Child of God*'s elements, as well as its setting, are indeed drawn from McCarthy's experience in Sevier County in 1962–1963. The rural house he lived in was not as rustic as the cabins in which the Holmes live, Culla trespasses, and Ballard is permitted to stay by his kindly neighbor Waldrop, yet these fictional cabins all derive partly from McCarthy's experience of living there rent free. He undoubtedly saw many rustic dwellings in East Tennessee and had already described Ownby's cabin and the log structure John Wesley and his mother occupy but do not own in *The Orchard Keeper.* The Sevier County floods of 1963, which McCarthy would have witnessed, also inform both *Outer Dark* and *Child of God,* where flooded rivers play pivotal roles (Luce, *Reading the World,* 153–55). In addition, McCarthy told Woodward that he based *Child of God* on news reports of a Sevier County murder case, still to be identified (Woodward, "Venomous Fiction" 31).

In *Reading the World: Cormac McCarthy's Tennessee Period* (2009), I show that sources for the novel include newspaper reports of James Blevins's murder trial in north Georgia and Ed Gein's serial killings in Wisconsin, as well as Robert Bloch's novel (1959) and Alfred Hitchcock's film (1960), both titled *Psycho.* Based on the information available then, I speculated that McCarthy's initial idea for a novel of a serial killer might have dated from as early as the late 1950s or 1960, when these cases and works were in local or national news (136–37). However, it is now clear that the strands of material woven into *Child of God* did not coalesce in a productive way until around January 1966, when McCarthy wrote Erskine from Europe (postmarked January 27, 1966) that he had nearly finished the second draft of *Outer Dark,* that he continued working on *Suttree,* and that he now had an idea for a fourth novel, almost certainly *Child of God.* The earliest archived typescript of *Child of God,* which McCarthy identifies as its "Middle Draft," is preserved in a file folder on which he penciled working dates for several page sequences, from September 28, 1970, to February 14, 1971. At least one draft of *Child of God* preceded the "Middle Draft," so it is possible that these dates had been recorded as he worked on an earlier version and that McCarthy reused the folder for his middle draft. But our best evidence now suggests that McCarthy decided to write the novel by January 1966, when he mentioned it to Erskine, composed his earliest draft(s) in Europe and then Tennessee between 1966 and 1970, and was intensively working on his "Middle Draft" by September 1970.

What we could not appreciate until his typescripts became available is that McCarthy's readiness to write *Child of God* emerged in conjunction with his reshaping *Outer Dark.* A significant factor in the genesis of Ballard's novel was McCarthy's having composed several scenes in the first draft of *Outer Dark* that he removed during its second draft stage and subsequently revised for *Child of God,* evidence of a compositional kinship and continuity between his more fabular novel of murder and his more realistic one, specifically between protagonists Culla Holme and Lester Ballard, both bereft of family, homeless, hunted, haunted, and homicidal. The *Outer Dark* draft passages McCarthy reconceived for *Child of God* include Culla's participation in a somewhat more fully articulated auction scene than the one mentioned in *Outer Dark* as published; his shooting the "High Sheriff of Sevier County"; a man's lighting a fire under his recalcitrant ox only to ignite his wagon; a child's chewing the legs off a half-frozen bird; and Culla's watching a talkative blacksmith sharpen an axe. Probably before the 1970–1971 working dates, McCarthy gave the heading "BALLARD (incl. Blacksmith) (leftovers)" to the folder that now contains the "Middle Draft" of *Child of God.* The label implies that he initially used the folder to hold the blacksmith episode and other "leftovers" from *Outer Dark* pending their revision for *Child of God.* Later he returned the original pages to his *Outer Dark* files.

Consequently, these scenes of Ur-*Child of God* material survive only in *Outer Dark*'s "Early Draft [B]," the photocopy typescript in which McCarthy preserved a variety of draft passages he had decided not to use, together with copies of used material. After deleting the incidents from Culla's novel or abbreviating them there, McCarthy refocused, recontextualized, and amplified them to develop the themes, effects, and structural patterns of Ballard's. Some passages reveal that McCarthy had initially conceived of Culla as a man more obviously like Ballard: dispossessed of his family land, seething with rage, armed and dangerous. Others show that as he worked concurrently on *Outer Dark, Child of God,* and *Suttree* in the 1960s, McCarthy absorbed East

Tennessee cultural practices and incidents from his reading, conversation, and observation as raw materials whose place in his work was yet to be determined. He repurposed some of that material from the early drafts of *Outer Dark* for Ballard's plotline and the oral tales of his neighbors, which partly structure *Child of God*. Judging from the Ur-*Child of God* material in the *Outer Dark* draft and the unused or superseded passages from earlier draft(s) of *Child of God* saved in its "Middle Draft," the narrative strands central to McCarthy's initial conception for Ballard's novel included the auction and eviction, the sheriff, and the unsympathetic anecdotes he and other members of the community tell. Ballard's serial killings and repeated acts of necrophilia so clearly indebted to the *Psycho* phenomenon of 1959/60 did not emerge until later but are present in the "Middle Draft."

# The Auction

C *hild of God*'s striking opening, the auction of the Ballard farm, evolved from an early fragmentary treatment of an auction in which Culla is hired to participate. Some of this auction material was composed on April 23–24, 1963, and because McCarthy regularly dated his work sessions in only the first-draft stage of *Outer Dark,* the dating of these pages identifies them as superseded first-draft material, now preserved in "Early Draft [B]." In these pages Culla sits on the porch of a country store eating crackers, the only meal he can afford. The Essary Auction Company wagon pulls up, driven by a man in black, who is so enormous that "the mule and the wagon . . . looked absurd, like a toy rig in a circus bearing some stately and monolithic clown" (*OD* "Early Draft [B]" 72/127; *OD* 139). This man proves to be Essary, and he urges Culla to attend his auction of the Speare place the next day, telling him the event will have "the Willis brothers and Little Aud, free prizes and lemonade"—details of the auction's attractions that appear in the published version of *Outer Dark* and recur in a more generalized description in *Child of God* (*OD* "Early Draft [B]" 73/128; cf. *OD* 142; cf. *CoG* 4). When Culla confirms that he is a stranger there, Essary initially considers him a potential buyer, a hint that the locals might be more reluctant to bid on a neighbor's property, as with the Ballard farm. Culla cannot buy but is seeking work. When the auctioneer asks if he has ever attended a land auction, Culla reveals that as a young child he saw the auction of his grandfather's place (73). Oblivious to what this may imply about Culla's sympathies, Essary offers him five dollars to pretend to be a buyer at the Speare auction without revealing they know one another. Culla's understanding of Essary's scam to drive up the bidding is that "Any time he says a figure will buy and then stops and says it'll buy it right I sing out the figure" (*OD* "Early Draft [B]" 75/130).

Given the structural patterns already emerging in McCarthy's early drafting of *Outer Dark*, it seems likely that as he first conceived it, Culla's reluctant colluding with Essary prepared for a scene at the auction in which an outraged crowd would threaten him, causing him to run and thereby forfeit his pay; and in a different context the flight motif remains in the revised store scenes. But as he honed his second draft of *Outer Dark*, McCarthy sharply reduced the auction references. The store owner and squire, renamed Clark, is still a fat-cat auctioneer, but he now wears white rather than black. In the margin next to his description of Essary's black suit, McCarthy had jotted "travesty of mourning"—a comment that would have been ironically apt for the auctioneer who would profit from Speare's death (*OD* "Early Draft [B]" 72/127). But the black clothing also might have linked Essary with the triune's leader, and in the revised scene McCarthy discarded the hint that the auctioneer is an avatar of the triune in favor of making him a victim of their violence. Now Clark hires Culla both to help him cheat the bidders and to dig graves, but Clark does not survive to officiate at the auction ("Early Draft [A]" 147). Culla works on the graves late into the night and returns to the store only to find it closed and no one to pay him for his labor. Sleeping in a field, he hears "something fearful about," and as he walks back toward town in the morning, he sees three hanged men, one of whom wears the soiled white suit associated with Clark ("Early Draft [A]" 149). When Culla reaches the store and finds Clark's mules standing untethered, he walks urgently on, finally breaking into a run ("Early Draft [A]" 150).

Had the auction material been fully developed in *Outer Dark,* it would have implied a less ambiguous motive for Clark's murder: that Culla harbors festering resentment over the forced sale of his family farm and the corruption of the auctioneer: the rage of the dispossessed that motivates Ballard. In a related unused passage Culla maintains a sullen silence when the assistant driving him to the auction site speculates that the heirs are selling because they do not get along ("Early Draft [B]" 75/130), a line that prompts the reader to question whether the Speares cannot tolerate sharing their property or whether it is sold to pay debts. When McCarthy rewrote the store scene for *Outer Dark,* he might easily have eliminated every reference to the auction. Instead he retained just enough trace of it to hint at Culla's mysterious rage against the auctioneer Clark. At some point in September 1963 or later, McCarthy also drafted an unused passage of Culla's dialogue with the triune that refers to the Holmes's experience of eviction by their neighbors. Culla complains, "They run us out of the county me and her. We wadnt but halfgrowed didnt have nobody to tend us" ("Rough/First Draft [B], np). If used, the passage would have established that Culla and Rinthy's neighbors expelled them from their midst when Rinthy became pregnant and that the siblings had found an abandoned cabin in which to stay, which would have further emphasized their poverty and homelessness. Indeed, the passage would have implied that the trauma of expulsion by the outraged community lies behind Culla's nightmare of the crowd that blames him for the eclipse.

Although in *Outer Dark* McCarthy only partially sketched the scene at the auction, heirs' being made homeless by legal but callous means was a significant focus of McCarthy's first draft. Perhaps he had witnessed such a land auction in Sevier County and was moved by the plight of the dispossessed, by the contrast between springtime rebirth and the death of a small farmer's hopes. The spring setting figures prominently in a one-paragraph scene of the auction site drafted in McCarthy's April 1963 work session on *Outer Dark*: a description of the broomstraw in the fields, the apple trees in bloom, and the log structure "chinked with mud of a nauseous orange color"—images he would later use in *Child of God* (*OD* "Early Draft [B]" 75/130; cf. *CoG* 3).

Two undated pages describing the auction further also survive in *Outer Dark*'s "Early Draft [B]," pages that are a first draft for the scene that opens *Child of God,* the scene of Ballard's dispossession and alienation from his neighbors that propel his descent into criminal madness. These *Outer Dark* leaves are narrated in a voice that objectively reports the auctioneer's patter but also makes subjective observations that could not derive from Culla's (or Ballard's) perceptions—a significant move toward the narrative stance of the first part of *Child of God*. For example, amplified through a megaphone, the auctioneer's voice echoes from the ridges "with a sombre quality and duplicated a Gregorian chorale chanting in the vespered shell of some old cathedral" (*OD* "Early Draft [B]" 97/131; cf. *CoG* "Middle Draft" 2; cf. *CoG* 5). Further comparing the carnivalesque auction to the sacred service, the narrator observes: "In the pines the ghost chorus chanted their litanies in voices lost and hollow" (*OD* "Early Draft [B]" 98/ 132; cf. *CoG* 6). Although in the first draft of *Outer Dark* Culla sometimes addresses a watchful and judgmental God, here the medieval Roman Catholic allusions, as well as the irony, are the thoughtful commentary of an authorial voice.

Deploying the auction scene in *Outer Dark* would have required that McCarthy cast it in the narrative perspective of Culla's unfolding experience, as he does the novel's other scenes that document obsolescent cultural realities. Indeed, only circumstantial evidence suggests that the two undated auction pages were composed as part of *Outer Dark*: McCarthy filed them with his discarded *Outer Dark* material, and their pagination is inconsistent with the placement of the auction scene at the opening of all the archived versions of

*Child of God.* In addition, Culla's first perceptions of the auction ("Essary stood in the bed of his wagon with a . . . megaphone in his mouth, and that was what he [Culla] had heard" ["Early Draft (B)" 75/130]) only roughly mesh with the description of the auctioneer on the undated page ("So he was standing in the wagon bed in the road before the old Squire's cabin" ["Early Draft (B)" 97/ 131]). The undated pages may be transitional, marking the point at which McCarthy first decided to compose an auction scene from a more ironic narrative stance, as in *Child of God*; perhaps more likely is that they record McCarthy's reaction to a scene he had witnessed, composed earlier than the dated pages leading up to the auction in *Outer Dark* and preserved for their novelistic potential. If so, he originally wrote them from an authorial perspective, then tentatively positioned them within the *Outer Dark* draft pending revision. Perhaps as McCarthy then began to rewrite the scene from Culla's perspective, he recognized that the authorial commentary was essential to it, even worthy of elaboration into a novel of the dispossessed related by a narrator whose complex compassion would counter the imperfectly informed judgments of the landowner's neighbors. Both sets of auction pages in *Outer Dark*'s "Early Draft [B]" reveal that McCarthy's early conception of dispossession as one motive for Culla's violence later evolved into the primal scene fanning Ballard's rage and setting him more deeply at odds with his community. In both novels or their drafts, eviction functions mythically as the loss of an innocent paradise, which casts the protagonists into emotional and spiritual darkness.

McCarthy's concern for the plight of the evicted had been pressing for expression early in the first-draft stage of *Outer Dark,* and it was implicit in the history of land acquisitions for the Great Smoky Mountains National Park and the Tennessee Valley Authority, which quietly informed *The Orchard Keeper* (see Luce, *Reading the World* 3–23). The issue may have troubled McCarthy since childhood as he struggled to reconcile his sympathy for East Tennessee's native sons with his father's role as the Tennessee Valley Authority attorney in charge of condemning and acquiring property. And McCarthy was also aware of the condemning of property for the construction of the Oak Ridge nuclear facility, which informs the family history of Bobby and Alicia Western in *The Passenger* and *Stella Maris*. Alicia tells Michael that their antebellum handcrafted family farmhouse "was condemned by the US Government. Flattened by bulldozers. In order to build a plant for the enrichment of nuclear fuel" (*Stella Maris* 71). Their maternal grandmother tells Bobby, "They was even families had been removed from their homesteads in the Great Smoky Mountains National Park in the thirties, TVA in the thirties again, and the atom bomb in the forties. By that time they didn't have nothin" (*The Passenger* 174). The distress of the dispossessed, a reality covered by local newspapers when it erupted in violence, may have been a topic of conversation within McCarthy's family and among his friends. It is not surprising that he tried to come to terms with this when he drafted *Outer Dark,* a novel partly focused on alienation and homelessness. When he chose to treat Culla's violence less sociologically and more ambiguously, the impulse to explore dispossession remained, and it became the beating heart of *Child of God,* where the displaced and disrespected man is the anti-hero. In keeping with the prominence of eviction and exclusion, the new novel would give greater emphasis to the community's role in fostering violence than *Outer Dark* had done, not only in its ostracism of Ballard but also in the gossipy oral tales through which the community, including the sheriff, speaks its judgments.

# The High Sheriff of Sevier County

In *Outer Dark*'s "Early Draft [B]" is a brief scene in which Culla shoots the Sevier County sheriff from the porch of a rustic cabin, much as Greer shoots Ballard. In this early unused passage, McCarthy conceived a seminal character of *Child of God,* the sheriff, interacting with the primary character of *Outer Dark,* Culla. The passage also reveals McCarthy's briefly toying with the idea of setting at least this portion of *Outer Dark* in Sevier County, where he conceived and began writing it. But as the novel's setting evolved into Culla's psychic terrain, McCarthy avoided identifiable place names and deployed only cultural references to East Tennessee to suggest a realistic setting, while complicating these with such ecological inconsistencies as swamps and alligators. Despite the early discarded reference to Sevier County, McCarthy wrote me in 1980 that he did not have a specific location in mind for the setting of *Outer Dark* (Luce, "Cormac McCarthy" 10).

Culla's firing at the sheriff is narrated from an angle of vision outside the cabin, with an image of the cabin door opening forcefully and Culla, armed, abruptly materializing in the doorframe, "simply become there full blown with his head . . . pressed to the stock" (*OD* "Early Draft [B]" 199). The image links him with the triune, who unexpectedly materialize in the superseded and published versions of the tinker's murder and in the published scenes when they murder Salter or the snake hunter ("Rough/First Draft [B]" 3; "Early Draft [A]" 234; "Middle Draft" 131; *OD* [51], [129], [231]). But it also links him with Ballard, whom Greer perceives as "an apparition created whole out of nothing and set upon him with such dire intent" (*CoG* 173). When Culla appears in the doorway, the sheriff freezes in the sloped yard, "his hands held out from his sides palmforward and his face tilted upward in an attitude [of] biblical supplication." Culla fires, and the sheriff falls as if nudged backward by an unseen hand (*OD* "Early Draft [B]" 199). In the next paragraph, a witnessing squire recalls the shooting, which suggests that the squire has summoned the sheriff to evict Culla.

By spring 1963, McCarthy had already drafted Culla's trial for trespassing in the cabin. On April 22 and May 2–4, he composed the trespassing episode up through Culla's arrest and introduction to the justice of the peace (*OD* "Rough/First Draft [A], 82/135–86/139; "Early Draft [B]," 71/134–86/139). So he was working on this portion of the trespassing scene very close to the time when he composed the Essary scenes that prepared for the auction. Both incidents recapitulate Culla's evictions from his family home and his community, and at some later point McCarthy considered having the triune kill the sheriff and possibly the justice of the peace as well. He inscribed a marginal note for a line to be added in the dialogue between Rinthy and the old woman about their fear of being alone: "Next/They done in the high sheriff hisself" ("Early Draft [A]" 120). So he was tentatively planning to link the death of the sheriff with the deaths of Salter, two hanged men, and another man, presumably Clark. But when he completed the trial-for-trespassing episode in "Early Draft [A]," McCarthy emphasized instead Culla's helplessness and passivity in the face of the law. Here he is unarmed, as he is throughout the published novel after he sells his father's gun. Far from killing the sheriff or the justice of the peace, Culla is evicted from the ramshackle cabin by its owner and sentenced to labor on the justice's farm (207–17; *OD* 197–208).

In *Outer Dark* as published, Culla is a violent man, but his aggression is enacted through his unacknowledged tripartite alter ego while he remains apparently docile in his interactions with others. He is symbolically emasculated, no longer armed with a rifle, and the triune usually commit his murders with the agrarian implements at hand. McCarthy explored Culla's armed resistance in defense of his shelter only in the discarded sheriff scene, and it would not finally have a role in *Outer Dark*. However, the idea was vital to the genesis of *Child of God*. Indeed, Culla's shooting the sheriff prefigures several incidents in *Child of God* in which a man is forced from his home and/or defends his dwelling from an intruder who invades the yard, as the auctioneer and bidders do in the opening scene of *Child of God,* prompting Ballard's resistance. When Sheriff Turner approaches Ballard's cabin to arrest him on rape accusations—the most benign of these scenes—Ballard mocks him from his porch but does not shoot him (*CoG* 50–51). More violently, Lester assaults Greer at the old Ballard home-place, and Greer shoots him at the threshold of the house, blowing him off the porch and blasting away his arm, literally disarming him (*CoG* 172–73).

When he composed the sheriff's murder for *Outer Dark,* McCarthy likely meant to reinforce Culla's resentment of his family's dispossession by auction. So when he decided to eliminate the auction scene from *Outer Dark,* it made sense to develop the trial for trespassing instead of the sheriff's murder at Culla's threshold. But it seems too that McCarthy had come to feel the auction and eviction scenes in *Outer Dark* would suggest reductive sociological motivations for Culla's violence and would depict his murders too directly, placing the novel's emphasis on the social injustice that provokes his assaults rather than his guilt-consciousness and mad evasion. As we have seen, McCarthy's invention of the triune in September 1963 allowed for the mysterious displacement of his violence. McCarthy's reconception of Culla's psychology contributed to his decision to write a separate novel addressing the plight of the evicted, with different narrative strategies for exploring the forces that determine each protagonist's fate. Culla's novel would focus on the murderer's alienation as a metaphysical condition, a corollary of his failure in love for his sister and their child; Ballard's would do that as well (the blacksmith's parable of human evil appears in both novels' drafts), but the latter novel would more fully explore the ways in which family history, communal judgment, and human nature coalesce to create the serial killer fatedly. At the same time, in *Child of God,* where the auction of Ballard's land might be seen as a sociological problem, eviction functions as a metaphor for his ostracizing from the human community, even for his metaphysical displacement.

In *Child of God,* the High Sheriff of Sevier County survives his encounters with Ballard to represent the community's official, legal antagonism to the evicted, even its front line of defense against crime. Yet McCarthy does not grant the sheriff the status of the detective hero of a mystery or a crime procedural. LaFayette Turner is neither as anonymous nor as hapless as the sheriff killed in the sketchy scene discarded from *Outer Dark,* nor as tragically impotent and humble about his courage to face down evil as Sheriff Bell in *No Country for Old Men.* Turner swaggers, full of the confidence conferred by his office. Still, in the deleted scene of *Outer Dark* and in *Child of God,* both high sheriffs fail to contain the dispossessed man turned violent; and in both novels as published, agents of the legal system are hypocritical, corrupt, and subject to ironic or even comic undercutting.

McCarthy conjoined elements from the sheriff's attempted eviction of Culla and from *Outer Dark*'s discarded auction scene as he composed the opening of *Child of God,* linking the sheriff to the auction (or sheriff's sale) and defining the as-yet-unnamed Turner's new role. In the "Middle Draft" version of the first oral reminiscence, the sheriff levels Ballard at the auction and drags him off by the shirt collar, so effectively neutralizing him that the auction of his land proceeds "like he never even of been there" (6). In the published version, the sheriff does not respond quickly enough to the auctioneer's summons (6–9), so another man strikes Ballard with the blunt side of an axe. Here the sheriff's failure to act becomes a subtle template for the rest of the novel, as Turner remains one step behind Ballard, even as he assertively carries out his official duties.

Little remains of the earliest draft(s) of *Child of God,* but some of the unused or superseded passages filed at the end of the "Middle Draft" suggest that the sheriff/antagonist was initially a more prominent figure in the novel, participating more often in community gossip and functioning more as Ballard's nemesis than he does in the published version. Two scenes involving the sheriff reveal that in an earlier stage of composition, Ballard had once been married.[1] The longer of the two describes the sheriff's recovery of his wife's body from a cave. The shorter scene is an unused conversation about Ballard among smokers gathered around a stove. It occurs after Ballard has assaulted the man who bought his property, and the talk is dominated by the "high sheriff of Sevier County," who shakes his head over Ballard's lawless behavior. The sheriff offers an uncomprehending summary of Ballard's life, a story constructed out of community knowledge and his own limited experience. This backstory reveals much about McCarthy's earliest conception of his protagonist's narrative arc. It dates from quite early in the composition process, as Greer is still named Collins (the name change is inserted here in holograph), and the sheriff refers to the Speare place, the property up for auction in the first-draft pages of *Outer Dark* filed in "Early Draft [B]." Furthermore, the sheriff voices no suspicion of Ballard's serial murders and necrophilia, and he muses only on Ballard's motivations for shooting Collins/Greer. We learn that when Ballard's wife left him, he let his farm go to ruin and lost his property to satisfy debts (*CoG* "Middle Draft" 9). This version of his history, then, reprises Ownby's backstory in *The Orchard Keeper* (151–56), except that Ownby does not lose his farm in a sheriff's sale: eventually he controls his grief and works to repay his uncle's loan. Ballard's early backstory may owe something too to Culla's sense that Rinthy has "run off" from him, which exacerbates his sense of homelessness and disconnection. In all three of McCarthy's first novels or their drafts, the loss of a farm conjoined with the loss of a woman creates an existential upheaval.

According to the sheriff in the early, unused passage, after his eviction Ballard lived "like some description of varmint" on the Speare property, which had belonged to his wife's family, and his alcoholism worsened. The sheriff believes "a steady diet of hard liquor will make a man pretty varmintish." But like the auctioneer Essary in the superseded material of *Outer Dark,* the sheriff is oblivious to the likelihood that a man in despair, cut off from his family and evicted from his family home, will learn to disrespect the law and desire vengeance against the buyer who legally dispossesses him. When the sheriff thinks of Ballard's resenting Collins/Greer "to the point of [shootin] him down pointblank," he admits more truly than he knows, "I guess I just dont understand this world" ("Middle Draft" 9). By the time he completed the "Middle Draft" of *Child of God,* McCarthy had reassigned the abandoning wife and the overtly self-destructive despair to Ballard's father and had given Lester the more outwardly directed rage of the evicted and abandoned. But the man driven to murder by the cold-blooded execution of property law was always central to McCarthy's conception.

Evidence in the "Middle Draft" suggests as well that McCarthy initially conceived the oral tale that describes the suicide of Ballard's father as another commentary by the unsympathetic sheriff. As in the published novel, the tale is a community member's first-person account of being summoned by the child Lester to respond to his father's death. At the time, the speaker himself was only fourteen or fifteen, and faced with the unsettling sight of the hanged suicide, he was reluctant to act. But he yielded to his companion's urging that they cut down the body. The speaker now is troubled that they did not prevent the body's dropping as if it were a butchered carcass, an act that resonates ironically with the sheriff's dragging the felled and unconscious Ballard from the auction site in the earliest surviving version of that incident. Both scenes seem designed to prefigure and even to condition Ballard's own treatment of inert bodies in the later sections of the book. Not until nearly the end of the tale of suicide do we learn that the trauma of this witness's early exposure to death and disfigurement is the sheriff's. When the speaker wishes that suicides would take poison so that survivors would not have to see such unnerving sights, and another comments that Ballard himself was a grisly sight after Greer shot him, the sheriff replies, "No. . . . But I dont mind honest blood. I'd rather to see that than eyeballs hangin out and such" ("Middle Draft" 1–a; cf. *CoG* 21–22). These lines and the passage as a whole reveal the sheriff's greater concern for his own adolescent squeamishness than for the child's loss, the child's own trauma of witnessing the horrifying spectacle of his father disfigured in death.

The sentence ambiguously identifying the sheriff as the speaker is the only evidence in this version that he was the young witness, and McCarthy placed angle brackets around it and marked it "N/U," not used ("Middle Draft" 1–a). Retaining the implication that the sheriff narrates this tale would have suggested an early experience and character traits that might have influenced Turner's later running for sheriff and his hard-won adaptation to the gruesome sights encountered in the investigation of murders—a self-willed hardening to death's realities strangely parallel to Ballard's. However, as McCarthy reduced the sheriff's presence in the novel, he also made his character less nuanced, allowing the reader to see him primarily in terms of his roles as Ballard's arrogant persecutor and the ineffectual, slow-acting representative of law and order.

The sheriff's narration of Ballard senior's suicide (1–a) is adjacent in the "Middle Draft" to old Gresham's bizarrely singing the chickenshit blues at his wife's funeral (16), and McCarthy merged the two blocks of material into one conversation in the "Late Draft" (16; cf. *CoG* 21–22). At the top of the Gresham page in the "Middle Draft" appears another reference to Lester's faithless wife: "I dont think he ever was right after his wife left him." The line is crossed out, but other material on this page also linked Gresham's loss of his wife with Lester's (rather than his father's). The speaker initially concluded that Lester was "ever bit as crazy" as Gresham, a comparison that worked only when the community believed that Lester was derailed because his wife abandoned him. But McCarthy's juxtaposition of the two leaves suggests that in the middle-draft stage he was already planning to combine the tale of Gresham with an account of Ballard senior's suicide, linked by the common thread of these two men's crazed grief for their lost wives, grief that would no longer apply to Lester. McCarthy revised the final line on the Gresham page to reflect the new idea that Lester's lunacy differs from his father's and Gresham's. When the speaker concludes that Gresham was not "a patch on Lester Ballard for craziness" ("Middle Draft" 16), he no longer alludes to Lester's loss of his wife but to his crimes of serial murder and necrophilia, belatedly revealed to the community.

The sheriff's youthful squeamishness in the "Middle Draft" account of Ballard senior's suicide is complemented by his relative unflappability in the longer of the two leftover scenes preserved at the end of the draft. This is a much more extended and humorous version of the recovery of a "moldy shecorpse" (3) than appears in the published novel (cf. *CoG* 196–97). The scene dates from an early stage of composition, when the corpse is not one of Ballard's many victims but is identified without irony as "Mrs Ballard." She has been killed by a blow to her face "with a blunt instrument" and laid out on a ledge in a sink-hole with her head cushioned on a pillow decorated with needlework "hearts and trees and the inscription I Pine For You and Balsam" (3). The passage reinforces the sheriff's account that Ballard was once married, and it suggests that he killed his faithless spouse and staged her corpse in a sleeping-beauty parody. This is, then, the earliest surviving deployment of necrophilia in the novel's drafts, marking its psychological emergence in Ballard's denial of his wife's death and in his mania to maintain possession of what is lost. And it reinforces the conclusion that in McCarthy's evolving conception of the novel, the faithlessness of Ballard's wife preceded that of his mother. In the novel as published, Ballard, unlike Ownby and Culla, loses not his sexual partner but his birth family, which makes him not the outraged husband but the bereft and stunted child, utterly orphaned in the world, clinging madly and pathetically to his forfeited farm and to the illusion of a reconstituted family.

In the superseded scene, the mawkish sentimentality and bad pun of the embroidered pillow placed beneath Mrs. Ballard's head introduce a ridiculous note that complements the scene's dark humor at the expense of the officers. Deputy Earl, the first to descend into the sinkhole, refuses to touch Mrs. Ballard because "She's covered with some sort of . . . gray shit and she's got mushrooms growin on her" ("Middle Draft" 2). Awkwardly hoisting the unnerved Earl, deputy Cotton declares, "The son of a bitch has gained weight down there" (2). Earl's squeamish horror of the moldering body means that the self-important sheriff, plagued by the ineptitude of his deputies, must himself go down into the sink to retrieve the body. When he descends, he observes with clinical detachment that the body "was covered over all with adipocere, a pale gray cheesy mold common to corpses in damp places" ("Middle Draft" 3; cf. *CoG* 196), and he "gamely" secures the rope around her, then drags her under the aperture for his "henchmen" to haul her up. As the corpse rises, a "sodden and dripping package," the sheriff seems imperturbable until he hears cursing from above and a leg splashes into the subterranean creek near him, causing him to stumble backward, drop his flashlight, and sit abruptly in the icy stream (3). The corpse remains wedged in the opening, and the deputies grapple with the rope and bicker because Earl still refuses to lay hands on her. Then she breaks free when her arm falls off. "I guess you sons of bitches have pulled her head off too," the sheriff calls up (5). Their discomfiture continues as they must now handle and draw up the rotted limbs. Finally, the sheriff wraps his own body in the befouled rope for the deputies to haul him out of the sinkhole.

In the margins of this scene, McCarthy identified some passages as either "used" or "N/U," and indeed, some of the language is retained in the much-abbreviated published episode of the retrieval of Ballard's dead from the cave. But when he revised, McCarthy stripped away the humorous dialogue and the dismemberment of the body, recast the scene in a more objective narrative stance, and gave Turner the willing assistance of his deputies in securing and raising the first corpse (*CoG* 195–97). Essentially, he excised the men's subjectivity, reporting their detached performance of their job duties and letting go of the scene's oblique commentary on the squeamishness of the sheriff when as a teen he cut down the corpse of Ballard's father. But repeated linkage of living and dead bodies and the ropes that haul them like meat is common to the unused material and the novel in its published form. The motif is developed in the hanged corpse of Ballard senior, in the rope still dangling from the barn rafters in the auction scene, in the hanging of Ballard's White Cap great-uncle, in Ballard's hauling one of his victims up and down a ladder on a rope, in his own near-hanging by the mob, and in the retrieval of his victims' bodies, who ascend "dangling" as the officers draw them from the sinkhole (*CoG* 196). The pattern comments both on Ballard's necrophilia and on models of handling others, living or dead, among the more respectable members of his community. Further, it suggests that humans are the puppets of deterministic forces.[2]

The larger number of oral tales involving the sheriff in the "Middle Draft" than in *Child of God* as published suggests that in McCarthy's earliest conception of the novel the sheriff was integral to his depiction of the unsympathetic community from which Ballard emerges. But the sheriff remained unnamed in the earliest draft scenes, which emphasized his impersonal role in the novel as another spokesman for the community. Not until late in the middle-draft stage did McCarthy pencil in his name, "LaFayette Turner," at the top of the fifth oral commentary and replace "Sheriff" with "Fate?" in its first line ("Middle Draft" 33; cf. *CoG* 44). The resonant name may have occurred to McCarthy as he worked on three versions of Ballard's assault on Greer. The "Middle Draft" is incomplete, and the cohesiveness of the narrative loosens after page 113, where Ballard watches the burgeoning spring and begins to cry. Following are an unpaginated first-person version of Ballard's dream of riding to his death and then three unnumbered leaves describing his attack on Greer. In the first two of these leaves, when Greer fires at the intruder on his porch, Ballard falls as the high sheriff does in the discarded scene of *Outer Dark*. Ballard gazes "at the welter of gore where his stomach had been[,] . . . his hands almost idle at his side on the floor." Then Greer "blew away the top of his head and flung him into the yard like a doll." In preparation for this version of Ballard's death and discarding, McCarthy wrote that when Greer's shovel deflects his bullet, Ballard hears it as "the gong of turned doom," a line that remains in the published novel but with different implications (cf. *CoG* 172). The third of these unnumbered leaves revises the nature of Ballard's doom twice, prolonging his life. Now Greer's first shot blasts the flesh from Ballard's bicep; his second severs the limb. Then in holograph McCarthy gave Greer a single shot: Ballard's arm goes "spinning off into the yard," he whirls and sits down "as if to watch it," and his rifle lands on the porch floor—an approximate echo of dead Mrs. Ballard's severed limbs, the dropped flashlight, and the sheriff's sitting down in the cave creek in that unused early scene. In the published version, Ballard anticipates his doom but does not learn its nature until he wakes in the hospital to find that he is a prisoner and that his arm is gone. He suffers the monster Grendel's fate, but the later century into which Ballard is born means that he is not fated to bleed out from his terrible wound, the sole benign intervention of fate or chance in his life. (McCarthy was aware of the Beowulf epic [Crews, *Books Are Made out of Books* 58–60], but probably he had drafted the three versions of Ballard's shooting by Greer in the "Middle Draft" before he requested that Erskine send him John Gardner's novel *Grendel* [letter, received September 24, 1971].)

The concept of a doom awaiting Ballard persisted across the variations in the assault scene, and the phrase "turned doom" may well have suggested the name Fate Turner for the sheriff. The moniker is both apt and ironic, for it is not the sheriff as legal authority who brings about Ballard's doom. Turner does not stop the serial killing; we do not see him arrest Ballard either at Greer's place or at the hospital where Ballard later turns himself in; Turner is never credited by the community for his detective work; and the mob takes Ballard out of his custody. Indeed, Turner is notably absent from the novel after Greer shoots Ballard. Instead, Ballard's fate has been gradually sealed ever more firmly when his mother abandons his father, his father kills himself, the family property is confiscated and auctioned, and Ballard lives on homeless and alienated within his community and turns to murder for the illusion of family. The sheriff functions as a fate turner only insofar as he is one representative of that negligent community, careless of its most vulnerable citizens.

# Contrary Oxen and the Unidentified Storytellers

The auction was not the only depiction of East Tennessee life that McCarthy first conceived as potentially part of *Outer Dark* but finally recast for *Child of God.* As ambiguously defined as he made the dreamlike locale of *Outer Dark,* McCarthy's strategy for the novel included realistic description of regional customs, often with a nightmarish twist. He had already documented local customs and folkways in the hunting, trapping, and whiskey-running scenes in *The Orchard Keeper,* and he would do so again in *Suttree* in the mussel-brailing, riverside baptism, jailhouse and roadhouse scenes, as well as an extended scene of a cockfight he deleted before publication. Especially before its final revisions at Erskine's behest, *Suttree* also would deploy anecdotes and tales related by a variety of unemployed or working-class characters as the novel explored male storytelling both as a cultural activity of East Tennessee and as an influence on Suttree as a developing writer (Luce, "Tall Tales"). Because the first draft of *Suttree* is not preserved in the archives, we cannot be sure just how early McCarthy started developing the storytelling motif in that novel he had begun in 1961 or 1962. But adumbrations of it surfaced in Ef Hobie's and Ownby's tales in *The Orchard Keeper* and in *Outer Dark*'s first draft, and it became a vital structural and tonal component of *Child of God*, where the male gossips trade stories about Ballard's activities and other local incidents.

It seems plausible that throughout his Tennessee period, when he was working with regional material in multiple novels whose composition overlapped, McCarthy recorded tales and incidents as he heard or witnessed them and sometimes filed them with his work-in-progress without necessarily having a definite plan for their place within a given work. For example, we find in *Outer Dark*'s "Early Draft [B]" a never-used incident dated August 7, 1960, in which two unwashed, overall-clad children torment a possum harnessed to a small wagon. As the creature tries to elude them, one child explains that at first the possum used to "sull," but now "you caint <u>make</u> him sull." Then the boy pokes the possum with a stick, trying to make it turn sullen and play dead rather than "baring its teeth and hissing" (200/198). This third-person narrative pre-dates the genesis of *Outer Dark* by more than two years. It may be a left-over from *The Orchard Keeper*, where it might have complemented such scenes as Warn's flying his buzzard on a tether. Or it may have been an incident that McCarthy had yet to situate within his fiction. Similar unused fragments, some of which have no clear relationship to *Suttree*, are filed in the "Left from Suttree" folder in the Cormac McCarthy Papers.

At least two of the oral tales in *Child of God* derived from experiences McCarthy's friends related to him. De Lisle reports that their social circle in Tennessee included many outgoing salesmen who were lively raconteurs (De Lisle, Conversations).[3] Goodman was one of them, and when McCarthy introduced him and another Knoxville friend, John Sheddan,[4] to Memphis novelist John Fergus Ryan, Ryan found them to be "fantastic storytellers" and extraordinarily funny (letter to Cormac and Annie McCarthy). Goodman claims as his own experience the incident of the man who hurriedly dons his trousers when the sheriff interrupts his sexual adventure in a car, only to step out of the vehicle and find himself wearing them inside out (*CoG* 44–45; Gibson, "Knoxville Gave Cormac McCarthy" 28).[5] And in a letter to *Tennessee Illustrated* editor George Spencer, McCarthy revealed that the boxing ape episode (*CoG* 58–60) originated with another friend, Billy Rhodes. "I wish I could have told it as well as he did," he added graciously (1–2).

We know too that McCarthy's neighbors in Sevier County shared local lore with him when he lived there in 1962 and 1963 and drafted *Outer Dark*. These included the "old moonshiners" he later took Anne to meet when he brought her to Tennessee from Ibiza (Gibson, "Knoxville Gave Cormac McCarthy" 30).

Thus, his idea to give the storytellers a prominent role in *Child of God* may have originated partly in his experience at Fox's store in Walden Creek (see Luce, *Reading the World* 154). A note he jotted at the bottom of the second oral tale in the "Middle Draft" reveals that he considered tying all the tales "together at store at end" (13). Fox's store appears in *Child of God* (99, 124–26) and may well be the implied setting of the leftover oral tale filed at the end of the "Middle Draft," in which the sheriff and others sit around a stove to smoke while the sheriff muses on the events that have led to Ballard's shooting Collins/Greer (9). However, McCarthy did not follow through on his idea to situate the storytellers at the store, either at the close of Section I, where all the oral tales appear, or at the end of the novel. Perhaps he changed his mind partly because he had ended *The Orchard Keeper* with a similar gathering of the men and teens who discuss Rattner's murder and John Wesley's reaction to it in Eller's store (235–37). Instead, in *Child of God* the storytellers are part of the "pocketknife society" who gather on the Sevier County courthouse lawn to "whittle and mutter and spit" (*CoG* 48).

Locating the raconteurs at the courthouse implicitly interrogates the community's formal and informal systems of justice, disengaged from the suffering of the criminal. The tales create an ironic frisson between the men's humor and delight in their shared storytelling and their casual judgments of Ballard and his crimes. McCarthy later reprised and modified the Sevier County whittlers who witness and comment on the community's fools and outlaws when he created the solitary whittler who attends McEvoy's hanging in *The Gardener's Son* and whose silence is a profound and sober statement about community and social class injustice (85–86). These varying treatments of communal gatherings, judgments, and storytelling suggest that McCarthy's interest in witnessing and bearing witness dates from his earliest works, indeed that bearing thoughtful witness to the dark side of human nature is for him one of the roles of the novelist.

The earliest version of any of the oral tales of *Child of God* is a holograph draft of the ox incident saved in *Outer Dark*'s "Early Draft [B]," where it appears together with passages and notes for Culla's novel. The passage begins after the unnamed driver has lit a fire under his ox, when the creature steps forward four paces, and the driver gazes at its "bovine eyes implacable w/ fraudulent piety." When it dawns on him that the ox has pulled the wagon over the fire, he swears and kicks out at the flames, then crawls beneath the wagon to flail at them with his hat and even his hands (*OD* "Early Draft [B]" 207/196). Culla is not mentioned, but the draft's narrative stance is consistent with the indirect discourse that narrates Culla's experience. This material is comic, however, and the tone McCarthy established for *Outer Dark,* with its humorless protagonist, was more consistently tragic and gothic than in either *Child of God* or

*Suttree,* where humorous or ribald tales and incidents contribute to the works' textures and complicate their tones. McCarthy did not develop the stubborn ox and burning wagon material further in the *Outer Dark* drafts, nor did he link it definitively to its plot. In that novel as published, rather than engaging in a power struggle with his ox, a teamster labors to repair a broken wagon wheel, another of the novel's realistic descriptions of vanishing skills (135–36).

For *Child of God,* McCarthy framed the ox material as one storyteller's anecdote of the foolish Trantham boy. Two versions of the scene appear in the "Middle Draft," the second hinged with tape over the first. Both locate the incident at a fair and establish that using oxen as draft animals is now "oldtimey." Both deploy the dialect of the tale teller. But through these successive versions, McCarthy refined the details of the burning wagon and its consequences for humorous effect. The first version ends with Trantham's discovering that his wagon is burning and creates a plausible explanation for its catching fire so readily: "Wagon had a bunch of hay hangin down from it and it caught fire . . . , they like to never got it out. Had to cut them oxes loose, they took off all right then. He was days catchin em" ("Middle Draft" 26).

This version is sketchier and less vivid than that in the *Outer Dark* draft, and likely McCarthy wrote it without consulting the earlier version. The revision taped over it carries forward some of the details of the *Outer Dark* draft and is nearly identical to the version published in *Child of God* (36). When Trantham realizes the oxen have drawn the wagon over the flames, he crawls under the wagon and "commenced a beatin at the fire with his hat and about that time them old oxes took off again. Drug the wagon over him and like to broke both his legs. You never seen more contrary beasts than them" ("Middle Draft" 26).

The humor is pleasurable for its own sake but even more effective for its implied commentary on Ballard and the community's superficial reactions to him. The Trantham tale is the last of three told in its subchapter. One man recounts a sobering incident of Ballard's angrily breaking the neck of his recalcitrant cow when he tied her to his tractor and yanked her forward at full speed: another image of ropes and bodies. This anecdote leads a second man to a near-acknowledgment of Ballard's desperate rage when he recalls that Ballard burned down the Waldrop cabin he had been living in. (The reader knows, though the speaker does not, that the damage was caused by Ballard's lack of foresight when he built a roaring fire in the throat of the chimney, and sparks rose into the attic.) But the men's serious consideration of Ballard's plight and what might be an appropriate response to such a troubled person within the community is short-circuited when the third speaker tells his Sut Lovingood-esque tale of the mayhem loosed by Trantham's contrary oxen and his ill-considered reaction. As sequential anecdotes shared in a group tend to be, the Ballard and Trantham tales are linked thematically (bovine stubborn-ness, human rashness, flaming consequences). Their juxtaposition raises seri-ous issues of humankind's short-sightedness in the face of stubborn reality, the sources of destructive behavior, and the responses of the offended commu-nity, prompting readers to probe beyond the intentions of these innocent and myopic storytellers. What had started as an incident sketched out for possible inclusion in *Outer Dark* became recontextualized and developed in *Child of God* as poignant indirect narrative commentary on its protagonist and on the genial community that ostracizes him and stokes his desperation and rage.

Draft evidence from the two novels suggests that the oral tales were es-sential to McCarthy's conception of *Child of God,* which relies for its effects on counterpointing the community's failures of compassion or mindfulness against the omniscient narrator's more contemplative treatment of the or-phaned, displaced, and alienated man and the evil he does. The men's conver-sations begin immediately after the auction scene in Part I, commenting on it; and the early, unused drafts of tales that give the sheriff a role as one of the novel's gossips suggest that the genesis of the tales may well have been con-current with the genesis of the sheriff. As McCarthy developed *Child of God,* he composed complementary plot incidents that further illustrated the commu-nity's failures in justice and empathy. Prominent among them are the scenes in which Sheriff Turner hounds and arrests Ballard, the church excludes him, the young women treat him with disdain and ridicule, and the mob threatens to hang him, prompting him to elude them in the caves, where he finds not a refuge but a prison.

McCarthy's idea to include humorous anecdotes may have originated in his experience with his friends and acquaintances of East Tennessee, and they provided authentic local color, but their more crucial functions would be to fill in details of Ballard's history and to characterize the callous community that casually excludes him and pulls the strings of his fate. McCarthy's sense of the importance of the oral tales to the effect of his novel is made even clearer by his reaction to Erskine's initial failure to appreciate their role. Erskine's suggestions appear in the editorial copy McCarthy labeled the "Late Draft," which is a carbon copy of the "Final Draft." The editor recommended deleting the anecdote of the boxing ape because after the cruel story of the rigged pi-geon shoot in the same section, he did not see how it would "contribute" ("Late Draft" 44). In McCarthy's revision notes responding to Erskine's suggestions, he reminded himself for typescript page 25 to discuss the "after the fact" sto-ries the men tell about Ballard (*CoG*: Revision notes: "LaFayette" [1]). It seems that McCarthy's explanation of the tales' narrative function convinced Erskine not only to retract his suggestion that the boxing ape anecdote be deleted but also to agree to the expansion of the tale-swapping motif. McCarthy later jotted in the margin of his revision notes that he was to write another such story to follow page 63, one that would draw on "leftover" White Cap material and reveal that Ballard's grandfather had been hanged (*CoG*: Revision notes: "LaFayette" [2]). Filed with the revision notes is his new page 63A: a draft of the oral tale about grandfather Leland Ballard and his hanged younger brother that connects the Ballard family with the shameful White Cap era in Sevierville's history,[6] extends the community's rejection of the Ballard family two generations back, prepares for old Mr. Wade's reminiscences about the White Cap and Blue Bill vigilante groups (*CoG* 165–68) and for the mob's threatening to lynch Ballard, and amplifies the trope of man as puppet, subject to fate.[7]

# The Child and the Frozen Robin

In addition to the related narrative strands concerning dispossession, the sheriff, and communal judgment of Ballard that seem to have formed the core of McCarthy's earliest conception, other scenes in *Child of God* also first appear in *Outer Dark*'s "Early Draft [B]." In an isolated incident that, like the tale of the oxen, explores human shortsightedness, a countryman gives his toddler a half-frozen bird, and the child chews off its legs. The passage appears on a leaf with holograph notes for the scene in which Culla abandons his baby, but probably McCarthy did not conceive this incident as part of *Outer Dark*. The passage is not focalized through Culla or Rinthy's eyes, and its narrative stance is more compatible with *Suttree* than with either *Outer Dark* or the rewritten scene in *Child of God*. An unidentified narrator tells the story of a farmer, Grey, who is his neighbor (*OD* "Early Draft [B]" 214). But the speaker's voice is highly literate, rendered without the dialect markers that would identify the passage as oral storytelling. The narrator segues from observations of Grey's unkempt appearance and shabby countryman's clothes to class-based judgments of the man as "lank jawed, tobacco chewing, the insolent obsequiousness of impoverished and beggary natured people, flatlander, given to lying, friendly, underhanded, indolent, generous, slatternwifed" (214). Thus Grey anticipates Reese, for whom Suttree feels contempt, and this description of the farmer would appear in neither *Outer Dark* nor *Child of God* when they were published. But the ensuing description of Grey's child and the bird's fate is an early draft of the incident we find in Ballard's novel. The child is a denizen of the floor, "beslobbered and benastied" (*OD* "Early Draft [B]" 214). Like Reese, who carves toys for his youngest daughter (*S* 357), Grey brings the toddler a "playpretty," the half-frozen bird. Only later does he notice the child's bloody mouth, the bleeding stumps of the bird's legs, and its "floundering helplessly" (*OD* "Early Draft [B]" 214; cf. *CoG* 77–79).

The refined and slightly condensed description of the filth-covered child in the "Middle Draft" of *Child of God* (61) is identical to the passage as published. The begrimed boy is now named Billy. The narrator identifies him as a "primate," linking him with the "simian" Ballard (*CoG* 77; 20). Now Billy is mentally disabled, which makes more explicit the implication of hydrocephaly in the reference to the child as "huge-headed" in the *Outer Dark* draft and slyly implies affinity with Ballard's limited mental acuity. The narrative voice retains the earliest version's subjective judgments of the child and his living conditions. However, here the scene is focalized at least partly through Ballard's perspective, and the larger context within which McCarthy sets the description of the toddler establishes Ballard's hopes to win over Billy's sister or failing that to kill and possess her. Ballard, rather than Billy's father, brings the robin to the boy, and his intuition that the child wants to prevent the bird from escaping is key to the effect of the scene, revealing as it does Ballard's frame of mind and his motivations for murder. When McCarthy completed the robin scene in the "Middle Draft" of *Child of God,* he had already discarded the idea that Ballard killed his wife to keep her from running off, but that motive for murder is inherent in the parable of the child and the robin, which immediately precedes Ballard's first premeditated murder to possess a young woman.

# The Blacksmith

On May 7–8, 1963, McCarthy wrote a nearly complete draft of the blacksmith's creation myth as an extended scene for *Outer Dark* in which Culla takes an axe to be sharpened. Although this is the most fully developed of the Ur-*Child of God* passages in the *Outer Dark* draft, it did not generate related plot material for Ballard's novel. Indeed, it functions as an ingenious set piece in both works. Since McCarthy composed it before he decided that the murders in *Outer Dark* would be performed by the triune, it seems likely the scene initially prepared for Culla's executing his condescending employer with the axe. However, three holograph lines at the top of the blacksmith scene's last page refer to Salter's murder by the triune:

Me? Me?

No, Earl.

Stand back now the S.[quire] said. . . . You hear? God. Please . . . (*OD*
"Early Draft [B]" 93/218)

These lines, added after McCarthy's choice to have the triune do the killings, reflect a new conception of Salter's murder that would make the blacksmith scene superfluous for *Outer Dark.*

In *Outer Dark* as published, Salter's mute employee turns the wheel so that Culla can grind the axe before sectioning the downed tree (42–43); and McCarthy had drafted this incident as early as March 24, 1963 ("Rough/First Draft [A]" 50). However, in the discarded pages dated May 7–8 and saved at the end of "Early Draft [B]," a Mr. Buchanan sends Culla to the nearest town to have the axe sharpened, and as the garrulous blacksmith works, he lectures on his craft. The metaphysical import of the blacksmith scene composed for *Outer Dark* establishes the smith as a precursor of the triune like the black-clad auctioneer Essary and the beehiver. When Culla enters the shop, he sees the smith "hulked in abject silhouette over the anvil," and eerily the blacksmith pivots to look at him "although he had made no sound" (90/215)—images that identify the smith with some sinister force. In the "Middle Draft" of *Child of God,* the diction is slightly softened to "the smith in silhouette hulked above his work," and his uncanny sense of his customer's presence has been deleted (55; cf. *CoG* 70).

In the *Outer Dark* draft, the smith's commentary reinforces the impression that he is about some pseudo-creative work, which McCarthy made more benign as well when he revised the scene for *Child of God.* The blacksmith instructs Culla that the fuel for the fire should be coal that has never lain in the sun: "We need no sunlight for such dark work" (*OD* "Early Draft [B]," 91/216; "dark" crossed out). In the "Middle Draft" of Ballard's novel, the smith initially advised that the iron should not be allowed to get white-hot: "This is dark work all the way" (57); but McCarthy drew parentheses around the sentence as he reconsidered the metaphysical implications the scene should develop in *Child of God,* and no reference to dark creation appears in its "Late Draft" (56) or the published novel (72). Similarly, as the smith in the *Outer Dark* draft tempers the axe head in the fire, he warns against leaving it there too long: "[S]ome smiths condemn a tool to long perdition but the proper thing is to reach em from the pit when they show the color of grace, and now we callin for a high red to salvation" ("Early Draft [B]" 91/216). The verb "condemn" here grants the creator/blacksmith will and agency in damning or saving his creation. Like the triune's challenges, the smith's comment probes Culla's sense of guilt and damnation and seems designed to amplify Culla's grievance against the watching God he argues with in other pages discarded in the second draft stage.

When McCarthy reworked this sentence for *Child of God,* he again removed the more sinister aspects, now suggesting the creator's negligence more than outright malevolence in the creation of the sinner: "Some people will poke around at somethin else and leave the tool they're heatin to perdition but the proper thing is to fetch her out the minute she shows the color of grace" (*CoG* 72). As McCarthy reshaped the blacksmith scene for *Child of God,* then, he maintained its metaphysical function, its suggestion that a human's nature is determined by the creator, but he made subtle changes that eliminated the darker implications he had explored in the *Outer Dark* draft. He eliminated as well the smith's habits of profane and racist speech.

On the last page of the blacksmith scene in his draft for *Outer Dark,* McCarthy jotted notes about the cost and quality of the smith's work relative to the machine-made axes sold in hardware stores, and he added the smith's resonant final statement: "The secret's in carin. . . . If you do everthing right but one you no better off than if you done every thing wrong" ("Early Draft [B]" 93/218). Probably he added these notations as he reworked the episode for *Child of God,* especially since that novel gives sustained attention to human negligence and lack of foresight. A revised version of the smith's assertion closes the scene in the "Middle Draft" of Ballard's novel (59); and in the "Late Draft" the section continues when the instructive smith asks Ballard if he thinks he could "do it now from watchin." The wary necrophile who has learned much from spying on couples asks, "Do what" (58; *CoG* 74), comically undercutting the smith's pretensions and commenting on Ballard's obliviousness to anything but his obsessions.

The blacksmith scene has fewer plot connections in *Child of God* than it once had in *Outer Dark,* where it complemented the scene in which Culla works with the axe to section the fallen tree and where it prepared for Buchanan or Salter's murder and perhaps the tinker's as well. At one time McCarthy considered deploying a series of axe references throughout *Outer Dark* that would have linked the deaths of the squire and the tinker with the birth of the child. On the leaf composed in November [1963], where the narrator says of the tinker's death, "Perhaps he heard the cleft wind sigh down the axe's pitted flank," McCarthy jotted: "See axe grinding—read histoire de l'axe /—axe under bed—ease childbirth" ("Rough/First Draft [B]" 197/190). But he may have decided that an extended axe motif would create too insistent a plot pun on the idea that Culla had an axe to grind, conveyed in Salter's line, "Every man to grind his own axe" ("Early Draft [A]" 41; cf. *OD* 42), and McCarthy tried out other agrarian implements for Salter's murder: a stock-blade, a scythe. The axe remained in the tree-sectioning scene, but in the published book it is no longer associated with Salter's murder. Although McCarthy initially conceived of the axe as a link between Culla and the murders of Salter and the tinker, when he decided to make that link less obvious by assigning the killing to the triune, the role of the axe became more incidental.

In the *Outer Dark* draft, the blacksmith's lecture complemented the garrulous ferryman's explanation of his current-driven ferry's workings. Both men want to talk about their work even when Culla is incurious. Additionally, the blacksmith's musings on human nature complemented the drovers' commentary on hog nature. When McCarthy decided to abandon the axe as Culla's murder weapon, to employ the triune to enact his will to violence, and to reduce the number of characters who mirror the triune, he may have seen that the blacksmith scene had a less vital role in *Outer Dark,* making it available for re-use in *Child of God.* But in the latter novel, as fine as the writing is, the episode may seem a more excrescent set piece, especially since here the East Tennessee cultural activities do not provide ballast for a dream narrative, and thus they tend to blend into the background of the realistic setting. Ballard chops wood for fuel, so the axe is an important survival tool for him, but it does not figure in his murders except in the grisly hint that he uses its well-honed blade to scalp one of his victims. The primary connection between the axe grinding scene and the main action of the novel is that one of the men strikes down Ballard with the blunt side of an axe in the auction scene—hardly a plot juncture. In McCarthy's early conception, this may have been the way Ballard murdered his wife, but in the published novel, no such connection remains.

McCarthy's friend Gary Goodman later remarked churlishly to Mike Gibson that the blacksmith scene in *Child of God* amounts to no more than McCarthy's showing off his knowledge (Gibson, "Knoxville Gave Cormac McCarthy" 30–31). Since McCarthy was living with him in Asheville in spring 1964, it is possible that Goodman first read the scene in the first draft of *Outer Dark.* Long after McCarthy had deleted the blacksmith scene, when Goodman read the carbon copy of *Outer Dark*'s final draft, he profanely objected to what he considered McCarthy's overuse of folklore. Because Goodman was impatient with McCarthy's incorporation of folk customs in *Outer Dark,* he may have disliked the blacksmith material in its first draft. And if he had already voiced his objection to the smith's scene in *Outer Dark,* he may have felt disregarded to find that McCarthy had repurposed it in *Child of God.* Erskine appreciated the incident in *Child of God* but found it "so long" and asked if it was necessary because it impeded the flow of the story (*CoG* "Late Draft" editorial copy 58). However, both Goodman's distaste and Erskine's uncertainty took inadequate account of the ways in which the blacksmith scenes function as metaphysical commentary on the mystery of evil in human nature and thus on the nature of the two protagonists' alienation. McCarthy followed his own judgment to keep the episode in *Child of God* despite the reservations of his cranky friend and his more objective editor. Its placement near the end of Section I effectively foreshadows and glosses Ballard's descent into psychopathology and his treading a path of evil that seems determined by the conditions of his creation as much as by his life experiences. The metaphysical creation myth complements and complicates the sociological origins of Ballard's plight.

Study of the Ur-*Child of God* passages from *Outer Dark* "Early Draft [B]" and of the earliest draft material that remains filed in the "Middle Draft" of *Child of God* reveals that in McCarthy's initial conception, Lester Ballard was a man bereft of his family home, mistreated by his community, and a wife-killer, but he was not yet a multiple murderer or necrophile. He evolved out of McCarthy's concern for those dispossessed by land auction to satisfy debt, which he had begun to explore as a motive for murder in *Outer Dark,* but which he reduced in that novel. Still, the evidence of the two novels' typescripts heightens our awareness of McCarthy's early concern for those who are victimized by their callous neighbors, especially by those in societally sanctioned positions of legal or economic power over others: sheriffs, constables, justices of the peace, social workers, and other government agents. Indeed, this is a prominent element of social realism that unites his works of the Tennessee period. Read on one level, these works stand as McCarthy's indictment of the social injustices and moral failures within an ostensibly Christian and egalitarian culture—of the disconnect between cultural values espoused and civic or individual actions. In all these works, members of the community sell their "*neighbors out for money*" (*OK* 215) or neglect, disparage, and ostracize those most at risk.

This aspect of McCarthy's work drew the attention of young director Richard Pearce, who invited him in 1975 to write *The Gardener's Son,* a screenplay that explores the patronizing and exploitative relationship of nineteenth-century textile mill owners to their workers. It also appealed to psychiatrist and social documentarian Robert Coles. However, McCarthy wrote to Coles in February 1980 that he disliked protest novels such as those by John Steinbeck and Upton Sinclair and even regarded Faulkner's *Light in August* a "poor effort" because it seemed to him too devoted to exposing the ills of a racist and repressive society (1). As important as the social problems addressed in McCarthy's work were, his own preference was to subordinate them to more essential philosophical issues of "fate and the existence of evil. Or the meaning of life, or of death" (3). He would reprise this statement of artistic principle four years later when he wrote Erskine that he considered the historical horrors that informed the plot of *Blood Meridian* "a framework upon which to hang a dramatic inquiry into the nature of destiny and history and the uses of reason and knowledge & the nature of evil and all these sorts of things which have plagued folks since there were folks" (letter, received c. Mar. 1984, 1–2).

In both *Outer Dark* and *Child of God,* McCarthy's deployment of social and economic injustices to address more universal and philosophical themes of human nature was an important focus of his composition and revision processes. In *Outer Dark,* Culla remains impoverished, resentful, and often callously mistreated, but McCarthy's revisions downplayed the eviction theme and made Culla's murders far more mysterious than acts of focused social protest. In contrast to Faulkner's treatment of Joe Christmas, McCarthy's objective narrative perspective on Culla left his psychology and motivations, even his deeds, more ambiguous, his choices puzzling to readers, his transgressions not fully explained by his experiences. McCarthy gradually implemented this strategy as he revised the novel, reducing instances of Culla's thoughts and inventing ways to project his interior life obliquely, finally representing his malevolence primarily in the triune, whose relation to himself Culla can scarcely acknowledge. In keeping with McCarthy's note in *Outer Dark*'s "Rough/First Draft [B]" that for the novel to function properly its "<u>events</u> must assume the shape of a character & . . . become . . . mere manifestations of the . . . coherent, logical, and immutable <u>deformation</u> of evolving fate" (195A), he treated Culla's evil acts as manifestations of his metaphysical fatedness, as the blacksmith's commentary on human nature had implied.

In the earliest draft(s) of *Child of God,* the auction, the sheriff, and the community gossips, all to some extent originating in *Outer Dark*'s earliest drafts, developed the motif of social injustice imposed on an orphan at the hands of his careless or hostile community. The reader gains a clear sense of the societal forces that have shaped Ballard, but again McCarthy resisted any reductionist attribution of evil to social causes. Ballard takes arms against Greer, who has purchased his farmstead at auction, but when McCarthy introduced the element of serial necrophilia, Ballard's other murders became acts not of protest or revenge but of his ongoing and desperate longing for connectedness, which strangely reconnected the murderer to universal human impulses.

Again a sense of fatedness overlies the novel, conveyed not only in the revised blacksmith's lecture on human nature, but also in the repeated rope metaphor, suggesting alternately that an individual is a puppet whose strings are manipulated by indifferent forces or that he or she is (not) mere meat; and like Culla, Ballard finds his own acts inexplicable. Both experience injustice and are treated callously, and both strike out in murderous struggle against their fates; but both novels also explore their specific experiences of suffering and crime as fundamental and mysterious aspects of the human condition which raise philosophical questions that have "plagued folks since there were folks."

# Domestic Life and Writing Life in Tennessee, 1967–1973

By the time McCarthy returned to Tennessee from Europe in 1967, he had completed the final draft of *Outer Dark* and one or more drafts of *Child of God* while continuing to work on *Suttree*. After their initial stay with Goodman, he and Anne settled first on the pig farm in Rockford and later in Louisville, both in Blount County. Consulting the Blount County Register of Deeds, Wesley Morgan has discovered that on September 24, 1969, the couple bought a barn with eleven acres of land on Light Pink Road in Louisville (pronounced Lewisville; email, Oct. 17, 2017). De Lisle remembers that Cormac surprised her with the purchase (De Lisle, Interview with Bryan Giemza and Dianne Luce). When they bought it, the structure was just "a cinder block shell on a concrete slab," McCarthy told Mark Owen. He repaired its broken casement windows, and they moved in, converting it to a home as they lived in it. This was time-consuming work which McCarthy did himself with the help of Anne and sometimes friends. McCarthy's design for his life allowed for interruptions to his writing, and he enjoyed working with his hands. "I've always been interested in architectural design and it gives me something to do in my spare time," he told Owen (Owen, "McCarthy Is One" 4B). De Lisle reports that "he was in charge of everything," and the house was entirely of his design (Interview with Bryan Giemza and Dianne Luce). Among other projects, McCarthy built stone chimneys and added a stone room to the structure (Williams, "Annie DeLisle" E2; Mick Brown, "On the Trail of the Lonesome Bard" 26). De Lisle recalls that they would be dressed up and driving somewhere, and Cormac would stop the car to pick up stones he could use. She remembers that he recovered a six-by-four-foot slate slab weighing about a thousand pounds that had slid down the mountain near Chilhowee Lake and transported it to their property on a septic-tank truck. Then with the help of friends he winched it up onto a wheeled contraption of his own devising and jockeyed it into place in the wide livestock doorframe at the end of the barn. With the magnificent hearthstone laid, he constructed the stone fireplace and wall around it (De Lisle, Conversations). The symbolism of this act was certainly not lost on him even though the hearthfire of their marriage would eventually die out.

The couple liked to refinish furniture together, and one piece was McCarthy's big writing desk, which they had found in an old "rag-shop" in Knoxville. It sat under a tarp at their house for some time until McCarthy decided to refinish it. When he removed the drawers and turned the desk upside down, a rain of silver dollars tumbled out—a welcome windfall. He cleaned the piece and applied seven layers of French polish (De Lisle, Conversations).

In summer 1971, McCarthy and Bill Kidwell collaborated for six weeks on the creation of two marble and river rock mosaics set in mortar in downtown Maryville, funded by an urban renewal grant from the US Department of Housing and Urban Development. Kidwell had secured the grant, De Lisle remembers, but he did not have the masonry skills to execute the project, so he asked for McCarthy's help. Kidwell reminisced that as they were constructing the mosaics in full view of the public on Main Street, passersby would stop and comment on their work. Kidwell wanted to engage them in conversation, but McCarthy asked him to keep still and listen. He was gathering speechways for his fiction. One mosaic, a serpentine shape that could not be preserved, is now gone; the other, a fifteen-foot circle, has been moved to the grounds of the new Blount County Public Library, where it is accompanied by a commemorative plaque with McCarthy's image (Kidwell, Conversation with Arnold and Luce; De Lisle, Conversations; Norris, "Piece of Art in Danger Downtown" 6A).

This was a period when McCarthy had a more settled domestic life than he often enjoyed. He had his writing, and Anne had her dancing. When the Maryville-Alcoa Civic Ballet started in 1972, Anne was a member of its Senior Company.[8] By 1973, she started a ballet school. The couple had a circle of friends including the people Anne was meeting through dance and theater as well as a local group of British expats, among them Oak Ridge physicist Richard Gammage and his wife. In about 1972, the McCarthys and Gammages went on a three-week trip to Mexico. They drove the Pan-American Highway through Laredo, Texas, to Mexico City, Taxco, and on to Acapulco and Puerta Angel on the Gulf, then back north to Oaxaca (De Lisle, Interview with Bryan Giemza and Dianne Luce). The McCarthys' friends of this period also included Bill Kidwell and his wife,[9] Frank and Carolyn Hare, and the rest of the lively group of storytelling salesmen. According to De Lisle, McCarthy listened avidly to the stories these men told and picked up details to use in his novels, just as he had listened to the storytellers of Sevier County. But he also participated in the storytelling, entertaining them in turn. At intervals Cormac and Anne also hosted out-of-town visitors at their home on Light Pink Road: Anne's mother, Leslie Garrett, Stacy Keach, and later Richard Pearce. Garrett was about to marry singer Linda Kerby, and Anne volunteered to coordinate a wedding for them at the Cheryl and Mickey Van Metre antebellum home in

Maryville. McCarthy was best man and Anne was matron of honor (De Lisle, Conversations).

McCarthy would usually write for four or five hours each day (Runsdorf, "Recognition Acceptable" 5). In the late afternoon, he would announce to Anne, "Well, it's cocktail time" and "take a shower as if washing all that stuff out of his hair," after which they would enjoy a candle-lit dinner (Williams, "Cormac McCarthy" E2). In the evenings, he would often read her some of what he had written that day. Even with Anne, McCarthy did not discuss his writing, but he enjoyed sharing it with her. She was encouraging, but she did not feel qualified to make suggestions (De Lisle, Conversations). Anne found adjusting to Tennessee a challenge, but she later remembered these years with Cormac as "the times when everything was right with the world" (Williams, "Cormac McCarthy" E2).

When Mark Owen interviewed McCarthy in 1971, he found him witty, un-cynical, and happy with the independent life he had created, a life of reading among his 1,500 books, writing his novels, and building his house. "I've always been horrified by the way people live their lives," McCarthy remarked. "On one hand there is a nine-to-five job you don't like and a totally artificial life. At the other end is the life of a hermit. But I don't want to be cut off from society and have to . . . compromise." He confessed that he was rather self-centered and hedonistic. His primary goal, however, was to write as well as he could. Everything else was subordinate to that (Owen, "McCarthy Is One" 4B).

Reading for pleasure and in service of his writing was always part of Mc-Carthy's adult life. It is not possible to reconstruct the full range of his wide reading during any period, although Michael Crews's survey of the literary and philosophical references in McCarthy's papers compiles evidence for much of it (Crews, *Books Are Made out of Books*). Other archival evidence exists in his correspondence with Erskine, who sent him copies of books he had edited or in which McCarthy expressed interest. On August 18, 1969, Erskine received McCarthy's thanks for some John O'Hara works. Previously McCarthy had read only O'Hara's *Appointment in Samarra* (1934) and *The Farmer's Hotel* (1951). Now he reported that he had enjoyed some of the new "stories," which suggests that Erskine had given him the collection *And Other Stories*, published in 1968. However, Erskine's reply of August 19 refers to the O'Hara as a novel, which suggests *Lovey Childs: A Philadelphian's Story*, published in 1969. It seems he had sent McCarthy both. The next fall, McCarthy thanked his editor for "the Bech book," probably John Updike's story collection *Bech: A Book* (1970) about a blocked writer. McCarthy wrote that it had made him laugh, and he found it better than Updike's other work, which he professed he found unreadable. At this time, he had also read "Bimini," an excerpt from

Ernest Hemingway's *Islands in the Stream* (1970), posthumously published in *Esquire.* McCarthy considered it "pretty bad" (letter received Oct. 8, 1970).

Early in 1971, in response to a catalogue of recent Random House publications that Beves had sent McCarthy with the offer that he could choose something, he requested three slim volumes in lieu of a larger one. The first of these was *Reason and Violence: A Decade of Sartre's Philosophy, 1950–1960* by psychiatrists R. D. Laing and D. G. Cooper. Their book is a summary/explication of Sartre's *Saint Genet, Question of Method,* and *Critique of Dialectical Reason,* and McCarthy's request adds to the evidence of his interest in French existentialism. He also asked for William Gass's *Fiction and the Figures of Life,* the writer/philosopher's volume of literary criticism. Finally, he requested *Zen in the Art of Archery* by Eugen Herrigel. All three were published by Random House affiliates in early 1971. McCarthy's choices speak to his interest in various ous philosophies. However, he confided to his editor that the catalogue's offerings did not do much credit to Random (letter to Erskine, received Mar. 3, 1971).

Later that year, McCarthy's letters to Erskine mentioned three other volumes. One was an unidentified nonfiction book on Thomas Hardy, sent by Beves along with other works that she and/or Erskine thought might interest him. This was likely Michael Millgate's *Thomas Hardy: His Career as a Novelist,* which Random published in 1971. Millgate was one of the writers to whom Erskine had sent an advance copy of *The Orchard Keeper* in hopes of eliciting an endorsement. McCarthy was reading the Hardy volume in May, and it piqued his interest in reading Hardy's own work. He had previously read only "a couple" of his novels several years earlier. McCarthy confessed that his knowledge of Hardy was limited but that he did not see the similarities to his own work that some reviewers mentioned (letter to Erskine, received May 20, 1971).

Erskine sent more books in the fall, one of which was a volume about Theodore Dreiser, likely Robert Penn Warren's *Homage to Theodore Dreiser on the Centennial of His Birth.* Not only was this a book that Erskine would have edited, but De Lisle recalls that she and Cormac had met Warren at Erskine's Westport home when they arrived from Europe in October 1967 (*Conversations*). For this reason, McCarthy might have found it of interest. He wrote Erskine that he had not initially thought he would read the book, an analysis of Dreiser's major novels, but he started with Warren's "invocations," three poems comprising its introductory "Portrait" section: "Psychological Profile," "Vital Statistics," and "Moral Assessment"; and they led him to finish the volume, which he found "very good." In the same letter, received on September 24, 1971, McCarthy asked for a copy of *Grendel,* which had just been published under the Knopf imprint. The novel by John Gardner is based on the eighth-century Old English epic *Beowulf,* and it retells the story from the point of view of the monster, Grendel, whose nihilistic or despairing pronouncements echo

Jean-Paul Sartre. In his request, McCarthy remarked that the book sounded "fascinating," and it may well have proved so to the writer who was deep into writing the "Middle Draft" about his monstrous, lonely, cave-dwelling child of God, largely from Ballard's indirect perspective. In *Grendel,* the omniscient Dragon tells the marauding protagonist, "You improve [men]. . . . You stimulate them! You make them think and scheme. You drive them to poetry, science, religion, all that makes them what they are for as long as they last. You are . . . the brute existent by which they learn to define themselves" (72–73).

In a letter Erskine received on April 17, 1972, McCarthy asked his editor to locate a copy of nature writer Edward Hoagland's most recent essay collection for him. McCarthy already knew Hoagland's work, probably at least his 1969 travel book *Notes from the Century Before* (Crews, *Books Are Made out of Books* 91–94), and he considered him "a very fine writer." As McCarthy was no doubt aware, Random was Hoagland's publisher, and Erskine arranged for *The Courage of Turtles* (1970) to be sent (Beves, Review Order). In the same letter, McCarthy wondered whether there might be anything by Harry Kressing (Harry Adam Ruber) other than *The Cook* (1965), a "blend of delicious black humor and Kafkaesque horror story," according to its publisher's description. A film based on it, *Something for Everyone,* had been released in the United States on July 22, 1970, and it seems likely that McCarthy had read the book and/or seen the film. Kressing's second work of fiction, *Married Lives,* was published by Faber and Faber in 1974, two years after McCarthy's inquiry, and no mention of it appears in his correspondence with Erskine.

As part of his compromise between creative focus and sociability, Cormac and Anne were also making time for trips within the United States such as their visits to his parents in Virginia, to the Hares in Kentucky, and to his brother Dennis in Soco Gap. In spring 1973, they traveled to a regatta at a friend's yacht club, Le Club, in Fort Lauderdale, Florida, where they were invited to sail to Cat Cay in the Bahamas. They dropped their lobster pots on the way, picked them up on the return trip, and cooked the fresh lobsters on the yacht for dinner. The group was to have included television personality Ed McMahon, who was the celebrity sponsor for the regatta, but who managed in his inebriation to fall off the pier, injuring himself (McCarthy to Caroline [Harkleroad]; De Lisle, Conversations). During this trip to Florida, the McCarthys also visited Palm Beach and Key West, where they toured the Hemingway Home and Museum.

Despite such pleasant distractions, McCarthy wrote steadily. Although he was working on both novels, he continued to think of *Suttree* as his next book rather than *Child of God.* In interviews published locally in October 1968, January 1969, and February 1971, he predicted that his next novel would be set in Knoxville ("Author Lives" F5; Jordan, "'Just Write'" 6; Owen, "McCarthy Is One"

4B ). As the dates on the "Middle Draft" folder of *Child of God* show, he took time off from *Suttree* from late September 1970 through mid-February 1971 to work on *Child of God,* and in February 1971 he still anticipated working on *Suttree* another year or two (Owen, "McCarthy Is One" 4B). After his initial mention of *Child of God* in 1966, McCarthy made no further reference to it in any of his letters to Erskine until he submitted it in February 1972; but as with *Outer Dark,* McCarthy's need for income may well have motivated him to finish the shorter novel first. Although Anne was working, they were living very modestly, and it may have weighed on him that his writing was not bringing in much. According to her, they did not discuss money, and McCarthy always provided for her (De Lisle, Conversations). Nevertheless, given the ways in which lack of income had contributed to the failure of his marriage to Lee, McCarthy may have felt anxiety that a similar fate would befall him with Anne.

The need for income may well have been exacerbated by their wish to become homeowners. On January 9, 1969, Erskine received a mildly testy letter from McCarthy complaining that *Outer Dark* was not available in bookstores in southern cities and asking for copies he could sell himself. Erskine took no offense, responding on the same day that although Random House records indicated that about 3,600 copies had sold, some 130 more than the figure Lane later quoted to Woolmer, he thought that by now many booksellers had sold out their initial modest orders and had neglected to reorder. His explanation to McCarthy is amplified in *At Random,* where Cerf writes that bookselling was not greatly profitable and that retailers were reluctant to buy books for which there was small demand—"first novels, poetry, essays, plays." Often booksellers would purchase only a copy or two and not reorder (Cerf, *At Random* 209).[10] But Erskine could not be certain about the sales numbers because their computer was then malfunctioning. He promised to investigate and did so throughout the spring. In the meantime, he arranged for McCarthy to receive a new advance of $1,000 on further sales of his two novels (Random House, "Draw Check" order, Feb. 6, 1969). It was forwarded to McCarthy on February 17 (Random House, Royalty check transmittal form).

On March 12, Erskine sent an internal memo to Dick Liebermann of the sales department (Cerf, *At Random* 289) indicating that 924 copies of *Outer Dark* had sold so far in 1969 and that they now had only about 500 in stock. In addition, interest in McCarthy's work generated by the new book had resulted in their selling out their remaining stock of *The Orchard Keeper,* Erskine thought, and he wanted to keep it in print. He apparently did not anticipate resistance to a second printing of *The Orchard Keeper* because on March 25 he sent to production McCarthy's 1966 list of corrections to be made and recorded the transmittal date on his copy of the list.

However, Liebermann was not in favor of reprinting *The Orchard Keeper* yet because sales of the first printing had dwindled from 660 in 1967, to 155 in 1968, and 65 in the first quarter of 1969. As for *Outer Dark*, his figures indicated that they still had 988 copies in stock—almost twice what Erskine had thought (Liebermann, Memo to Albert Erskine, Apr. 1, 1969). However, ten days later a hand count revealed that 750 copies were on hand (Singer, Memo to Leon Peikin, Apr. 11, 1969), and on April 17 Erskine again wrote Liebermann to say that while he agreed there was no urgency for a second printing of *Outer Dark,* he had "a strong feeling" that *The Orchard Keeper* should be reprinted. With so few copies in stock, it was "effectively out of print," and he worried that sales might already have been lost due to insufficient numbers in the storeroom. Since sixty-five had sold in the first quarter of 1969, he pointed out, they could project sales of more than two hundred for the year if they had them on hand. He did not remind Liebermann that the Ballentine paperback would soon be issued. Perhaps they would not have considered that relevant to the hardcover sales since hardcover books were sold through independent bookstores in the 1970s, while mass-market paperbacks were designed to be sold from magazine displays in supermarkets and similar outlets (Kiefer, "Striking the Fire of Commerce" 16). Erskine's persistence paid off. By early May, a small second printing of 750 copies *The Orchard Keeper* was approved. The price was to rise significantly, from $4.95 to $6.95. Originally the corrected printing was planned for July 1 delivery, but at some point it was delayed until fall (Goldstein, Form memo to Suzanne Beves; Erskine, Letter to Anne McCarthy, Sept. 11, 1969).

It seems that McCarthy did not know a second printing of *The Orchard Keeper* was in the works. No surviving correspondence indicates that Erskine informed him of the plans before mid-August, and this slip in communication apparently led to McCarthy's additional frustration about the way Random was handling his books. To judge from Erskine's reply on July 14, in summer 1969 McCarthy had sent Erskine a postcard from a road trip, communication that prompted the editor to ask why he had not come on to New York but also to wonder how much work he was getting done. He nudged McCarthy to send a progress report. McCarthy took a month to answer, and then his tone was sometimes cordial, sometimes disgruntled. He and Anne had been in Virginia for a wedding, he reported. However, De Lisle does not remember this wedding, which could not have been the marriage of one of Cormac's siblings (De Lisle, Conversations). Possibly McCarthy was inventing a cover story for his slow response. Meanwhile, he had received a letter from a New York bookseller who had paid fifteen dollars for a copy of *The Orchard Keeper,* and now McCarthy suspected that the novel had been remaindered with no prior notice to him. He wondered if there might be any copies left that he could have for his own collection. Turning to *Outer Dark,* he reminded Erskine that his most recent statement from Random indicated that 2,240 copies had sold in the first half of 1969, which he guessed was okay for a novel that seemed not to have been in the bookstores. He made no mention of his progress on *Suttree* (received Aug. 18, 1969).

Erskine replied on August 19, 1969, diplomatically ignoring McCarthy's irritation. *The Orchard Keeper* had not, in fact, been remaindered and was about to be reprinted. Erskine had learned, however, that booksellers had returned 278 books in less-than-new condition, and Random had sent them to a bargain outlet in fall 1966. Far from being distressed at the sale of a first printing for fifteen dollars, Erskine declared he was pleased to see McCarthy's work entering the rare book market, a hint that McCarthy too should be gratified for what this said of his growing reputation.

Erskine was right, but this took no account of the fact that the profit from a book sold at collectors' prices went to the dealer, not to the author; and McCarthy seems to have realized that his remaining books might just as well be sold through him. However, it was too late to do much with the first printing of *The Orchard Keeper.* Random located one copy for McCarthy, but the stock was by then completely depleted (Erskine, Letter to Anne McCarthy, Sept. 11, 1969). A week later, Anne wrote to ask that any other first printings which might come back from booksellers be set aside for her to buy (Anne McCarthy to Erskine, Sept. 18, 1969); but none was found until March 1972, when a beat-up copy surfaced (Beves, Memo to Anne McCarthy, Mar. 10, 1972).

In April 1970, Erskine initiated payment to McCarthy of yet another $1,000 advance (Random House, "Draw Check" order, Apr. 16, 1970). On October 8, he received a letter McCarthy wrote upon receiving a new royalty statement. He wanted news about his other potential sources of income: the forthcoming Ballentine paperback and French editions of *Outer Dark,* the German-language edition of *The Orchard Keeper,* and the likelihood that Parallel would exercise its film option for *Outer Dark,* which he recalled would expire in December. Implicit in this letter were his disappointment in his royalties and the fact that despite the advances Random had approved in 1969 and 1970 and his receipt of the Guggenheim award in 1969, he needed money. He reported that his construction work on both the house and his novel were coming along well but not rapidly.

By early 1971, McCarthy and Goodman had devised an arrangement for Goodman to sell his books. On February 4, Erskine received McCarthy's letter asking how many hardcover copies of *Outer Dark* were left. It seems they communicated further by phone, and on February 23, Erskine sent his blessings for Goodman's endeavor and detailed the discount schedule Random could offer him. McCarthy served as go-between, forwarding Goodman's payment for fifty books (forty-five of *Outer Dark* and five of *The Orchard Keeper,* presumably the second printing; McCarthy, Letter to Albert Erskine, received Mar. 17, 1971). McCarthy signed some or all of the forty-five first edition copies of *Outer Dark,* and Goodman offered them for sale at $12.50 each (Owl Books advertisement [1971]; since the advertisement provides a post office box in lieu of a street address, it may be that Owl Books had no storefront.) By May, Goodman had sold the books on hand and needed two more of *The Orchard Keeper* (McCarthy, Letter to Albert Erskine, received May 20, 1971). If Goodman sold all fifty books at $12.50 each, that would have netted $650, out of which Goodman would be reimbursed for his investment of $205 (fifty books at $6.95 each, less the 41 percent bookseller's discount). Random and McCarthy would receive their contractual payments, as for any books sold. There is no evidence of McCarthy and Goodman's agreement about the proportions of the profit each would receive from the signed editions. But even if all the proceeds went to McCarthy, it could not have amounted to substantial income—$445 at most, and their experiment in selling signed copies seems to have ended.

By fall 1970, when McCarthy's primary focus was revising *Child of God,* Erskine had again begun to function as McCarthy's de facto agent in hopes of placing episodes from his work in periodicals. Clearly McCarthy recognized that there were no stand-alone narratives in the spare and challenging *Child of God.* However, the Knoxville novel-in-progress was more episodic even though on closer look, as Guy Davenport would later write, its structure was "tight as the strings on a guitar" (Davenport, "Silurian Southern" 368). Now it seems the editor was trying to help McCarthy earn enough for him and Anne to live on and improve their house until he published his next book. Erskine had been reading through a draft of Joseph Blotner's biography of William Faulkner, and he was likely thinking a great deal about the financial difficulties his extraordinarily talented but long-undervalued author had suffered and about Faulkner's strategy of shaping episodes in novels such as *The Unvanquished* (1938), *The Hamlet* (1940), and *Go Down, Moses* (1942) so that they could generate income from magazines as he worked (Erskine, Letter to Willie Morris, Sept. 14, 1970). Selling excerpts years in advance of *Suttree*'s publication might not improve the book's sales, but it might make it possible for McCarthy to finish it.

McCarthy selected pieces from the "Middle Draft" of *Suttree,* which were retyped and repaginated as self-contained stories. Erskine first tried Willie Morris of *Harper's Magazine,* whom he had introduced to *Outer Dark* in 1968. On September 14, 1970, Erskine sent Morris an episode McCarthy titled "Harrogate and the Flittermouses" (see *S* 207–19). But Morris replied on September 29 with a brief note of rejection. On October 21, Erskine sent the excerpt to *Esquire*'s Gordon Lish, who replied graciously on October 26, apologizing that he had not thought to request new McCarthy material even though he held his work in high esteem. Lish did not find that the excerpt worked as a short story, however. Despite its "notable" writing and lush prose style, it was finally "more anecdotal than dramatic" (Lish, Letter to Albert Erskine, Oct. 26, 1970). But he added in a separate note of the same day that he was receptive to looking at other pieces by McCarthy (Lish, Note to Albert Erskine, Oct. 26, 1970). Erskine sent him an untitled excerpt three weeks later (Beves, Memo to Gordon Lish, Nov. 17, 1970). Later correspondence from Willie Morris reveals that this was the early chapter in which Suttree sells his fish and then meets his friends in the Huddle, becomes horribly drunk, and wakes in jail after his dream of the flayed man (Morris, Letter to Albert Erskine, Feb. 22, 1971; see *S* 63–86). Lish's response to the Huddle excerpt was warm. He was still convinced of McCarthy's enormous talent, still hoping for other offerings, but he turned this one down too. And now he complained about what he saw as the excesses of McCarthy's prose style: he wished McCarthy would write with more restraint and "let the silences speak" (Lish, Letter to Albert Erskine, Nov. 20, 1970). McCarthy would find Lish's comments "strange," and he was not sure how to interpret them since he did not know to which of the two excerpts Lish referred (McCarthy, Letter to Albert Erskine, received Mar. 3, 1971).

Erskine now planned to send Morris the Huddle episode Lish had rejected, and if *Harper's* did not take it, he would try *Playboy* as a "last resort." There was also the underground magazine *Rolling Stone,* and he wondered how McCarthy would feel about publishing there (Erskine, Letter to Cormac McCarthy, Dec. 30, 1970). True to his word, Erskine sent Morris McCarthy's "impressive new story" just after the new year (Erskine, Letter to Willie Morris, Jan. 4, 1971), but *Harper's* kept the manuscript for more than six weeks before turning it down. Morris reported that the editors were impressed with the bar scene and McCarthy's talent and that they still hoped to accept something eventually (Morris, Letter to Albert Erskine, Feb. 22, 1971).

Encouraged by Erskine's ongoing efforts, McCarthy sent him another excerpt early in February. This was the episode of the freezing Thanksgiving Day during which Suttree checks on his friends and later ends up stranded at the end of the streetcar line and walking home in the cold (see *S* 167–79; Beves, Letter to Cormac McCarthy, Aug. 1971).[11] In his cover letter, McCarthy thanked his editor for his attempts to place the stories. But money was still on his mind. He asked when he would receive copies of the Ballentine paperback of *Outer Dark* and proceeds from that edition or any other source (McCarthy, Letter to Albert Erskine, Feb. 4, 1971). However, unless Erskine had unsuccessfully tried the Thanksgiving excerpt with Lish, perhaps hand-delivering it when they met for lunch as Lish had suggested, Erskine did not resume his efforts to place the

*Suttree* episodes until mid-May, soon after he received, in April, a fourth ex-cerpt from McCarthy, the chapter detailing Suttree's Sunday excursion down-river to visit his aunt and uncle and to see the deserted family mansion (see *S* 119–36; Beves, Letter to Cormac McCarthy, Aug. 1971). Then Erskine submitted the four "self-contained sections" he had in hand to Robie Macauley, who now edited *Playboy* (Erskine, Letter to Robie Macauley, May 11, 1971; Erskine, Letter to Cormac McCarthy, June 8, 1971). But Macauley felt that he needed a differ-ent kind of fiction for *Playboy* than he had earlier published in *Kenyon Review,* and he found the submissions from the new novel too unrelievedly dark and sordid: "the depression of slow death on skid row." Like Morris and Lish, he acknowledged McCarthy's ability and hoped to see something more suitable from him in the future (McCauley, Letter to Albert Erskine, May 27, 1971). But it was clear that this could not be from *Suttree.*

While his episodes were under consideration at *Playboy,* McCarthy wrote Erskine that his third novel, which he estimated he could pare down to about 200,000 words or 700 pages, was then about 70 percent finished. This was a progress report on *Suttree,* then, rather than the shorter *Child of God.* He won-dered how large an advance he might now receive and whether discussions then underway with an unidentified production company had yielded a new film option on *The Orchard Keeper* (McCarthy, Letter to Albert Erskine, re-ceived May 20, 1971). When the Parallel option had expired, it seems, Random's subsidiary rights department had attempted to sell the film rights elsewhere. Two weeks later, Erskine had been unable to convene the decision-makers at Random House to discuss an advance, nor had he shown them the *Suttree* excerpts because he feared they might provide too disjointed an impression of the novel. Perhaps, too, he was influenced by Macauley's perception that it was all too unrelievedly a study of life at its most degraded. To better prepare him to plead McCarthy's case, Erskine hinted that he could use an account of the overall structure and movement of the book to provide context for the sec-tions he had, and he asked McCarthy to put a figure to the advance he needed. He also wondered what other excerpts and magazines McCarthy wanted him to try (Erskine, Letter to Cormac McCarthy, June 8, 1971).

Clearly no advance was immediately forthcoming, and around June 20 Mc-Carthy sent a new episode from *Suttree* with the suggestion that it go to Lish at *Esquire.* This was what would become the final chapter of the book, which hinted at Suttree's transcendence of his death-haunted and lonely life in Knox-ville (see *S* 448–71; Beves, Letter to Cormac McCarthy, Aug. 1971). However, Lish refused this excerpt on the grounds, once again, that despite its elegant prose, the piece was not structured as a story (Lish, Letter to Suzanne Beves, Aug. 5, 1971).

It seems that the unsuccessful attempts to sell novel excerpts led to McCarthy's later decision not to allow his work to be anthologized. As early as his revisions of *The Orchard Keeper* for his editors, McCarthy had recognized that given the intricate interweaving of his narratives, "whenever anything is moved, something else falls over," and the repeated reaction of periodical editors that the excerpts could not masquerade as self-contained short stories reinforced his awareness of the complicated structures of his novels. Agent Amanda Urban's efforts to sell excerpts from his later works have in fact been successful. However, she honors McCarthy's feeling that his work is not well-represented in disconnected extracts, and as instructed, she has consistently refused permission to represent him in anthologies.

After Erskine failed to place any of the *Suttree* episodes, McCarthy wrote in September 1971 to answer a question his editor had posed in June. Although he recognized that the editor might be alarmed by his request, he told Erskine he would need an advance of $15,000 to complete the construction work on his house, clear his debts, and settle in "for a year or so in the privacy" he needed to polish off his next book (McCarthy, Letter to Albert Erskine, received Sept. 24, 1971). Notes among Erskine's papers reveal that this request prompted Random to draw up a contract for a third novel, providing for an advance of $6,000 upon McCarthy's signing and another $6,000 on delivery of the manuscript by September 1973 (Erskine, notes for communication with John Gallagher). This was not as much as McCarthy had requested, but it was a substantial increase over his previous advances, which had never been more than $1,500 at a time. There was a tone of desperation in McCarthy's terse plea, a hint that he was encountering too many distractions to his writing: his and Anne's active social life, the pressure to finish construction on the house, and perhaps even the distraction of living with a lively young wife who loved him and wanted his attention. There is also a hint that he was planning to escape these pressures by leaving, if only temporarily. Indeed, once *Child of God* reached publication in January 1974, McCarthy would use what was left of his advance to go west for a year to try to finish *Suttree* and to begin exploring the historical and geographical terrains that would inform *Blood Meridian*. He may have freed himself of debt with the advances, but according to De Lisle he never fully completed his work on the house (Conversations). His defaulting on that goal, which may have been something he had wanted to do for her, may be a measure of his need for solitary working conditions and of the absolute primacy he placed on his writing.

# Representation by the Robert Lantz-Candida Donadio Literary Agency

When Erskine sent "Harrogate and the Flittermouses" to Willie Morris in September 1970, he confided that because he believed so strongly in McCarthy's talent, he had offered to function as his agent. However, by late summer 1971, Erskine, McCarthy, or the two in concert had decided that Erskine should no longer serve in that capacity. In a letter to Robert Coles explaining his unhappy financial circumstances in 1979, McCarthy wrote that "Albert [is] literate and interested and shakes his head . . . over the present Literary Situation—as he well may. But other than continue to publish my books there's not a lot he can do" (McCarthy, Letter to Robert Coles, [Feb.-Mar. 1979]). Erskine continued to serve him well as his editor, but despite his successes with placing excerpts from *The Orchard Keeper,* he was either overextended or ill-suited to function as McCarthy's literary agent. He championed McCarthy's work, but he relied on his own circle of contacts among magazine editors and may not have had the wider network or the salesman's instincts to be successful in marketing McCarthy's work to periodicals more broadly.

At first McCarthy tried representing himself, but probably he was already seeking a literary agent. Beves sent him a lead in August 1971, writing that *Evergreen Review* was paying $45 per filled page. McCarthy did not follow up on this right away, but in November he composed his own submission letter and sent it to Beves, asking that she forward it with "Harrogate and the Flittermouses" and the Huddle chapter to *Evergreen* editor Fred Jordan. McCarthy felt that the remuneration would not be good, but he had heard that the "exposure" would be beneficial (McCarthy, Letter to Suzanne Beves, received Nov. 29, 1971). Beves recorded on McCarthy's letter that she had sent both excerpts to *Evergreen* on November 29. Two weeks later, Erskine heard from John Gallagher of the Robert Lantz-Candida Donadio Literary Agency that Gallagher had agreed "with enthusiasm" to represent McCarthy and that he would like to phone to discuss his work (Gallagher, Letter to Albert Erskine, Dec. 14, 1971). In February 1972 Beves asked Gallagher if he had heard any decision about

McCarthy's submissions (Beves, Memo to John Gallagher, Feb. 28, 1972). Gallagher investigated and replied on March 1 that, strangely, *Evergreen* had no record of having received the submissions—another disheartening outcome, possibly arising from slippage in communications as the handling of periodical submissions shifted from Erskine's office to Gallagher's.

In September 1971, McCarthy and Erskine had discussed the terms of the contract for *Suttree,* and it reached McCarthy that fall. However, he delayed signing it, probably because he hoped to acquire an agent's help or advice. He responded near the end of November with a new assertiveness, bargaining for more favorable terms. He indicated that should the new book be issued in paperback under Random's Modern Library or Vintage imprints or as a mass-market book, he wanted a royalty of 10 percent rather than the 7½ percent stipulated in the contract. And again he wanted to strike the standard clause that allowed Random to dispose of his manuscripts and proofs (McCarthy, Letter to Albert Erskine, received Dec. 1, 1971). In late February, Beves sent Gallagher copies of the presumably revised contract for McCarthy to approve.[12] And on March 22, Random sent Gallagher the $6,000 advance due on the signing of the contract (Beves, Memo to John Gallagher, Mar. 22, 1972).

When Erskine delivered the news at the end of 1970 that Parallel's film option for *Outer Dark* had lapsed on December 18 without a sale (Erskine, Letter to Cormac McCarthy, Dec. 30, 1970), it freed McCarthy to make other arrangements. By the following September, when he wrote Erskine about his contract for the third novel, he expected that *Outer Dark* would be made into a film, with payment for the new option due by December 1972. He wrote that he did not want his advances for the third novel repaid to Random out of the sale of the film rights (McCarthy, Letter to Albert Erskine, received Sept. 24, 1971). Since McCarthy informed Erskine of this sale and since there is no further documentation of it in Erskine's papers, it may have been handled by Gallagher. But likely it was first arranged by McCarthy himself. In 1981, McCarthy wrote to John Fergus Ryan that his friend, actor Stacy Keach, had owned the rights to *Outer Dark* for several years but had not secured funding to make the film (McCarthy, Letter to John Fergus Ryan, received Oct. 30, 1981).

De Lisle remembers that she and Cormac interacted with Keach at one of Erskine's gatherings during the period when Keach was living in New York City with his girlfriend, singer/songwriter Judy Collins, and that they might have met the couple on an earlier occasion (Conversations). Their meeting was no earlier than 1969, when Keach and Collins were performing Ibsen's *Peer Gynt* in one of Joseph Papp's Central Park productions; and the pair were still together in 1973 (Keach, *All in All* 66, 108). The two men shared enough interests to cement a friendship. Keach played pool, at which McCarthy excelled, and he liked race cars and horses (Keach, *All in All* 80, 116, 150). Although his first love was live theater and especially Shakespeare, he had acted in western-themed plays and films before McCarthy began writing of the southwest. Keach starred in the role of Buffalo Bill on stage in Arthur Kopit's *Indians* (1969) and as Doc Holliday on film in *Doc* (1971; Keach, *All in All* 73, 79). In *The Life and Times of Judge Roy Bean* (1972), Keach played opposite Paul Newman as his arch-enemy Bad Bob (Keach, *All in All* 88–89). Together with his brother James, from 1971 to 1979 Keach wrote, developed, and acted in *The Long Riders* (1980; Keach, *All in All* 133–36). Moreover, through his film work on *That Championship Season* (1982), Keach became friends with Bruce Dern, who would later take the small role of the compassionate Texas judge in Billy Bob Thornton's 2000 adaptation of *All the Pretty Horses* (Keach, *All in All* 140).

If Keach's relationship with McCarthy was still active in later decades, the two would also have shared their interests in science and religion. Keach had been raised Episcopal, but he became Roman Catholic when he married Malgosia Tomassi in 1986. Doing voice work on the science documentary *The Search for Solutions* reinforced his reading in science, and soon he became one of the directors of Environmental Communications, where a friend hosted weekly meetings to discuss *Scientific American* articles. Later Keach became the voice of PBS's long-running series *NOVA* (Keach, *All in All* 186–88).

Keach had long admired the work of Ernest Hemingway, whom he credits with first awakening his appreciation of modern literature. His performance in the television series *Hemingway* garnered him an Emmy nomination and a Golden Globe award in 1988 (Keach, *All in All* 179–81). And as Keach finished his memoir, *All in All,* published in 2013, he was co-writing a one-man show about the writer, "who remains fascinating to me in both his glory and his tragedy" (238). Hemingway is another shared interest Keach and McCarthy would likely have enjoyed.

In his memoir, Keach records that he himself composed the adaptation of *Outer Dark*: "I loved McCarthy's characters and his sense of suspense," he writes (*All in All* 78). He may also have appreciated *Outer Dark*'s resonances with *Macbeth,* since Keach had played the role of Banquo in the television movie released in the same year as McCarthy's novel. When he visited Cormac and Anne for several days in Louisville, as De Lisle recalls, it seems likely that one reason was to discuss the screenplay and plans for producing the film (De Lisle, Conversations). However, Keach's memoir mentions neither of the meetings De Lisle remembers, and intriguingly, it does not include McCarthy in its index, as if to give him some measure of anonymity.

During the filming of *Fat City* (1972), Keach approached his young co-star Jeff Bridges about playing the role of Culla (Keach, *All in All* 87). But to Keach's disappointment, he could never make the film: "it was foolhardy to think someone would finance a gothic horror story set in Appalachia that starts with incest then moves on to murder and cannibalism," he writes. He changed the resolution to make it less shocking, but still the story was too "relentlessly dark" to find backing (Keach, *All in All* 78, 87).[13] As Stacey Peebles shows in her concluding chapter of *Cormac McCarthy and Performance,* similar concerns have frustrated several attempts to film *Blood Meridian.*

By January 1972, Random had learned that the Ballentine paperback editions of McCarthy's first two novels were out of print, and now they thought of doing a reissue of *The Orchard Keeper* under their new Vintage imprint (Tom Lowry, Memo to Don Pace, Jan. 31, 1972). Vintage had been started by Alfred A. Knopf Jr., and it had reprinted a few Random House titles before the two companies merged in 1960. After the merger, Vintage greatly expanded under the leadership of Jason Epstein, who had previously developed the Anchor paperback series for Doubleday (Cerf, *At Random* 201–202). However, Vintage did not then reissue *The Orchard Keeper* or *Outer Dark. Suttree* would be released under the Vintage Contemporaries imprint in 1986,[14] but McCarthy's novels would not regularly be issued as Vintage paperbacks until 1993—after Erskine's retirement, McCarthy's move to the Knopf imprint, and Gary Fisketjon's becoming his editor.

Although McCarthy now had an agent, Gallagher did not seem to be contributing much to increased sales of excerpts, reprint rights, or film rights. By December 1973, Hy Cohen had replaced him as McCarthy's agent at Lantz-Donadio, and although McCarthy found him "enthusiastic" and wrote to Caroline Harkleroad of Random's publicity department that Cohen would have better ideas than he about how to market *Child of God,* it seems than no agent before Amanda Urban worked with McCarthy for long or advanced his career very successfully. Cohen left to start up his own agency in 1975, and McCarthy would sever his relationship with Donadio's agency in 1978.

# Revising *Child of God* in the Middle and Late Draft Stages

**M**cCarthy began a sustained push on *Child of God* on September 28, 1970. His notes on the file folder of its "Middle Draft" reveal a certain urgency, evidence that by then McCarthy had decided he needed to complete a new draft of this shorter book before returning to work on *Suttree*. In the top right corner of the file folder is the notation "120 page book 35,000 words 90pp to go = 45 days (Nov. 15?)." Apparently he was hoping that starting around the first of October he could write or revise two pages a day to finish the "Middle Draft" in mid-November. But the working dates on the file folder reveal that, as usual, it took him longer than anticipated. By February 14, 1971, he had completed 100 "actual pages." When McCarthy spoke with Mark Owen before February 26, he did not mention *Child of God* even though he had been working on it regularly since September (Owen, "McCarthy Is One" 4B). Clearly he recognized that *Child* would need yet another revision before he was ready to send it to Erskine, but he may also have been unwilling to discuss the shocking subject of his novel in advance of its publication.

The book would also prove to be longer than anticipated. The incomplete "Middle Draft" contains about 130 leaves, and below McCarthy's projection on the file folder that it would reach 120 pages, he jotted a revised figure, "160 pp book." He probably made this notation after he completed his "Late Draft" of 161 pages. McCarthy's notes on page 35 of the "Middle Draft" reveal that he worked on the "Late Draft" from about November 1971 through early February 1972, and he estimated that if he revised and retyped thirty-five more pages each week, he could manage the remaining 135 pages by December 2, [1971]—a date he successively revised to December 11, [December] 28, [January] 25, and [February] 2, 1972. He submitted the "Late Draft" to Erskine in mid-February 1972.

The scenes of necrophilia in the published novel have undergone little revision from the "Middle Draft," where they are fully realized. They are handled with considerable restraint compared with the scenes of sexual activity or dialogue among the living, such as the dumpkeeper's mounting one of his daughters and the young women's sexual flirting with men or taunting of Ballard. The necrophilia scenes are narrated from Ballard's perspective, and they include little graphic description of the victims' bodies as sexual objects or of Ballard's intercourse with them. Indeed, Ballard's perspective casts an almost romantic aura over his partners, revealing that he is not only a man whose sexual instincts have been deformed by his fate but also a man of deeply thwarted emotional need and such terrible loneliness that he takes what comfort he can in the inanimate. A minor revision in the "Middle Draft" shows McCarthy moving toward this delicacy of treatment. When Ballard kneels between the thighs of the dead girl in his cabin, McCarthy originally wrote that he "spat in his hand," which prompts the reader to imagine a graphic sexual image. Then he crossed out the line. He also deleted the second part of Ballard's address to the dead girl: "You been wantin it, he told the corpse, and now you're goin to get it" (79; cf. *CoG* 103). The deletion transforms an expression of sexual aggression to a more pitiful revelation of Ballard's fantasy life.

Although passages with coarse sexual references remain in the novel, even in Ballard's maladroit attempts at courting the living, McCarthy reduced such material in the middle and late drafts. In the "Middle Draft" scene of the asphyxiated couple, Ballard reacts verbally and gesturally to the dead man's still-erect penis. Like the young woman's breasts, which peek at him in a reversal of his own voyeurism, the man's penis points at him as if in accusation. Dismayed at the man's persistent erection even in death, Ballard utters, "They godamighty . . . It's stiff as a goddamned poker" (67), but the simile does not appear in the published novel (*CoG* 88). When Ballard finishes with the woman, he sees that the man is still erect, and he shakes his head, perhaps in disapproval of his dead double's priapism, perhaps in sheer astonishment at the dead's persistent readiness for sex, an idea he sustains as he acts out his fantasy with his female victims ("Middle Draft" 68; cf. *CoG* 89). McCarthy placed angle brackets around Ballard's headshake and did not carry it into the finished novel. The deletions eliminated Ballard's rather comic wonder and disapproval but retained his telling interpretation of the dead's gestures toward him, peeking and pointing and watching. McCarthy would make further reductions in sexual imagery and coarse sexual language during the editorial stage.

In the "Middle Draft," McCarthy composed Ballard's story up through his being shot by Greer and waking in the hospital. At the bottom of this page, he forecast Ballard's incarceration in the asylum, penciling in two sentences about Ballard and the cannibal housed there, with whom Ballard feels he has nothing in common (np; cf. *CoG* 193). However, at this point the narrative continuity becomes ragged, and the full asylum scene, which culminates in Ballard's death and autopsy, is not in the "Middle Draft." On eight subsequent unpaginated leaves at the end of the "Middle Draft," McCarthy composed Ballard's conversation with the hospital nurse as well as the lynch mob scene up through Ballard's telling the men that he knows where the bodies are. But there is nothing about his eluding them in the caves and his imprisonment there, his slow digging out, or his return to the hospital.

Except for these final scenes of the novel, most of its incidents appear in the "Middle Draft," yet McCarthy also made a few additions and did some restructuring during the middle-draft stage. For instance, a line in one of the oral tales suggests that Ballard's living in the caves was not part of McCarthy's earliest conception. The speaker remarks that even after Ballard burned down Waldrop's cabin, "he let him hole up in the barn like some description of varmint" ("Middle Draft" 26). This line appears to be left over from an earlier draft since the "Middle Draft" also includes the scenes of Ballard's postfire removal to the caves and descriptions of his living there with his growing family of murder victims. Furthermore, the passage reuses the phrase that he lives like a varmint from the sheriff's early discarded account of Ballard's backstory, filed at the end of the "Middle Draft" (9). This suggests that page 26 was composed after McCarthy had discarded the sheriff's account but before he hit upon the idea that Ballard would move underground. In the deleted lines, the speaker unintentionally stresses Waldrop's enduring charity toward Ballard, which differentiates Waldrop from the rest of the community. The speaker can only imagine that Ballard must have something on Waldrop to coerce such hospitality. When McCarthy revised to make the passage consistent with the plot as it had evolved, he maintained the implication of Waldrop's inexplicable charity: "Even after he burnt his old place down he [Waldrop] never said nothin to him about it that I know of" (*CoG* 35).

In the "Middle Draft" McCarthy also rearranged scenes of the sheriff's investigations and Ballard's murder of Billy's sister. Originally, Ballard's moving into the caves after the cabin burns and he loses his first, found partner ("Middle Draft" 84; cf. *CoG* 107–108) immediately preceded Turner's finding the abandoned car of a missing couple (85–87; cf. *CoG* 145–48). Since Ballard has left the male corpse of the asphyxiated couple in the car, this sequence implied that Ballard has already turned to murder to acquire replacement bodies, male as well as female. Ballard's second arrest and interrogation followed Turner's investigation of the car ("Middle Draft" 88–89; cf. *CoG* 121–23). But as he worked further on the draft, McCarthy inserted a new scene on pages 84A–84E, in which Ballard murders the neighbor girl and burns down her house, having learned through experience that he enjoys having a dead girlfriend and that fire will consume all evidence of his wrongdoing (cf. *CoG* 115–120). McCarthy also shifted the sheriff's investigation of the abandoned car forty pages later, placing it at the opening of section III *(CoG* 145–48). So now the sequence in section II is as follows: Ballard moves to the caves; Ballard murders the girl and child; sheriff arrests Ballard for questioning about the burning of Waldrop's cabin, but not the murders and arson at the girl's house. Spacing out the sheriff's scenes of detection and interrogation reduced the sense that his investigation might be effective enough to stop Ballard, and the new placement of Ballard's arrest before the abandoned car is found removes the implication that Turner arrests Ballard to question him about the missing couple. The new sequence invites readers to see Turner missing the leads that they know point to Ballard. Indeed, at the bottom of "Middle Draft" page 88, McCarthy noted to himself that the arrest scene should focus on "the falsely accused man." It would be an indictment of the sheriff's detecting abilities while also, ironically, an exoneration of his instincts about Ballard, whose actual crimes exceed Turner's suspicions.

Until this point in McCarthy's composition, it seems, he had thought all of Ballard's murders would depend on the happenstance of his finding vulnerable couples parked on the mountain road. The new scene built on Ballard's bringing the frozen robin to the child in hopes of interacting with his sister and introduced Ballard's premeditated murder of a victim who is known to him. In this added scene, as Ballard ineptly tries to engage the girl sexually by accusing her of being Billy's unwed mother, he leers at her, and the narrator comments, "Oft in dreams he'd hung gobbets of hot clabber from her womb's door" ("Middle Draft" 84B; see *CoG* 116). Again McCarthy did not carry the graphic line forward into the "Late Draft," thereby maintaining stronger emphasis on Ballard's emotional needs than on his sexual frustration. When the girl rebuffs him, Ballard retrieves his rifle from the yard, where he has left it ready to hand, and he approaches the house to murder her.

In this initial draft of the murder scene, when Ballard shoots through the window at the back of the girl's head, he misses. The girl stands up at the sounds of the gunshot and the shattered glass, and he fires again ("Middle Draft" 84D). In scenes composed earlier, McCarthy had taken pains to establish Ballard's infallible aim: he shoots rats for the dumpkeeper ("Middle Draft" 27–28), he can shoot a spider out of a tree, and he wins so many prizes in the carnival shooting gallery that he is denied further chances ("Middle Draft" 44). So Ballard's uncharacteristic failure to hit his target in this version of the scene suggests his nervousness, even a conflictedness about murder reminiscent of Culla Holme's. In contrast, in the published novel, the girl's unexpected movement causes Ballard's miss: just as he squeezes the trigger, she rises and turns toward the window (118), a revision that makes the scene nicely parallel to his missing Greer when, as Ballard fires, Greer's shovel arcs up and deflects the bullet. In both scenes as published, Ballard's plans do not anticipate the moves of his victims, and because he does not learn the unpredictability of the world from his missed shot at the girl, his missing Greer as well leads to his doom.

Other evidence in the "Middle Draft" supports the conclusion that McCarthy was working toward pairing these murders of selected victims. At the top of page 84A of the girl's murder scene, he noted "GREER? / See 100," and on "Middle Draft" page 100, the first paragraph of which describes how Ballard watches Greer throughout the winter and imagines shooting him through the kitchen window, McCarthy jotted, "This should go <u>before</u> he kills the girl in the house." He carried through on this change, making the Greer paragraph a free-standing section positioned a few pages before the girl's murder (*CoG* 109). The new placement implies that Ballard's mental practice for ambushing Greer, his self-willed numbing of his conscience, has also served as rehearsal for his killing the girl.

McCarthy also reversed the scenes of Ballard in his cave with his dead family and his attempt to sell his victims' watches when he wrote a new scene to prepare for them both. Following page 89 in the "Middle Draft" are three un-paginated leaves on which he drafted the store scene in which Fox computes how much Ballard owes him and concludes that at the rate that Ballard is go-ing, Fox will not live long enough to be repaid (see *CoG* 124–26). This is a newly drafted or redrafted and repositioned scene since these unpaginated leaves are placed in the draft to be pages 90–92, but the scene of Ballard in the cave, with overlapping pagination 92–93, already existed in the "Middle Draft" (cf. *CoG* 133–35). "Middle Draft" pages 94 and following are the barter of watches (cf. *CoG* 127–32), which McCarthy shifted before the cave scene in both the draft and the published novel. Fox's denying Ballard further credit prompts him to cross the mountain to sell his collection of watches, and McCarthy reinforced this when he juxtaposed the two store scenes and their financial negotiations instead of letting the cave scene intervene. Because the scene in the cavern culminates with the striking image of Ballard's multiple vic-tims arrayed on the stone ledges, newly revealing the scale of his serial mur-ders, it seems likely that McCarthy initially felt it should precede the barter of watches, a scene which emphasizes the many timepieces Ballard has gleaned from the dead. But the new sequence invites readers to surmise the source of the watches in the bartering scene and then confirms their dread with the revelation of the bodies in the cave.

Also in the "Middle Draft" is a first-person version of the experience of riding toward death through the autumn woods. It appears on an unnum-bered leaf placed between Ballard's weeping in the spring ("Middle Draft" 113) and the unpaginated draft of his ambushing Greer, the same position Ballard's dream occupies in the published novel (see *CoG* 170–72). Although there is less solid evidence that this first-person passage describes one of McCarthy's own dreams than there is for the eclipse dream that informs *Outer Dark,* it seems a possibility, especially since this version of the dream is more strik-ingly and specifically relevant to McCarthy than to Ballard. If the first-person premonition of death and resolution to "ride" or write on despite that terrible knowledge are a record of McCarthy's own dream or perception of his life, the leaves he passes are a symbol of his own writing: "Each leaf . . . deepened my . . . sadness and dread and the leaves were many. Each leaf I passed I'd never pass again" ("Middle Draft" np). As McCarthy worked on the late portions of his "Middle Draft" in 1971, he was approaching forty. Although he would write on for many productive decades, at that stage in his career he may have felt that he was nearing a midpoint of his life but had achieved no financial sta-bility and limited recognition. So far, he had published only two novels while, for example, Philip Roth, also born in 1933, had published five books. Even more sobering, by age thirty-eight Faulkner had produced twelve novels and several volumes of stories and poems. Yet McCarthy had indeed composed a great many leaves for his first four novels, two of which were still in progress. Those leaves were behind him, and he would never again experience the particular joy of their creation.

The first-person draft of the ride through the woods continues that he steeled himself to go on without dwelling on death because he "could not turn back," which seems an expression of stubborn but not mindful resignation to the doomed process of life. But McCarthy reconsidered these implications, jotting in pencil that he had resolved himself "& kept resolving?" to ride on ("Middle Draft" np). Pondered as a statement about his writing, McCarthy's revised first-person passage becomes an affirmation of his ongoing commitment to his life and work, a daily resolution to write on with courageous persistence. Thus, the passage resonates with one of Suttree's most unsettling challenges: his unrelenting awareness of death, which threatens to undermine his potential as a writer-in-the-making.

Aside from recasting the dream passage in Ballard's indirect third-person point of view in his "Late Draft," McCarthy made relatively few changes as he adapted it for *Child of God.* He made it explicit that this is Ballard's "dreamt" experience, while the earlier version may be read either as a dream or as some other symbolic rendering of an emotional state. Instead of the little burro that the first-person speaker rides, Ballard rides a mule, more consistent with his experience of farm life and with the creature he has watched in the valley below earlier that day. Ballard's sadness and dread are less explicitly of his ride—his past and future—but the subtle implication remains; now the yellow leaves he passes, never to pass again, are the fleeting and rare experiences of beauty in his life. Finally, McCarthy carried forward the idea of resolve, but not heroic commitment to a valued goal: "He had resolved himself to ride on for he could not turn back" (*CoG* 171). Ballard's thought faintly echoes Samuel Beckett's "I can't go on, I'll go on" from *The Unnameable* (Beckett, *Three Novels* 407) but with more poignant resignation to his fate, a sense that Ballard dreads punishment and death but cannot free himself from his compulsion or undo the acts that have led him to this point.

However, Ballard reacts against this sense of entrapment in his own needs and deeds in a scene that does not appear in the published novel. In the "Late Draft," McCarthy added a brief, horrifying scene immediately following Ballard's dream of riding through the woods. Under the influence of his distressing dream, Ballard performs a terrible self-punishment, an act designed to alter the condition in which he rides on. Draping his testicles over a fallen log, he slices them away with his knife in near-unconscious repudiation of his sexual drive—or like an animal who amputates its leg to free itself from a trap. The language of the castration passage emphasizes that Ballard recognizes his act as one of feminization, and it prepares for his adopting feminine clothing for his final act of violence when he assaults Greer, as if he has introjected the avenging Mother or as if he has adopted the identity of his female victims in atonement for his violations of them: looking down he sees his penis resting in the wound, "a cleanlipped little cuntlet welling blood. . . . Had his hand done it? Been told," he wonders. Then in pain and despair, he exclaims, "Oh god. . . . Oh godalmighty" (137). Ballard's act is a profound reversal of what may be McCarthy's own dreamed or experienced affirmation of his creative desire.

The sequence of these scenes in the middle and late drafts speaks to Ballard's growing despair and self-destructiveness. On the seasonal anniversary of his loss of his home, witnessing the spring rebirth from his removed and lonely vantage point in a mountain pass, Ballard bows his head and weeps ("Middle Draft" 113); lying underground that night, he imagines he hears the whistling of his mourned father, "a lonely piper" ("Late Draft" 136; *CoG* 170), who has not for years returned home to his son, leaving him alone, orphaned, and unhoused; later that night Ballard dreams he is riding to his death but feels helpless to change his course; then he castrates himself ("Late Draft" 136–37), seeking freedom from his compulsion or at least its forbidden sexual component. These incidents culminate in his reckless assault on Greer in feminized form and garb, the attack which results in Ballard's death as originally drafted and then in revision occasions his further emasculation through the blasting away of his arm and his capacity to wield his rifle. It may be that McCarthy conceived the self-castration as one of two essential moves toward the novel's resolution of Ballard's crimes: Ballard's sacrifice of his testicles would close down his necrophilia, mark his despair at reconnecting with a family through congress with the dead, and suggest his desire not to do wrong; and the loss of his arm would similarly close down his ability to murder. Further, the self-castration strongly implies that Ballard has given up on his life and rides on only to his destination in death. The self-mutilation reinforces the implication that Ballard's attempt to murder Greer is an act not only of revenge but more pointedly of suicidal despair, of his opening himself to death, rather like the displaced and dispossessed John Grady's knife-fight with Eduardo in *Cities of the Plain* (253).

Moreover, the novel's ending repeats Ballard's repudiation of his past life implicit in the paired scenes of his castration and his attack on Greer. Ballard laboriously digs free of his captivity in the cave system, thus saving himself from death, but returns to the hospital and thence to the asylum, where he is fed and housed and lives out his death-in-life ironically reabsorbed into the community that repudiates him—contained by it. Again we find a strange parallel with *The Border Trilogy*, where Billy abandons his struggle against his tragic fate and settles for a constricted life on Mac's ranch, hoping just to "minimize the pain," until the murder of John Grady sets him on the road again

(*Cities of the Plain* 78). But Billy finally achieves the grace of joining a family who treat him as a grandfather and who respect and love him as he gently ages into death. As a ward of the state, Ballard remains physically alive but emotionally without succor, an orphan still. His whole life has been a tragic distortion of his fate, a diminishment of what he might have been in other circumstances, but the end of it is more pathetic than tragic, perhaps because he accedes to his fate as the perennial outsider.

We have seen that in the second drafting stage for *Outer Dark,* McCarthy added a passage of narrative commentary comparing his primary characters to wanderers in purgatory, trapped in their fates. Because such interpretive commentaries from the narrator are rare in McCarthy's work, they take on special emphasis. Often they predict a character's future, as when the narrator of *Child of God* says "more's the fool" (*CoG* 116) of the girl who lets Ballard into her home, or when the narrator of *The Crossing* tells us cryptically and ominously that during the winter when Billy takes the wolf back to Mexico, "A cold wind [came] down from the north with the earth running under bare poles toward a reckoning whose ledgers would be drawn up and dated only long after all due claims had passed, such is this history," which proves to forecast not only Billy's disastrous losses, but also America's development and deployment of the atomic bomb (5). Not until he was composing the "Late Draft" of *Child of God* did McCarthy add the narrator's speculation about what factors sustain Ballard in the flooded creek or metaphorically in the flume of his life. The middle draft's line, "His wrath seemed to buoy him up," is immediately followed by Ballard's reaching the shallows where he can stand (108), as if he is simply too enraged to drown, the kind of joking and dismissive response more characteristic of the local men's commentaries than of the narrator's.

In the "Late Draft," the narrator meditates more thoughtfully on Ballard's fate as he flounders in the waters, and the movement of the new passage dramatizes the narrator's unfolding analysis: He begins with the observation that "Some halt in the way of things" keeps Ballard afloat, and he exhorts the reader and himself to "See him"—that is, to ponder Ballard's mystery more deeply. One possibility is that Ballard is buoyed by his evocative memories of his father and by his illusion that others want him, that he has imaginatively "peopled the shore with them calling to him." But the narrator recognizes too that given his crimes and mental illness, promoted by his very ostracism, the people Ballard longs to connect with are not the nurturing family of his needy imagination, but "A race that gives suck to the . . . crazed, that wants their wrong blood in its history. . . ." This is as close as the narrator will come to an explicit indictment of the community's engendering and fostering its criminals, not least through its enshrining them in its more horrifying legends. Finally, the narrator recognizes that although the community has created its

Frankenstein's monster in Ballard—perhaps because like Gardner's *Grendel,* he is the "brute existent" against which self-flattering humanity defines itself—it pursues his life. In his guilty and fearful imagination, Ballard "has heard them . . . seeking him with lanterns and cries of execration." So the narrator remains questioning: Fated to live in an indifferent natural world and a hostile community, how is Ballard "borne up" ("Late Draft" 123; *CoG* 156)?

As they read forward, readers too are prompted to wonder how Ballard can sustain his life except through brute persistence or perhaps through a dim sense that he remains a child of God, however ironic that may be. So the late addition of narrative commentary, composed well after McCarthy had decided that Ballard would not die when Greer shoots him, foreshadows Ballard's remaining life, his persistence in the life of the community, walled away until he dies of natural causes and present to others only in their uncomprehending stories. The narrator's meditation also poses the question Ballard must answer about his future path. As pathetic as his ending is, he achieves a limited measure of self-determination when he chooses self-castration, when he evades the lynch mob in the caves, and then when he delivers his stunted life to the care of his society's institutions, a forcing of their care-without-empathy. McCarthy's carefully constructed unfolding of Ballard's end defeats genre expectations that the murderer will die or be apprehended in sentimental reaffirmation of communal order, or alternatively that he will return to thrill the community with its impotence in the face of evil—as in James Franco's film adaptation. Franco ends with the scene of Ballard's emergence from the underground, a film cliché that constitutes a profound unravelling of the implications of McCarthy's resolution.

# The Editing Stage

**M**cCarthy's contract with Random specified delivery of a third novel, which he had expected would be *Suttree,* by fall 1973. However, the long Knoxville novel would not see publication until 1979. He continued working on *Suttree* throughout the 1970s, but *Child of God* took precedence. McCarthy mailed a letter to Woolmer on June 28, 1973, reporting that his forthcoming third novel was a briefer project which had interrupted his writing the long Knoxville book. McCarthy had submitted *Child of God*'s finished draft by late January 1972. With the typescript in hand and ready for editing, Erskine contacted McCarthy's agent John Gallagher with details for a new contract and projected publication in September 1973 (Erskine, Notes for communication with Gallagher, Jan. 27, 1972). McCarthy signed the contract before March 22, when his first advance for *Child of God* was forwarded to Gallagher (Beves, Memo to John Gallagher, Mar. 22, 1972).

Given its subject, *Child of God,* could have been problematic for Erskine, but there is no evidence of his earliest reactions. It is almost certain that McCarthy would have discussed the project with his editor when they met in October 1967 on his return from Europe, and possibly Erskine read an early, partial draft then. The *Child of God* draft Erskine might have seen in 1967 may not have included the serial murders and necrophilia that appear in the "Middle Draft" of 1970–1971, but if not, it seems likely that McCarthy subsequently discussed this bold new direction with Erskine by telephone.

Although we cannot know what might have transpired when and if Erskine read an earlier draft, on one of three photocopies of the "Late Draft" appear some terse suggestions for revision of the kind that fell under Erskine's purview and almost certainly are his. They are addressed to "Mac," but they appear to be recorded in McCarthy's holograph script, which suggests either that someone dictated them to him over the phone or that he transcribed them from notes affixed to his draft. The discussion below is predicated on the premise that they are indeed Erskine's. Many of McCarthy's responses to these editorial comments appear in the first and longest of his three sets of revision notes, a list headed "LaFayette" and keyed to the pagination of the "Late Draft."

Although the editorial suggestions often seem to reflect first-reading confusion, they offer no evidence that Erskine was either surprised or squeamish about the necrophilia, a central metaphor of *Child of God.* Indeed, a note on the scene of Ballard's first necrophilic act reads, "Mac: Here I would expand; describe; too abrupt—Done right, this could have real impact—dimension" (67). McCarthy jotted "elaborate" in his revision notes but only slightly expanded by adding the line, "Who could say she did not hear?" The addition emphasizes that Ballard is acting out his fantasy as he speaks to the body, lost in his illusions (Revision notes: "LaFayette" [2]; cf. *CoG* 88–89). By declining to expand further, McCarthy preserved the impact of his next scene, in which Ballard's staging a date with the dead woman reveals the pathos and bathos of his romantic and sexual longings (*CoG* 91–92). The dimension and impact that Erskine asked for are fully developed in this later scene, which he had yet to read when he made his suggestion. McCarthy also silently rejected the editorial prompt that he add "dimension" and "details" to the scene in which Ballard is falsely accused of rape ("Late Draft" 37; see *CoG* 51–52).

Among the other substantive revisions Erskine suggested were deletions of several scenes or passages. As discussed earlier, he questioned whether the blacksmith scene and the oral tale of the boxing ape were necessary. McCarthy considered revising the opening of the blacksmith scene, which moves Ballard into the smith's shop with little preparation ("Late Draft" 58). In his revision notes, McCarthy queried "Rewrite 1st ¶ ?" (Revision notes: "LaFayette" [2]). Yet he revised neither scene, and he drafted the new story of White Capping in the Ballard family history to give the motif of community legends such as the boxing ape tale even more prominence.

Erskine did not fully grasp the functions of the anecdotes interpolated in Section I, and in addition to the boxing ape tale, he questioned the need for the sheriff's mildly humorous account of the "sick" hunting dog Suzie. Since the story emphasizes Turner's inept participation in the community tale-swapping and his tendency toward self-aggrandizement as he makes himself the hero of his anecdote of one-up-manship, McCarthy did not delete it. As a relatively ineffective tale, it undercuts the sheriff and differentiates him from the other men. Nevertheless, McCarthy noted that he should "Simplify & shorten" the sheriff's anecdote (Revision notes: "LaFayette" [1]). In the "Late Draft," Turner recounts that when he and Suzie's owner hunted with her, they "killed four-teen birds over old Ben and he shot one over Suzie that had laid low out of a covey" (35). In his notes, McCarthy made a start toward concision, jotting, "We hunted all day & she never pointed a bird," a revision that eliminated the more successful bird-dog Ben and made the hunt entirely unproductive (Revision notes: "LaFayette" [1]). Finally, he settled on "We . . . hunted all afternoon and killed one bird" (*CoG* 49). His cuts were minimal, but they made the story punchier while retaining its revelations of Turner's character.

If Erskine had seen an earlier draft, he may have been surprised to encounter the late addition of Ballard's self-castration. On reading it in the editorial copy of the "Late Draft," he found the scene "arbitrary; not set up. OK if you motivate it earlier . . . , but as it comes it is unprepared for. He has haunting guilts for what he did? OK; but foreshadow it, or you'll lose the reader." And he suggested that McCarthy talk it over with him (137). As discussed above, a case can be made that Ballard's preceding dream effectively foreshadows his despairing self-mutilation. Erskine was enthusiastic about the following scene, in which Ballard appears in Greer's yard "in frightwig and skirts." He found it "true in that way beyond ordinary true" but reiterated that "the key is properly motivating that castration scene" ("Late Draft" 138). Clearly Erskine recognized the crucial connection between the castration and Ballard's subsequent cross-dressing, but as when he had edited *The Orchard Keeper,* he asked for more explicit revelation of character motivation than McCarthy was willing to provide, especially after he had made extraordinary innovations in the deployment of narrative objectivity in *Outer Dark.* If McCarthy and Erskine discussed the function of the castration scene, either in a phone call or in April 1972, when the two saw one another on Erskine's trip to Tennessee (McCarthy, Letter to Albert Erskine, received Apr. 17, 1972),[15] it seems likely that McCarthy would have argued that his narrative reticence about Ballard's motives opened interpretive space for the reader and invited deeper engagement. It was, after all, a strategy he had employed throughout *Child of God*. In any event, rather than making Ballard's motives more explicit, McCarthy struck the castration scene. In the revision notes he recorded that he had deleted it (Revision Notes: "LaFayette," [4]). The shooting away of Ballard's arm was sufficient to end his criminal career without the parallel loss of his testicles, and clearly McCarthy preferred not to belabor Ballard's self-destructiveness.

In both the "Late Draft" and the published novel, the passage describing Ballard's dream before his self-mutilation ends with the tonally effective sentence: "He had resolved himself to ride on for he could not turn back and the world that day was as lovely as any day that ever was and he was riding to his death" (136; *CoG* 171). But Erskine felt that the final clause "telegraphed" the novel's ending, and he asked McCarthy to delete it ("Late Draft" 136). Erskine seems not to have appreciated McCarthy's subtle characterization of Ballard, that Ballard himself knows that he is riding to his death and dreams a premonition that projects his despair. There is nothing here to surprise a reader, for all know that we are always riding toward death, and we can conclude as readily as can Ballard that his criminal path will lead to disaster. How, after all, is he borne up? Ballard's premonition may slightly reduce the mystery of the novel, but it contributes to the suspense, giving Ballard and the reader foreknowledge and consequent dread that heighten the impact of the scenes in which he is threatened by the lynch mob and trapped in the cave. But in fact, Ballard does not come to the violent end the reader may expect; he dies in the asylum of pneumonia, not with a bang but a whimper. One wonders if Erskine would have called for deleting this passage if he had already read to the end of the typescript.

Given that Erskine asked for more character motivation for the castration scene, it is surprising that he missed the point of Ballard's comment that the toddler who chews off the robin's legs wants to prevent its running away, which economically projects Ballard's own motives for murder. Erskine called for deleting the lines from "The bird floundered on the floor" to the end of the scene. Possibly he was distracted by the partial repetition from three or four lines earlier, "It fluttered on the floor and fell over" ("Late Draft" 63; cf. *CoG* 79). There is no evidence in the revision notes that McCarthy gave Erskine's suggestion serious consideration, and wisely he left the scene intact.

Another scene Erskine questioned was the one in which Ballard steals shelled corn, a chicken, and eggs from his old homeplace, now owned by Greer (*CoG* 137). Erskine noted that "this rather ordinary violence vitiates previous acts of violence—diminishes them by its ordinariness." Then as if he thought the scene's only purpose was to provide further evidence of Ballard's criminality,

Erskine added, "we know the man is evil," and he suggested deleting the scene ("Late Draft" 109). But this passage too plays an important characterizing role, as well as explaining how Ballard eats after Mr. Fox denies him further credit for groceries. Ballard's scavenging for food even though he could hunt is consistent with his opportunistic scavenging for sexual partners. In the fall, he gleans the remnants of corn from a harvested field, for instance (*CoG* 40). Crucially, however, his returning to his old homeplace reveals that he feels entitled to the fruits of the farm that once belonged to his family, and thus it prepares for the more murderous offense against Greer to come. Finally, the episode hints of his pathetic longing to return to the domestic space of his childhood nurturing. The scene mitigates his evil, as Erskine observed, but designedly so. Again, no evidence in the revision notes suggests that McCarthy considered deleting it.

However, McCarthy's pondering this scene appears to have prompted him to revise the paragraph in which at night Ballard watches Greer through the lit window of his old home, a passage Erskine did not flag for revision unless they discussed it during his April visit. In the "Late Draft" the paragraph begins, "It was at this time that he took to visiting Greer" (84). In his revision notes, McCarthy began redrafting this opening to imply more clearly that Ballard stalks Greer because he broods over the loss of his home and resents the man who has displaced him: "Shortly after he moved into the *cave,* Ballard took to watching his *old house.*" Above "house" he jotted, "its *new tenant*" (emphasis added; Revision notes: "LaFayette" [2]). When he typed up his new version on replacement page 84, the opening read, "The weather did not change. Ballard took to wandering . . . through the snow to his old homeplace where he'd watch the house, the house's new tenant" ("Setting Copy" 84; *CoG* 109). Now McCarthy had increased the pathos of the scene, placing Ballard outside in the snow and cold and dark as he gazes into the warm, well-lit kitchen from which he has been excluded and forced underground.

One characteristic of McCarthy's prose style is his deployment of the indeterminate and informal "some" to introduce a simile or metaphor, especially when the comparison is to something drawn from history, mythology, or artistic representations, something outside of contemporary experience. This occurs twenty or thirty times in both *The Orchard Keeper* and *Outer Dark,* but only eight in *Child of God.* However, Erskine now objected to the practice, pointing out four instances in the first half of the "Late Draft": "faces watching into the dark for some midnight contest to begin" (49; cf. *CoG* 65); "rapt below the . . . pitchlight of some medieval fun fair" (50; *CoG* 65); "he looked like a man beset by some ghast succubus, the dead girl riding him with legs bowed akimbo like a monstrous frog" (120; *CoG* 153); "like some demented hero or bedraggled parody of a patriotic poster" (123; *CoG* 156). Erskine now seems to have regarded this an intrusive style tic, and he directed McCarthy to "avoid the word" ("Late Draft" editorial copy 50).

However, McCarthy made no move toward doing so, and he seems to have found the phrasing vital to achieving his narrative ends. In the first two passages above, "some" signals economically that the narrator speaks imaginatively, figuratively. In the second pair, "some" joins with "like" to emphasize the fanciful simile. The indeterminate "some" signals that the narrating mind is searching for a satisfactory image to convey his conceit and calls the reader's attention to the narrator's active, somewhat tentative feeling his way toward meaning in the story he tells, as the sequence of two alternative images in the latter two examples also implies. In all McCarthy's novels, the "some" similes and metaphors characterize the pensive, questing narrative mind, but in *Child of God* they also heighten our awareness of the narrator's function as a corrective to the complacent, unsearching mode of the community storytellers. It may be that Erskine's questioning the use of "some" in figurative passages led to McCarthy's rethinking his rationale for the practice and to his articulating more clearly for himself and for his editor why he found it effective. In McCarthy's next two novels, the stylistic strategy is even more prevalent, with fifty instances in *Suttree* and over eighty in the much shorter *Blood Meridian,* where the narrator engages in a quest to comprehend history and fully to imagine the unimaginable. McCarthy's narrators do not always stand back, paring their fingernails, and the rhythmic foregrounding of the narrator's voice, interrupting and punctuating the more objective narrative perspective in most of his novels, is one key to their effects.

In a few instances, Erskine objected to obvious literary borrowings. If he and McCarthy discussed the emasculation scene, they may have realized that it seemed derivative of a story Versh tells Quentin in Faulkner's *The Sound and the Fury* (143), which might have contributed to McCarthy's willingness to omit the plot echo. Moreover, in *Suttree,* Trippin Through the Dew tells a similar story of the vitriolic evangelical who "trimmed hisself" (111). If McCarthy had already drafted this anecdote for *Suttree,* it might have made him even more willing to delete Ballard's castration scene despite its contribution to revealing his character. However, McCarthy was apparently less reluctant to echo others' diction. Erskine wondered if the "womanchild" Ballard watches at the fair was a "Faulkner transfer" ("Late Draft" editorial copy 50), but McCarthy did not change it (*CoG* 65). On the other hand, when Erskine labeled the phrase "sawdust streets" a cliché ("Late Draft" editorial copy 46), perhaps because it reminded him of T. S. Eliot's "half-deserted streets" lined with "sawdust restaurants" in "The Love Song of J. Alfred Prufrock" (ll. 10; 13), McCarthy revised it to "sawdust lanes" (Revision notes: "LaFayette" [2]; *CoG* 61). Since the scene was the fairgrounds, "sawdust" was neither a cliché nor a literary borrowing but a literal designation of the material on the path underfoot. But "streets" did not have the right connotation for the unpaved walkways of the fairgrounds, and "lanes" was the better choice.

Although several reviewers of his first two books had charged McCarthy with mannered writing, Erskine questioned only two passages of *Child of God* on those grounds. He thought the description of Ballard's toting one of his victims on his back, "like a man beset by some ghast succubus, the dead girl riding him with legs bowed akimbo like a monstrous frog" was "forced" ("Late Draft" 120; *CoG* 153). The images are startling, but they bring a grotesque or even black comedic tone to Ballard's laboring over the mountain with his prey, and the similes effectively convey that he is "beset" and hag-ridden by his terrible need. Erskine also objected to the description of Ballard in his white hospital gown as a "false acolyte or antiseptic felon, a practitioner of ghastliness, a part-time ghoul" ("Late Draft" [140]; *CoG* 174). The first two elements seem natural enough images since they are predicated on the purity or sterility of the white gown, but Erskine underlined the final two elements for revision. However, the four-stage sequence is another instance of the narrator's evolving thought as he seeks the most apt comparison, and his mental linkage suggests that white-coated medical practitioners also deal appallingly with the human body, living or dead. McCarthy reinforces this idea in the scene of Ballard's autopsy, where medical students examine his entrails like "haruspices of old [who] perhaps saw monsters worse to come in their configurations" (*CoG* 194). Both passages that troubled Erskine, and that might be accused of needlessly calling attention to the writing, work effectively to convey the narrator's perceptions economically and without direct pronouncement. McCarthy revised neither.

As usual, Erskine queried some of McCarthy's diction. Not fully recognizing the humorous undercutting of several tale-tellers, the editor took too seriously the sheriff's wish that "if a man wanted to hang hisself he'd do it with poison," and he suggested that "kill" might be the more appropriate word ("Late Draft" 16; *CoG* 21). But the sheriff's careless expression to hang oneself with poison was a source of zany humor in the passage, and McCarthy did not revise it. In other suggestions about diction, Erskine thought the phrases "tiers of prizes" and "fires licked" were clichéd ("Late Draft" 46; 93; *CoG* 61; 120). Similarly, he objected to the "sea" of faces that "floated" past Ballard at the fair; he underlined these words and placed a terse "No" beside each ("Late Draft" 48; cf. *CoG* 65). In the same scene, he indicated "No" for the verb "sang" in the sentence, "Step right up . . . sang the shooting gallery man" ("Late Draft" 47–48 cf. *CoG* 64). Erskine thought that to say that a dog "worried" the ears of a dead boar was perhaps "weak" and also that it might be "stronger" to have the boar hunters "hurrying against the light" than against the "fading light" ("Late

Draft" 53; *CoG* 69). He wondered too whether another verb would be better in the description of Ballard, exhausted from his struggle to haul a corpse into the attic, resting on the floor with "his breath exploding whitely" ("Late Draft" 72; *CoG* 95). Eskine underlined and queried "went" in McCarthy's line: "He stirred as he went the weight of dimes in . . . his pocket" ("Late Draft" 47; *CoG* 63). Perhaps he found the verb too bland and imprecise, or perhaps he was calling McCarthy's attention to the fact he had used the same verb three lines earlier. Confident of his own instincts, McCarthy changed none of these.

While Erskine was comfortable with McCarthy's undertaking to explore the psychology and metaphysics of necrophilia in *Child of God*, he questioned some—but not all—of the coarse language and anatomical or scatological imagery in the "Late Draft." He objected to the description of the dumpkeeper's daughters as "gangling longtitted progeny" because he thought it "degrade[d]" McCarthy's prose, and McCarthy deleted "longtitted." Yet on the same page, Erskine judged "O.K." the line about country boys with "long cocks and big feet" ("Late Draft" 19; *CoG* 26–27). And when Ballard visits the house of his first murder victim and sees her "all tits and plump young haunch," this also received the editor's okay ("Late Draft" 60; *CoG* 76). One might wonder whether the first of these feminine images seemed too pejorative or misogynistic to him, while the masculine image sounded complimentary. Although the generalized reference to the boys' large members was fine with him, Erskine asked if McCarthy was certain that he wanted to include the more particular image from the first necrophilia scene, when Ballard sees "The dead man's penis, sheathed in a wet yellow condom, . . . pointing at him rigidly" ("Late Draft" 66; *CoG* 88). McCarthy had clearly already given serious thought to the tone of his novel, and he kept the image that captured Ballard's sense of being watched or judged; but Erskine may well have been aware that reviewers might object.

Since he had been giving his opinion about each coarse word, Erskine made a point of noting that the reference to "Small lumps of yellow shit wrapped up and laid by" in the dumpkeeper's house teeming with his daughters and their illegitimate babies was also "O.K." ("Late Draft" 20; *CoG* 27). But references to literal or figurative spit seemed to offend Erskine. He objected to the line that the shooting gallery rifles "cracked and spat" and to the similar expression that flames "spat" from the axehead in the forge, even though the contexts make it clear that the words refer to sound and movement and not saliva ("Late Draft" 47; *CoG* 63; "Late Draft" 55; *CoG* 71). Erskine read as a visual image the line that "it had begun to spit rain," noting that this too "cheapen[ed]" the language ("Late Draft" 28; *CoG* 39). In his notes, McCarthy wrote that this was "A type of rain, not a metaphor" (Revision notes: "LaFayette" 1). He revised no instance of spit or spat.

McCarthy's "LaFayette" revision notes also address issues that were not raised in the editorial comments on the "Late Draft," some of which may have been Erskine's later queries and some McCarthy's own concerns. Although it is not marked on the "Late Draft" page, it appears that Erskine questioned the word "husbanding" when McCarthy wrote that Ballard "went husbanding" through the cornfields to gather what the mechanical harvester had missed (24), and Erskine may have suggested the alternative "harvesting." In his revision notes, McCarthy carefully thought through the word choice. He wrote that Ballard was more accurately a "gleaner" than a "harvester" since he is "salvaging the remnants, hence the connotation of frugality, thrift, prudence." But then for each of these adjectives he superscribed asterisks keyed to the skeptical note "Our Lester?"—questioning whether "gleaning" would be the appropriate word after all. And he added that it "usually refers to grain. Cant think of gleaning anything as large as an ear of corn." Finally he returned to his first choice, quoting the *OED*'s cite: "We were obliged to husband our ammunition" ("LaFayette" notes 1; *CoG* 40).

McCarthy's note for a scene of Ballard in Waldrop's cabin reveals that at this late stage he thought of rendering it in present tense rather than the past and past perfect of the "Late Draft" (51; "LaFayette" [2]). In the novel as published, the scene alternates between the present tense of Ballard's described action and present perfect tense for previously completed action (*CoG* 66–67). McCarthy's shifting the scene into the present tense is an interesting experiment that mimics cinematic effects. We see Ballard feeding into his fireplace the bracken and beanpoles that he has previously brought in. That is, the viewer is situated in the cabin, and infers Ballard's prior acts of gathering fuel for his fire, as in a film scene that would show him building the fire but imply his prior gathering through the presence of the fuel. We see him remove his shoes and socks and clean his rifle in present time; then the scene cuts to his eating the cornbread that he has by now already baked on his hearth. It is a way of eliding the narration comparable to McCarthy's overall strategy for the novel: narrating in discontinuous sections that open abruptly upon discrete scenes. But McCarthy's deployment of present and present perfect tenses for this section gives it the "real-time" feel of the cinematic mode. Like the occasional intrusive comment from the narrator and the "like some" similes, this section of mixed present and present perfect tense narration draws attention to the narrator's imaginative act: he visualizes Ballard in his domestic life with the immediacy of his filmic inner eye.

McCarthy worked on his revisions over the course of a year and sent a marked copy of the typescript to his editor in February 1973. In his letter of transmittal, which Erskine received on February 22, McCarthy informed him that the addition of the White Caps in Ballard's family history and the deletion of the castration episode were the most substantive revisions he had made, but he reported that he had also added the new description of Ballard's stalking Greer at his old homestead to make the scene clearer. This was the revision that emphasized Ballard's sense of cold exclusion from his warm home. He invited Erskine to telephone him if he had questions about his "chicken scratching" or if he disliked anything in the revision.

On a second, one-leaf set of revision notes, McCarthy responded to further editorial queries posed when the editor was in the process of preparing the setting copy. These include a minor question about the new page 63A, the White Cap story McCarthy had added in his first round of revisions. Several questions about line spacing, page breaks, and word choices were easily resolved, but Erskine also raised two substantive issues. First he wondered what Ballard lost in the flooded river (see *CoG* 155–57). In his revision notes, McCarthy wrote, "What does he have in crate & what does he lose?" The question had arisen when Erskine read the line, "The only thing he recovered was the crate" ("Late Draft" 124). But lower on the page of notes, McCarthy wrote that he had specified the crate's contents on "Late Draft" page 122 (Revision notes: List B). Since Ballard loses everything but the crate, no revision was needed. Second Erskine found it a loose end that Ballard does not retrieve his incriminating rifle shell from the burning house where he has murdered Ralph's daughter (see *CoG* 119–20). Penciled with the notation about the shell are McCarthy's thoughts that he might address the issue in the dialogue in Ballard's hospital room but also that "Hitchcock would just leave it"—a private reference to *Psycho,* which had influenced his conception of Ballard (Revision notes: List B). McCarthy inked in the margin of his notes two brief, unused passages that establish Sheriff Turner's having found the shell. The first of these is dialogue between Ballard and one member of the lynch mob. When the accuser tells him that the sheriff found the rifle shell, Ballard feigns innocence; then the accuser says, "Hell fire . . . it dont take Dick Tracy to figure out somebody . . . is been a killin people"—a line that minimizes the sheriff's competence. McCarthy crossed out this interchange. In his second attempt, either the accuser or Ballard says that he knows the sheriff has found the shell, and Ballard defends himself by pointing out that he had been shooting rats for Ralph beside the house, as Ralph can attest (Revision notes: List B). This would have solved the problem neatly, except that in these notes McCarthy was conflating two neighbors with desirable daughters: Ballard's rat-shooting for the dumpkeeper Reubel had been established earlier in the novel but not for Ralph. Finally McCarthy decided to go with his first instinct and to let the apparent loose end stand for the reader to ponder. In doing so, he kept the focus off the sheriff's detective work and made the lynch mob's kidnapping Ballard less logically motivated, more a result of their communal impulse for scapegoating.

# Publication and Reception

The setting copy was prepared by March 22, 1973, when it was mailed to Haddon typesetters (Random House, *Child of God* Composition Order). The published book carries the copyright date of 1973, but it did not appear until January 2, 1974, a month before McCarthy left Tennessee and went west to begin research for *Blood Meridian* (Anonymous, Review of *Child of God, Publishers Weekly*; De Lisle, Conversations). At some point after the proofs were printed, either Erskine or agent Hy Cohen sent a set to Gordon Lish at *Esquire*. Lish was impressed by *Child of God* and proposed running it serially in *Esquire* but "was overruled" by its managing editor (McCarthy, Letter to Caroline [Harkleroad] [Dec. 1973], 1). Despite Lish's criticism of McCarthy's stylistic extravagance in the excerpts of *Suttree* he had read in 1970, it seems he came to embrace McCarthy's talent more wholeheartedly as he read more of his work. In 1985 he would make an exuberant assessment to Leon Rooke for his "Author, Author!" radio series: "This guy will knock your socks off. Your . . . socks will run a four-minute mile just by themselves. . . . [W]e are talking genius and the long march into eternity" (Rooke, "'Author! Author!'" 11). Lish was by then an editor at Knopf, the prestigious Random House affiliate that would publish McCarthy's novels from *All the Pretty Horses* on, but his enthusiasm in 1985, while unrestrained, is not inconsistent with his earlier recognition of McCarthy's promise.

No documentation of the preparation of the jacket copy survives. The author's note on the back flyleaf is brief, but it mentions Anne's name, which the jacket of *Outer Dark* had not. This may have been Erskine's doing, or it may have been McCarthy's considered, public acknowledgment of her. The back of the jacket features a full-page photo of McCarthy in three-quarter view, taken at his home in Louisville by David Styles, who did design work for some of the Maryville Ballet's stage sets. Styles recalls that the photo shoot went very quickly since McCarthy had thought out what he wanted and knew how to pose. The picture was taken outdoors, with the house he had been creating in the background. McCarthy stands with casually crossed arms, gazing pensively into the distance. His expression is unsmiling but relaxed. He wears a light-colored geometric print shirt and sports the mustache and longer hair and sideburns common in the early 1970s. The photo was likely to be attractive to readers browsing in a bookstore yet compatible with the tragic aspects of

Ballard's story. Indeed, McCarthy's thoughtful, far-seeing pose is an apt representation of the contemplative narrator whose voice is intermittently heard in the novel. And its rural backdrop implied McCarthy's familiarity with the setting of his novel.

Although McCarthy willingly participated in securing the photo for the jacket, it does not appear that he collaborated with Erskine on the first edition's rather ungraceful description. Indeed, the piece seems to reflect the lack of perception about some aspects of the novel that surfaces in Erskine's editorial comments. Since it emphasizes the horror and violence of the story, presented with "unstinting realism," the jacket description may well have contributed to some reviewers' negative responses. In the description, Ballard is characterized as violent, degraded, and sordid, his scenes perverse and grotesque. But it ends with an expression of wonder that McCarthy could depict such a character "with taste, dignity, and humor." What it does not mention is the empathy and understanding with which McCarthy depicts his child of God and which he evokes in the reader. Nothing in the description addresses Ballard's necrophilia or the role the community plays in his abject alienation. But it does stress McCarthy's craftsmanship and lyrical power.[16]

*Outer Dark* received slightly fewer reviews than had *The Orchard Keeper,* and *Child of God* was noticed still less. Again, several years had elapsed between the books' publications, making it difficult for McCarthy to sustain attention in the press, which in any case he had not actively cultivated. Of those who reviewed *Child of God,* only Robert Coles and Jonathan Yardley had assessed McCarthy's previous work, and some appraisers seemed defeated by the extremity of Ballard's crimes and the novel's shocking or repellent incidents. (To be fair, *Child of God,* like *Outer Dark,* is a deceptively simple novel that may require more than one open-minded reading fully to appreciate McCarthy's aims and achievement.) *Child of God* did receive thoughtful praise, notably from Coles, from fiction writer Anatole Broyard, and from novelist Doris Grumbach, all in influential publications with national distribution, and McCarthy also received a sincere, congratulatory letter about the novel from Guy Davenport.

Predictably, the most negative reviews came from those whose serious contemplation of the novel's merits had been short-circuited by its frank exploration of taboo subjects. Earlier writers had expanded the definition of the tragic hero for a democratic audience, but these reviewers, perhaps like Erskine, did not accept McCarthy's implicit attempt to stretch that definition toward inclusion of the most criminally deranged of the children of God. Richard Brickner, a teacher of writing at the New School, who wrote for the *New York Times Book Review,* was so offended by Ballard and the novel that he resisted the recognizably tragic elements of its plot structure and character treatment. For

Brickner, Ballard was one of those characters "so flattened by fate before they crawl into our view that they exist beneath the reach of tragedy." Thus he considered *Child of God* "sentimental" and "morose" rather than "tragic." Contributing to Brickner's wholly negative reaction was McCarthy's "nasty 'writing'" (perhaps an objection to the anatomical and scatological language) and the novel's "cold, sour diction," which Brickner took as evidence of McCarthy's "hostility toward the reader" (Brickner, "A Hero Cast out, Even by Tragedy" 7). The anonymous writer for *Kirkus Reviews,* too, was unsympathetic with Ballard and with McCarthy's fictional project, which he or she rejected as a waste of time and of the awards McCarthy had received. Virgil Miller Newton Jr. dismissed Ballard as "a deranged hillbilly, who won't work." At the end of his review for the *Tampa Tribune,* he wondered, "why waste talent on such a macabre subject?"—a query that could have been a productive starting point for serious consideration of the novel (Newton, "From English Tycoons to Arsonist Roaches" 5C). Peter Prescott compared *Child of God* unfavorably to Toni Morrison's *Sula* in his review of both for *Newsweek,* and he found Ballard "an entirely numb man, . . . only barely alive," ignoring McCarthy's painstaking if understated exploration of Ballard's terrible awareness of his losses and his struggle against his fate ("Dangerous Witness" 63). Robert Leiter wrote a more considered survey of McCarthy's three novels for *Commonweal;* nevertheless, he concluded that Ballard, with his "extravagant violence . . . is all there is to *Child of God,* and for all his mystery, he is not enough" (Leiter, Review of *Child of God* 92).

Once more, those who were most out of sympathy with McCarthy's achievement in *Child of God* tended to pigeon-hole the novel as Southern gothicism, a genre they disliked. Peter Prescott found the setting less a realistic rendition of Tennessee than a "caricature of a Faulknerian landscape: a place that lends itself to incest, murder, necrophilia" (Prescott, "Dangerous Witness" 67). *National Observer*'s Bill Perkins dismissed the novel as a decadent mid-century parody embodying all the "heavyhanded" clichés of the genre: "This is Gothic Concentrate, boiled down to violence, perversions, and body functions." In a remarkable display of first-reading incomprehension, Perkins complained that McCarthy had wasted no time "on explaining why the characters are shiftless and depraved, or on . . . a coherent story line, or on building a metaphor that might" mitigate the novel's "sordidness" (Perkins, "Mined-out Territory" 21).

Although in *Child of God* McCarthy had allowed himself more narrative commentary than in *Outer Dark* and had structured his third novel to create meaningful counterpoint between the oral commentaries of Ballard's unsympathetic neighbors and Ballard's own experience, some reviewers were perplexed by his narrative objectivity, his reluctance to force his readers' responses or to pontificate. In his column for the Knoxville *News-Sentinel,* Carson

Brewer found Ballard more believable than the one-dimensional, sexually violent mountaineers of James Dickey's *Deliverance* (1970), yet he complained
that McCarthy had provided little evidence of Ballard's emotional life (Brewer,
"This Is Your Community," 19). Leiter faulted the novel for failing consistently
to place Ballard within a broader social context and thought McCarthy should
have carried the community's oral commentaries into the later sections of the
novel. He speculated that the work might come to be considered "a bad novel
written by a good writer" (Leiter, Review of *Child of God* 92).

McCarthy's reliance on strategic opacity contributed to British reviewers'
consensus that the novel was morally facile—although they may have adopted
this idea from one another, as reviewers are wont to do. Lorna Sage recognized
in her review for *The Observer* that Ballard's perverse behaviors are learned
from his community, that "his murderous underground career is made to ape
and echo at every point the cruel hints of normality," yet she declared that
McCarthy's point that "Lester only takes to his grisly pranks for lack of love"
constitutes "a neat, circular device which ties up the moral business." "'Child
of God' is gripping stuff," she concluded, "but its myth is banal." Robert Buckler echoed Sage in his brief review in the *Listener* three weeks later, when he
conceded that *Child of God* was "compulsive reading" but lacking in "moral
sophistication." Apparently misled by McCarthy's coupling of narrative reticence with his unflinching gaze at humanity at its most damaged, Buckler
declared, "Understatement is the last thing Cormac McCarthy strives for in
*Child of God.*" In his assessment for the *Times Literary Supplement,* Roy Foster
was more admiring of McCarthy's ability to evoke compassion for Ballard:
"McCarthy's sense of the tragic is almost unerring. Ballard becomes a monster,
yet he never loses his disturbing, understated pathos." Yet he found the novel
lacking in "the universal vision" that Faulkner's works supplied. Foster did not
explain this, but one wonders if he, too, found Ballard too beyond the pale to
be representative of human nature (Foster, "Downhill-billy" 445).

Unique among the mixed reviews is William Parrill's for the Nashville *Tennesseean,* in which he argues for more opacity and less historical or sociological context. Parrill observed plausibly that while *Outer Dark* had delineated
a purely gothic realm, in *Child of God* McCarthy establishes "historical context" for his protagonist. However, Parrill complained that McCarthy explains
Ballard reductively through hereditary and environmental factors. Parrill preferred the more mysterious treatment McCarthy had given to Culla Holme.
"Ballard is an authentic revenant" he concluded; "the problem is that McCarthy seems to think that he is a mountain man who has been badly treated"
(Parrill, "McCarthy's Gift Akin to Poe's" 7F). Of course, he can be both.

More appreciative reviewers, such as the anonymous writer for the *Atlantic,* admired McCarthy's courage in focusing on necrophilia "without being

gratuitously grotesque or . . . inadvertently comic." The reviewer recognized that McCarthy "suggests that the worst depravity is not inhuman, merely the far end of the continuum. . . ." He or she also praised McCarthy's "lean prose alive to the natural world, speech, and to the tenuous civilization that fails to contain Ballard" (Anonymous, "Depraved" 128).

The strongest reviews tended to ponder more broadly what McCarthy had achieved in *Child of God,* and all of them started from the just position that grants the writer his subject and acknowledges the challenges it presents to author and reader alike. One such was by short story writer and literary critic Anatole Broyard, whose collection of reviews, *Aroused by Books,* would be published by Random in 1974, and who might have been influenced to review *Child of God* by his association with the publisher. His review appeared in the *New York Times* a month before the novel itself. Still, Broyard seems genuinely appreciative of *Child of God,* and he would later review *Suttree* favorably as well. What impressed him foremost was the way that McCarthy had induced him to extend his compassion to the morally "bad" Ballard: "I cared about Ballard and very nearly forgave him his sins because . . . his actions flow so naturally from what he is. He murders, rapes, vandalizes corpses, sets fires and steals—yet Mr. McCarthy has convinced me that his crimes originated in a reaching for love." Broyard implicitly acknowledged that such a purpose in fiction could easily slide into sentimentality and make one impatient, but in talented hands like McCarthy's, "the magic of art . . . can make you contradict yourself, surprise yourself, discover charities you blush to confront" (Broyard, "'Daddy Quit,' She Said" 45).

Novelist Doris Grumbach, professor of American literature and creative writing, was literary editor of *The New Republic* from 1972 to 1974. Her long, entirely enthusiastic review in its pages is unique in its affirmation of *Child*'s startling originality. The novel impressed her as so "'new,' so clearly made well that it seems almost to defy the easy esthetic categories" (26). She recognized it as an "extraordinary quest-novel" that encompasses a dark "unreasonable comedy at the heart of [its] tragedy." Far from offended by the novel's unlikely protagonist, Grumbach declared that the reader feels "*privileged,* oddly enough, to watch him . . . as he moves toward his crazed, inevitable death . . . in the presence of sometimes cruel, sometimes beneficent Nature" (Grumbach, "Practitioner of Ghastliness" 26–27; emphasis in original). Indeed, she observed, "The natural world and the world of violence and madness are united in Ballard" (27). She praised, too, the mystery McCarthy had achieved through his decision to narrate Ballard almost entirely through an objective point of view. Like voyeurs, readers come to know him only through what we see, and both Ballard and the "cutting, touching, harsh beauty of his landscape . . . are equally immune to our comprehension." Yet, she concludes, "every sentence

[McCarthy] writes illuminates, if only for a moment, the great dark of madness and violence and inevitable death that surrounds us all" (28).

In his appreciative assessment for the *Charlotte Observer*, English professor Scott Byrd echoed Broyard and Grumbach's praise for McCarthy's ability to evoke empathy for his protagonist. Byrd wrote that although Ballard is a grotesque, McCarthy treats him neither ironically nor condescendingly: he "illuminates him and causes the reader to love him, for in his own way . . . Ballard . . . [exemplifies] endurance and affection, even if he must wander too deeply into the forbidden kingdom of death." Byrd recognized that, as shocking as Ballard is, "his solitary instincts and needs are often less perverse than those of the townspeople who contemptuously begrudge his very existence" (Scott Byrd, "Grotesque Plot Is Compelling" 9B). He placed McCarthy among the best writers of the region.

Robert Coles reviewed *Child of God* favorably and with understanding in the *New Yorker*, and he reprinted the review, "The Stranger," the following year in his collection *The Mind's Fate*. Coles reiterated and elaborated some points he had made about *Outer Dark*. Again he compared to Greek tragedy McCarthy's reluctance to explain away his protagonist's acts by attributing them to "understandable causes." *Child of God* was not "yet another novel about the corruption of society," and McCarthy, Coles thought, "seems not to wish our twentieth-century psychological sensibility to influence his work" (Coles, "The Stranger" 87). It seems to me that Coles, like Grumbach, underplays McCarthy's indirect methods of addressing the sociological and psychological factors at work in Ballard's fate ("Lester destroys and is destroyed, but we have not a clue as to why," Coles writes [89]), but both reviewers do so in service of praising the novel's foregrounding the mystery and complexity of human motivation. Coles had written in his 1965 review of Krafft-Ebing's *Psychopathia Sexualis* (itself a likely source for *Child of God*): "There are, perhaps, more bruised, lonely, desperate people in any century than we dare realize" (Coles, "Eros erraticus" 3.) Reviewing *Child of God,* Coles observed that McCarthy's works intimate the limits of our ability to comprehend "the riddles of human idiosyncrasy" (89). Ultimately, he argued, "McCarthy resembles the ancient Greek dramatists and medieval moralists—a strange, incompatible mixture: Ballard blind to himself and driven by forces outside his control, and Ballard the desperately wayward one whose vagrant life is one day to be judged by God" (89). Coles found in McCarthy's novels a humanism and spirituality that spoke to his own.

Although it could have no effect on the public reception of the novel, Guy Davenport's enthusiastic letter to McCarthy upon first reading *Child of God* must also have been highly encouraging, and it deserves mention with the most favorable responses. Davenport declared McCarthy had again written a "masterpiece." While he thought its subject bore comparison with fifteenth- or sixteenth-century Scotland's notorious multiple murderer Sawney Bean and his incestuous clan, cave-dwelling and cannibalistic, the form of McCarthy's novel seemed to Davenport "Japanese in its spareness"—"as lean and clear and penetrating as a poem." He proclaimed that McCarthy's mastery of tone exceeded any other writer's (Davenport, Letter to Cormac McCarthy, Dec. 22, 1973).

   Not all reviewers admired McCarthy as a master of tone and poetic prose, however. Reviews of McCarthy's earlier books had had much to say about his diction and style(s), sometimes harshly critical, sometimes admiring, and this attention recurs in the assessments of *Child of God.* Reviewers who were put off by the novel or afraid to endorse it tended to fault its prose as well. As we have seen, Brickner complained of the novel's offensive writing, which surely had more to do with its frank approach to gritty subjects than with McCarthy's lyrical style. Sage charged McCarthy with writing "narcissistic prose" (Sage, "The Edge of Hysteria" 30). Similarly, the *Kirkus* reviewer found the narrative "artificially stylized," as if McCarthy's lyrical or meditative passages should not coexist with his more earthy material (Anonymous, Review of *Child of God* 1225).

   On the other hand, a few reviewers who had mixed reactions to the novel found McCarthy's style a strength. Foster, the most generous of the British reviewers, did not consider McCarthy's writing self-indulgent; rather he observed that the "lyrical prose never sacrifices necessary economies" (Foster, "Downhill-billy" 445). Knoxville's Brewer deemed *Child of God* neither good nor bad but "terrible," a book of both "mental-physical squalor and beauty," and he warned that it was for sale locally for "10 dirty words per penny," except in the Baptist Book Store. Yet he acknowledged that it was beautifully written and that, like its details of East Tennessee life, the dialogue "ring[s] true" (Brewer, "This Is Your Community" 19). Parrill, who faulted the author for treating Ballard's madness reductively, nevertheless had high praise for McCarthy's masterful writing, which in *Child of God* was "more compressed and beautiful than ever." *Child of God* is "a marvel," he declared (Parrill, "McCarthy's Gift Akin to Poe's" 7F). Lee Winfrey, writing for the *Philadelphia Inquirer,* found the novel "troublesome" despite its "artistry" because it seemed too "reminiscent" of Faulkner's *Sanctuary* (1930), another novel that dares to explore shocking material. However, Winfrey did not find McCarthy derivative of Faulkner. McCarthy had developed his own distinctive voice and created a "prose of gorgeous beauty but tough and brain-testing complexity." Neither did Winfrey find the novel's erudite diction a liability as had some reviewers of *The Orchard Keeper* and *Outer Dark*. Rather, "these rarely-seen words [are] eased so smoothly into their places in this shimmering prose that they seem the only possible ones to use, never emptily pretentious" (Winfrey, "No Ordinary Hero, Exactly" 6F).

Not surprisingly, once again the fiction writers and literary scholars who reviewed *Child of God* appreciated McCarthy's mastery of his flexible prose styles and assessed the novel more highly overall. In his review for *Newsday*, Hal Burton, conservationist and author of the Walton Boys series of children's adventure books, praised McCarthy's "power over words" and the spareness of his prose, as if McCarthy "had learned his trade from Hemingway" rather than Faulkner, to whom he had been tiresomely compared in earlier reviews. He concluded: "What a writer this young man is!" (Burton, "A Masterly Novel"). Grumbach also admired McCarthy's "rare, spare, precise yet poetic prose" (Grumbach, "Practitioner of Ghastliness," 27) and his "achievement of vividness" (26). Byrd observed that McCarthy could range from "mountain dialect to Biblical eloquence" with "almost never a lapse in mastery" (Scott Byrd, "Grotesque Plot Is Compelling" 9B). New Orleans native Broyard declared that McCarthy "has the best kind of Southern style, one that fuses risky eloquence, intricate rhythms and dead-to-rights accuracy" and exploits the "sonorousness and musicality" of the language. He was inclined to forgive McCarthy's Latinate diction and instances of inverted syntax, such as "knew not," as "overflowings . . . from a brimming imagination" (Broyard, "'Daddy Quit,' She Said" 45).

Although reviews of *Child of God* were sparser and indicative of narrowing interest in McCarthy's work in the years since his debut novel won the William Faulkner Foundation award, the best of them contributed to his *succes d'estime*. But in light of the concerns that were foremost in McCarthy's mind as he composed the novel, it is also notable that very few reviewers commented on his strategy of contrasting the biased views of Ballard revealed in his community's shared stories with the more intimate view revealed, if obliquely, as the indirect discourse follows his activities. Few noticed the intrusions of the subjective narrative voice that implies its own conclusions, except for the most obvious one, in which the narrator tells the reader that Ballard is "much like yourself perhaps" (*CoG* 4), a line that may have offended Brickner as evidence of the author's hostility to the reader (Brickner, "A Hero Cast out, Even by Tragedy"). The notable outlier was Broyard, who was struck by the narrator's "apostrophe to fate" when he wonders how it is that Ballard does not drown (*CoG* 156), but Broyard thought it "belongs in somebody else's book" (Broyard, "'Daddy Quit,' She Said" 45). Even this observation, then, proves the rule that the early readers of the novel did not recognize the presence of a narrating mind who sees Ballard differently than either Ballard or his neighbors do, and who contributes to the philosophical underpinnings of the novel.

Few reviewers except for Ralph Hollenbeck in *Parade of Books* and southerners Byrd in the *Charlotte Observer* and B. H. H. in the *Anniston (Alabama) Star* focused on the sequence of losses Ballard suffers with his parents' devastating abandonments and then at the hands of the law and his neighbors. Instead, most grappled with the task of coming to terms with Ballard's egregious acts, the plot incidents that were for the most part added after the first draft. Perhaps this is where all readers must begin with *Child of God*, as McCarthy's challenge to accommodate an individual such as Ballard, to see him, is central to his aims in the book.

Apparently discouraged by the poor sales of McCarthy's first two novels in paperback and perhaps put off by the necrophilia and the graphic representations of human decomposition in *Child of God*, Ballentine did not offer to issue it in paperback. In February or March 1979, when McCarthy replied to Robert Coles's query about the paperback issues of his books, he recalled that Warner Books might have been interested in *Child of God*, but their offer had been so meager that he had turned them down (McCarthy, Letter to Robert Coles [Feb./Mar. 1979]). Probably it was Warner's bid for the book to which McCarthy referred when he wrote Erskine in mid-March 1974 that he thought an unidentified paperback offer was "asinine."[17]

# Afterword

## 1974

One might identify various watersheds to demarcate significant periods in McCarthy's writing life. Usually, scholars have distinguished his Tennessee period from his western period, as I do in *Reading the World*, since McCarthy's physical move west in 1974 to begin his work on *Blood Meridian* also marked a move west in the settings and subjects of most of his later novels. Other significant career-shaping events were Erskine's retirement after the publication of *Blood Meridian,* followed by McCarthy's finally acquiring an effective agent in Amanda Urban at International Creative Management, who interested Knopf in publishing him (Lisa Chase, "To Binky Urban"). One might also differentiate the sixteen years in which his work was entirely in fiction from the later years when he also wrote for film and stage, the long period of dramatic writing starting in 1975, admirably treated by Stacey Peebles in *Cormac McCarthy and Performance.* McCarthy's receiving a five-year fellowship from the MacArthur Foundation in 1981 and the long-awaited financial return on his writing when *All the Pretty Horses* (1992) and his subsequent novels acquired bestseller status both marked turning points in his wider reception as a writer. And his becoming a bestselling author and his new ability to sell film rights to his work inaugurated a period of welcome financial independence from foundations. One might also consider his acquiring the role of writer-in-residence at the Santa Fe Institute, where he is now a trustee, as marking yet another stage in his writing life. And there is his late-career turn to the contemporary west and its border conflicts centering on the drug cartels. But in fact, any of these distinctions is an artificial imposition of order on a six-decade career that has unfolded continuously and organically, and these phases have overlapped significantly.

Still, I want to close with a few observations about the year 1974, the year inaugurated with the publication of *Child of God,* as a turning point that evolved naturally in the flow of McCarthy's writing life. When *Child of God* was published, it left him with only *Suttree* in his pipeline of active work. He may well have conceived *The Passenger* by then, but he would not turn serious attention to it until 1980. As he wrote to Robert Coles in early January 1980, and as we have seen in this study, McCarthy always ensured he had a couple of projects to work on at a time, and he tended to let one rest as he turned to another to keep himself interested and to give him perspective on his work. So 1974 was a natural time for him to begin cultivating his ideas for his western novel, *Blood Meridian,* even while he was laboring to finish *Suttree,* the Knoxville novel that he hoped would be some kind of career breakthrough but that would not see print for five more years.

As noted earlier, on Thanksgiving 1964 he had recorded on a draft page of *Outer Dark* "writing = happy" (*OD:* "Rough/ First Draft [B]" 198/26/191). In 1971 McCarthy told Maryville interviewer Mark Owen that his writing was what everything else in his unconventional life revolved around (Owen, "McCarthy Is One" 4B). And at the time of *Child of God*'s publication, McCarthy confessed to Kingsport interviewer Martha Byrd that his writing was "a compulsion" (Martha Byrd, "East Tennessee Author" 9C). His sacrifices over the next years, mostly lean ones, would bear out the implications of these self-consistent statements.

On Anne's birthday, January 31, 1974, McCarthy took his wife of almost eight years out to dinner at The Orangerie, an upscale restaurant in Knoxville, and moved west without her the next day. He had been packing up his belongings all month. Some time before he left, McCarthy inscribed a copy of *Outer Dark* to Anne, naming her "the love of my life" but apologizing that he could not offer her all that she deserved. Anne was uncertain whether her marriage would survive the stresses it had been and still was under. But at Cormac's invitation, in mid-August she joined him in Tucson, where they lived together in his apartment for two weeks before making an extended trip that fall, driving in McCarthy's outfitted Volkswagen bus to El Paso, Chihuahua, Babicora, Casas Grandes, Guerrero, Janos, and back to El Paso. After resting there a few days, they made another excursion by train across the Sierra Madre and the Copper Canyon to Los Mochis and Topolobampo, then by boat to the Baja peninsula: La Paz and south to Cabo San Lucas. Except for her anxiety about their future, to Anne the trips seemed much like their travel across western Europe in the first months of their marriage, exciting adventures filled with new people, places, and food. McCarthy was not writing on their excursions in Mexico, but he was absorbing the culture and landscapes of the borderlands that would inform five of his eight subsequent novels and his screenplay *The Counselor.* When his money ran out (probably the last installment of his advance for *Child of God*), the couple returned to El Paso in mid-October, where Cormac put Anne on a plane back to Tennessee, telling her that he might see her at Christmas. He did return at intervals, and he would send batches of revised pages of *Suttree* for her to type and return to "some strange clandestine address." However, their marriage was never secure again (De Lisle, "The Dream"; De Lisle, Conversations).

McCarthy started his writing career in 1959 full of youthful confidence that he could write well and possessed of the maturity and discipline to work steadily at his novels even though he was making little money from his writing. His parents were dubious about his career path, but his confidence in his talent was validated along the way by friends, sympathetic editors, other fiction writers, reviewers, and the financial support of prestigious foundations. Further, McCarthy must have been highly satisfied with what he was learning through practicing his craft and what he had achieved so far in his fiction. He may have been discouraged from time to time by the delays in bringing his first three novels to completion, some caused by the complicated editing process, some by his own standards of perfection, and some by his desire to live a full and active personal and social life concurrent with his writing. Indeed, in the first fifteen years of his career, he published only three novels, averaging five years per book. *Suttree,* which he considered his masterwork of the period, had begun in 1961 or 1962 but had yet to reach completion. His frustration that he had composed so many leaves but not yet fully accomplished that book is evident in his comment to Erskine in 1971 that he needed to get away and to find the privacy in which to work. When McCarthy moved west in 1974 to revise *Suttree* and to begin his research for *Blood Meridian,* he sacrificed much of the personal and domestic life he had built with Anne in Tennessee. The move west was not only a new direction; it was a profound act of recommitment to his writing career.

# Notes

**Part One.** *The Orchard Keeper,* 1959–1965

1. According to De Lisle, she and McCarthy did not attend church when they were together. She found him to be "spiritual" but not religious (De Lisle, Conversations).

2. For further discussion of the genesis of *The Passenger*, its place within McCarthy's career, and its likely theme of creativity thwarted, see my "Creativity, Madness, and 'the light that dances deep in Pontchartrain': Glimpses of 'The Passenger' from McCarthy's 1980 Correspondence." *The Passenger* and its companion work, *Stella Maris,* are scheduled for publication in October and December 2022, respectively.

3. Woodward implies that *Suttree* was begun in 1959 (Woodward, "Venomous Fiction" 36), but when McCarthy applied to the Rockefeller Foundation in March 1966, he indicated that he had begun the novel five years earlier, or in 1961; and when he applied to the Guggenheim Foundation in fall 1968, he reported that he had been writing *Suttree* for six years, or since 1962 (McCarthy, Letter to Gerald Freund, September 23, 1968).

4. McCarthy changed this in holograph revisions on his carbon copy of the "Final Draft." See, for instance, pages 4, 11, 22.

5. For detailed study of these tales in *Suttree*, see my "Tall Tales."

6. The dynamic between them is reprised in the relationship between Llewellyn and Carla Jean Moss in *No Country for Old Men*, particularly in the scene when Moss comes home late at night (20–22).

7. The other two deleted leaves in the folder of revision notes are a letter from Kenneth Rattner to his "Mamaw" (130), which probably originated in an earlier draft, and a page of dialogue between John Wesley and Ownby about the old man's shooting at the government tank (264).

8. The interlude becomes hallucinatory and death-haunted, haunted by the specter of World War II, as it questions the old man: "We dream . . . visionary dreams of the race that was. . . . [R]eceding on the eve of pillage . . . we . . . saw from the final promontory before the void . . . your forms veiled and indistinct." It concludes with a phrase which McCarthy reused in *Suttree*: In these dreams of past people, their forms are so divorced of their functions that they could be "posts or trees, or prophets sealed in glass" (210; cf. *S* 305).

9. McCarthy's creation in *The Orchard Keeper* and *Suttree* of retrospective narrators who imaginatively recreate or "write" their own lived and witnessed histories is one of the strategies he borrowed from Melville's *Moby-Dick*, in which the narrating Ishmael remembers his younger, more naïve self.

10. Because Plimpton was in New York City and often unresponsive, Bensky found managing *Paris Review* very taxing. In 1966 he returned to the United States to edit the

*New York Times Sunday Book Review,* where his leftist ideas and anti-war activism soon put him at odds with some of his colleagues. Bensky became managing editor of *Ramparts* magazine in San Francisco, a journal that was more compatible with his own politics, in 1968. His interest in political journalism took him from print media to radio, and he is most recognized for his work as a national affairs correspondent for Pacifica Radio in the late 1980s and 1990s, for which he won numerous honors, including a lifetime achievement award from the Society of Professional Journalists. Beginning in 1998 he taught journalism and political science courses at Stanford University; California State University, East Bay; and Berkeley City College. In 2007 he retired from radio broadcasting to produce and host the web site *Radio Proust,* sponsored by Bard College (Bensky, e-mail to the author, Mar. 7, 2012; Lilley, "A Tribute to Larry Bensky"; Peter M [*sic*], "Hidden in Plain Sight").

11. Drawing on studies of the US publishing industry, King points out that just before and during McCarthy's association with Random, the publisher underwent a series of transformations, first with the public sale of its stock in 1959, which reduced the owners' and editors' autonomy; then with its absorption by conglomerates RCA in 1965 and S. I. Newhouse in 1980. These buyouts made it accountable to corporate interests not entirely in sympathy with the values of writers and their editors (King, *Cormac McCarthy's Literary Evolution* 21–23). McCarthy's comment to Woolmer reflects his awareness of some of these changes (McCarthy, Letter to Howard Woolmer, postmarked Nov.5, 1979).

12. Erskine became Ellison's editor after Frank Taylor left Random, and he guided *Invisible Man* to its publication in 1952 (Rampersad, *Ralph Ellison* 211).

13. Bensky identified him to Josyph (Josyph, Email to the author, Jan. 4, 2017). Jellinek later worked, like Bensky, at the *New York Times Book Review* (Josyph, "Damn Proud" 27).

14. In his letter of November 14, 1963, Erskine explained that he had begun marking the typescript before copying it, so some of his marks appeared black and thus were indistinguishable in color from those made by McCarthy or Bensky. On the photocopy, Erskine had gone back over those he wanted to highlight for McCarthy in red (5).

15. Later he would write into the text of *Suttree* the explanation that the word "yegg" is one Suttree has seen only in the Knoxville newspapers (*S* 235).

16. Soon McCarthy would replace this typewriter with an Olivetti Lettera 32. When the Lettera was auctioned in 2009, he recalled at first that he had purchased it in a pawn shop in 1958, probably conflating it with his Royal portable. Subsequently he realized that he had acquired it "a few years later" than that. His letter to Erskine documents that he was still using the Royal portable in 1964. Typewriter collector Robert Messenger writes that the Olivetti Lettera 32 was not available in the United States until summer 1964. He argues plausibly that McCarthy likely replaced his Royal with a used Olivetti, which weighed only eight and a half pounds, as he was preparing for his summer 1965 trip to Europe (Messenger, "Unreliable Memories").

17. *The Reporter* was an influential liberal magazine published bi-weekly in New York between 1949 and 1968. It commented on national and international politics and regularly published book reviews.

18. The interview was for a radio script about McCarthy, which Rooke was preparing for the Canadian Broadcasting Corporation's State of the Arts series. Rooke re-quotes Erskine in his "Rash Undertakings" (306).

19. McCooe remembers that her father also read poems to her from *The Oxford Book*

*of American Verse*, but since this volume, edited by F. O. Matthiessen, was first published in 1950, Bobbie and Cormac would have been well into their teen years by then.

20. "Tony" Wimpfheimer was the stepson of Random co-owner Donald Klopfer (Cerf, *At Random* 276). He eventually became a vice president of the firm.

21. Halpern had started *Antaeus* in Tangier in 1969, with the encouragement of his mentor Paul Bowles and with Bowles's financial backing for its inaugural issue. In 1972 in New York, Halpern founded Ecco Press (Dana, "Daniel Halpern" 155, 151).

22. McCooe indicates that the nickname was taken from the line of cartoon character Bugs Bunny: "What's up, Doc?"

23. In *The Passenger*, Western lives in an apartment on St. Philip [*sic*] Street in New Orleans until he moves to evade his pursuers.

24. McCarthy would receive a travel award from the American Academy of Arts and Letters by summer 1965, but there is no evidence that he was aware of this before February.

25. As this letter to Bensky demonstrates, McCarthy composed his impromptu autobiographical sketch for Bensky in 1962, not at Erskine's request in 1964 as King claims (*Cormac McCarthy's Literary Evolution* 26).

26. Zachary Turpin and I have compiled these newspaper interviews, with an introduction and annotations, in "Cormac McCarthy's Interviews in Tennessee and Kentucky, 1968–1980," forthcoming in the Fall 2022 issue of the *Cormac McCarthy Journal*, 105–32.

27. For ample documentation and thoughtful discussion of McCarthy's collaboration with film and theater people, see Stacey Peebles, *Cormac McCarthy and Performance*. For his relationships with visual artists, see my "Landscapes as Narrative Commentary in *Blood Meridian*" and "Creativity, Madness" (91–92).

28. McCarthy's reluctance to talk about his writing, as opposed to his life, seems to derive from other concerns. John Sepich, author of *Notes on Blood Meridian*, recalls one of his first conversations with McCarthy: "I said he must go into a heightened state to be able to write the way he does. And McCarthy told me a story of a wingshot, a dove hunter, who could hit any bird that flew, and that a farmer, on whose land he was hunting, stopped him and asked did he keep his left eye open when he shot, or did he hold it closed? And that man said he didn't know, but he'd think about it. And McCarthy said the man never hit another dove again" (quoted in "Cormac McCarthy: The World's Greatest Living Writer"). McCarthy cooperated generously with Sepich by identifying many of the historical sources he had consulted for *Blood Meridian*, but it seems that he was willing to do so because Sepich did not press him to talk further about his writing methods.

29. The annual award, which rotated among fiction, nonfiction, and poetry, was established in 1984 but discontinued after a decade (Huxtable, "1978–1987" 253).

30. The Institute, established in 1898, was the more inclusive branch of the bi-cameral Institute/Academy. The Academy, created in 1904, was a smaller subgroup elected by the Institute's members. The Institute and the Academy merged their governance and budgets in 1976 and in 1996 adopted the name American Academy and Institute of Arts and Letters (Updike, "Foreword" i–x).

31. The funds for awards accrued slowly through endowments and donations over the Institute's first eight decades. In 1977, it distributed $130,000 in prize money, but by 1997, this had grown to $750,000 (Beeson, "1968–1977" 220).

32. In his retrospective of the year's best books, O'Leary ambiguously backed away from this assessment, as if embarrassed by his initial enthusiasm. He reminded his readers

that *The Orchard Keeper* had struck him as "by far the best first novel" of the year, but since other reviewers were less keen, he now wondered if he might have been too impressed ("In Retrospect" 6H).

33. Erskine sent Byerly's and Trachtenberg's reviews to McCarthy on October 14, 1965, "in spite of their plus-minus attitudes."

### Part Two. *Outer Dark*, 1962–1968

1. I am grateful to Wesley Morgan for sharing a local newspaper announcement of a boy born at the Presbyterian Hospital to Mr. and Mrs. Charles Joseph McCarthy of Sevierville (email to the author, Apr. 13, 2018).

2. She would also publish in *Great River Review, Solo,* and *Third Coast* ("About the Poet"). I have been unable to identify her contributions to these literary journals. Lee McCarthy's books were donated to the library at California State University in Bakersfield, where they were absorbed into the general collection, but the location of her papers is unknown. It seems likely that they remain in her son Chase McCarthy's possession.

3. Later Lee taught English at Wasco Union High School in Bakersfield, California, where she remained for the rest of her career. She had earned her master's degree at San Francisco State University ("Lee McCarthy").

4. In his next draft, McCarthy shortened the passage and then deleted it, marking it "N/U" for "Not Used" ("Early Draft [A]" 14).

5. My dating of this passage represents a change from that in my "Projecting Interiority" (14), a revision in my thinking based on further study of the typescripts' dates, pagination, and the relationships between the drafts of specific scenes.

6. In "Rough/First Draft [A]," one finds triune scenes that were composed later placed before the campfire scenes he drafted in September 1963: 297/213 follows page 42, and 324/209 follows page 59, with the notation that it had been transferred on "July 17 [?]."

7. The "U" in Uriah seems to have been penciled over a "B," and the "h" is ambiguous and could be read as an "n," so possibly the name was initially Brian.

8. Lee states that her son was named by his father ("Stories" 83), which McCarthy may have seen as an enduring act of claiming and acknowledging him.

9. Another partial version of the ferry scene appears on a holograph page composed on January 12, 1965, and preserved in "Early Draft [B]." Here Culla touches the horse on the far riverbank, it shies, and the rider tells him to "keep your goddamned hands off my horse" (205). Given its date and higher page number, this passage is later than the "Early Draft [A]" page on which McCarthy planned that the rider would die in the river. It may be that McCarthy briefly reconsidered the events because he was weighing writing a scene in which the triune kill the rider.

10. McCarthy drafted the triune's opening section in May 1964 ("Rough First Draft [B]" 272/212 [?]).

11. This bank was established in 1933, before McCarthy's family moved to Knoxville. McCarthy was living in New Orleans by November 1964, but he may have taken the typescript page to Knoxville on a visit to his family before his move or mailed it to his parents to place in a safe deposit box together with his first draft of the novel. It is also possible that he returned to Knoxville for Thanksgiving that year but dined in Walgreen's instead of with his parents.

12. In 1979 McCarthy asked that a complimentary copy of *Suttree* be sent to Britton, "a strong supporter" (McCarthy, Letter to Cheryl Mercer). For most of the 1970s, Britton

had been an employee of the Strand Bookstore in New York, where he commissioned many of the sketches he would include in his 1976 book, *Self-Portrait: Book People Picture Themselves*. So it seems plausible that McCarthy's self-portrait was drawn at the Strand and certain that it dates from before 1976. In 1978, Britton founded his own bookstore, Books & Company. He once claimed to be "the greatest reader alive, at least in fiction," and at both bookstores, he often recommended his favorite novels to customers, saying, "It's just as easy to read something good —why don't you read this book?" (Barron, "Burt Britton, 84" A22).

13. McCarthy also numbered the first three of his triune interludes sequentially in addition to paginating the second and third of these to reflect their placement in the evolving structure of the novel ("Early Draft [B]" 1, 34, 50).

14. However, McCarthy gives the suicidal Alicia Western a crucial role in *The Passenger*, and she is the protagonist of *Stella Maris*. Both focus on her extraordinary intelligence and on the projections of her unconscious.

15. Except for the glade where Culla abandons the baby, this paragraph is the earliest reference to a swamp in the drafts, and it is significant that here the noxious swamp is associated with despair, death-in-life, as is the swamp Culla comes to at the end of the novel. Indeed, McCarthy may have consulted this early passage when he drafted Culla's swamp scene; in "Rough/First Draft [B]" the leaf is followed by a passage of Culla's dialogue with the blind man (8) and then by a description of the swamp composed on March 5, 1965, during the second-draft stage (208/197).

16. Similarly, the tinker may have been conceived as the objective correlative of McCarthy's fear of the alienation and wandering that followed on his separation from his child and the "malediction" he expected or experienced from others.

17. I sent McCarthy a preliminary draft of my article about him for the *Dictionary of Literary Biography*, and he graciously read it and made a few corrections. Where I referred to Culla as "one of the main characters," he penciled, "not the main?" (Luce, "Cormac McCarthy" 10).

18. In a deleted passage in "Early Draft [A]," Culla suggests that his sister would take the baby, and the leader replies, "Even Harmon knows that aint goin to happen" (238; cf. *OD* 236).

19. McCarthy's conception of the purgatorial nightmare also derives from William Butler's Yeats's play *Purgatory* (1939), which envisions a closed circuit in which the characters are doomed to endless repetition.

20. I am grateful to Dustin Anderson for sharing his extensive list of biblical passages relevant to the sacrifice of children to Moloch, from which I have expanded my treatment here.

Another influence on the child's fate is likely *Macbeth*, with its own trope of infanticide. In her attempt to shame Macbeth into murdering Duncan, Lady Macbeth imagines the unthinkable: that she would dash out the brains of her nursing baby if she had sworn to do so (1.7.54–58). Adding cannibalism to infanticide, into the witches' hell-broth go the finger of a "birth-strangled babe" (4.1.30) and the blood of a sow "that hath eaten/Her nine farrow" (4.1.64–65). *Outer Dark* refers to the sow that consumes her young when the "crone," wrongly suspecting Rinthy of infanticide, tells her, "Yon sow there might make ye a travelin mate that's downed her hoggets save one" (*OD* 112).

21. In *Moby-Dick*, which McCarthy has frequently named one of his favorite works of fiction, Ishmael thinks of several ill omens he encountered before boarding the doomed

Pequod. One of these is the black cauldrons on the sign of the Try Pots Inn, where he rooms in Nantucket. These cook-kettles rather perversely remind Ishmael of "Tophet" and thus prefigure the crew of the Pequod as children sacrificed to Ahab's madness (*Moby-Dick* 72). Ishmael's personal fear of cannibalism is aroused yet domesticated through his encounter with Queequeg, the affectionate cannibal who shares his room early in the novel. In *Outer Dark*, McCarthy imaginatively links the kettles of the Try Pots with the witches' caldron in *Macbeth*, associating both with cannibalistic child sacrifice.

22. She also vividly recalls seeing the marble sculpture *Ugolino and His Sons* (1867) by Jean-Baptiste Carpeaux at the Louvre in Paris in 1965 or 1966. It was purchased in 1967 by the Metropolitan Museum of Art in New York, where it now resides (Draper and Papet, *The Passions of Jean-Baptiste Carpeaux* 315). The sculpture is based on the story in Dante's *Inferno*, Canto XXXIII, of the nobleman Ugolino, imprisoned with his four sons and grandsons and starving to death. Driven mad by his hunger, Dante's Ugolino has eaten his dead children and is condemned eternally in the ninth circle of hell, reserved for traitors. Carpeaux's sculpture shows seated Ugolino surrounded by his young boys, with his fingers to his agonized mouth. It reflects the moment when his sons beg him not to eat his fingers, but to eat their remains instead, the moment when that horrific alternative enters his mind. De Lisle reports that she and McCarthy were both "mesmerized" by the work (Conversations).

McCarthy may also have been familiar with Auguste Rodin's *Ugolino and His Sons*, another work on the theme of child cannibalism, although De Lisle reports that she and McCarthy did not visit the Rodin Museum together when they were in Paris. Rodin's sculpture, first conceived as part of his *Gates of Hell* series, shows the children lying dead or nearly lifeless and their father crouched over them on all fours with more confirmed intention than in Carpeaux's work. The imagery of these Ugolino sculptures is not echoed in *Outer Dark*, but McCarthy may have had Rodin's piece partly in mind when he wrote of the hungry hermit hovering ominously over the sleeping kid in *Blood Meridian* (20).

23. McCarthy picks up this idea in the discarded scene of Ballard's self-castration in *Child of God.*

24. McCarthy revisits this miserable wet dog washed up out of the night in *The Crossing*, when, as if he cannot bear this correlative of his own misery, Billy drives out the misshapen dog who, like him, has sought shelter from the rain in a shack (423–25).

25. Years later, in *The Stonemason*, Ben Telfair will conduct his own self-appraisal and ask himself, "Where are the others?" (113).

26. In the published version, Rinthy makes this plaint about herself but not as an excuse for her choices (*OD* 29).

27. It also adumbrates Ballard's moral blindness in *Child of God* and the father's dream of the blind cave-dwelling creature in *The Road* (4-5).

28. McCarthy did not retain the word "sleech" for *Outer Dark*, but he used it in *Suttree's* "claggy sleech" (*S* 403).

29. Bobby Western's friend Debussy Fields lives on Dumaine Street in *The Passenger* (362).

30. Knoxville interviewer Pat Fields reported that when he finally sailed, "the draft and notes and portable typewriter [made] up a large part of his luggage" ("Knox Native" A8).

31. Since Shrapnel's review appeared on March 17, McCarthy would not have seen it before he wrote to Erskine (Shrapnel, "Echoes from the Corridors" 10).

32. For a study of this relationship and the two writers' mutual influence, see my "Cormac McCarthy and Leslie Garrett."

33. In "Creativity, Madness," I discuss the ways in which McCarthy's friendships with these troubled creative men may have influenced his thinking about *The Passenger*, to which he turned in earnest in 1980. McCarthy refers to de Hory and thus indirectly to Irving in *The Passenger* when Bobby Western, sitting in an outdoor café in Ibiza, tells an old acquaintance, "There used to be some interesting criminals living here. A first class art forger. One of the greats" (374).

34. "Anthroparians" appears in the first hospital scenes in *Suttree*, when Suttree's concussed brain dreams of them "scuttling" through the night streets (188). In the same paragraph, he dreams of the city's skyline as a "horde of retorts and alembics ranged against a starless sky," an association that suggests Suttree conceives of the anthroparians as alchemical creations.

35. The sentence was again revised, somewhat awkwardly, for the back cover of the Vintage International edition: "Both brother and sister wander separately through a countryside being scourged by three terrifying and elusive strangers, heading toward an eerie, apocalyptic resolution." McCarthy does not seem to have written this revised version.

36. Lane's letter to Woolmer lists the publication date of August; and review copies were mailed in the middle of that month (Erskine, unsigned letter to McCarthy, Aug. 13, 1968). However, a note Erskine wrote to McCarthy on September 23, 1968 indicated that publication day would be September 24.

37. According to De Lisle, Frank continued to work as a salesman of real estate in Gatlinburg and was quite nomadic, so they also saw him and Carolyn in Tennessee periodically (Conversations).

38. On a separate occasion, the Hares also introduced Lee McCarthy to Davenport. Davenport's papers include both Cormac and Lee's letters to him. Lee's are especially fine letters, but they reveal little about her life with McCarthy.

39. When Beves sent Corrington's review to McCarthy on November 11, 1968, she reported that she and Erskine found it "both interesting and good" and added that she admired Corrington for his novel, *The Upper Hand*. McCarthy replied that he had earlier received a letter from Corrington, in which he asked him to submit something for a journal he edited in New Orleans and forecast that his review in the *National Observer* would write "kind things" (McCarthy, Letter to Suzanne [Beves], received Dec. 7, 1968). Perhaps the two had met when McCarthy was in New Orleans.

40. In February 1972, Beves sent Guggenheim's Steven Schlesinger a copy of 178 draft pages of *Suttree* as documentation for McCarthy's application for further support, which was unsuccessful.

### Part Three. *Child of God*, 1966–1973

1. These are the scenes Travis Franks refers to as the "Middle Draft Compendium." He reads the sheriff's narration of Ballard's life as a "coda" to or extension of the "Middle Draft" (Franks, "'Talkin about Lester'" 94). I see this material saved at the end of the "Middle Draft" as leftover from an earlier typescript, not an integral part of the "Middle Draft."

2. The conception of man as a puppet appears in *Outer Dark* as well, when the tinker in firelight appears "like an effigy in rags hung by strings from an indifferent hand" (189).

3. According to De Lisle, these salesmen included Ted (Joe Toddy) Cook, Bob Crenshaw, Frank Hare, John Holley, Lambert and Paul Holme, and J. W. Lawrence, in addition to Goodman. In storytelling mode, these men were wildly entertaining. "A light shone upon them," she remarks (De Lisle, Conversations).

4. Sheddan features as an important character in *The Passenger*, one of Bobby Western's friends from East Tennessee with whom he converses in New Orleans bars and restaurants. Sheddan claims that Western thinks of him as a psychopath and that he may be right about that (31). In the novel, Sheddan is a petty criminal, but he is also highly intelligent and well-read. Of their friendship, Sheddan says, "I will tell you Squire that having read even a few dozen books in common is a force more binding than blood" (143). Wesley Morgan has learned from one of their classmates that McCarthy and Sheddan met in an American Literature course at the University of Tennessee, where Sheddan was the more vocal of the two.

5. De Lisle thinks the story of the sheriff's confronting the couple may derive from an experience she and Cormac had; she recalls, however, that once when Goodman and Cormac were sledding on a hillside near their house, Goodman lost control and skidded into a bush with such force that his pants and boots were torn off (De Lisle, Conversations).

6. For information about the White Cap era in Sevier County and McCarthy's source material for it, see my "White Caps, Moral Judgment, and Law."

7. McCarthy mailed the final version of the new story to Erskine with his revised draft ("Setting copy" 63A-63B; letter to Erskine, received Feb. 22, 1973). Franks assumes that the revision notes date from earlier than the "Final Draft" and the carbon copy of it labeled "Late Draft." As a result, he claims that pages 63A and 64A "do not persist in the final copy" ("'Talkin about Lester'" 93). In fact, they were composed *after* the "Final Draft," as evidenced by the numbering of the revision notes to match the pagination of the "Late" and "Final" Drafts and by the new pages' appearance in the "Setting Copy."

8. For photographs of her with other members of the ballet company, see Segroves ("There's a Touch of England" G7) and Betsy Morris ("Also Have a Great 'Motoring Act'" F12). De Lisle began dance training in England when she was six. After passing all the examinations of the Royal Academy of Ballet, she enrolled in the Southampton School of Ballet at thirteen, where she studied under Daphne Turner and Nellie Potts of the Royal Academy. She began dancing professionally at age seventeen, and in 1961 she formed a singing and dancing duo with her partner Nicky Banks, with whom she performed throughout Europe, Africa, the Middle East, and Asia. The two also recorded for EMI and worked in radio and television. In Tennessee, De Lisle danced in many Maryville-Alcoa Ballet productions and performed the lead roles in "The Nutcracker" in 1975 and "Coppelia" in 1977 (Segroves G1, G7), as well as "La Sylphide," "Sleeping Beauty," "Carmen," and "Swan Lake. She also taught at her De Lisle School of Ballet at Maryville College. In 1991, she was affiliated with Ballet Florida and the Jupiter School of Dance in West Palm Beach. In 2007, she taught ballet, tap, and musical theater there at the Keldie Academy and the Academy of Dance, Music and Theatre (De Lisle, Conversations).

9. For biographical information about Bill Kidwell, see Tumblin, *Bill Kidwell Fountain City Artist*, and Pickle, "Artistic Return."

10. Cerf's assessment of bookselling was approximately contemporaneous with the exchange between McCarthy and Erskine. *At Random* was published posthumously in

1977, edited by Cerf's widow Phyllis Cerf Wagner and Albert Erskine. It was based on oral history sessions Cerf had done in 1967 and 1968 with Mary R. Hawkins, and Cerf had begun writing notes to update the interviews in March 1971. *At Random* was based on these interviews and notes. To complete the unfinished book, the editors drew from his detailed diaries and scrapbooks, his correspondence, and other published work (Wagner and Erskine, "Editors' Note" ix).

11. Beves's letter of August 1971 provides a useful listing of all the excerpts McCarthy sent Erskine between September 1970 and June 1971.

12. Random may not have agreed to the royalty stipulation, however. When Random and the Lyndhurst Foundation drew up a preliminary budget in 1984 for a paperback reissue of *Suttree* in the Vintage Contemporaries series, it called for McCarthy to receive a 6 percent royalty for the first 30,000 copies, and 7½ percent thereafter ("Proposal for Co-Publishing Arrangement").

13. In fall 2021, award-winning Hungarian director László Nemes and his French co-writer Clara Royer wrote an adaptation of *Outer Dark* with hopes of securing funding to make the film.

14. For the history of how the Vintage Contemporaries publication of *Suttree* came about, see my "Robert Coles and Cormac McCarthy." Since this article was published, I have learned that although the Lyndhurst Foundation is credited in the paperback's front matter with subsidizing the reprint, Random/Vintage did not finally accept Lyndhurst's proffered support (Montague, Interview with Dianne Luce).

15. De Lisle does not remember Erskine's visit, and she thinks the house was never finished enough for them to have hosted the Erskines, so it is probable that he and Cormac met elsewhere when he passed through Knoxville (De Lisle, Conversations).

16. A revised, compressed, and improved version of the description appears on the back cover of the Vintage paperback. It reduces the negatively loaded diction of the first edition's description of character and subject, and it hints at Ballard's necrophilia, "the strange lusts" that cause him to prey on others.

17. I date the letter in mid-March 1974 because in it McCarthy refers to his brother William's not having received copies of *Child of God*. On March 21, Harkleroad replied to McCarthy, apologizing and saying that William's books had been mailed that day.

# Works Cited

Albert Erskine Random House Editorial Files, 1933–1993 (AEF). Accession # 13497. Special Collections, University of Virginia Library, Charlottesville.

Alcorn, Alfred. Review of *The Orchard Keeper*. *Montgomery Advertiser,* July 26, 1965: 4A.

Alighieri, Dante. *The Divine Comedy.* Translated and edited by Thomas G. Bergin. Arlington Heights, IL: Harlan Davidson, 1955.

American Academy of Arts and Letters. https://artsandletters.org/awards/. Accessed Dec. 14, 2020.

"Americans in Debt." *Times Literary Supplement* (London), Mar. 10, 1966: 185.

Anonymous. "Depraved." Review of *Child of God. Atlantic,* May 1974: 128.

———. "Notes on Current Books." *Virginia Quarterly Review* 45 (Winter 1969): viii.

———. "Notes on Recent Books." *Virginia Quarterly Review* 41 (Summer 1965): lxxx.

———. Review of *Child of God. Kirkus Reviews* 41 (Nov. 1, 1973): 1224–25.

———. Review of *Child of God. Publishers Weekly* 204 (Oct. 29, 1973): 31.

———. Review of *The Orchard Keeper. Cleveland Plain Dealer*, May 16, 1965. Compilation of news clippings. Box 29, folder 7, AEF.

———. Review of *Outer Dark. Publishers Weekly* 194 (July 1, 1968): 53–54.

———. Review of *Outer Dark. Kirkus Reviews* 36 (July 1, 1968): 714.

———. "A Southern Parable." *Time* 92 (Sept. 27, 1968): E5.

Apicella, Vincent F. Letter to Joseph Levy, Nov. 24, 1964. Ts. Box 1, folder 1, Cormac McCarthy Papers (CMP).

Arnold, Edwin T. "Cormac McCarthy's *The Stonemason*: The Unmaking of a Play." In *Myth, Legend, Dust: Critical Responses to Cormac McCarthy*, edited by Rick Wallach, 141–54. Manchester, UK: Manchester University Press, 2000.

———, and Dianne C. Luce. "Introduction." *Perspectives on Cormac McCarthy*, 1–16. Jackson: University Press of Mississippi, 1999.

"Author Lives in Blount." *News-Sentinel* [Knoxville, TN], Oct. 6, 1968: F5.

Bankowsky, Richard. *On a Dark Night: Three Canticles.* New York: Random House, 1964.

Barron, James. "Burt Britton, 84, Book Lover Who Collected Author Sketches," *New York Times,* Aug. 13, 2018: A22.

Baskin, Suzanne [Beves]. Letter to Andrew Lytle, Oct. 1, 1964. Ts. Box 29, folder 4, AEF.

———. Letter to Cormac McCarthy, Mar. 6, 1964. Ts. Box 29, folder 3, AEF.

———. Letter to Cormac McCarthy, Jan. 8, 1965. Ts. Box 29, folder 5, AEF.

———. Letter to Cormac McCarthy, Jan. 22, 1965. Ts. Box 29, folder 5, AEF.

———. Letter to Cormac McCarthy, May 21, 1965. Ts. Box 29, folder 5, AEF.

———. Letter to Cormac McCarthy, Aug. 11, 1965. Ts. Box 29, folder 5, AEF.

———. Letter to Cormac McCarthy, Mar. 22, 1968. Ts. Box 29, folder 8, AEF.

———. Letter to Elizabeth Chitty, Jan. 15, 1965. Ts. Box 29, folder 5, AEF.

———. Letter to Robie Macauley, Oct. 1, 1964. Ts. Box 29, folder 4, AEF.

———. List of magazines receiving galleys of *The Orchard Keeper*, November 12, 1964. Ms. Box 29, folder 4, AEF.

———. Memo to Albert Erskine, Aug. 10, 1964. Ts. Box 29, folder 4, AEF.

———. Memo to C. A. Wimpfheimer, Sept. 17, 1964. Ts. Box 29, folder 3, AEF.

———. Memo to [C. A.] Tony Wimpfheimer, Apr. 9, 1968. Ts. Box 29, folder 8, AEF.

———. Memo to Natalie Bates, Sept. 11, 1964. Ts. with holograph note added Sept. 15, 1964. Box 29, folder 4, AEF.

———. Note, Sept. 16, 1964. Ms. Box 29, folder 4, AEF

———. Note, unsigned, Feb. 4, 1965. Ms. Box 29, folder 5, AEF.

———. Note of reminder. Sept. 29, 1964. Ms. Box 1, folder 1, CMP.

———. Notes on American Academy of Arts and Letters traveling fellowship, [1965]. Ts. and ms. Box 29, folder 6, AEF.

[Bates], Natalie. Letter to Susan [Suzanne Baskin], Nov. 6, 1964. Ts with holograph note by Baskin. Box 29, folder 4, AEF.

Beck, Warren. *Faulkner*. Madison: University of Wisconsin Press, 1976.

———. Letter to Albert Erskine, Feb. 19, 1965. Ts. Box 29, folder 5, AEF.

———. Letter to Albert Erskine, Apr. 16, 1965. Ts. Box 29, folder 5, AEF.

———. Review of *The Orchard Keeper*. *Chicago Tribune*, May 19, 1965. *Books Today* sec.: 7.

Becket, Margaret. "Random House (New York: 1927– )." In *Dictionary of Literary Biography 43: American Literary Publishing Houses, 1900–1980: Trade and Paperback*, edited by Peter Dzwonkoski, 305–11. Detroit: Gale, 1986.

Beckett, Samuel. *Three Novels: Molloy; Malone Dies; The Unnameable*. New York: Grove Press, 1958. (Original work published 1953)

Beeson, Jack. "1968–1977: Housekeeping in a Messy World." In *A Century of Arts and Letters: The History of the National Institute of Arts and Letters and the American Academy of Arts and Letters as Told, Decade by Decade, by Eleven Members*, edited by John Updike, 198–237. New York: Columbia University Press, 1998.

Bell, Vereen. *The Achievement of Cormac McCarthy*. Baton Rouge: Louisiana State University Press, 1988.

Bensky, Lawrence M. Email to the author, Mar. 7, 2012.

———. Letter to Albert Erskine, May 21, 1962. Ts. Box 29, folder 3, AEF.

———. Letter to Albert Erskine, July 9, [1963]. Ts. Box 29, folder 3, AEF.

———. Letter to Cormac McCarthy, June 12, 1962. Ts. Box 29, folder 3, AEF.

———. Letter to Cormac McCarthy, with list of editorial suggestions, Oct. 9, 1962. Ts. Box 29, folder 3, AEF.

———. Letter to Cormac McCarthy, Dec. 13, 1962. Ts. Box 29, folder 3, AEF.

———. Letter to Cormac McCarthy, Jan. 25, 1963. Ts. Box 29, folder 3, AEF.

———. Letter to Cormac McCarthy, Feb. 19, 1963. Ts. Box 29, folder 3, AEF.

———. Letter to Cormac McCarthy, May 21, 1963. Ts. Box 29, folder 3, AEF.

———. Letter to Cormac McCarthy, June 25, 1963. Ts. Box 29, folder 3, AEF.

———. Letter to Cormac McCarthy, Aug. 6, 1963. Ts. Box 29, folder 3, AEF.

———. Letter to Cormac McCarthy, Aug. 22, 1963. Ts. Box 29, folder 3, AEF.

———. Letter to Cormac McCarthy, Sept. 13, 1963. Ts. Box 29, folder 3, AEF.

———. Letter to Cormac McCarthy, Oct. 3, 1963. Ts. Box 29, folder 3, AEF.

Berg, A. Scott. *Max Perkins: Editor of Genius*. New York: E. P. Dutton, 1978.

Beves, Suzanne Baskin. Letter to Cormac McCarthy, May 23, 1969. Box 29, folder 6, AEF.

———. Letter to Cormac McCarthy, Aug. 1971. Ts. Box 29, folder 10, AEF.

———. Letter to Stephen Schlesinger, Feb. 3, 1972. Ts. Box 29, folder 2, AEF.

———. Memo to Anne McCarthy, Mar. 10, 1972. Ts. Box 29, folder 2, AEF.

———. Memo to Cormac McCarthy, Nov. 15, 1968. Ts. Box 29, folder 8, AEF.

———. Memo to Cormac McCarthy, Dec. 13, 1968. Ts. Box 29, folder 8, AEF.

———. Memo to Gordon Lish, Nov. 17, 1970. Ts. Box 29, folder 2, AEF.

———. Memo to John Gallagher, Feb. 28, 1972. Ts. Box 29, folder 2, AEF.

———. Memo to John Gallagher, Mar. 22, 1972. Ts. Box 29, folder 2, AEF.

———. Review Order, Apr. 17, 1972. Ts. Box 29, folder 2, AEF.

Bingham, Mary. "From the South: Mixed Bag." *Courier-Journal* (Louisville, KY), Aug. 15, 1965: D5.

Bloch, Robert. *Psycho.* New York: Simon and Schuster, 1959.

Blotner, Joseph. "Albert Erskine Partly Seen." *Sewanee Review* 113, no. 1 (2005): 139–61.

———. *Faulkner: A Biography.* 2 vols. New York: Random House, 1974.

———. *Robert Penn Warren: A Biography.* New York: Random House, 1997.

"Books–Authors." *New York Times,* Mar. 17, 1966: 36.

Bowker, Gordon. *Pursued by Furies: A Life of Malcolm Lowry.* New York: St. Martin's Press, 1995.

Boyle, Kay. Letter to [Tom] Gervasi, Mar. 26, 1965. Ms. Box 29, folder 5, AEF.

Brewer, Carson. "This Is Your Community." Review of *Child of God. News-Sentinel* (Knoxville), Dec. 31, 1973: 19.

Brickner, Richard P. "A Hero Cast out, Even by Tragedy." *New York Times Book Review,* Jan. 13, 1974, sec. 7: 6–7.

Brown, Mick. "On the Trail of the Lonesome Bard." *Telegraph Magazine,* Apr. 16, 1994, 23–27.

Brown, Paul F. *Rufus: James Agee in Tennessee.* Knoxville: University of Tennessee Press, 2018.

Brown, Robert. Letter to Albert Erskine, [Sept. 12–14, 1964]. Ts. Box 29, folder 4, AEF.

Broyard, Anatole. "'Daddy Quit,' She Said." *New York Times,* Dec. 5, 1973: 45. Rpt, slightly revised, in *Aroused by Books,* 281–83. New York: Random House, 1974.

Brunelleschi, Filippo. *The Sacrifice of Isaac.* 1401–02. Competition door panel, bronze. The Baptistery, Florence, Italy.

Buckler, Robert. "Eleri and Greenery." *Listener* 93 (May 1, 1975): 590. Buckner, Tom. "Allegorical Narrative Set in Faulkner Land." *Lexington Herald* [KY], Dec. 1, 1968. Newspaper clipping. Box 29, folder 8, AEF.

Burton, Hal. "A Masterly Novel." *Newsday* [Garden City, NY], Dec. 20, 1973. Newspaper clipping. Box 29, folder 1, AEF.

Byerly, Mary. "Haunting Memory." *North American Review* 250, no. 4 (Sept. 1965): 62.

Byrd, Martha. "East Tennessee Author Talks about His Works and His Life." *Kingsport* [TN] *Times-News,* Dec. 16, 1973: [9C].

Byrd, Scott. "Grotesque Plot Is Compelling but Very Grim." *Charlotte Observer,* May 12, 1974: 9B.

Caravaggio. *The Sacrifice of Isaac.* 1603. Oil on Canvas. Uffizi, Florence.

Carpeaux, Jean-Baptiste. *Ugolino and His Sons.* 1967. Marble. Metropolitan Museum of Art, New York.

Casey, Thomas. "Drill Ye Tarriers, Drill." Ed. Norm Cohen. *Long Steel Rail: The Road in American Folk Life.* 1980. Champaign: University of Illinois Press, 2000, 554.

Cerf, Bennett. *At Random: The Reminiscences of Bennett Cerf,* edited by Phyllis Cerf Wagner and Albert Erskine. New York: Random House, 1977.

"Charles McCarthy Gets $125 Writing Award." *News-Sentinel* [Knoxville, TN], Feb. 10, 1959: 5.

Chase, Lisa. "To Binky Urban, 'Power' Is a Male Word." *New York Magazine,* Oct. 16, 2018. Accessed May 5, 2021.

*Child of God.* Dir. James Franco. Perf. Scott Haze, Tim Blake Nelson. RabbitBandini Productions, 2014.

Chitty, Elizabeth N. Letter to Albert Erskine, Jan. 12, 1965. Ts. Box 29, folder 5, AEF.

Coles, Robert. *Children of Crisis.* 5 vols. Boston: Atlantic-Little Brown, 1967–77.

———. "The Empty Road." *New Yorker,* Mar. 22, 1969. Rpt. in *Farewell to the South,* 119–26. Boston: Atlantic-Little Brown, 1972.

———. "Eros erraticus." Review of *Psychopathia Sexualis* by Richard von Krafft-Ebing. *Book Week,* Mar. 21, 1965: 3.

———. *Migrants, Sharecroppers, Mountaineers.* Vol. 2 of *Children of Crisis.* Boston: Atlantic-Little Brown, 1971.

———. "The Stranger." *New Yorker,* Aug. 26, 1974: 87–90. Rpt. *The Mind's Fate: A Psychiatrist · Looks at His Profession,* 217–21. Boston: Atlantic-Little Brown, 1975.

Comans, Grace P. "Beyond Time and Space." *Hartford Courant,* Nov. 17, 1968. Sunday Magazine sec.: 21.

Cormac McCarthy Papers (CMP). Southwestern Writers Collection, The Wittliff Collections, Albert B. Alkek Library, Texas State University–San Marcos.

"Cormac McCarthy: The World's Greatest Living Writer." Edgar Daily.com. Web. Accessed Jan. 27, 2015.

Corrington, John William. "Cormac McCarthy's Novel Reaches for Infinity." *National Observer* 7 (Nov. 11, 1968): 23.

Cowley, Malcolm. Letter to Albert Erskine, Jan. 26, 1965. Ts. Box 29, folder 5, AEF.

Craig, David. "Tanks, Trees." *New Statesman* 71 (Mar. 11, 1966): 347–48.

Crews, Michael Lynn. *Books Are Made out of Books: A Guide to Cormac McCarthy's Literary Influences.* Austin: University of Texas Press, 2017.

Cruttwell, Patrick. "Plumbless Recrements." *Washington Post Book World,* Nov. 24, 1968: 18.

Csikszentmihalyi, Mihaly. *Creativity: The Psychology of Discovery and Invention.* New York: Harper Perennial Modern Classics, 2013. (Original work published 1996)

Cutrer, Thomas W. *Parnassus on the Mississippi: The "Southern Review" and the Baton Rouge Literary Community, 1935–1942.* Baton Rouge: Louisiana State University Press, 1984.

Dana, Robert. "Daniel Halpern." In *Against the Grain. Interviews with Maverick American Publishers,* 151–64. Iowa City: University of Iowa Press, 1986.

Davenport, Guy. "Appalachian Gothic." *New York Times Book Review* Sept. 29, 1968: 4.

———. Letter to Cormac McCarthy, Dec. 22, 1973. Ts. Box 29, folder 8, AEF.

———. "Silurian Southern. *National Review*, Mar. 16, 1979: 368.

De Lisle, Anne. Conversations with the author, 2018–2021.

———. Interview with Bryan Giemza and Dianne Luce. Film. Charlotte, NC, Nov. 21, 2021.

———. "The Dream." Unpublished drafts of a memoir, 2019–2020.

Derleth, August. "Books of the Times: A Superb First Novel." *Capital Times* (Madison, WI), June 10, 1965: 8.

"Diary of a Madman." Stageplay. Adapted from Gogol by Richard Harris and Lindsay Anderson. Perf. Royal Court Theater, 1963.

Diogenes Verlag. Postcard to Miss Curry, postmarked June 4, 1966. Box 29, folder 6, AEF.

Donoghue, Denis. "Teaching *Blood Meridian.*" In *The Practice of Reading,* 259–77. New Haven: Yale University Press, 1998.

Doré, Gustave. "Forest of Suicides" (1861). In *The Doré Illustrations for Dante's Divine Comedy*, 37. New York: Dover, 1976.

Draper, James David, and Edouard Papet. *The Passions of Jean-Baptiste Carpeaux*. New York: Metropolitan Museum of Art, 2014.

"Drill Ye Tarriers, Drill." Recorded by The Tarriers. 1957.

Dykeman, Wilma. "Cormac McCarthy's Book Impressive." *News-Sentinel* [Knoxville, TN], May 30, 1965: F2.

Ecco Press Records, 1963–2014. Mss Coll. 111. New York Public Library, New York.

Edelstein, Arthur. "In the South, Two Good Stories, One Stereotype." *National Observer* 4 (July 5, 1965): 17.

Eliot, T. S. "The Love Song of J. Alfred Prufrock." In *The Complete Poems and Plays, 1909–1950*, 3–7. New York: Harcourt, Brace & World, 1971.

Ellis, Jay. *No Place for Home: Spatial Constraint and Character Flight in the Novels of Cormac McCarthy*. New York: Routledge, 2006.

Ellison, Ralph. Comments for dust jacket of *The Orchard Keeper*, recorded by Albert Erskine, [Feb. 1965]. Ms. Box 29, folder 5, AEF.

———. Letter to Gerald Freund, Apr. 5, 1966. Ts. Box 29, folder 6, AEF; *The Rockefeller Foundation: A Digital History*. Web. Accessed Dec. 14, 2020.

Erskine, Albert. "About the Author" draft for jacket of *The Orchard Keeper* [before Oct. 15, 1964]: holograph revision to McCarthy's ts. [c. Jan.–Feb. 1963]. Box 29, folder 4, AEF.

———. "About the Author" for *Outer Dark*, June 21, 1968. Printer's proof. Box 29, folder 8, AEF.

———. "Back ad" draft for *Outer Dark* dust jacket, [1965–68]. Ts. Box 29, folder 8, AEF.

———. "Confidential Report on Candidate for [Guggenheim] Fellowship." Dec. 17, 1968. Ts. Box 29, folder 2, AEF.

———. "Cormac McCarthy." Reading notes for *The Orchard Keeper*, [May/June1962]. Ms. Box 29, folder 4, AEF.

———. Draft of jacket copy for "The Harrow" [*Outer Dark*], [June 1968]. Ts. with ms revisions by Cormac McCarthy. Box 29, folder 8, AEF.

———. "Editor's Note." *A Robert Penn Warren Reader*, xi–xiv. New York: Random House, 1987.

———. Letter to Andrew Lytle, Oct. 5, 1964. Ts. Box 29, folder 4, AEF.

———. Letter to Andrew Lytle, Nov. 6, 1964. Ts. Box 29, folder 4, AEF.

———. Letter to Andrew Lytle, Jan. 5, 1965. Ts. Box 29, folder 5, AEF.

———. Letter to Anne McCarthy, Sept. 11, 1969. Ts. Box 29, folder 6, AEF.

———. Letter to Cormac McCarthy, Oct. 29, 1963. Ts. Box 29, folder 3, AEF.

———. Letter to Cormac McCarthy, Nov. 14, 1963. Ts. Box 29, folder 3, AEF.

———. Letter to Cormac McCarthy, Dec. 27, 1963, with cover note of Dec. 31, 1963. Tss. Box 29, folder 3, AEF.

———. Letter to Cormac McCarthy, Jan. 7, 1964. Ts. Box 29, folder 3, AEF.

———. Letter to Cormac McCarthy, Feb. 11, 1964. Ts. Box 29, folder 3, AEF.

———. Letter to Cormac McCarthy, Mar. 4, 1964. Ts. Box 29, folder 3 AEF.

———. Letter to Cormac McCarthy, Mar. 18, 1964. Ts. Box 29, folder 3, AEF.

———. Letter to Cormac McCarthy, Mar. 31, 1964. Ts. Box 29, folder 3, AEF.

———. Letter to Cormac McCarthy, Apr. 9, 1964. Ts. Box 29, folder 3, AEF.

———. Letter to Cormac McCarthy, June 2, 1964. Ts. with ms. list of copy-editing issues. Box 29, folder 3, AEF.

———. Letter to Cormac McCarthy, June 30, 1964. Ts. Box 29, folder 3, AEF.

———. Letter to Cormac McCarthy, July 14, 1964. Ts. Box 29, folder 3, AEF.

———. Letter to Cormac McCarthy, Aug. 13, 1964. Ts. Box 29, folder 4, AEF.

———. Letter to Cormac McCarthy, Sept. 9, 1964. Ts. Box 29, folder 4, AEF.

———. Letter to Cormac McCarthy, Sept. 10, 1964. Ts. Box 29, folder 4, AEF.

———. Letter to Cormac McCarthy, Oct. 5, 1964. Ts. Box 29, folder 4, AEF.

———. Letter to Cormac McCarthy, Oct. 20, 1964. Ts. Box 29, folder 4, AEF.

———. Letter to Cormac McCarthy, Dec. 16, 1964. Ts. Box 29, folder 4, AEF.

———. Letter to Cormac McCarthy, Dec. 30, 1964. Ts. Box 29, folder 4, AEF.

———. Letter to Cormac McCarthy, Jan. 20, 1965. Ts. Box 29, folder 5, AEF.

———. Letter to Cormac McCarthy, Feb. 19, 1965. Ts. Box 29, folder 5, AEF.

———. Letter (unsigned) to Cormac McCarthy, Mar. 4, 1965. Ts. Box 29, folder 5, AEF.

———. Letter to Cormac McCarthy, Mar. 23, 1965. Ts. Box 29, folder 5, AEF.

———. Letter to Cormac McCarthy, May 12, 1965. Ts. Box 29, folder 5, AEF.

———. Letter to Cormac McCarthy, Aug. 3, 1965. Ts. Box 29, folder 5, AEF.

———. Letter to Cormac McCarthy, Oct. 14, 1965. Ts. Box 29, folder 5, AEF.

———. Letter to Cormac McCarthy, Jan. 31, 1966. Ts. Box 29, folder 6, AEF.

———. Letter to Cormac McCarthy, Feb. 16, 1966. Ts. Box 29, folder 6 AEF.

———. Letter to Cormac McCarthy, Mar. 3, 1966. Ts. Box 29, folder 6, AEF.

———. Letter to Cormac McCarthy, June 15, 1966. Ts. Box 29, folder 6, AEF.

———. Letter to Cormac McCarthy, July 14, 1966. Ts. Box 29, folder 6, AEF.

———. Letter to Cormac McCarthy, Aug. 17, 1966. Ts. Box 29, folder 6, AEF.

———. Letter to Cormac McCarthy, Jan. 16, 1967. Ts. Box 29, folder 2, AEF.

———. Letter to Cormac McCarthy, Mar. 15, 1967. Ts. Box 29, folder 8, AEF.

———. Letter to Cormac McCarthy, May 23, 1967. Ts. Box 29, folder 8, AEF.

———. Letter to Cormac McCarthy, Aug. 8, 1967. Ts. Box 29, folder 2, AEF.

———. Letter to Cormac McCarthy, Nov. 28, 1967. Ts. Box 29, folder 8, AEF.

———. Letter to Cormac McCarthy, Jan. 11, 1968. Ts. Box 29, folder 8, AEF.

———. Letter to Cormac McCarthy, Feb. 1, 1968. Ts. Box 29, folder 8, AEF.

———. Letter to Cormac McCarthy, Feb. 17, 1968. Ts. Box 29, folder 8, AEF.

———. Letter to Cormac McCarthy, Apr. 9, 1968. Ts. Box 29, folder 8, AEF.

———. Letter (unsigned) to Cormac McCarthy, Aug. 23, 1968. Ts. Box 29, folder 2, AEF.

———. Letter to Cormac McCarthy, Oct. 1, 1968. Ts. Box 29, folder 2, AEF.

———. Letter to Cormac McCarthy, Oct. 17, 1968. Ts. Box 29, folder 2, AEF.

———. Letter to Cormac McCarthy, Jan. 9, 1969. Ts. Box 29, folder 2, AEF.

———. Letter to Cormac McCarthy, July 14, 1969. Ts. Box 29, folder 2, AEF.

———. Letter to Cormac McCarthy, Aug. 19, 1969. Ts. Box 29, folder 6, AEF.

———. Letter to Cormac McCarthy, Dec. 30, 1970. Ts. Box 29, folder 2, AEF.

———. Letter to Cormac McCarthy, Feb. 23, 1971. Ts. Box 29, folder 2, AEF.

———. Letter to Cormac McCarthy, June 8, 1971. Ts. Box 29, folder 2, AEF.

———. Letter to Elizabeth Chitty, Jan. 20, 1965. Ts. Box 29, folder 5, AEF.

———. Letter to Enzo Angelucci, May 19, 1966. Ts. Box 29, folder 6, AEF.

———. Letter to Gerald Freund, Mar. 24, 1966. Ts. Box 29, folder 6, AEF; *The Rockefeller Foundation: A Digital History.* Web. Accessed Feb. 7, 2018.

———. Letter to Gordon Lish, Oct. 21, 1970. Ts. Box 29, folder 2, AEF.

———. Letter to readers of advance copies of *The Orchard Keeper*, Jan. 15, 1965. Ts. Box 29, folder 5, AEF.

———. Letter to Robie Macauley, May 11, 1971. Ts. Box 29, folder 2, AEF.

———. Letter to Saul Bellow, Jan. 21, 1965. Ts. Box 29, folder 5, AEF.

———. Letter to Sidney Jacobs, June 17, 1964. Ts. Box 29, folder 4, AEF.

———. Letter to Willie Morris, Apr. 10, 1968. Ts. Box 29, folder 8, AEF.

———. Letter to Willie Morris, Sept. 14, 1970. Ts. Box 29, folder 2, AEF.

———. Letter to Willie Morris, Jan. 4, 1977. Ts. Box 29, folder 2, AEF.

———. Manuscript Transmittal Data Sheet for *The Orchard Keeper*, Nov. 6, 1964. Box 29, folder 3, AEF.

———. Memo to Dick Liebermann, Mar. 12, 1969. Ts. Box 29, folder 2, AEF.

———. Memo to Dick Liebermann, Apr. 17, 1969. Ts. Box 29, folder 2, AEF.

———. Memo to Neil Van Dyne/ Tere LoPrete, Sept. 30, 1964. Ts. Box 29, folder 3, AEF.

———. Memo to Sidney Jacobs, Feb. 5, 1968. Ts. Box 29, folder 8, AEF.

———. Note to Cormac McCarthy, Sept. 23, 1968. Ms. Box 29, folder 8, AEF.

———. Notes for communication with John Gallagher, Jan. 27, 1972. Ms. Box 29, folder 2, AEF.

———. Notes on revised opening of *The Orchard Keeper*, [Nov. 1963]. Ms. Box 29, folder 3, AEF.

———. Notes on titles for *Outer Dark*, [Feb. or Mar. 1968]. Ms. Box 29, folder 8, AEF.

———. Publishing Summary for *The Orchard Keeper*, Oct. 12, 1964. Box 29, folder 3. AEF.

———. Schedule of solicitations to and replies from readers of advance copies of *The Orchard Keeper*, [1964–65]. Ts. with ms. notations. Box 29, folder 5, AEF.

———. Setting copy for *Outer Dark* copyright page. May 9, 1968. Box 29, folder 8, AEF.

———. Telegram to Cormac McCarthy, May 5, 1965. Box 29, folder 5, AEF.

———. *The Orchard Keeper* front flap copy, drafts [A] and [B]), [early spring 1965]. Tss. with ms. revisions by Cormac McCarthy. Box 29, folder 5, AEF.

———. *The Orchard Keeper* front flap setting copy, [spring 1965]. Ts. Box 29, folder 3, AEF.

Faulkner, William. *Absalom, Absalom!* New York: Modern Library, 1964. (Original work published 1936)

———. "Albert Camus" (1961). In *Essays, Speeches and Public Letters*, edited by James B. Meriwether, 113–14. New York: Random House, 1965.

———. *As I Lay Dying*. New York: Vintage, 1964. (Original work published 1930)

———. "Barn Burning." *Collected Stories of William Faulkner*, 3–25. New York: Random House, 1950.

———. *The Hamlet*. New York: Random House, 1940.

———. *Light in August*. New York: Random House, 1932.

———. *Sanctuary*. New York: Modern Library, 1932.

———. *The Sound and the Fury*. New York: Jonathan Cape and Harrison Smith, 1929.

Fields, Pat. "Knoxville Author Gets Award for Writing." *Knoxville Journal,* May 19, 1965: 13.

———. "Knox Native McCarthy's 'Outer Dark' Second Novel Gets Good Reviews." *Knoxville Journal*, Oct. 7, 1968: A8.

Foote, Shelby. Letter to Bob Loomis, Apr. 12, 1965. Box 29, folder 5, AEF.

Foster, Roy. "Downhill-billy." *Times Literary Supplement,* Apr. 25, 1975: 445.

Franks, Travis. "'Talkin about Lester': Community, Culpability, and Narrative Suppression in *Child of God*." *Mississippi Quarterly* 76 (Winter 2014): 75–97.

Frazer, James. *The Golden Bough: A Study in Magic and Religion*. 1 vol. abridged ed. New York: Macmillan, 1951. (Original work published 1922)

Freud, Sigmund. *The Ego and the Id and Other Works. The Standard Edition of the Complete*

*Works of Sigmund Freud,* Vol. 19, edited by James Strachey. London: Hogarth, 1949. (Original work published 1923)

Freund, Gerald. Letter to Albert Erskine, Mar. 22, 1966; with Rockefeller Foundation "Literature Program" enclosure, Jan. 1966. Tss. Box 29, folder 6, AEF.

———. Letter to Albert Erskine, July 5, 1966; with "Rockefeller Foundation Proposed Grantees 1966-1967 Literature Program" enclosure. Ts. Box 29, folder 6, AEF.

———. Letter to Cormac McCarthy, June 2, 1966. Ts. Box 29, folder 6, AEF; *The Rockefeller Foundation: A Digital History.* Web. Accessed Dec. 14, 2018.

———. Letter to Cormac McCarthy, Sept. 17, 1968. Ts. *The Rockefeller Foundation: A Digital History.* Web. Accessed Dec. 14, 2018.

———. Letter to potential Rockefeller Advisory Committee, [1967]. Ts. Box 8, Gerald Freund folder. Robert Coles Papers. Michigan State University.

———. Letter to Robert Coles, Nov. 27, 1968. Ts. Box 3, folder 151, Robert Coles Papers, 1954–1999. University of North Carolina.

———. *Narcissism and Philanthropy: Ideas and Talent Denied.* New York: Viking, 1996.

Gallagher, John. Letter to Albert Erskine, Dec. 14, 1971. Ts. Box 29, folder 2, AEF.

———. Letter to Suzanne Beves, Mar. 1, 1972. Ts. Box 29, folder 2, AEF.

Gardner, Howard. *Creating Minds: An Anatomy of Creativity Seen Through the Lives of Freud, Einstein, Picasso, Stravinsky, Eliot, Graham, and Gandhi.* New York: Basic Books, 1993.

Gardner, John. *Grendel.* New York: Vintage, 1989. (Original work published 1971)

Gass, William. *Fiction and the Figures of Life.* New York: Knopf, 1971.

Gervasi, Tom. Letter to Albert Erskine, Jan. 6, 1965. Ts. Box 29, folder 5, AEF.

———. Memo to Jean Ennis, Albert Erskine, et al., Mar. 22, 1965. Ts. Box 29, folder 5, AEF.

Ghiberti, Lorenzo. *The Sacrifice of Isaac.* Bronze door panel. 1401–02. The Baptistery, Florence, Italy.

Gibson, Mike. "Knoxville Gave Cormac McCarthy the Raw Material of His Art. And He Gave It Back." In *Sacred Violence,* 2d ed., vol. 1, edited by Wade Hall and Rick Wallach, 23–34. El Paso: Texas Western Press, 2002.

"A Gift Bag of Favorites." *San Francisco Examiner,* Dec. 5, 1965: Book Week sec.: 12.

Givner, Joan. *Katherine Anne Porter: A Life.* Rev. ed. Athens: University of Georgia Press, 1991. (Original work published 1982)

Gogol, Nikolai. "Memoirs of a Madman." Translated by Claud Field. New York: Frederick A. Stokes, n.d.

Goldstein, H. Form memo to Suzanne Beves, with information added by Beves, May 5 and May 9, 1969. Ts. Box 29, folder 6, AEF.

Gough, Paddy. "Darkness Inside as Well." *Greensboro News* [NC], Nov. 10, 1968. Newspaper clipping. Box 29, folder 8, AEF.

Goya, Francisco. *Saturn Devouring His Son. c.* 1819–23. Oil mural transferred to canvas. Museo Nacionel del Prado, Madrid.

Greenblatt, Stephen. *Will in the World: How Shakespeare Became Shakespeare.* New York: W. W. Norton, 2005.

Grimshaw, James A. "Robert Penn Warren and Albert Russel [*sic*] Erskine, Jr.: A Sixty-Year Friendship." *South Carolina Review* 39, no. 2 (2007): 110–28.

Groffsky, Maxine. Note to Larry Bensky, [May 1962]. Ms. Box 29, folder 3, AEF.

Grumbach, Doris. "Practitioner of Ghastliness." *New Republic* 170 (Feb. 9, 1974): 26–28.

Guy Davenport Papers. MS-4979. Harry Ransom Center, University of Texas, Austin.

Gwynn, Frederick L. and Joseph L. Blotner, eds. *Faulkner in the University: Class Conferences at the University of Virginia, 1957–1958.* Charlottesville: University of Virginia Press, 1959.

H., B. H. "Misery in the Hills with 'Child of God.'" *Anniston (AL) Star*, Jan. 27, 1974: 2D.

Hall, Wade, and Rick Wallach, eds. 1995. *Sacred Violence.* 2nd ed., 2 vols. El Paso: Texas Western Press, 2002.

Hardy, Tomas. "In Tenebris." In *The Complete Poems of Thomas Hardy*, edited by James Gibson, 167–69. New York: Macmillan, 1976.

Hare, Carolyn. Conversations with the author, October 2019.

Hawthorne, Nathaniel. "Ethan Brand: A Chapter from an Abortive Romance." In *The Complete Novels and Selected Tales of Nathaniel Hawthorne*, edited by Norman Holmes Pearson, 1184–96. New York: Modern Library, 1937.

Hayes, John P. *James A. Michener: A Biography.* Indianapolis: Bobbs-Merrill, 1984.

Hazelman, Mary Frances. "McCarthy's Mountain Tale about the Passage of Time." *Greensboro Daily News* [NC], May 16, 1965. Newspaper clipping. Box 29, folder 7, AEF.

Hemingway, Ernest. "Bimini." Excerpt from *Islands in the Stream. Esquire* 74 (Oct. 1, 1970): 122–37 +.

———. *The Sun Also Rises.* New York: Scribner, 1926.

Herrigel, Eugen. *Zen in the Art of Archery.* New York: Vintage, 1971. (Original work published 1948)

Hersey, John. Letter to Gerald Freund, Apr. 7, 1966. Ts. *The Rockefeller Foundation: A Digital History.* Web. Accessed Dec. 14, 2020.

Hicks, Granville. "Six Firsts for Summer." *Saturday Review* 48 (June 12, 1965): 35–36.

———. "Literary Horizons." *Saturday Review* 51 (Dec. 21, 1968): 22.

Hoagland, Edward. *The Courage of Turtles.* New York: Random House, 1970.

———. *Notes from the Century Before.* New York: Random House, 1969.

Hollenbeck, Ralph. Review of *Child of God. Parade of Books,* Jan. 6, 1974: 2–3.

Huxtable, Ada Louise. "1978–1987: Holding the High Ground." In *A Century of Arts and Letters: The History of the National Institute of Arts and Letters and the American Academy of Arts and Letters as Told, Decade by Decade, by Eleven Members,* edited by John Updike, 238–63. New York: Columbia University Press, 1998.

Jackson, Dot. "Cast into 'Outer Dark': Woman, Incestuous Brother Reap Horror's Harvest." *Charlotte Observer* [NC], Oct. 13, 1968: 6G.

Jackson, Katherine Gauss. "Books in Brief." *Harper's* 231 (July 1965): 112.

J[ellinek], R[oger]. "Ideas for Possible Titles for Cormac McCarthy Novel." Aug. 7, 1964. Ts. Box 29, folder 4, AEF.

———. Memo to A[lbert] E[rskine], Nov. 14, 1963. Ts. Box 29, folder 3, AEF.

Jordan, Richard. "'Just Write' Says Successful Author." *Daily Beacon* [University of Tennessee] Jan. 28, 1969: 6.

Josyph, Peter. "Damn Proud We Did This: A Conversation with Larry Bensky." Unpublished interview. New York City, June 30, 2015.

———. Email to the author, Jan. 4, 2017.

Joyce, James. *Ulysses.* New York: Modern Library, 1934.

Jung, C. G. *Memories, Dreams, Reflections.* Recorded and edited by Aniela Jaffé. Translated by Richard and Clara Winston. Revised ed. New York: Vintage, 1965.

Kaminsky, Howard. Memo to Albert Erskine, Aug. 22, 1968. Ts. Box 29, folder 2, AEF.

———. Memo to Albert Erskine, Oct. 16, 1968. Box 29, folder 2, AEF.

Keach, Stacy. *All in All: An Actor's Life on and off the Stage.* Guilford, CT: Lyons Press, 2013.

Kidwell, Bill. Conversation with Edwin T. Arnold and Dianne C. Luce, Aug. 5, 2000. Maryville, TN.

Kiefer, Christian. "Striking the Fire of Commerce: How Big Money, the Trade Paperback, and Jay McInerny Taught Us to Love *Blood Meridian*." In *They Rode On:* Blood Meridian *and the Tragedy of the American West*, edited by Rick Wallach, 11–24. Casebook Studies in Cormac McCarthy, vol. 2. [Miami]: Cormac McCarthy Society, nd.

King, Daniel Robert. *Cormac McCarthy's Literary Evolution: Editors, Agents, and the Crafting of a Prolific American Author.* Knoxville: University of Tennessee Press, 2016.

"Knox Author Going to Europe." *News-Sentinel* [Knoxville], May 19, 1965: D7.

Krafft-Ebing, Richard von. *Psychopathia Sexualis: A Medico-Forensic Study*, translated by Harry E. Wedeck. New York: Putnam, 1965. (Original work published 1886)

Krantz, Bertha. List of compound and hyphenated words in *The Orchard Keeper*, with holograph notes by Cormac McCarthy, [May 1964]. Ms. Box 29, folder 3, AEF.

Kressing, Harry. *The Cook*. Richmond, VA.: Valancourt Press, 1965.

———. *Married Lives*. London: Faber and Faber, 1974.

Kreyling, Michael. *Author and Agent: Eudora Welty and Diarmuid Russell.* New York: Farrar, Straus, and Giroux, 1991.

Kushner, David. "Cormac McCarthy's Apocalypse." *Rolling Stone*, Dec. 27–Jan. 10, 2008, 43, 46, 48, 52–53.

Laing, R. D., and D. G. Cooper. 1964. *Reason and Violence: A Decade of Sartre's Philosophy, 1950–1960.* New York: Pantheon, 1971.

Lambert, Bruce. "Albert R. Erskine, 81, an Editor for Faulkner and Other Authors." *New York Times*, Feb. 5, 1993. A18.

Lane, Sharon. Letter to J. Howard Woolmer. July 25, 1983. Ts. Box 1, folder 5, Woolmer Collection of Cormac McCarthy.

Lanning, George. Letter to Mr. Erskine, Oct. 22, 1964. Ts. Box 29, folder 4, AEF.

———. Postcard to Miss Baskin, Oct. 3, 1964. Ts. Box 29, folder 4, AEF.

Lask, Thomas. "Southern Gothic." *New York Times* 118 (Sept. 23, 1968): 33. "Lee McCarthy." Obituary. *Bakersfield Californian,* Mar. 29, 2009. Web. Accessed Dec. 16, 2020.

Leiter, Robert. Rev. of *Child of God. Commonweal* 100 (Mar. 29, 1974): 90–92.

Lewis, R. W. B. "1898–1907: The Founders' Story." In *A Century of Arts and Letters: The History of the National Institute of Arts and Letters and the American Academy of Arts and Letters as Told, Decade by Decade by Eleven Members,* edited by John Updike, 1–27. New York: Columbia University Press, 1998.

Liebermann, Dick. Memo to Albert Erskine, Apr. 1, 1969. Ts. AEF.

Lilley, Sasha. "A Tribute to Larry Bensky: Award-Winning Broadcaster Larry Bensky Retires." KFPA.org. Pacifica Foundation, 2007. Web. Accessed July 28, 2011

Lish, Gordon. Letter to Albert Erskine, Oct. 26, 1970. Ts. Box 29, folder 2, AEF.

———. Letter to Albert Erskine, Nov. 20, 1970. Ts. Box 29, folder 2, AEF.

———. Letter to Suzanne Beves, Aug. 5, 1971. Ts. Box 29, folder 10, AEF.

———. Note to Albert Erskine, Oct. 26, 1970. Ts. Box 29, folder 2, AEF.

Longley, John. Letter to Albert Erskine, Feb. 17, 1965. Ts. Box 29, folder 5, AEF.

Lowry, Malcolm. *Under the Volcano.* New York: Reynal and Hitchcock, 1947.

Lowry, Tom. Memo to Don Pace, Jan. 31, 1972. Ms. Box 29, folder 2, AEF.

Luce, Dianne C. "The Archives and the Tennessee Years, I: *The Orchard Keeper* and *Outer Dark.* In *Cormac McCarthy in Context*, edited by Stephen Frye, 273–80. Cambridge: Cambridge University Press, 2020.

———. "The Archives and the Tennessee Years, II: *Child of God*, *The Gardener's Son*, and *Suttree*. In *Cormac McCarthy in Context*, edited by Stephen Frye, 281–88. Cambridge: Cambridge University Press, 2020.

———. "Ballard Rising in *Outer Dark*: The Genesis and Early Composition of *Child of God*." *The Cormac McCarthy Journal* 17, no. 2 (Fall 2019): 87–115.

———. "Cormac McCarthy," Feb. 1980. Photocopied ts., with penciled notes by Cormac McCarthy. Postmarked Lexington, KY, Feb. 14, 1980.

———. "Cormac McCarthy and Albert Erskine: The Evolution of a Working Relationship." *Resources for American Literary Study* 35 (2012): 303–38.

———. "Cormac McCarthy and Leslie Garrett: A Literary Friendship." In *Cormac McCarthy*, edited by Christine Chollier and Edwin T. Arnold. Special Issue of *Profils Américains* 17 (2004): 27–59.

———. "Cormac McCarthy in High School: 1951." *Cormac McCarthy Journal* 7, no. 1 (Fall 2009): 1–6.

———. "Creativity, Madness, and 'the light that dances deep in Pontchartrain': Glimpses of 'The Passenger' from McCarthy's 1980 Correspondence." *Cormac McCarthy Journal* 18, no. 2 (2020): 85–99.

———. "Landscapes as Narrative Commentary in *Blood Meridian or the Evening Redness in the West*." *European Journal of American Studies* 12, no. 3, (2017): 1–25. (Special Cormac McCarthy issue, edited by James Dorson and Julius Greve).

———. "Projecting Interiority: Psychogenesis and the Composition of *Outer Dark*." *Cormac McCarthy Journal* 16, no. 1 (Spring 2018): 2–37.

———. *Reading the World: Cormac McCarthy's Tennessee Period*. Columbia: University of South Carolina Press, 2009.

———. "Robert Coles and Cormac McCarthy: A Case Study in Literary Patronage." *Resources for American Literary Study* 41, no. 2 (Fall 2019): 221–61.

———. "Tall Tales and Raw Realities: The Late-Stage Deletions from McCarthy's *Suttree*." *Resources for American Literary Study* 38 (2015): 213–56.

———. "'They aint the thing': Artifact and Hallucinated Recollection in Cormac McCarthy's Early Frame-Works." In *Sacred Violence*. 2nd ed. Vol. I, edited by Wade Hall and Rick Wallach, 21–36. El Paso: Texas Western Press, 2002.

———. "White Caps, Moral Judgment, and Law in *Child of God*, or, The 'Wrong Blood' in Community History." In *Cormac McCarthy: Uncharted Territories,* edited by Christine Chollier, 43–59. Reims, France: Presses Universitaires de Reims, 2003.

Lyndhurst Foundation Records, 1970–2013. #04723. Southern Historical Collection, The Louis Round Wilson Special Collections Library, University of North Carolina at Chapel Hill.

Lytle, Andrew. Letter to Albert Erskine, Nov. 2, 1964. Ts. Box 29, folder 4, AEF.

M [*sic*], Peter. "Hidden in Plain Sight: Media Workers for Social Change, Chapter 7." *Indymedia*. San Francisco Bay Area Independent Media Center. Oct. 17, 2010. Web. Accessed July 28, 2011.

Macauley, Robie. Letter to Albert Erskine, May 27, 1971. Ts. Box 29, folder 2, AEF.

Madden, David. Review of *The Orchard Keeper*. In *Masterplots 1966 Annual,* edited by Frank N. Magill, 218–21. New York: Salem Press, 1967.

Maddocks, Melvin. "A Few Fine Fish That Almost Got Away." *Life Magazine,* Dec. 20, 1968: 6.

Marius, Richard. "*Suttree* as Window Into the Soul of Cormac McCarthy." In *Sacred*

*Violence*. 2nd ed. Vol. I, edited by Wade Hall and Rick Wallach, 113–29. El Paso: Texas Western Press, 2002.

Matthews, Jack. Review of *Outer Dark*. In *Masterplots 1969 Annual: Magill's Literary Annual*, edited by Frank N. Magill, 258–60. New York: Salem Press, 1970.

Matthiessen, F. O., ed. *The Oxford Book of American Verse*. Oxford: Oxford University Press, 1950.

May, Stephen J. *Michener: A Writer's Journey*. Norman: University of Oklahoma Press, 2005.

McCarthy, Anne De Lisle. Letter to Albert Erskine, Sept. 18, 1969. Ts. Box 29, folder 6, AEF.

"McCarthy, Cormac." *Who's Who in America*, vol. 35 (1968  69): 1447. Chicago: Marquis.

McCarthy, Cormac. *All the Pretty Horses*. New York: Vintage International, 1993. (Original work published 1992)

———. "All the Pretty Horses." Excerpt from *All the Pretty Horses*. *Esquire*, Mar. 1992: 121–36.

———. Application for Guggenheim fellowship in creative arts, [Sept. 23, 1968]. Ts. Box 29, folder 2, AEF.

———. Application for Rockefeller grant in Imaginative Writing and Literary Scholarship, March 15, 1966. Ts. Box 29, folder 6, AEF.

———. *Blood Meridian or The Evening Redness in the West*. New York: Random House, 1985.

———. *Blood Meridian*: Reading notes. Photocopied ms. of unpaginated spiral notebook leaves. Box 35, folder 5, CMP.

———. "Bounty." Excerpt from *The Orchard Keeper*. *Yale Review* 54 (March 1965): [368]-74.

———. Cartoon self-portrait. *Self-Portrait: Book People Picture Themselves: From the Collection of Burt Britton*. Comp. Burt Britton, 33. New York: Random House, 1976.

———. *Child of God*. New York: Vintage International, 1993. (Original work published 1973)

———. *Child of God*: "Middle Draft" in marked file folder, [1970–71]. Ts. Box 16, folder 2, CMP.

———. *Child of God*: "Late Draft." [1972]. Photocopied ts. with editorial notes in McCarthy's hand. Box 16, folder 5, CMP.

———. *Child of God*: Revision notes keyed to the "Late Draft": "LaFayette." [1972–1973]. Ms. Box 16, folder 1, CMP.

———. *Child of God*: Revision notes keyed to the "Late Draft": List B. [1973]. Ms. Box 16, folder 1, CMP.

———. *Child of God*: "Setting copy." 1973. Ts. Box 16, folder 6, CMP.

———. *Cities of the Plain*. New York: Vintage International, 1999. (Original work published 1998)

———. *The Crossing*. New York: Vintage International, 1995. (Original work published 1994)

———. "The Dark Waters." Excerpt from *The Orchard Keeper*. *Sewanee Review* 73, no. 2 (April–June 1965): [210]–16.

———. Draft of letter to Albert Erskine, [early June 1964]. Ts. Box 1, folder 1, CMP.

——— (C. J. McCarthy). "A Drowning Incident." *The Phoenix* [University of Tennessee *Orange and White* Literary Supplement], Mar. 1960: 3–4.

———. *The Gardener's Son*. Hopewell, NJ: Ecco, 1996.

———. *The Gardener's Son*: Research materials, [1975]. Photocopies. Box 18, folder 2, CMP.

———. "Harrogate and the Flittermouses," [1970]. Excerpt from "Middle Draft" of *Suttree*. Ts. Box 30, folder 1, AEF.

———. Interview with Oprah Winfrey. "The Exclusive Interview Begins." *Oprah's Book Club*. July 2007. Web. Accessed July 17, 2007.

———. "The Kekulé Problem." *Nautilus* 47: Consciousness. Apr. 20, 2017. Web. Accessed Dec. 19, 2017.

———. Letter to Albert Erskine, [late Dec. 1963]. Ts. Box 29, folder 3, AEF.

———. Letter to Albert Erskine, received Jan. 13, 1964, noted on verso. Ts. Box 29, folder 3, AEF.

———. Letter to Albert Erskine, [late Jan./early Feb. 1964]. Ts. Box 29, folder 3 AEF.

———. Letter to Albert Erskine, received Mar. 6, 1964. Ts. Box 29, folder 3, AEF.

———. Letter to Albert Erskine, received Mar. 31, 1964. Ts. Box 29, folder 3, AEF.

———. Letter to Albert Erskine, received Apr. 9, 1964. Ts. Box 29, folder 3, AEF.

———. Letter to Albert Erskine, received mid–late Apr. 1964, on verso. Ts. Box 29, folder 3, AEF.

———. Letter to Albert Erskine, received May 1964. Ts. Box 29, folder 3, AEF.

———. Letter to Albert Erskine, received June 8, 1964. Ts. Box 29, folder 3, AEF.

———. Letter to Albert Erskine, received June 26, 1964. Ts. Box 29, folder 3, AEF.

———. Letter to Albert Erskine, received July 7, 1964. Ts. Box 29, folder 4, AEF.

———. Letter to Albert Erskine, received Sept. 2, 1964. Ts. Box 29, folder 4, AEF.

———. Letter to Albert Erskine, received Sept. 9, 1964. Ts. Box 29, folder 4, AEF

———. Letter to Albert Erskine, postmarked Atlanta, received Oct. 15, 1964. Ts. Box 29, folder 4, AEF.

———. Letter to Albert Erskine, received Nov. 5, 1964. Ts. Box 29, folder 4, AEF.

———. Letter to Albert Erskine, received Nov. 18, 1964. Ts. Box 29, folder 4, AEF.

———. Letter to Albert Erskine, received Dec. 4, 1964. Ts. Box 29, folder 4, AEF.

———. Letter to Albert Erskine, received Dec. 23, 1964. Ts. Box 29, folder 4, AEF.

———. Letter to Albert Erskine, postmarked Jan. 29, 1965. Ts. Box 29, folder 5, AEF.

———. Letter to Albert Erskine, [late March 1965]. Ts. Box 29, folder 5, AEF.

———. Letter to Albert Erskine, received May 10, 1965. Ts. Box 29, folder 5, AEF.

———. Letter to Albert Erskine, received May 20, 1965. Ts. Box 29, folder 5, AEF.

———. Letter to Albert Erskine, received June 4, 1965. Ts. Box 29, folder 5, AEF.

———. Letter to Albert Erskine, received Aug. 11, 1965. Ts. Box 29, folder 5, AEF.

———. Letter to Albert Erskine, postmarked Paris, Nov. 12, 1965; received Nov. 15, 1965. Ts. Box 29, folder 5, AEF.

———. Letter to Albert Erskine, postmarked Jan. 27, 1966, received Jan. 31, 1966. Ts. Box 29, folder 6, AEF.

———. Letter to Albert Erskine, received Feb. 25, 1966, dated on verso. Ts. Box 29, folder 6, AEF.

———. Letter to Albert Erskine, postmarked Mar. 15, 1966. Box 29, folder 6, AEF.

———. Letter to Albert Erskine, received May 10, 1966. Ts. Box 29, folder 6, AEF.

———. Letter to Albert Erskine, received June 15, 1966. Ts. Box 29, folder 6, AEF.

———. Letter to Albert Erskine, received Aug. 12, 1966. Ts. Box 29, folder 6, AEF.

———. Letter to Albert Erskine, received Aug. 29, 1966. Ts. Box 29, folder 6, AEF.

———. Letter to Albert Erskine, received Jan. 8, 1967. Ts. Box 29, folder 2, AEF.

———. Letter to Albert Erskine, received Jan. 23, 1967. Ts. Box 29, folder 8, AEF.

———. Letter to Albert Erskine, received Apr. 10, 1967. Ts. Box 29, folder 8, AEF.

———. Letter to Albert Erskine, received Aug. 7, 1967. Ts. Box 29, folder 2, AEF.

———. Letter to Albert Erskine, received Oct. 11, 1967. Ts. Box 29, folder 2, AEF.

———. Letter to Albert Erskine, with revision list, received Dec. 22, 1967. Tss. Box 29, folder 8, AEF.

———. Letter to Albert Erskine, received Feb. 15, 1968. Ts. Box 29, folder 8, AEF.

———. Letter to Albert Erskine, received Mar. 11, 1968. Ts. Box 29, folder 8, AEF.

———. Letter to Albert Erskine, [May 1968]. Ts. Box 29, folder 8, AEF.

———. Letter to Albert Erskine, received Oct. 11, 1968. Ts. Box 29, folder 2, AEF.

———. Letter to Albert Erskine, received Nov. 8, 1968. Ts. Box 29, folder 2, AEF.

———. Letter to Albert Erskine, received Jan. 9, 1969. Ts. Box 29, folder 2, AEF.

———. Letter to Albert Erskine, received Aug. 18, 1969. Ts. Box 29, folder 6, AEF.

———. Letter to Albert Erskine, received Oct. 8, 1970. Ts. Box 29, folder 2 AEF.

———. Letter to Albert Erskine, received Feb. 4, 1971. Ts. Box 29, folder 2, AEF.

———. Letter to Albert Erskine, received Mar. 3, 1971. Ts. Box 29, folder 2, AEF.

———. Letter to Albert Erskine, received Mar. 17, 1971. Ts. Box 29, folder 2, AEF.

———. Letter to Albert Erskine, received May 20, 1971. Ts. Box 29, folder 2, AEF.

———. Letter to Albert Erskine, received Sept. 24, 1971. Ts. Box 29, folder 2, AEF.

———. Letter to Albert Erskine, received Dec. 1, 1971. Ts. Box 29, folder 2, AEF.

———. Letter to Albert Erskine, received Apr. 17, 1972. Ts. Box 29, folder 2, AEF.

———. Letter to Albert Erskine, received Feb. 22, 1973. Ms. Box 29, folder 8, AEF.

———. Letter to Albert Erskine, [early Mar. 1974]. Ts. Box 1156, Random House Records, 1925–1999.

———. Letter to Albert Erskine, received c. Mar. 1984. Ms. Box 29, folder 8, AEF.

———. Letter to Bill Kidwell, postmarked Nov. 6, 1968. Heritage Auctions. Apr. 10, 2013. Accessed May 23, 2016. Web.

———. Letter to Caroline [Harkleroad], [Dec. 1973]. Ts. Box 1156, Random House Records,1925–1999.

———. Letter to Cheryl Mercer, [1979]. Ms. Box 1611, Random House Records, 1925–1999.

———. Letter to Deaderick Montague, [late Aug. 1980]. Ms. Box 15, Cormac McCarthy folder, Lyndhurst Foundation Records, 1970–2013.

———. Letter to Deaderick Montague, received Oct. 6, 1986. Ms. Box 15, Cormac McCarthy folder, Lyndhurst Foundation Records, 1970–2013.

———. Letter to Ecco Press, [April 7, 1982]. Ms. Box 32, folder 12, Ecco Press Records.

———. Letter to Fiction Editor, received May 3 [1962]. Ts. Box 29, folder 3, AEF.

———. Letter to George Spencer, postmarked Jan. 5, 1988. Ms. "36187 Cormac McCarthy Autograph Letter Signed. El Pa." *Live Auctioneers*. Web. Accessed Jan. 28, 2021.

———. Letter to Gerald Freund, Sept. 23, 1968. Ts. *The Rockefeller Foundation: A Digital History*. Web. Accessed Jan. 20, 2021.

———. Letter to Howard Woolmer, postmarked June 28, 1973. Ts. Box 1, folder 1, Woolmer Collection of Cormac McCarthy.

———. Letter to John Fergus Ryan, received Oct. 30, 1981. Ms. Box 1, folder 38, Cormac McCarthy Correspondence [with John Fergus Ryan], 1976–1985. MS # 3762. Betsey B. Creekmore Special Collections and University Archives, University of Tennessee Knoxville.

———. Letter to Lawrence M. Bensky, July 12, 1962. Ts. Box 29, folder 3, AEF.

———. Letter to Lawrence M. Bensky, [late Oct.–Nov. 1962]. Ts. Box 29, folder 4, AEF.

———. Letter to Lawrence M. Bensky, [early Dec. 1962]. Ts. Box 29, folder 3, AEF.

———. Letter to Lawrence M. Bensky, [Feb. 1963]. Ts. Box 29, folder 3, AEF.

———. Letter to Lawrence M. Bensky, May 16, 1963. Ts. Box 29, folder 3, AEF.

———. Letter to Lawrence M. Bensky, [Aug./Sept. 1963]. Ts. Box 29, folder 3, AEF.

———. Letter to Lawrence M. Bensky, [Sept. 1963]. Ts. Box 29, folder 3, AEF.

———. Letter to Megan Ratner, [late April 1982]. Ms. Box 32, folder 12, Ecco Press Records.

———. Letter to Robert Coles, [Feb.–Mar. 1979]. Ms. Box 5, folder 288, Robert Coles Papers, University of North Carolina.

———. Letter to Robert Coles, [early Jan. 1980]. Ts. Box 5, folder 288, Robert Coles Papers, University of North Carolina.

———. Letter to Robert Coles, [late Feb. 1980]. Ms. Box 5, folder 288, Robert Coles Papers, University of North Carolina.

———. Letter to Suzanne [Beves], received Dec. 7, 1968. Ts. Box 29, folder 8, AEF.

———. Letter to Suzanne Beves, received Nov. 29, 1971. Ts. Box 29, folder 10, AEF.

———. *No Country for Old Men*. New York: Vintage International, 2006. (Original work published 2005)

———. *The Orchard Keeper*. New York: Random House, 1965; New York: Vintage International, 1993.

———. *The Orchard Keeper*. Corrected final proof pages. Nov. 6, 1964. Box 7, CMP.

———. *The Orchard Keeper:* "Editorial Copy." 1963–64. Photocopied ts., with editorial comments and McCarthy's ms. revisions. Box 2, folder 2. CMP.

———. *The Orchard Keeper*: "Final Draft" [1962–63]. Onion skin carbon copy of the ts., with new pages and holograph revisions. Box 1, folder 5, CMP.

———. *The Orchard Keeper*: Corrected galley proofs, Sept. 23, 1964. Box 7, CMP.

———. *The Orchard Keeper*: Deleted leaves. Box 1, folder 2, CMP.

———. *The Orchard Keeper*: Galley proofs for "Toilers at the Kiln," [Aug. 11, 1964]. Box 4, CMP.

———. *The Orchard Keeper*: "Late Draft," [1961–62]. Ts. Box 1, folder 3, CMP

———. *The Orchard Keeper*: "<u>Red Mtn.</u>" Box for "Late Draft." Box 1, item 4, CMP.

———. *The Orchard Keeper*: Revision notes, [1963–64]. Box 1, folder 2, CMP.

———. *Outer Dark*. 1968. New York, Vintage International, 1993.

———. *Outer Dark*: "Early Draft [A]." 1966. Ts. Box 9, folder 1, CMP.

———. *Outer Dark*: "Early Draft [B]." 1963–65. Photocopy ts. Box 9, folder 2, CMP.

———. *Outer Dark:* "Final Draft." 1967. Ts. Box 9, folder 3, CMP.

———. *Outer Dark*: "Late Draft." 1967. Carbon copy of the "Final Draft" ts., with editorial comments and holograph revisions. Box 10, folder 2, CMP.

———. *Outer Dark:* "Middle Draft." [c. 1966–1967]. Ts. Box 8, folder 3, CMP.

———. *Outer Dark*: Revision list, Dec. 22, 1967. Ts. Box 29, folder 8, AEF.

———. *Outer Dark:* "Rough/ First Draft [A]." Dec. 16, 1962– c. Dec. 14, 1963. Ts. Box 8, folder 1, CMP.

———. *Outer Dark:* "Rough/ First Draft [B]." Dec. 16, 1962– c. Dec. 14, 1963. Ts. Box 8, folder 2, CMP.

———. *Outer Dark:* "Setting Copy" [1967–68]. Ts. Box 11, folder 1, CMP.

———. Postcard consent form to Albert Erskine, postmarked Nov. 2, 1968. Ms. signature. Box 29, folder 2, AEF.

———. *The Road*. New York: Vintage International, 2006.

———. *The Stonemason*. New York: Vintage International, 1995. (Original work published 1994)

———. *The Sunset Limited: A Novel in Dramatic Form*. New York: Vintage International, 2006.

———. *Suttree*. New York: Random House, 1979; Vintage Contemporaries, 1986; Vintage International, 1992.

———. *Suttree*: Excerpts from the "Middle Draft." 1970–71. Tss. Box 30, folder 1, AEF.

———. *Suttree*: "Final Draft," 1977. Ts. Boxes 23–24, CMP.

———. *Suttree*: "Middle Draft." [1970–74]. Photocopied ts. Box 22, CMP.

——— (Charlie McCarthy). "Two Hour Scholar Loses His Dollar." Clipping from *Gold and Blue* [Catholic High School student newspaper]. Sept. 29, 1950: np. Catholic High School archives, Knoxville.

——— (C. J. McCarthy). "Wake for Susan." *The Phoenix* [University of Tennessee *Orange and White* Literary Supplement] Oct. 1959: 3–6.

———. "The Wolf Trapper." Excerpt from *The Crossing. Esquire*, July 1993: 95–104.

"McCarthy, Lee Holleman." *Who's Who in America* 56 (2002): 3459. Chicago: Marquis.

McCarthy, Lee. "About the Author." In *Desire's Door*. Brownsville, OR: Story Line Press, 1991.

———. "About the Poet." In *Good Girl*. Ashland, OR: Story Line Press, 2002.

———. *Desire's Door*. Brownsville, OR: Story Line Press, 1991.

———. "It's in the Cards." In *Desire's Door*, 22–23. Brownsville, OR: Story Line Press, 1991.

———. "Mother Outlaw." In *Combing Hair with a Seashell*, 28–29. Memphis: Ion, 1992.

———. "Only Child." In *Desire's Door*, 13–14. Brownsville, OR: Story Line Press, 1991.

———. "Stories." In *Desire's Door*, 80–83. Brownsville, OR: Story Line Press, 1991. "McCarthy Wins Award for Novel." *News-Sentinel* [Knoxville], Mar. 12, 1966: 12.

McCooe, Barbara. Interview with Bryan Giemza and Dianne Luce. Film. Ridgewood, NJ, Aug. 4, 2021.

McDowell, David. Letter to Albert Erskine, [c. Sept. 10, 1964]. Box 29, folder 4, AEF.

McKinney, Ruth Ann. "McCarthy Measures Up to First Novel." *Fort Worth Star–Telegram*, Sept. 29, 1968: 7F.

Melville, Herman. *Moby-Dick*. New York: Harper, 1852.

Messenger, Robert. "Unreliable Memories: Why the McCarthy Olivetti Lettera 32 Story Is Full of Holes." oz. Typewriter. Blog. Feb. 24, 2015. Web. Accessed Jan. 29, 2021.

Michener, James. Letter to Albert Erskine, Feb. 12, 1965. Ts. Box 29, folder 5, AEF.

———. *Sayonara*. New York: Random House, 1954.

Millgate, Michael. Letter to Albert Erskine, Feb. 15, 1965. Ts. Box 29, folder 5, AEF.

———. *Thomas Hardy: His Career as a Novelist*. New York: Random House, 1971.

"Miss McCarthy Marries Mr. James A. Jacques III." *Knoxville Journal*, June 10, 1963: 10.

Montague, Deaderick. Interview with Dianne Luce. Film. Chattanooga, TN, Mar. 6, 2020.

Montesi, Albert J. *Historical Survey of* The Southern Review*, 1935–1942: Radical Conservatism*. Lewiston, NY: Edwin Mellen, 1999.

Moody, Minnie Hite. "Novels of the South Have a Common Flaw." *Dispatch* [Columbus, OH], Nov. 3, 1968. Newspaper clipping. Box 29, folder 8, AEF.

Morgan, Kay. "Tennessean's Novel Explores Rural Morals." *Memphis Press–Scimitar*, Oct. 25, 1968. Newspaper clipping. Box 29, folder 8, AEF.

Morgan, Wesley. "Cormac McCarthy and *The Yearling*." *Cormac McCarthy Journal* 17, no. 1 (2019): 70–72.

———. Email to the author. Oct. 17, 2017.

———. Email to the author. Apr. 13, 2018.

———. Email to the author. Apr. 25, 2018.

Morris, Alice S. Letter to Natalie Bates, Dec. 15, 1964. Ts. Box 29, folder 4, AEF.

Morris, Betsy. "Also Have a Great 'Motoring Act.'" *News–Sentinel* [Knoxville], Feb. 29, 1976: F12.

Morris, Willie. Letter to Albert Erskine, Sept. 29, 1970. Ts. Box 29, folder 2, AEF.

———. Letter to Albert Erskine, Feb. 22, 1971. Ts. Box 29, folder 2, AEF.

Morrow, Sara Sprott. Review of *The Orchard Keeper*. *Tennesseean* [Nashville], May 16, 1965: 12D.

Murray, James G. Review of *The Orchard Keeper*. *America* 112 (June 12, 1965): 866.

Newton, Virgil Miller Jr. "From English Tycoons to Arsonist Roaches." *Tampa Tribune,* Jan. 20, 1974: 5C.

Norris, Robert. "Piece of Art in Danger Downtown: Mosaic of Famous Author, His Friend in Way of Road." *Daily Times* [Maryville, TN], July 16, 2000: 1A, 6A.

O'Leary, Theodore M. "In Retrospect, a Few Books Begin to Loom Large in Importance." *Kansas City (MO) Star,* Dec. 5, 1965: 4H, 6H.

———. "Once in Long, Long While There Comes Such a Novel." *Kansas City (MO) Star,* May 9, 1965. Newspaper clipping. Box 29, folder 7, AEF.

Ortega y Gasset, José. "Notes on the Novel." In *The Dehumanization of Art*, translated by Helene Weyl, 55–103. Princeton: Princeton University Press, 1968. (Original work published 1925)

Owen, Mark. "McCarthy Is One of Nation's Most Remarked Young Authors." *Maryville–Alcoa Times* [Maryville, TN], Feb. 26, 1971: 4B. Newspaper clipping. Box 29, folder 8, AEF.

Owl Books advertisement, [1971]. Unattributed clipping. Box 29, folder 2, AEF.

Palmer, John. Letter to Albert Erskine, Sept. 29, 1964. Ts. Box 29, folder 4, AEF.

———. Letter to Albert Erskine, Apr. 10, 1968. Ts. Box 29, folder 8, AEF.

Parrill, William. "McCarthy's Gift Akin to Poe's." *Tennessean* [Nashville], Jan. 27, 1974: 7F.

Pearce, Richard. "Foreword" to *The Gardener's Son*, by Cormac McCarthy, v–vi. Hopewell, NJ: Ecco, 1996.

Pearre, Howell. "About New Books: Superior Novel Should Be Prize-Bound." *Nashville Banner,* Oct. 4, 1968. Newspaper clipping. Box 29, folder 8, AEF.

Peebles, Stacey. *Cormac McCarthy and Performance: Page, Stage, Screen.* Austin: University of Texas Press, 2017.

Perkins, Bill. "Mined-out Territory." *National Observer* 13 (Jan. 12, 1974): 21.

Pickle, Betsy. "Artistic Return: Bill Kidwell Has Painted His Way around the World and Back Home Again." *News–Sentinel* [Knoxville, TN], Dec. 1, 1988: B1–2.

Plutarch. "On Superstition." *Moralia*. Translated by F. C. Babbitt. Loeb Classical Library, 1928. II. 452–95. Web. Accessed Dec. 15, 2020.

Pouder, G. H. "A Folklore Study." *Morning Sun* [Baltimore, MD], Jan. 15, 1969. Newspaper clipping. Box 29, folder 8, AEF.

Powers, James. "Book Reviews." *Hollywood Reporter,* Oct. 11, 1968. Newspaper clipping. Box 29, folder 8, AEF.

Prescott, Orville. "Still Another Disciple of William Faulkner." *New York Times,* May 12, 1965: M49.

Prescott, Peter S. "Dangerous Witness." *Newsweek* 83 (Jan. 7, 1974): 63, 67.

"Proposal for a Co-Publishing Arrangement." [1984]. Ts. with holograph notations. Box 15, Cormac McCarthy folder, Lyndhurst Foundations Records, 1970–2013.

*Psycho.* Film. Dir. Alfred Hitchcock. Paramount, 1960.

Quiller-Couch, Arthur, ed. *The Oxford Book of English Verse, 1250–1918.* New York: Oxford University Press, 1939.

Rampersad, Arnold. *Ralph Ellison: A Biography.* New York: Knopf, 2007.

Random House. "Random House Congratulates Cormac McCarthy." *New York Times Book Review,* May 9, 1965. Advertisement clipping. Box 29, folder 6, AEF.

——. *Child of God* Composition Order, Mar. 22. 1973. CMP, box 16, folder 6.

——. Contract [for *Outer Dark*], Jan. 4, 1965. Box 29, folder 2, AEF.

——. Draw Check order, Feb. 6, 1969. Box 29, folder 2, AEF.

——. Draw Check order, Apr. 16, 1970. Box 29, folder 2, AEF.

——. Reprint Rights Data Sheet, Nov. 22, 1968. Box 29, folder 8, AEF.

——. Revised Manufacturing Schedule for "Toilers at the Kiln" [*The Orchard Keeper*], Nov. 6, 1964. Box 29, folder 3, AEF.

——. Royalty check transmittal form, to Suzanne Baskin, Feb. 17, 1969. Ms. Box 29, folder 2, AEF.

——. Royalty Statement [for *The Orchard Keeper*], Fall 1966. Box 29, folder 6, AEF.

——. Publicity release, 1966. Ts. Box 29, folder 6, AEF.

Random House Records, 1925–1999. Ms # 1048. Rare Book and Manuscript Library, Columbia University, New York.

Random House Royalty Department. Memo to Suzanne Baskin, Feb. 17, 1969. Ms. Box 29, folder 2, AEF.

Ratner, Megan. Letter to Cormac McCarthy, Apr. 13, 1982. Ts. Box 32, folder 12, Ecco Press Records.

Rawlings, Marjorie Kinnan. *The Yearling.* New York: Modern Library, 1939.

Rembrandt van Rijn. *The Sacrifice of Isaac.* 1635. Oil on canvas. Hermitage Museum, St. Petersburg.

Ritalin, Thane. "A Brilliant, Vital First Novel." *Chicago Daily News,* May 15, 1965: Panorama sec. Newspaper clipping. Box 29, folder 7. AEF.

Robert Coles Papers, 1954–1999. # 04333. Louis Round Wilson Special Collections Library, University of North Carolina at Chapel Hill.

Robert Coles papers. MSS 323, Special Collections, MSU Libraries, Michigan State University, East Lansing.

Rockefeller Foundation. "Imaginative Writing and Literary Scholarship Program Grantees Literature Program." Ts. Enclosure in Freund letter to Erskine, July 5, 1966. Box 29, folder 6, AEF.

Rodin, Auguste. *Ugolino and His Sons.* c. 1881–82. Plaster; bronze casting. Musée Rodin, Paris.

Rooke, Leon. "'Author! Author!': Leon Rooke on Cormac McCarthy." Script for State of the Arts. CBC, Victoria, BC, broadcast Dec. 1, 1985. Ts. Box 28, folder 7, AEF.

——. "Rash Undertakings." In *The Brick Reader,* edited by Linda Spalding and Michael Ondaatje, 304–308. Toronto: Coach House, 1991.

Rubens, Peter Paul. *Saturn Devouring His Son.* c. 1636–38. Oil on canvas. Museo Nacionel del Prado, Madrid.

Runsdorf, Blithe. "Recognition Acceptable, Says Author McCarthy." *Lexington (KY) Herald-Leader*, Nov. 27, 1968: 5. Online, via Newspapers.com. Accessed Mar. 17, 2022.

Sage, Lorna. "The Edge of Hysteria." *Observer,* Apr. 6, 1975: 30.

Segroves, Gerald. "There's a Touch of England in the Maryville-Alcoa Ballet." *News–Sentinel* [Knoxville], Mar. 13, 1977: G1, G7.

Sepich, John. *Notes on Blood Meridian.* Rev. and expanded ed. Austin: University of Texas Press, 2008. (Original work published 1993)

Shakespeare, William. *The Complete Works of William Shakespeare*, edited by Hardin Craig. Glenview, IL: Scott, Foresman, 1961.

———. "Hamlet, Prince of Denmark." In *The Complete Works of William Shakespeare*, edited by Hardin Craig, 903–43. Glenview, IL: Scott, Foresman, 1961.

———. "Macbeth." In *The Complete Works of William Shakespeare*, edited by Hardin Craig, 1046–70. Glenview, IL: Scott, Foresman, 1961.

Shrapnel, Norman. "Echoes from the Corridors." *Guardian Weekly* (Manchester), Mar. 17, 1966: 10.

Singer, Don. Memo to Leon Peikin, Apr. 11, 1969. Ts. Box 29, folder 2, AEF.

"Solo Actor Like Piece of Mobile Sculpture." *The Times* (London), Mar. 8, 1963: 15.

*Something for Everyone.* Dir. Harold Prince. Perf. Angela Lansbury, Michael York, Anthony Higgins. Cinema Center Films. 1970.

Spearman, Walter. Review of *Outer Dark. Rocky Mount (NC) Telegram,* Dec. 1, 1968: 7D.

Styles, David. Conversation with the author. Nov. 1, 2019.

Sullivan, Walter. "'Where Have All the Flowers Gone?' Part II: The Novel in the Gnostic Twilight." *Sewanee Review* 78 (Oct. 1970): 654–64.

———. "Worlds Past and Future: A Christian and Several from the South." *Sewanee Review* 73 (Autumn 1965): 719–26.

"The Three Ravens." In *The Oxford Book of English Verse, 1250–1918*, edited by Arthur Quiller-Couch, 449–50. New York: Oxford University Press, 1939.

Tibbetts, A. M. "A Fiction Chronicle." *Southern Review* n. s. 3 (Jan. 1967): 186–96.

Titian (Tiziano Vecellio). *The Sacrifice of Isaac.* 1542–44. Oil on canvas. Santa Maria della Salute, Venice.

Trachtenberg, Stanley. "Black Humor, Pale Fiction." *Yale Review* 55 (Oct. 1965): 144–49.

Tumblin, Jim. *Bill Kidwell Fountain City Artist.* KnoxTNtoday.com. Web. Feb. 15, 2022. Accessed Feb. 21, 2022.

"The Twa Corbies." In *The Oxford Book of English Verse,* 1250–1918, edited by Arthur Quiller-Couch, 450–51. New York: Oxford University Press, 1939.

"Two from Area Get Fellowships." *News–Sentinel* [Knoxville], Apr. 4, 1969: 21.

Updike, John. "Appendix: Academy Members, Past and Present." In *A Century of Arts and Letters: The History of the National Institute of Arts and Letters and the American Academy of Arts and Letters as Told, Decade by Decade, by Eleven Members,* edited by John Updike, 293–326. New York: Columbia University Press, 1998.

———, ed. *A Century of Arts and Letters: The History of the National Institute of Arts and Letters and the American Academy of Arts and Letters as Told, Decade by Decade, by Eleven Members.* New York: Columbia University Press, 1998.

———. "Foreword." In *A Century of Arts and Letters: The History of the National Institute of Arts and Letters and the American Academy of Arts and Letters as Told, Decade by Decade, by Eleven Members,* edited by John Updike, vii–xii. New York: Columbia University Press, 1998.

———. "1938–1947: Decade of the Row." In *A Century of Arts and Letters: The History of the National Institute of Arts and Letters and the American Academy of Arts and Letters as Told, Decade by Decade, by Eleven Members,* edited by John Updike, 105–35. New York: Columbia University Press, 1998.

Van Troyen, Rombout. *King Ahaz Sacrifices His Son to Moloch.* 1626. Oil on wood.

Wagner, Phyllis Cerf, and Albert Erskine. "Editors' Note." In Bennett Cerf, *At Random: The Reminiscences of Bennett Cerf,* edited by Phyllis Cerf Wagner and Albert Erskine, ix. New York: Random House, 1977.

Wallach, Rick, ed. *Myth, Legend, Dust: Critical Responses to Cormac McCarthy.* Manchester, UK: Manchester University Press, 2000.

———. "Prefiguring Cormac McCarthy: The Early Short Stories." In *Myth, Legend, Dust: Critical Responses to Cormac McCarthy,* edited by Rick Wallach, 15–20. Manchester, UK: Manchester University Press, 2000.

Warren, Robert Penn. *Eleven Poems on the Same Theme.* Norfolk, CT: New Directions, 1942.

———. *Flood: A Romance of Our Time.* New York: Random House, 1964.

———. *Homage to Theodore Dreiser, August 27, 1871–December 28, 1945, on the Centennial of His Birth.* New York: Random House, 1971.

———. "R[obert] P[enn] W[arren] re THE ORCHARD KEEPER," [Feb. 1965]. Ts. Box 29, folder 5, AEF.

Williams, Don. "Annie DeLisle [*sic*]: Cormac McCarthy's Ex-Wife Prefers to Recall the Romance." *News–Sentinel* [Knoxville], June 10, 1990: E1–2.

———. "Cormac McCarthy: Knoxville's Most Famous Contemporary Writer Prefers His Anonymity." *News–Sentinel* [Knoxville], June 10, 1990: E1–2.

———. "An Interview with Leslie Garrett." *Poets & Writers Magazine* 21 (Mar./Apr. 1993): 48–55.

Winfrey, Lee. "No Ordinary Hero, Exactly." *Philadelphia Inquirer,* Dec. 30, 1973: 6F.

Woodward, Richard B. "Cormac Country." *Vanity Fair,* Aug. 2005: 98, 100, 103–104.

———. "Cormac McCarthy's Venomous Fiction." *New York Times Magazine,* Apr. 19, 1992: 28–31+.

Woolmer Collection of Cormac McCarthy. Southwestern Writers Collection, Albert B. Alkek Library, Texas State University–San Marcos.

Wylie, John Cook. List of William Faulkner Foundation Award finalists, [1966]. Ts. Box 29, folder 6, AEF.

Yeats, William Butler. "Purgatory." *The Collected Plays of W. B. Yeats,* 429–36. New York: Macmillan, 1953.

# Index